Career Education: New Approaches to Human Development

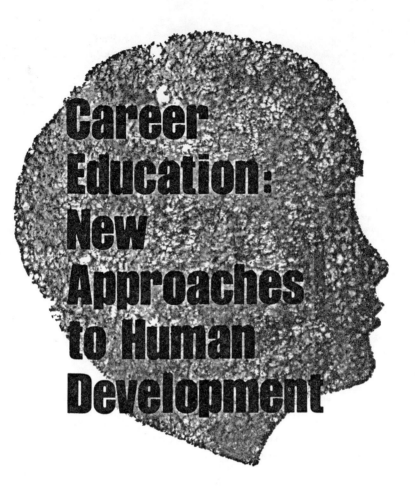

Career Education: New Approaches to Human Development

LARRY J. BAILEY
RONALD W. STADT
Southern Illinois University at Carbondale

McKNIGHT PUBLISHING COMPANY
BLOOMINGTON, ILLINOIS

McKNIGHT
McKNIGHT
McKNIGHT
McKNIGHT
McKNIGHT
McKNIGHT
McKNIGHT
McKNIGHT

Copyright 1973

PUBLISHING COMPANY/BLOOMINGTON, ILLINOIS 61701

FIRST EDITION
Lithographed in U.S.A.

Ronald E. Dale, Vice President — Editorial, would like to acknowledge the skills and talents of the following people and organizations in the preparation of this publication:

Donna M. Faull
Production Editor

Bettye King
Copy Editor

Elizabeth Purcell
Art Editor

Sue Whitsett
Proofreader

William McKnight, III
Manufacturing

Gary Kailey
Dunlap, Illinois
Cover Artist

Gorman's Typesetting
Bradford, Illinois
Compositor

Illinois Graphics, Inc.
Bloomington, Illinois
Preproduction

Library of Congress
Card Catalog Number: 73-75120

SBN: 87345-601-7

To Jackie and Lorraine for their role
in the authors' career development

Table of Contents

Foreword

Better than most, the authors of this book are cognizant of the changing form and function of schooling. They have examined a wealth of literature in a number of relevant fields and have, themselves, been involved in the emergence of career education.

Educators and laymen should be pleased with the blend of logic and chronology which has been used to structure the book. The book begins with a succinct analysis and synthesis of educational criticism and recent responses to outside forces. It concludes with a similar analysis of change theory as applicable to education and recommendations for the several kinds of people who can contribute to a self-starting organization, committed to providing career education experiences.

The core of the book entails brief historical and thorough theoretical treatment of three interrelated matters: career development, the foundations and evolution of career education, and models for career education and curriculum development. It is exciting to ponder the implications of this material. For many years much professional labor will be devoted to pursuing major issues in career development and career education. Convention programs, periodical literature, and books will work and rework this fertile ground. Experiences for children and youth and the organizational structure of schools will become more functionally oriented. Preservice and inservice preparation of professionals will be affected by career development theory and career education practice. Finally, schools will again become *community* schools, enjoying widespread support for programs which serve the developmental needs of each of the children of all of the people respective to the several major aspects of life but especially to wholesome earning. Because this book lays good bases for understanding these trends, it is recommended to professional development, preservice teachers

and practicing management and instructional personnel across the
board, regardless of subject matter or grade-level affiliation.

Elmer Clark, Dean
College of Education
Southern Illinois University
at Carbondale

Preface

The publisher selected authors Larry J. Bailey and Ronald W. Stadt to research and construct a supportive framework for analyzing the topic of refocusing the elementary and secondary school curriculum with career development and career education as a theme. The authors' prime objective is to support the implementation of a valid approach to human development in the American education system. They assigned Kenne Turner the task of researching and abstracting current publications and special group position papers that support human development needs in establishing individual lifestyles through an accommodating career development.

The content of this book is a digest of individual and group philosophies, research, and recommendations. It provides a knowledge base for the reader concerning the evolution and implementation of a systematic career development and education model which facilitates human development, tentative selection, and the realization of careers that lead to the achievement of individual lifestyle attitudes and environments.

The publisher and authors agree that successful implementation of new, more valid approaches to personal growth and career education largely depends on the combined efforts of the United States Office of Education, business and industry, publishers, and the educational communities throughout each state and school district. Therefore, this book was conceived to:

1. describe the social and education conditions that fostered the need for career education;
2. describe a synthesis of career development theory and research;
3. describe the foundation of curriculum content that precedes the refocusing of education to any new approach to human development in the educational system;

4. describe the principles of curriculum development; and
5. suggest systematic implementation of career development and career education with a curriculum model that articulates progressively with the maturity of children, teenagers, and adults.

No single individual or organization can successfully achieve a major refocus of education. However, the combined efforts of all individuals and organizations can result in successful implementation of these concepts to further the individual development of the American youth in our education system.

The Publisher

Acknowledgments

The authors are deeply indebted to colleagues without whom the book could not have been written. Kenne Turner was responsible for researching the majority of reference material and for maintaining order and consistency throughout. Without his direct personal cooperation and support, the wealth of reference materials could not have been synthesized. Fellow researchers Bill Van Rooy, Barbara Zimmermann and Mary Antholz reviewed early drafts and made many valuable contributions. Mary Roush and Sharon Fischmar typed the several drafts. Together with Dorothy Thompson, they helped to coordinate the authors' time for manuscript preparation with other professional obligations. As in the case with many projects of this magnitude, the authors' families have sacrificed time together to allow the book to be completed.

The writers also gratefully acknowledge the many authors and publishers who have granted permission to reproduce quotations and/or other materials. Specific credit lines have been requested by selected publishers as follows:

Chapter 3, page 64: Thorndike, R. and Hagen, E. *10,000 careers.* New York: John Wiley, 1959, pp. 50 and 323. Copyright 1959 by John Wiley and Sons, Inc. and reproduced by permission.

Chapter 3, page 70: Reprinted by permission of the publisher from Donald Super, John Crites, Raymond Hummel, Helen Moser, Phoebe Overstreet and Charles Warnath, *Vocational development: a framework for research.* (New York: Teachers College Press, copyright 1957 by Teachers College, Columbia University), pp. 40 and 41.

Chapter 3, Table 3-1, page 73: Reprinted with permission from the *Industrial and Labor Relations Review*, Vol. 9, No. 4, July 1956. Copyright 1956 by Cornell University. All rights reserved.

The Climate
for Change

CHAPTER 1

Criticism and Crisis in Education

Introduction

For more than a decade, even casual observers of the American scene have known that the institution of education is seriously ill. Perhaps because of the good which the enterprise is alleged to have done in the past, and certainly out of loyalty to their disciplines, most critics have prescribed new regimens of traditional subjects and massive transfusions of expensive technology. In rather recent times, critics have prescribed alternate forms of experiences and delivery systems. Illich (1970a, 1970b, 1971) has carried criticism to the extreme by proposing that the first article of a bill of rights for a humanist society should "... correspond to the First Amendment of the U. S. Constitution: 'The State shall make no law with respect to the establishment of education,'" (Illich, 1970a, p. 11). The president of Teachers College, John H. Fischer (1972, p. 23) submits: "We are in the beginning stages of a sweeping redefinition of the purposes and functions of education in our society." Critics within and without the profession of education agree that schools are sick. They disagree, however, on the nature of the malady and the appropriateness of various corrective measures.

The purpose of this chapter is to review recent statements regarding the need for change in education and to introduce the case for focusing schooling on *career education*.[1] The argument is that allocation of educational resources must be in accord with the recognition that sooner or later each citizen must work for survival, maintenance, or mobility; that preparation for the world of work must become an integral component of the central structure

---

[1]An understanding of this phenomenon is the primary purpose of this book.

of curriculum if schools are to recapture the promise of the total learning process; and that the notion that some young people should prepare for higher education while others, who are alleged to be less capable, are oriented toward work should be dismissed once and for all.

The History of Criticism

American education has always had its critics. From time to time, people within and without the profession of education, who range from the irresponsible to the honestly sincere, have assessed schools and found them wanting. McNally and Passow (1960) categorized the proposals of responsible critics into four categories: (1) that education neglects the individual, (2) that schools do not maintain standards, (3) that priorities are not put on important learnings, (4) and that the most effective organization and methods of instruction are not used in schools.

The *first* complaint, that schools neglect individuals, has always been the most significant. This complaint has traditionally come from within the profession. But, as the next section will show, it is now leveled by an increasing number of social critics in several sectors of society. In the 1950's and early 1960's educators showed great concern to serve students of wider ability and interest ranges. The homogeneous vs. heterogeneous grouping controversy raged. Fortunately, the concern to serve individuals is part of most other forms of complaint. Even the most fanatic advocates of disciplined subject matter orientation prescribe better service to "talented" individuals.

The *second* kind of complaint is that education does not maintain high standards. In his first course in professional education, one of the authors was required to read Bestor (1953) and Lynd (1953) who were foremost among those who condemned progressive education, "frills," colleges of education, and the lack of rigor in traditional subjects. For such critics, all there is to teaching is learning disciplines in a university, getting a teaching job, and insisting on high scholastic standards. Fortunately, almost no critics put matters so simply today.

Several critics made great impact on schooling by emphasizing the high standards prescription. Foremost among these was Conant (1959). Conant advocated individualized programming; elimination of defined tracks for college bound, commercial, and other kinds of students; ability grouping in all subjects; and a rigorous program for the top three percent of the academically talented. A more outspoken advocate for rigor was Admiral Rickover (1959). He proposed that a council of scholars establish standards for both teacher competence and the secondary school diploma. The Science Advisory Committee, appointed by President Eisenhower, advocated improving the competence of teachers and updating materials. It decried automatic promotion and "life adjustment" education.

As the treatment of excellence in Chapter 2 will indicate, much of this kind of complaint was a response to the threat of Russian military might. Like most institutions in the postwar period, the schools deserved reassessment. Many recommendations of Conant's voluminous works, the efforts of the National Science Foundation, and later projects, such as those funded under the National Defense Education Act, improved many features of many schools.

The *third* kind of complaint, that schools do not put enough emphasis on the most important learnings, is nearly always laid by people outside the profession. University administrators, liberal arts and science professors, and some laymen (usually lawyers and M.D.'s) who sit on school and college governing boards, advocate major doses of the "hard" subjects. This kind of complaint is often coupled with the second type. Conant, for example, advocated lots of mathematics and foreign language for the talented at the same time as he advocated high standards.

Taken as a group, there is a comical feature about critics who prescribe emphasis on allegedly important learnings. Taken together, their prescriptions cancel each other. Utilitarians and scientists suggest lots of science and mathematics. Humanists suggest that lots of literature, art, and music are essential to the educated man. The schools cannot hope to expose youngsters to anywhere near the sum of the several recommendations. It is forced to compromise some of everyone's demands, including citizenship, evils of drugs and alcohol, and lots of other add-ons. Surely, complaints of this type shall plague schools forever. After all, there is an endless array of subjects and of people who want what they studied and/or what they have since discovered they missed, taught to the current generation. School people are plagued no end by all manner of citizens who want emphasis on this or that subject(s).

The *fourth* kind of complaint identified by McNally and Passow (1960) is more basic and more closely related to the concerns of this book. This is the complaint that schools do not use the most effective forms of organization and instruction. When McNally and Passow wrote their insightful book, there was a lot of experimentation with, and discussion about, variations on the 8-4,

6-3-3, 3-3-3-3, methods of housing students and programs. Non-graded schools, various combinations of large classes and small group patterns, flexible-modular scheduling, and lots of other schemes were offered up as significant innovations. Most ideas of this sort have merit, i.e., are successful in some applications. But, as shall be seen in this chapter and later in this book, the proposals of the late 1960's and early 1970's were to deal in much more fundamental ways with the structure of the educational enterprise.

Complaints about methodology have been mostly well-taken. On occasion, educators are over-zealous about audiovisual aids. But, in the main, schools continue to lag behind other media in realizing the full meaning of the principle that learning success is better assured by presentations which involve all senses than by traditional classroom techniques which appeal to only one or two senses. Although the incidence of television and many other media has increased in most American schools, many presentations in classrooms, in the armed services, in the advertising industry, and on public educational television are more sophisticated than most of what youngsters confront in the schools.

Just as later sections will show that criticisms regarding the inflexible structure of educational enterprises have taken on new dimensions, so will they demonstrate that a few contemporary critics have recommended approaches to bridging the gap between the quality of experience in schools and the vitality of learning outside classrooms and laboratories. Criticisms of education seem to grow in three ways. (1) They grow in magnitude and intensity. (2) They deal increasingly with the foundation structure of schooling. (3) They are more and more positively prescriptive. Many contemporary critics recommend changes which have wide appeal. As shall be seen in this chapter, from the early 1950's to the early 1970's, criticism went half-cycle from reactionary (teach the traditional subjects rigorously) to revolutionary (use altogether different delivery systems and don't have schools as we know them).

Issues

McNally and Passow (1960) predicted that the future course of American education would depend upon resolution of five issues. The reader is encouraged to consider these issues as he reads the treatment of contemporary criticism. The chapter summary will outline how career education would resolve these issues.

1. Shall the schools place their greatest emphasis on social adjustment or upon intellectual development?
2. Shall the schools organize so as to emphasize the interrelationships between and among the fields of knowledge and facilitate integration in the learning of them, or shall we organize to teach the various "disciplines" (i.e., subjects) separately?
3. Shall the schools concentrate on a curriculum of basic, relatively unchanging subject matter, or shall we continue to make significant curriculum changes designed to adapt education to a rapidly changing world?
4. Shall all the schools adopt the same goals and the same curriculum, or shall there continue to be freedom to adapt goals and curriculum to local needs and conditions?
5. Who shall make the curriculum? (1960, pp. 22-24)

Contemporary Criticism

No less a figure than Sidney P. Marland Jr. (1972, pp. 14-15) U. S. Commissioner of Education in 1971-72 has said "...no intelligent person can question that we are deeply and constructively engaged with concerns that must — by any standards — be called revolutionary." The number of professionals who defend the public schools is greatly diminished. The number of critics is even more greatly increased. Analysis of the literature of educational criticism is a task larger than a single individual can accomplish. Unfortunately, no group has been commissioned to conduct continuing analyses of criticism.

A gross grouping of criticisms serves as an outline for this section. Purpel and Belanger (1972, p. 485) deal with "...three central themes of educational criticism — knowledge, school-society, and person." Table 1-1 illustrates the approximate relationship of these categories of concern to McNally and Passow's earlier analysis of criticism. Fischer (1972, p. 27) categorizes all but extreme proposals such as Illich's into three "fairly well-defined lines." As Table 1-1 indicates, these are (1) equal educational opportunities, which is the contemporary form of earlier concern for individuals; (2) accountability, which is in some senses a new concern but treatable as an extension of criticism of organization and methods; and (3) free schools, which is obviously relatable to Purpel and Belanger's school-society category and to older proposals about methods and structure. It seems appropriate, then, to treat (1) concern for individuals and equal educational opportunity, (2) concern for important learnings, and (3) concern for the structure of schooling and the school-society relationship. Lest this become a book dealing only with educational criticism, several of the major critics only can be treated under each of these categories.

TABLE 1-1

THEMES OF CRITICISM OF SCHOOLING

McNally and Passow	Individuals	Academic standards	Important learnings	Organizations and methods
Purpel and Belanger	Person	Knowledge		School - society
Fischer	Equal educational opportunity	Accountability		Free schools

Concern for Individuals and Equal Educational Opportunity

There is ample evidence to support the contention that concern for individual human beings is at the base of nearly all contemporary educational criticisms. Since the late 1960's, there have been many cogent arguments for schooling which is vastly more humanizing than the jailhouse existence to which millions of young are subjected 180 or so days a year. Prominent among these treatises is *Education and Ecstasy* by Leonard (1968). Leonard maintains that education, at its best, is ecstatic. "When joy is absent, the effectiveness of the learning process falls and falls until the human being is operating hesitantly, grudgingly, fearfully at only a tiny fraction of his potential" (1968, p. 20). Leonard lays out very good arguments for the learning potential of humans, for technology, and for their combination in schools which are the natural extension of successful educational enterprises, sans inhibitions which professionals have not yet been willing to give up. After submitting that credentials are screening devices by which employers, who care not what people have learned but know that people have survived it, Leonard dismisses the teaching of traditional subjects such as English after grade seven. He is pleased that schools fail in their present task which is ". . . to teach a few tricks and otherwise limit possibilities, narrow perceptions and bring the individual's career as a learner (changer) to an end"

(1968, p. 115). On the premises (1) that highly interactive and regenerative technology requires mass genius, mass creativity and lifelong learning, and (2) that "... schools *as they now exist* are already obsolete" (1968, p. 115), Leonard describes a very exciting and humanizing education, showing throughout that:

1. The human potential is infinitely greater than we have been led to believe.
2. Learning is sheer delight.
3. Learning itself is life's ultimate purpose (1968, pp. 215-216).

Leonard is very familiar with the literature of educational criticism and quick to illustrate that Conant (1959) was remiss to assume that the structure of schooling was given. The open and highly mechanized school he prophesies entails new school-society relationships. Students and parents come and go as they please, participating in varied experiences when and for as long as they wish. Learning is free. In a real sense, *Education and Ecstasy* is a fetching argument for the kinds of schools advocated in this book.

Another poignant reprisal of traditional classroom conduct and a brilliant suggestion for reform in behalf of student welfare and creativity is *Teaching as a Subversive Activity* (Postman and Weingartner, 1969). Because of its styles, this book has to be read to be appreciated. It is filled with item-by-item suggestions for conducting discussions which permit young people to develop rather than be stifled. Suffice it here to cite five suggestions which Postman and Weingartner (1969, p. 151) submit are acceptable to teachers whom they have had in classes.

1. Eliminate all conventional "tests" and "testing."
2. Eliminate all "courses."
3. Eliminate all "requirements."
4. Eliminate all full-time administrators and administrations.
5. Eliminate all restrictions that confine learners to sitting still in boxes inside of boxes (1969, p. 151).

One can see that individualized education, different from the vogue in many ways, would remain.

Needless to say, much of the concern for education to be more personalized has come together with the larger concern for alleviating urban and rural poverty and consequent disadvantages in employment, education, housing and other conditions. Many of the people who managed government programs for disadvantaged peoples in the 1960's challenged traditional definitions of the form and function of education. One of the more coherent presentations regarding meaningful learning for youth from poverty areas is *On the Outskirts of Hope* by Helaine Dawson (1968). Dawson describes an unorthodox approach to reaching the disassociated. She contends that success depends upon (1) awareness of the problems of the poverty stricken, of historical attitudes toward ethnic groups, and of living conditions in the ghetto; (2) teachers and educational administrators who foster innovation and service and are not shocked by atypical behavior; (3) learning experiences which are not restricted by walls, established course outlines, and preconceived notions about appropriate behavior patterns; (4) instructional techniques which are more like those used by clinicians than those used by authoritarian teachers; and (5) evaluative techniques which demonstrate learning successes and stimulate employment tests. Dawson's suggestions should be taken in light of the fact that they stem from her personal successes during three years of teaching Manpower Development and Training Act (M D T A) students in San Francisco. Too few theoreticians have this base of experience.

Clark (1969) is one of the more articulate spokesmen for better education in ghettos. He deems contemporary education to be very inadequate.

...The present level of public school inefficiency has reached an intolerable stage of public calamity. It must be demonstrated that minority group children are not the only victims of the monopolistic inefficiency of the present pattern of organization and functioning of our public schools.

It must be demonstrated that white children — privileged white children whose parents understandably seek to protect them by moving to suburbs or by sending them to private and parochial schools — also suffer both potentially and immediately.

It must be demonstrated that business and industry suffer intolerable financial burdens of double and triple taxation in seeking to maintain a stable economy in the face of the public school inefficiency which produces human casualties rather than constructive human beings.

It must be demonstrated that the cost in correctional, welfare, and health services is intolerably high in seeking to cope with consequences of educational inefficiency — that it would be more economical, even for an affluent society, to pay the price and meet the demands of efficient public education.

It must be demonstrated that a nation which presents itself to the world as the guardian of democracy and the protector of human values throughout the world cannot itself make a mockery of these significant ethical principles by dooming one-tenth of its own population to a lifetime of inhumane futility because of remediable educational deficiencies in its public schools. (1969, pp. 120-121).

Another prominent appeal to reorient schooling is Glasser's *Schools Without Failure* (1969). Glasser is a psychiatrist who has had experience with ghetto peoples in correctional institutions. In keeping with many other critics, he submits that present schooling is failure-oriented. He proposes that his theory of *reality therapy* be applied in schools. This would involve increased involvement, relevance, and thinking at the expense of memory and drill. Schools have to be changed so that responsibility and success will replace failure and the tendency toward withdrawal and delinquency.

Among Glasser's proposals are elimination of punishment, the development of discipline in individuals, progression from small successes to larger ones, no excuses, and positive involvement. He advocates classroom group counseling, led by the teacher. Daily time devoted to developing social responsibility is necessary to solving behavioral and educational problems of people who evidence the negative effects of poverty and bad social conditions. Glasser's successes in correctional education are reflected in detailed proposals regarding testing, heterogeneous classes, homework, and student classification. In keeping with some of the more successful ghetto community colleges, he proposes a grading system which reports success and eliminates failure labels.

Glasser's is a very simple, logical, and realizeable proposal for taking disadvantaged and delinquent or potentially delinquent youngsters, meeting them more than half way with love and the promise of forgiving past but not future misbehavior, introducing learning successes, and building on these successes. For the reader, *Schools Without Failure* develops the very compelling realization that the procedures for moving misbehaving young people to reliable and mature, healthy and learning, and sociable and proud people are not only convincingly tempting but already tested and proven in a variety of educational settings from kindergarten to graduate school. In the main, this is an appeal for respecting people and orienting schooling toward individuals instead of toward subject-matter and shallow establishment goals. "All students must be accepted as potentially capable, not as handicapped by their environment" (Glasser, 1969, p. 199).

In a book entitled *Human Teaching for Human Learning,* Brown (1970) describes the results of an experiment and the theory behind experiences which teachers at all levels can use to foster self-awareness. To promote *affective education,* Brown worked regularly with teachers to plan and evaluate experiences which couple intellectual, and emotional, and spiritual learning. Brown submits that the conference of these learnings can assure relevance without revolution. His book is typical of many which emphasize refocusing on individuals.

There have been a great many positive responses to concern for the development of several facets of individuals. Many in-school and perhaps as many out-of-school educational programs have focused on personal growth. These and a great many more articles and books in the contemporary literature of educational criticism make proposals such as: (1) psychological education for long-term life changes at the expense of short-term subject-matter gains, (2) experiences which develop understanding of fantasies, (3) exploration of the effect of emotions on behavior, (4) sensitizing experiences such as meditations, improvisations, and expressive dance, (5) elimination of harmful habits via self-understanding and living highly active and full existences, (6) challenging experiences, such as Outward Bound, which tax individual physical and emotional strengths, (7) group counseling via seminars and practicums, (8) experience with resolving confrontation and conflict, and (9) open education. The literature of *psychological education* or *affective education* or *education for self-awareness and development* — whatever it may come to be called — is voluminous, fascinating, and not to be taken lightly. It appears that forces are already well-collected for marrying education and psychology to assure the welfare of the individual human in a world with man-woman, ghetto-suburb, work-play, and many other increasingly intense relationships. The marriage can be accomplished through experiences which are liberalizing not in the sense formerly espoused by classicists who advocated intimate familiarity with the great books but in the sense personified by Carl Rogers and other behavioral scientists. Put another way, critics are demanding (and schools are beginning to provide) experience modes which foster human growth and understanding. The trend is toward focusing on human problems as dominant and on material problems *and* organized content from the disciplines as secondary.

Part II, Career Development, of this book is based, in part, on the same principles of human development that are the foundation of psychological education. Together with Part II, the reader is encouraged to become familiar with the literature of psychological education. It would be well to begin with Part Four of Purpel and Belanger (1972) and with *Open Education and the American School* by Barth (1972).

Concern for Important Learnings

"The overemphasis of abstract knowledge and deemphasis of the arts of the practical have left the curriculum reform movement open to justifiable charges of social and moral irresponsibility" (Purpel and Belanger, 1972, p. 486). *There are almost no remaining critics of education who submit coldly that curriculum should consist of organized disciplines alone.* Prior to World War II, a great many influential people advocated schooling consisting almost exclusively of theoretical disciplines in the secondary school. Dewey (1916), who is often interpreted oppositely, was to the careful reader such a critic. Martin (1972) treats the organized disciplines issue very adequately. In current curriculum theory, the disciplines principle of content selection functions together with the principles of structure and inquiry and becomes "teach the structure of the disciplines as inquiry" (Martin, 1972, p. 102). There is a tendency to call all school subjects or those which one likes "disciplines." This must be avoided. Only disciplines — by some acceptable definition — must be considered. Otherwise, the principle cannot be used to differentiate; it is vitiated. But, the discipline principle is too limiting because it rules out the teaching of such things as foreign language, art, physical education, and typing. Thus, it is not an acceptable principle by itself. It is better to select subject matter from the disciplines than to select only subjects which are disciplines. Put another way, ". . . education ought not misunderstand or distort the disciplines . . ." and ". . . advocates of the disciplines ought not be allowed to misunderstand or distort education" (Martin, 1972, p. 121).

It appears that critics who advocate disciplines studied exclusively and for their own sake are soon to be, if not already, extinct. Present concern for important learnings is better understood by analysis of the meanings of knowledge in curriculum. Lamm (1972, p. 124) identifies three formulae: "(1) Knowledge is meant for use. (2) Knowledge has intrinsic value. (3) Knowledge is a means in the process of individualization." According to the *first* formula, an individual can function acceptably only if he has specified understandings and values. Validity of knowledge is determined by utility. Knowledge permits imitation of a behavioral mode.

The *second* formula which holds that knowledge has intrinsic value is important to advocates of education for acculturation. Transition from one society or culture to another is acculturation. Many educators are concerned with "cross-cultural" approaches to educating sundry groups. Knowledge is the product of the most "human of human beings" and the means for transforming people into human beings. Knowledge has no value beyond cultivation of human qualities; this is knowledge for its own sake.

Lamm (1972) submits very convincingly that these two approaches to defining important learnings have a common denominator. Both see instruction as a bridge between knowledge and the learner; instruction mediates between knowledge and the learner. Knowledge is laws and models of behavior, and the learner lacks discipline until he has knowledge. Because of this common denominator, most schools use both the disciplinary and the instrumental approach to instruction. Internalization and conditioning are thought to be justified because the learner has voids.

The *third* approach to defining important knowledge is the formula: "Knowledge is a means in the process of individuation" (Lamm, 1972, p. 127). This approach assumes that the structure, the form and the substance of knowledge can and should be manipulated and that the learner cannot and should not be manipulated. Adoption of this formula makes big differences. Instead of acculturating or manipulating students, schools would be concerned with development of the self-concept and self-actualization. Lamm (1972) is beautifully clear on the implications of this conception of the relationship of knowledge, individuals and schooling:

. . . We do not learn humanity by acquiring social roles or by internalizing the principles, values, and norms of a specific culture. Humanity is a given datum present in human beings, and education is the process designed to enable the individual to actualize his own humanity, which is unique to him as an individual different from others. We thus arrive at a further assumption. The imparting of knowledge whether as a means of socialization or as a means of acculturation is a process designed to make people alike (or at least to mold them according to patterns of given social roles or cultural groups). Society with its patterns and mechanisms and culture with its values and norms are designed to serve as common denominators for individuals who are different from one another. The differences among people make it necessary to adapt the means of imparting knowledge, but as far as ends are concerned, all people are considered equal. Knowledge must be imparted differently to gifted children and to ordinary children, but the role which it is expected to play is the same for both. In this sense, the difference between people is something which has to be overcome in order to include everyone in the common denominator which is given in society (according to those whose end is socialization) or in culture (according to those whose end is acculturation).

According to the radical conception of education, diversity is not an obstacle to be overcome but a basic premise defining the humanity of human beings (1972, pp. 128-129).

Lamm's treatment of creativity, subjectivity, self-awareness, self-regulation, motivation and other characteristics of the kind of schooling which views knowledge as a resource for individuals rather than as a means to molding uncommon novices into common citizens is succinct and prophetic. Suddenly, there looms the prospect for defining important learnings in a way compatible with critics who advocate schooling focused on personal growth and development. Gattegno (1970) supports the notion that knowledge is not something which exists prior to learning. Rather, knowledge should be a consequence of learning. Learning, not teaching, should be the concern of schooling. Gattegno's thesis is that *because children have eyes, professionals should aid and abet their seeing by clearing out the rubbish and pointing them in right directions.* This is in contrast to blindfolding children and requiring memorization of outdated information about the world.

Purpel and Belanger (1972) submit that because of curriculum projects in the physical sciences "... the concept of knowledge has been updated, away from the conceptualization of knowledge as a finished product isolated from any human activity and toward a view of knowledge as open and continually subject to human reinterpretation and reinvention" (1972, p. 485). Given this new concept of knowledge, schools may be able to respond to the third category of criticism.

Concern for the Structure of Schooling and the School-Society Relationship

Whereas concern in the early 1960's dealt with educational methodology and features of institutional structure, such as grouping and class scheduling, these dimensions have now been expanded. Critics now make more basic challenges to the structure of schooling. In the extreme, contemporary complaints recommend altogether new relationships between school and society.

A number of very positive suggestions for changing the structure of classroom activities have resulted from practices which have been perfected in selected schools in the United Kingdom. One major voice in this regard has been Joseph Featherstone. In *Schools Where Children Learn*, Featherstone (1971) reprinted a series of pioneering articles and afterthoughts about teaching. His suggestions are very specific and include descriptions of the following characteristics of "infant schools" in the United Kingdom: (1) use of a great quantity and variety of materials, (2) emphasis on concrete experiences, (3) great reduction of rote learning, (4) effective utilization of all manner of building areas and grounds, (5) multiple activities moment-to-moment, (6) socio-psychological climates of cooperation and friendliness, and (7) emphasis on resource allocation rather than instruction and discipline. Featherstone's proposal is hidden from some observers by the level of detail of his descriptions. The scope of the proposal is clearest when the reader considers the mature teacher's responsibility in the infant school. Professionalism becomes a measureable matter. The quality of relationship established with individuals in a doctor-client kind of setting determines, in large part, the effectiveness of educational experiences. Focus on children and the process of learning *and* changes in the physical and organizational structure of the enterprise are more basic than the changes which first and second generation curriculum projects ushered in in the 1970's. One of the authors recently discussed curriculum reform with the staff of an infant school outside Birmingham. These professionals would not consider a carefully patterned curriculum and were quick to supply advantages (always from the children's view) of the freer methods and environment over traditional schools. Although they appreciated the fundamental and far-reaching contrasts between open and traditional primary schooling, they underscored the ease of modification to, and conduct of, child-centered curricula.

One of the major contributors to the practice and literature of open or free schooling in America is Herbert R. Kohl. In *The Open Classroom*, Kohl (1970) draws generalizations from observations made in his own teaching and consulting. He is quick to condemn American education as consisting, for most children, of one authoritarian and oppressive system. Everywhere the teachers' foremost concern is to establish and maintain discipline. Only in the best schools are there genuine attempts to cover planned curricula. In these, rigid sequences are boring, degrading, and misguided. Kohl proposes the open classroom because children's learning is episodic rather than vertical or linear. Working together in an open classroom means responding to expressed interests and moving freely in the community. Kohl gives many practical suggestions for working within the existing structure of physical facilities, required textbooks, grading, and reporting. At base, it is the structure of authority and prescription that Kohl challenges. This is more far-reaching than earlier complaints about the inadequacies of hard and soft material. Like Featherstone and many others, Kohl speaks for a new student-professional relationship and introduces the concept of community education which is treated later in this section.

One of the monuments of educational criticism is Silberman's (1970) *Crisis in the Classroom.* Silberman advocates alleviation of what he calls "Education for Docility." Several kinds of criticisms of schools, including the concept that schools should be eliminated, have persisted over several centuries because of several characteristics which are displayed by nearly all schools. These are:

1. Compulsion. By law or by parental insistence, American children must be in school.
2. Duration. Five or six hours a day, five days a week, thirty or forty weeks a year, for twelve or more years.
3. Collective experience. Economy of scale requires a crowd.
4. Evaluation. Constant assessment differentiates power and authority between student and teacher.

From classroom visits by himself and his staff during the *Carnegie Study* and from the literature of educational criticism,

Silberman (1970) cites many items and incidents which support the contentions (1) that these characteristics are ubiquitous over time and place and (2) that they impede learning and foster docility. Silberman also demonstrates the failures of team teaching, instructional television, ungraded or nongraded primaries, and massive curriculum projects which were accelerated by Sputnik, and generally irrelevant content. He lays a great deal of the failure at the feet of reformers who were unaware that their proposals had been made by theorists in the 1920's and 1930's and had been tried by well-meaning professionals. Because modern reformer-scholars have been mostly professors who look *down* on schools and want to bypass teachers and because they assumed that given content with "proper" structure students will learn it, curriculum reform has been doomed — if for no other reason than teacher sabotage but also because of the maneuvering of competing efforts in chemistry, biology, etc. Silberman treats innovations in educational technology with the same keen analysis that he applies to curriculum reform. He is to be respected for not condemning good features. He is strong in pointing out (1) that reform is meaningless if it assumes educational establishment instead of individual goals and (2) that technology is suspect unless it is under-girded by a thorough theory of teaching. He concludes that the pressing educational problem ". . . is not how to increase the efficiency of the schools; it is how to create and maintain a humane society. A society whose schools are inhumane is not likely to be humane itself" (1970, p. 203). The bulk of *Crisis in the Classroom* is devoted to how schools should be changed. In short, this entails eliminating unexamined practices.

The preoccupation with order and control, the slavish adherence to the timetable and lesson plan, the obsession with routine qua routine, the absence of noise and movement, the joylessness and repression, the universality of the formal lecture or teacher-dominated "discussion" in which the teacher instructs an entire class as a unit, the emphasis of the verbal and de-emphasis of the concrete, the inability of students to work on their own, the dichotomy of work and play — none of these are necessary; all can be eliminated (1970, pp. 207-208).

Silberman describes new English primary schools and goes into detail concerning how elementary and secondary schooling and teacher preparation should be liberated in America. We hope and trust that the present book is in keeping with this astute, sincere, and positive proponent of public education and the welfare of professionals who are basic to its cause.

In a milestone article, "End of the Impossible Dream," Peter Schrag (1970a, p. 94) submits that we should have learned in the

1960's that "... there is no magic in the single school system or in any set of curricular prescriptions, and that the most successful motivating device may simply be the sense that one has chosen what he wants to learn and under what conditions." He argues for multiple options and values, i.e., for separate schools, which are accountable to their clients. This could be possible by the "voucher system" proposed by Christopher Jencks. By "impossible dream," Schrag means the concept that everyone could be successful by reason of education, i.e., the promise of equality and opportunity. Alluding to statistics regarding dropouts and ethnic groups, he concludes that "... nothing in school makes as much difference as economic background of the student and the social and economic backgrounds of his peers" (1970a, p. 68). Perhaps because of simplicity, Schrag more convincingly than most, dismisses the linear standard from bright to slow and the competitive spirit of schooling. More than anything else, schools "certify and legitimize success and failure" (1970a, p. 92). Credentialism is worse in higher education. "Cash and power . . . can be converted into degrees, then reconverted into more cash and power" (1970a, p. 92). Therefore, we fight about schools. More tactfully than most, Schrag challenges the concept that technological advance signals education which is more and more utilitarian. Even if schools could prepare people for a world inaccurately described as technological, they should not be so idolatrous. Rather, technology suggest pluralism, greater leisure, and resourcefulness. In a second article Schrag identifies the source of disillusionment.

The instrument of oppression is the book. It is still the embodiment of the great mystery; learn to understand its secrets and great things will follow. Submit to your instinctive and natural boredom (lacking either the skills to play the game or the security to revolt), and we will use it to persuade you of your benighted incompetence. (1970b, p. 61).

People should be independent rather than dependent in the technology-education-people relationship. Schrag's advocacy of alternate forms of schooling goes beyond the recommendations of authors previously cited and foreshadows some that follow. That there will be new relationships between school and society and basic changes in the form and function of schooling is a commonly held idea.[2]

    One of the more manageable proposals for overcoming inadequacies of schoolhouse education has been made by Vacil M. Kerensky, a well-known community education specialist, and

[2]See for example Burns and Brooks (1970, p. 31).

Ernest O. Melby, who has had a number of leadership positions in teacher education. In *Education II: The Social Imperative,* Kerensky and Melby (1971) analyze the inadequacy of schools in much the same fashion as have critics already cited and propose actions which alter school-community relationships. They cite Schrag and Silberman, showing similarities and agreeing that schools are the final destructive forces for many children. The gist of the underlying argument for *Education II* (1971, pp. 27-28) is paraphrased as follows:

1. Even if present schools could be successful with poor, Black and rural youth, education acquired in childhood and youth will not be longlasting.
2. Therefore, educating adults is as important as educating children.
3. Individuals should review their responsibility and practice participation in their own community.
4. Thus, schools should be community schools.
5. Personality development, also emphasis on cognitive learning, utilization of a variety of professional and non-professional instructional personnel, and other, new features are necessary to community schools.

Kerensky and Melby identify two basic characteristics of schoolhouse education, which contribute to its inadequacy. *First* is the sequence of daily demands, which everyone knows many youngsters will fail. (We have heard this from many other authors). *Second* is failure to educate all of the people of the community. (Ditto). Educators have responded to failure with more of the same content and technology which have failed to resolve problems in the past. Kerensky and Melby submit that all individuals have intellect, that each may have an exciting intellect, and that learning can be fun and intellectual. They challenge the following assumptions:

a. That some chilcen will inevitably fail.
b. That the schoolroom is the child's entire education.
c. That knowledge is the end of education.
d. That present administration and control are satisfactory.

Kerensky and Melby agree with other authors that schools have failed most with the children of the poor and underscore the fact that awareness of inner city problems has had the advantage of magnifying concern to improve. Again, in concert with many contemporary critics, the authors assess what is known of human growth and development and conclude (1) that educational measurement has fostered elitism, (2) that the new psychology presents a more hopeful view of human growth, (3) that education must involve children and youth and adults in self-actualization, (4) that creativity exists in all children, (5) that teachers must relate to individual children, (6) that all can learn, (7) that no two children are alike, (8) that community education is essential and (9) that school management can achieve change only if it has "... belief in people and assumes the leadership in developing a staff that can take children and adults where they are and assist them in setting and achieving higher aspirations" (1971, p. 67).

The last half of *Education II* describes community education. Community education is essential if all of the children of all of the people are to be educated and if we are to alleviate the present situation, wherein one million inadequately prepared youngsters are dumped on society each year. Community education will have the following features:

1. Leaders who think not only of schools but also of all manner of educational resources in the community. Professionals, children, and parents will grow together in the education-centered community.
2. Orientation to subject, or school, or tradition will be replaced by focus on individual children.
3. Failure will be replaced by reliance on the self-concept and new attitudes regarding human potential.
4. Variability of people will be valued and no method of segregation will be tolerated.
5. Marking will be banished and reporting will entail descriptions of people and their accomplishments.
6. Schools will be ungraded and individuals will work at appropriate levels, at their own rates, successfully as they go.
7. Teachers will seek and be rewarded by the hard tasks.
8. The class size will depend upon student need.
9. Teachers will have decision-making power. This will require basic organizational change (Kerensky and Melby, 1971, pp. 99-100).

The latter chapters of *Education II* suggest forms of school finance, mobilization of community sources, a more integrated society, and professional development which are necessary to America's survival. The descriptions and arguments are simple, cogent, and acceptable, especially because they are realizable. The present authors submit that the description of career development and models of career education described in this book are compatible with *Education II*.

Few would challenge the statement that Ivan Illich (1970a, 1970b, 1971) is the extreme, contemporary critic of education. In "The False Ideology of Schooling" (1970b) he reviews a number of criticisms concerning poverty, equality, international competition, and other such concerns, stating as have almost all critics of

note that in school, the rich win and the poor lose. As do many other observers, Illich abhors the belief that schools can label people correctly for life roles. "School inevitably gives individuals who . . . dropout, as well as those who don't make it at all, a rationale for their own inferiority . . . To buy the schooling hoax is to purchase a ticket for the back seat in a bus headed nowhere" (1970b, p. 58). In *Deschooling Society* (1970a), Illich calls for a cultural revolution. After challenging the belief that ever-increasing production, consumption, and profit are measures of the quality of life, he suggests four guarantees to protect individuals (1970a). The first was mentioned in the introduction to this chapter. (1) " 'The State shall make no law with respect to the establishment of education.' There shall be no ritual obligatory for all." (1970a, p. 11), (2) To facilitate disestablishment, there must be a law which forbids discrimination in voting, working, and learning. This would not exclude appropriate performance tests but would prevent favoritism to people who learn skills at the largest public expenditure. (3) The third reform would guarantee each individual equal public educational resources. This would be a generalized GI bill, an "edu-credit card" for each citizen. (4) The fourth legal guarantee would prohibit inquiries into previous school performance. This would protect people from the education monopoly and detach competence judgments from curriculum labels.

Unlike most of the reformers who have been cited thus far, Illich does not go into step-by-step detail regarding reform. He provides guidelines. For example, in an ideal system ". . . there should be no obstacle for anyone at any time of his life to be able to choose instruction among hundreds of definable skills at public expense" (1970a, p. 14).[3] All who want to learn should be provided resources throughout life. Technology can foster independence and learning or bureaucracy and teaching. Technology can be a liberating educational method via (1) reference services to educational objects, (2) skill exchanges, (3) peer matching, and (4) reference services to educators at large. Elsewhere Illich (1971) says that the end of schooling may usher in the "global schoolhouse." His proposals are more compatible with contemporary, leading-edge thought in education than most of his many critics are aware; only his introductory remarks regarding the four

[3]Note that this is a proposal for achieving equality of opportunity, respecting individual initiative and interest, and relating to technology and the work-a-day world via career education. This is not a new proposal. Vocational educators have made it for at least a century. Note also that this is *schooling* not *deschooling* society if schools without walls count as schools.

approaches to matching students and learning resources can be included here.

1. Reference Services to Educational Objects — which facilitate access to things or processes used for formal learning. Some of these things can be reserved for this purpose, stored in libraries, rental agencies, laboratories, and showrooms like museums and theaters; others can be in daily use in factories, airports, or on farms, but made available to students as apprentices or on off-hours.
2. Skill Exchanges — which permit persons to list their skills, the conditions under which they are willing to serve as models for others who want to learn these skills, and the addresses at which they can be reached.
3. Peer-Matching — a communications network which permits persons to describe the learning activity in which they wish to engage, in the hope of finding a partner for the inquiry.
4. Reference Services to Educators-at-Large — who can be listed in the directory giving the addresses and self-descriptions of professionals, paraprofessionals, and free-lancers, along with conditions of access to their services. Such educators, as we will see, could be chosen by polling or consulting their former clients. (Illich, 1970ab, pp. 78-79)

Some authors[4] pooh-pooh vast parts of Illich's analysis and suggestions. The authors take him seriously, especially because he foresaw models and delivery systems in many ways similar to the United States Office of Education proposals regarding career education models and because he envisions pluralistic educational systems for life, not pigeonhole education. Given careful reading, Illich can be seen to say that it is the *monopolistic delivery system not the essence of schools as institutions that he challenges.* Whereas he would deschool society, he would, at the same time, school *it.*

The views of two of the more widely known critics have been saved for last. These are Ivar Berg (1970) and Paul Goodman (1969, 1970). These authors agree with many of the complaints leveled by other critics and are noted for a special observation. They challenge, with good evidence and logic, the commonly held conceptions regarding the relationship of education and employment. Goodman (1970, p. 67) submits that it is ironic to have schools that estrange students when the function of education in advanced countries is to help each youngster find his calling:

...the majority of so-called students in college and high schools do not want to be there and ought not to be. An academic environment is not the appropriate means of education for most young people, including most of the bright.[5]

Because there is strong empirical evidence that schools have little effect on citizenship and vocational ability, because school-

[4]See, for example, Fischer (1972, pp. 23-24).
[5]Emphasis added.

ing has so many negative results, and because tutelage is against nature and arrests growth, formal schooling should be drastically reduced. From ages six to eleven, children should go to small, neighborhood schools, moving freely from home to school. Education should be incidental.

For adolescents, education should vary (Goodman, 1969). Some should attend college preparatory academies. Some should be supported in apprenticeships, travel, browsing, and self-directed study, research, and programs such as VISTA.

The belief that a highly industrialized society requires twelve to twenty years of prior processing of the young is an illusion or a hoax. The evidence is strong that there is no correlation between school performance and life achievement in any of the professions . . . (Goodman, 1969, p. 98).

Schooling exists to police the young and to occupy the young unemployed. Thus, youth lobby for free choice by resisting authority. "By multiplying options, it should be possible to find an interesting course for each individual youth, as we now do for only some of the emotionally disturbed and troublemakers" (Goodman, 1969, p. 103). Each must know he is taken seriously as a person. It is after adolescence that people have need of academic withdrawal.

Obviously, Goodman *condemns the jailhouse existence of schooling, envisages continuing and community education, and conceives of different delivery systems for preparing people for changing jobs.* His ideas unify the less systematic criticisms of schools which are not integral with the larger society. Several of his challenges are worthy of long professional soul-searching and research. For example:

. . . learning to learn usually means picking up the structure of behavior of the teachers . . . (1970, p. 78).
The problem of knowing is to have attentive experience . . . Schools are bad at this. Interesting reality is good (1970, p. 81).
. . . I don't agree with the theory of Head Start, that disadvantaged children need special training for their intellectual faculties to prepare them for learning (1970, p. 83).

Goodman's (1970) "reformation" thinking regarding education is put succinctly.

1. Incidental education, taking part in the on-going activities of society, must again be made the chief means of learning and teaching.
2. Most high schools should be eliminated, with other kinds of youth communities taking over their sociable function.
3. College training should generally follow, rather than precede, entry into the professions.
4. The chief occupation of educators should be to see to it that the activities of society provide incidental education, rather than exploitation or neglect.

If necessary, we must invent new useful activities that offer educational opportunities.
5. The purpose of elementary pedagogy, through age twelve, should be to relay socialization, to protect children's free growth, since our families and community both pressure them too much and do not attend to them enough (1970, pp. 85-86).

These ideas are compatible with the several kinds of relationships career educators recommend for young people, older employees, employers, and schools. The several models described in Chapter 8 are grounded in some of the same ideas as are Goodman's proposals and are certainly responses to the social conditions which he has observed.

Ivar Berg's (1970) *Education and Jobs: The Great Training Robbery* has received renewed attention because of the employment difficulties of recent graduating classes. Cramer (1971) and Frum (1971) are representative of the many pulp and slick magazine writers who have underscored the plight of arts, science, and some professional school graduates. Faltermayer's (1970) earlier discussion of "excess credentialism" challenges universities and colleges in many of the ways in which previously cited authors challenge the schools. His article supports the contention that contemporary schooling is not nearly as directly related to employability as school men would have us believe.

Berg's book is a report of careful and, in many instances, numerical study. It does not bear as directly on criticism or crisis in schools as do many other studies. But it deals with the employability aspect of the school-society relationship like no other. The gist of Berg's analysis of this relationship is appropriate to present concerns. Berg is, above all, concerned to point out that higher education should enrich people's lives and not masquerade as a means of getting a job. Like Faltermayer, he challenges the validity of the B.S. degree. People leave universities in increasing numbers, go to work, become influential, and insist in more and more instances that job holders have degrees. The B.S. degree generates its own demand. (The same cycle affects the high school diploma.)

Berg is to be admired for rigorous comparison of educational attainments of job holders. Some of his conclusions are: (1) that the United States of America produces more B.S. degree holders than it needs, (2) that even if employers' specifications re education are accepted, educational attainment in the population surpassed job requirements in 1968, (3) that available evidence suggests that excess credentialism results in lower morale, higher turnover, and lower productivity, (4) that what is learned in college has little relationship to success and promotion, (5) that education and income are not nearly as highly correlated as many researchers suppose, (6) that worker dissatisfaction increases as educational levels increase for lower skilled jobs as well as for upper and middle level jobs, (7) that quality of ghetto education is not necessarily improved by teachers with better paper credentials, and (8) that paying teachers according to credits toward degrees encourages movement to other jobs in education and industry and deters upgrading of teachers.

Berg would reverse the long-term tendency of employers to raise job entry requirements, challenge the credentials monopoly which schools enjoy and reform schools to find a balance between too much for some and not enough for others. These concepts are basic to contemporary thinking re career education. Judicious career education people are deeply interested in striking new relationships between school and the employment community — for purposes of instruction and employment throughout life. As later chapters show, career education entails new school-society partnerships.

Limitations

Before summarizing criticism and crisis in education, it is appropriate to point out several limitations of this chapter: *First*, even though Table 1-1 might suggest otherwise, there has been little mention of free schools. From time to time on campuses and in other places, such as storefronts, there are honest attempts to experience many of the kinds of learnings which are advocated by reformers. Of course, these are variously successful, good, and longlived. Many have been reported in weekly newsmagazines and elsewhere. Collectively, free schools tell tax-supported education the same kinds of things that published critics tell it. Educators should heed the messages of the free school movement. *Second*, there has been no mention of student underground movements or of overt dissent. Schoolmen would do well to heed the obvious and subtle messages of student papers — especially the underground ones — as seriously as they respond to open revolt. Above all, they should not be complacent when students are complacent. So long as educational practice persists in archaic forms, students shall rise again. *Third*, even though Table 1-1 suggests otherwise, there has been only casual mention of "accountability." Accountability is treated at length in the next chapter, which looks at modern education in another, revealing way.

Summary

One could conclude from the foregoing review that schools are doomed beyond salvage. The more judicious conclusion is that it is fortunate that criticism has finally come to challenge the system at its very bases. In "Who Needs Schools?" (1970), Fischer points out that if all of the children of all of the people are to be educated, the idea that there need not be schools is an idle one. The question, Fischer says, is how to assure that schools do not ". . . reject psychologically and physically, vast numbers of children whose potentiality is neither determined nor developed" (1970, p. 91). It is as if schools and their mentors are at their knees, wanting to know ways out of the dilemma.

Career education is, in every conceivable sense, a new response to (1) contemporary concern for individual students and equality of educational and other life opportunities, (2) contemporary conceptions of knowledge, storage and retrieval systems, and the value of practical and applied versus theoretical and purely academic pursuits, (3) evidenced concern of young, Black, female, and other "target groups," and (4) complaints about the nonconnectedness of school and society. Contemporary complaint cries out for a more natural and easy transition from childhood to adulthood. Education is caught in the middle. In-school and out-of-school youth and adults of many ilks cry out with increasing frequency and volume for structured but meaningful and humanizing experiences which will help rather than hinder individual growth and development in a world where technology and jobs and forms of play change, but where what is human and humanizing changes little. As later chapters will show, many educational leaders and other influential people submit that career education is a proper bridge between youth and responsible adulthood, i.e., between discontent and the human condition.

Answers to McNally and Passow's questions (1960, pp. 22-24) summarize this chapter and project what is to follow.

1. Shall the schools place their greatest emphasis on social adjustment, or upon intellectual development?

Educational critics and advocates of career education prefer not to address clear cut alternatives. Obviously, both alternatives are important. Intellectual development has been overemphasized because it has been the primary or glory road. It should remain the major concern for some. But, for many the emphasis should be on other aspects of growth and development, for life roles do not distinguish between social and intellectual development. Schools and related agencies must foster both kinds of development, according to *changing* individual needs — moment-to-moment and over the long haul.

2. Shall the schools organize so as to emphasize the interrelationships between and among the fields of knowledge and facilitate integration in the learning of them, or shall we organize to teach the various "disciplines" (i.e., subjects) separately?

Study of the disciplines as such will lose ground in the school curriculum. It is already doing so — even in universities. Career education will move appropriate numbers of people to rarified study and research for new knowledge in universities and "think tanks." But no longer will studying disciplines as such be the glory road or the only means of access to higher education. The curriculum of schools will be oriented to individual and societal problems, not to transmitting pre-ordered knowledge.

3. Shall the schools concentrate on a curriculum of basic, relatively unchanging subject matter, or shall we continue to make significant curriculum changes designed to adapt education to a rapidly changing world?

Obviously, the latter. Complaints and suggestions about schooling say this in spades.

4. Shall all the schools adopt the same goals and the same curriculum, or shall there continue to be freedom to adapt goals and curriculum to local needs and conditions?

Teachers are becoming more professional. Professionals keep abreast of new techniques and practices and adjust delivery systems for individual clientele. Pluralism must prevail in schooling. Not only the day-to-day experiences of students but also the kinds and characteristics of delivery systems (which involve various community agencies) will vary, according to the individual short- and long-range plans. Milton Freidman says in response to the school busing issue, "The right solution is to give all parents a wide range of choice" (1972, p. 69). He favors the voucher system. Financial plans are not our present concern. The point is that society is ready for the multiple delivery systems which are essential to career education. Competition and differences among approaches to individual development should be encouraged.

5. Who shall make the curriculum?

There will be multiple curricula — the effort of hardware-software producers, practicing professionals, and university based or other curriculum developers. Employers, students, and professionals will have ever more impact on curricula. The communications vehicles need only be put to the task.

BIBLIOGRAPHY

Barth, R. S. *Open education and the American school.* Agathon Press, 1972.
Berg, I. Education and jobs: *The great training robbery.* New York: Praeger Publishers, 1970.
Bestor, A. *Educational wastelands.* Urbana: University of Illinois Press, 1953.
Brown, G. I. *Human teaching for human learning: An introduction to confluent education.* New York: Viking Press, 1971.
Burns, R. W. and Brooks, G. D. (eds.). *Curriculum design in a changing society.* Englewood Cliffs, New Jersey: Educational Technology, 1970.
Clark, K. Alternative public school systems. In B. Gross and R. Gross (eds.) *Radical school reform.* New York: Simon and Schuster, 1969, 116-125.
Conant, J. B. *The American high school today.* New York: McGraw-Hill, 1959.
Cramer, A. You've got a degree, so what? *Weekend Magazine,* 1971, 21(6), 15-16.
Dawson, H. *On the outskirts of hope.* New York: McGraw-Hill, 1968.
Dewey, J. *Democracy and education.* MacMillan, 1916.
Faltermayer, E. Let's break the go-to-college lockstep. *Fortune,* 1970, 82(5), 98-103+.
Featherstone, J. *Schools where children learn.* New York: Liveright, 1971.
Fischer, J. H. Who need schools? *Saturday Review,* 1970, 53(38), 78-79+.
————. Public education reconsidered. *Today's Education,* 1972, 61(5), 22-31.
Friedman, M. Busing: The real issue. *Newsweek,* 1972, 80(11), 69.
Frum, B. Class of 71. *Maclean's,* 1971, 84(6), 14-21+.
Gattegno, C. *What we owe children: The subordination of teaching to learning.* New York: Outerbridge and Dienstfrey, 1970.
Glasser, W. *Schools without failure.* New York: Harper & Row, 1969.
Glines, D. E. *Creating humane schools.* Mankato, Minnesota: Campus Publishers, 1972.
Goodman, P. *New reformation: Notes of a neolithic conservative.* New York: Random House, 1970.
————.Visions: The school in society. In B. Gross and R. Gross (eds.) *Radical school reform.* New York: Simon and Schuster, 1969, 98-115.
Gross, B. and Gross, R. (eds.) *Radical school reform.* New York: Simon and Schuster, 1969.
Illich, I. *Deschooling society.* New York: Harper & Row, 1970. (a)
————. The false ideology of schooling. *Saturday Review,* 1970, 53(42), 56+58+. (b)
————. The alternative to schooling. *Saturday Review,* 1971, 54(25), 44-48+.
Kerensky, V. M. and Melby, E. O. *Education II: The social imperative.* Midland, Michigan: Pendell Publishing, 1971.
Kohl, H. R. *The open classroom: A practical guide to a new way of teaching.* New York: Random House, 1970.
Lamm, Z. The status of knowledge in the radical concept of education. In D. E. Purpel and M. Belanger (eds.) *Curriculum and the cultural revolution.* Berkeley, California: McCutchan Publishing, 1972, 124-142.
Leonard, G. B. *Education and ecstasy.* New York: Dell Publishing, 1969.
Lynd, A. *Quackery in the public schools.* Boston: Little, Brown and Company, 1953.
Marland, S. P. Jr. A splendid discontent. Speech before the annual Convention of the American Association of School Administrators, February 15, 1972, Atlantic City, New Jersey.

Martin, J. R. The disciplinaries and the curriculum. In D. E. Purpel and M. Belanger (eds.) *Curriculum and the cultural revolution.* Berkeley, California: McCutchan Publishing, 1972, 100-123.

McNally, H. J. and Passow, A. H. *Improving the quality of public school programs.* New York: Teachers College Press, 1960.

Pucinski, R. C., and Hirsch, S. P. (eds.). *The courage to change: New directions for career education.* Englewood Cliffs, New Jersey: Prentice-Hall, 1971.

Postman, N. and Weingartner, C. *Teaching as a subversive activity.* New York: Dell Publishing, 1969.

Purpel, D. E., and Belanger, M. (eds.) *Curriculum and the cultural revolution.* Berkeley, California: McCutchan Publishing, 1972.

Rickover, H. G. *Education and freedom.* New York: E. P. Dutton, 1959.

Schrag, P. End of the impossible dream. *Saturday Review,* 1970, 53(38), 68-70+. (a)

————. Growing up on mechanic street. *Saturday Review,* 1970, 53(12), 60-61. (b)

Silberman, C. E. *Crisis in the classroom: The remaking of American education.* New York: Random House, 1970.

Wasserman, M. *The school fix, NYC, USA.* New York: Outerbridge and Dienstrfrey, 1970.

Excellence, Relevance and Accountability

Introduction

In the late 1960's various individuals and groups began to confront school officials with new demands because of increasing taxes, inflation and unemployment, spurred by the Nation's efforts to conduct a costly war and to continue with domestic programs in education, health, transportation and other institutions. In many communities, parent and citizen's groups demanded information about the quality of educational output. Data from standardized testing programs *revealed widespread failure to impart even basic communication and numerical skills.*

In earlier times, when educators were confronted with evidence that Johnny could not read, they blandly attributed deficiencies to home influences, inadequate facilities, and the dearth of curriculum research and development activity. Contemporary parent and citizen's groups, joined by legislators and government agency people, refuse to accept such shallow explanations.

For several reasons, domestic and foreign issues in the 1960's and early 1970's caused many people to believe that support of schools should continue or grow only if there is evidence of learning. Believing that their taxes are high enough, taxpayers submit that continued support of public schooling is warranted only if concrete results can be demonstrated. This stance is aided and abetted by the Office of Management and Budgets in the Federal government, which requires that agencies which are responsible for such things as highways and defense show *clearly* what tax dollars purchase in the way of material goods, safety, and other intangibles such as national image and support from friendly nations. The concern for demonstrable results is further spurred by the electronic age. The explosive speed of communication via mass media informs laymen about educational successes or failures in diverse schools everywhere. In the cyberneted age, it is very easy to know nearly all that we wish to know of the conduct of primary institutions, such as government and finance.

Taxpayers are perfectly reasonable in their insistence upon a day's worth of learning progress for a day's expense. Taxpayers have always made similar demands. But, the intensity of such demands has soared to new heights in recent times. Because taxpayers are currently demanding economic accountability for success or failure of public education, the educational institution is in a state of near revolution. *This chapter tells how we have come to assume that accountability is an established right of the American public and how the trend toward accountability has impinged upon thinking regarding the function and substance of schooling.* The chapter has three sections. Each section represents a recent era of thought and change. Understanding is given to three terms or watchwords which are the collected attempts of educators to fix the function of schooling clearly and acceptably in the public's eyes. These three terms can be thought of as thesis, antithesis, and synthesis.

1. The *thesis* of "excellence" was thought to be the obvious theme for schools which would respond (1) to the postwar Russian threat and (2) to demands of the new technology which would spur us to new prosperity levels.
2. The *antithesis* of "relevance" was created as the theme for those who would *redirect* education in the interest of sundry disassociated peoples.
3. The *synthesis* of "accountability" appears to be the theme for the 1970's. This term may guide the American educational institution as it becomes characteristically "for all of the people all of the time." Accountability focuses on definite objectives which can be measured in performance terms in much the same way that accountability of business, industry, and commercial enterprises is assessed.

Thesis: Excellence

The first watchword of modern education came to the fore shortly after what was feared to be a National emergency. Many would have it that the most traumatic and direction-changing event ever for American education was the successful orbit of Sputnik in October of 1957. One of the more astute observers of the educational scene was quick to point out that Sputnik's beeps merely made earlier demands upon education more audible (Broudy, 1968). National defense and the vigor of the industrial revolution, spurred by World War II had long since knelled the doom of educational watchwords such as *life adjustment.* Sputnik served to underscore two indictments which were being made with increasing vigor:

1. As contrasted to Russian and European education, the college preparatory track was identified as "inadequate preparation for engineering and scientific pursuits."

2. Because inadequate numbers of youth were engaged in rigorous study of science, mathematics and foreign language, America could not be assured of winning the "Cold War" battles of sophisticated armaments, support for dependent nations,[1] and so-called police actions like the Korean conflict.

Outside Forces

Very soon after Sputnik, there were scramblings in the legislative and administrative branches of the Federal and many State governments and in universities, colleges and schools to correct our competitive disadvantage via education. Journalists, industrialists, military men led by Admiral Rickover, scientists and other laymen leveled incisive attacks on schoolmen. Efforts at curriculum planning shifted from educationists to military men, scientists, and engineers.

Inside Forces

Soon the hue and cry among schoolmen and laymen became *excellence.* Many speeches and articles extolled the virtues of "programs of excellence" in education. By the early 1960's, convention programs of educator's associations were sure to deal wholly or in large measure with excellence. Issues of professional journals were replete with articles which alleged that this or that curriculum or curriculum component could be excellent if the author's remedies could be injected.

Giants in educational theory, such as Harry S. Broudy (1964), featured the word in the titles of books. Whereas people outside of education tended to be concerned only with technological competence, Broudy stressed concern for excellence in all subjects and in problem-solving. "One now has to study formally and systematically a good deal of economics, sociology, and physics in order to undertake fruitful problem-solving and discussion. Good citizen-

---

[1]Do not be confused by the fact that these are mostly called *independent* nations.

ship in a modern democracy demands conceptual readiness as well as appropriate attitudes and procedures" (Broudy, 1968, p. 58).

Broudy and many others encouraged the downward trend of rigorous study in the disciplines. "Or, to put it another way, the minimum cognitive achievement needed for good citizenship is today nearer to what the graduate of a four-year undergraduate college is presumed to have than to what a high school diploma represents" (Broudy, 1968, p. 58).

It must be noted that whereas Broudy was then and is now a strong advocate of rigorous study of organized disciplines in the secondary school, he was careful to point out, at the onset of the excellence movement, the need to be excellent in terms of (1) pedagogical strategy, (2) the organization of instruction for a large variety of special groups, and (3) motivation or levels of aspiration. These concerns foreshadowed the antithesis to excellence which was *relevance* and will be treated in the next section of this chapter.

The Long and Short of It

The sum and substance of the clamor and stampede for excellence was not anywhere near as widespread as early and astute observers such as Broudy had hoped. As with earlier reform movements (in education and other institutions), practitioners took only the obvious and missed several of the important aspects of the proposals. As might have been expected, educators were more adoptive than adaptive. That is, they swallowed the recommendations of military and university leaders too blindly.

(1) Excellence came to mean: We must have all the *mathematics and science* we can, as early as we can, so that we may catch up to the USSR in engineering and scientific manpower and productivity for defense. People in university science departments and professional schools fanned this part of the fire. Mamas and papas joined in because it was comforting to feel justified in prodding Johnny to become a Ph.D., M.D., or L.L.D.

This syndrome was prevalent almost everywhere. In a drama which one of the authors recalls, the principle character was a teen-age boy who had committed murder and the principle scenes were in a courtroom. In one of the final scenes, the boy, his mother, and the defense attorney were seated in an anteroom while the jury was out.

Mother: "How do you think the jury will decide?"

Attorney: "We have made a good case, but the evidence is overwhelming. They'll rule guilty on the first ballot."

Mother: "Oh! That's terrible!" (weeping) "There'll be no college for Johnny!"

This epitomizes the syndrome which the excellence movement fostered throughout nearly all facets of the population.

(2) **Excellence also came to mean:** "Let's have all the *foreign language* we can get." A clear cut analysis of this part of the fire is not possible. The impetus for foreign language study was prob-ably not so much the idea that we would benefit from the work of foreign scientists as it was that we would benefit politically at the international bargaining tables. Some had it that we should study Russian and Chinese for the day when we would have to speak nicely to them.

In the main, those who might later become Birchers prevented the teaching of these languages. Thus, French, Spanish, and Ger-man rose to new heights in the curriculum. Although the supply of foreign language teachers was inadequate in the early and mid-1960's, much of the available supply was in these traditional (not to be confused with ancient) languages. Of course, many university people fostered foreign language study in the schools on the old premise that it trained minds and assured that only the "best" could go to college.

(3) **Excellence also came to mean:** "Let's use every resource to assure *excellence in facilities, instructional materials, and the teachers* of these subjects." Great booms resulted in several sec-tors of education. Not without motivation from earlier eras or with-out additional reasons, the hardware, software, and human re-sources of education became much more adequate to the enter-prise. This was the era of language laboratories, programmed instruction, and many other developments. Commercial interests were quick to capitalize on the willingness of taxpayers almost everywhere to buy material improvements for education. The num-ber of commercial and other agencies developing, producing, and marketing hardware and software systems grew like Topsy. Pro-fessional associations had to meet in larger and larger convention facilities not just to house themselves, but primarily to house commercial exhibits.

It followed that teachers and others in the educational enter-prise had to be updated. This movement took the forms of in-creased standards for subject matter competence in teacher edu-cation; workshops and institutes sponsored by National Science Foundation, National Defense Education Act, and (later) Education Professions Development Act legislation and involving stipends for participants and a wealth of in-service updating activities associated with new curriculum materials. In a word, education, especially in the "hard" subjects, got a massive transfusion.

(4) **Excellence also came to mean:** *Woe be it for those whose gullets refuse to swallow* what used to constitute a college education by the time they finish high school. They would be unemployed in the cybernated age. Science and the technology of automation and space would eliminate menial jobs. Somehow pedagogy had to assure that all achieved very high-level facility with words, numbers, and abstract reasoning. Educational psychology (specifically experimental study into the learning processes of large varieties of people, coupled with even larger varieties of methodologies) would have to discover how to assure that all could excel in new levels of achievement in the omnipotent subjects of mathematics, science, and language.

Thus, educational psychology came to be the king in professional teacher preparation. People in educational theory or philosophy were reduced to second class citizenship (and pay) in the educational family. Educational psychologists had a heyday. Carefully controlled studies of the impact of endless varieties of audio-visual aids, inductively and deductively organized mini-goodies of knowledge, and myriad styles of teacher-pupil relationships and other sociopsychological arrangements — these and many other variables — were studied to death.

Heyday of Excellence

Excellence was one of the longer lived, nondemocratizing and nonliberating watchwords which has served as an oversimplified descriptor of the hopes of the American educational enterprise. Like most hathooks, it was at once good, bad, rallying and clarifying, and misunderstood. *In the end, it was its own worst enemy.*

All manner of adults thought it was great. Traditional university, college, and school departments had all to gain and little to lose, so they embraced the term and its corollaries. Nearly every parent wanted Johnny and Mary to go to college. Somehow college would assure easy, nonmanual work, affluence, leisure, and other features of the good life as defined by parents who had sacrificed to win WW II.

Superintendents of schools could easily sell excellence to school board members who, themselves, had been deeply steeped in the same stuff. After all, many school board members were college trained and those who weren't were alert citizens who saw, at least, the surface occupational and avocational advantages of higher education in war time and peace time pursuits. Thus, *the*

TABLE 2-1

EXPENDITURES FOR ALL PUBLIC EDUCATION RELATED TO EXPENDITURES FOR VOCATIONAL EDUCATION, 1958-1968

Year	All Public Education	Vocational Education
1958	$13,569,163	$ 209,745
1960	15,613,255	238,812
1962	18,373,339	283,948
1964	21,324,993	332,785
1966	26,248,026	779,895
1968	32,977,182	1,192,863

SOURCE: U. S. Department of Health, Education, and Welfare, Office of Education, *Digest of Educational Statistics: 1970 Edition.* Washington: U. S. Government Printing Office, September, 1970, pp. 56 and 58.

excellence prescription was easily swallowed. They paid dearly for science and language laboratories, new textbook and supplementary materials in mathematics, language arts, foreign language, and selected other subjects. Table 2-1 illustrates overall and vocational education expenditures. Note that gains for vocational education were only a small fraction of the total expenditures for all of education.

Although many of the proponents of excellence saw intelligent citizenship in an ever more complex industrial democracy and other honest purposes as the motivation for the movement, the simple, obvious, and measureable motivation for laymen and local school people became raising the percentage of a school system's graduates which entered universities and colleges. Guidance departments flourished if they were able to demonstrate increases in this and in the number of graduates who received plush scholarships, advanced placement, and other recognitions of the institution's excellence. Much was invested in the few.[2] And many more than heretofore were encouraged to qualify for college entrance. The "closing college door" became the enemy of donation campaigns. Entrepreneurs set up shop, promising to get Johnny or Mary into an

[2]This is not to say that much was not done for other groups. For example, special education made great advances with the mentally and physically handicapped as well as the gifted during this same period.

appropriate college. Meanwhile, higher education fared very well. The concrete never set on most old campuses, and many new campuses were constructed. Some even had visions of the day when all young people would go to school until they were 20 years old or older.

Excellence Wanes

But, as is always the case when too many eggs are put in too few baskets, this facet of the American dream did not come true for some peoples. Especially, as Black peoples organized to become powerful and articulate, it became obvious that large numbers of disassociated peoples were not taking the pill of excellent education. Observations of social scientists, which had been largely ignored, were heard with increasing intensity in many quarters. It began to be noticed that lots of kinds of people remained educationally, economically, and socially disadvantaged. Not only Blacks, but females, middle class whites, and others were (1) not benefitting from the rejuvenated curriculum and (2) demonstrating via new dress modes, sex codes and, in some instances, violence, that they were more than passively resistive of the curriculum. Although their antics were heralded around the world, the subtle message of their revolt did not penetrate the quarter inch of skull of many members of the establishment. The final blow to the simplified excellence syndrome came with the realization that a lot of affluent kids did not embrace it either. As Studer (1971, p. 49) put it, the "bite-the-bullet syndrome" had run its course. Masses of kids were crying out in many misunderstood forms that they were not willing to grin and bear it until they were finished with the *rite de passage.*

The excellence era came to a close. This was certainly not so much because of the way it was conceived by knowledgeable professionals such as Broudy and by government agencies which fostered torrents of monies for myriads of special programs, but more so because of (1) residuals of the earlier influences of university entrance requirements in the liberal arts and sciences, (2) the fledgling character of rapidly expanding school guidance services, and (3) the oversold populace.

After all, the percentage achieving the baccalaureate degree, the percentage dropping out of high school, the percentage of 19-25 year olds unemployed — none of these had changed for the better during the excellence era. For a complexity of reasons we shall never understand but, surely in part because of extremes of educational programs of excellence, many societal problems had, if anything, worsened. The rate of teenage crime grew three times as fast as the youthful population in the 1960's. Drug addiction and other indexes of cultural unrest increased during the very time when more material resource was invested in the welfare of youth than at any prior time, anywhere.

Even the best of pedagogy could not deliver the pill of excel-lent education. The newer technologies of education were as mis-understood and misused as the new curricula. That torrents of money for improving teachers and classrooms and materials would improve learning simply did not prove out. In a very good article, the well-known economist, Roger A. Freeman, (1969) made abundantly clear to laymen what those who even earlier had begun to cry for relevance sensed through other than numerical analysis.

... While the country's business and other private investment tripled over the past 20 years, investment in education increased eightfold, reaching about $52 billion in the school year 1967-68. Public school revenues account for more than half of that, having increased by more than 150 percent in the last decade. (Only a tenth of the increased funds came from the federal govern-ment.) Congress has passed 40 major educational laws in the past four years.

Three years have passed since Title I of the 1965 bill provided for 'compensatory' programs across the country, time enough for signs of success or failure to have appeared. The signs have indicated, alas for the children involved, failure. A nationwide Associated Press survey in May 1968 found that both critics and supporters now agree that it is not working. 'A monumental flop,' said Rep. Roman Pucinski (D. Ill.), one of the bill's original sponsors. Said Assistant U. S. Commissioner of Education Joseph Fromkin: 'We still have little evidence that the problem is being licked; in fact, we may even be falling be-hind.' Edmund Gordon, writing in *College Board Review*, ascribed one funda-mental difficulty to the programs: 'They are based on sentiment rather than on facts.' Actually, the programs were designed and authorized in the face of over-whelming evidence that they could not produce what their sponsors promised, and such evidence continues to pour in.

A statistical table published by the U. S. Office of Education in 1967 revealed that in 19 tests ranging from reading comprehension to arithmetic, the educational lag of children in Title I programs had been slightly reduced on ten tests but had actually increased on the other nine. The next year's report disclosed that the average disadvantaged child was farther behind national norms in reading and arithmetic *after* going through Title I programs than he had been before (pp. 9-10).

. . .

Or consider Project Headstart, the most enthusiastically received of all the war-on-poverty programs. More than 600,000 children have participated in each of the past four years at a cost of more than $300 million annually. But while initial results showed an average gain of eight to ten points on IQ verbal tests, the gain disappeared within a few months. Studies found no lasting progress when Headstart children were compared with other groups.

A recent report by the U. S. Commission on Civil Rights found that none of the many compensatory education programs 'appear to have raised signifi-cantly the achievement of participating pupils,' and noted that the programs tended to strengthen growing de facto racial segregation in the schools (pp. 10-11).

• • •

The Coleman report, based on a USOE-sponsored study in 1965 of 4,000 schools, stated that 'The evidence revealed that within broad geographic regions, and for each racial and ethnic group, the physical and economic resources going into a school had very little relationship to the achievements coming out of it.' Among the specific findings was that pupil-teacher ratios 'showed a consistent lack of relation to achievements among all groups under all conditions.'

The burden of the Coleman report was a repudiation of the entire mode of thinking that holds environment entirely responsible for whatever short-comings are apparent in individual pupils.

Parents whose children attend schools with low average scores on testing increasingly tend to blame school boards, administrators, teachers, and curriculums, a trend that is resulting in demands that school control in urban poverty areas be transferred to local communities. The theory is that parents, with their children's interests at heart, will see to it that the schools provide a good education. While this idea has some merits, its widely-publicized translation into practice in three New York City 'disadvantaged' areas has not only resulted in no improvement in the children's education, but has created chaos and caused the skill and knowledge of New York's school children to fall farther behind.

Christopher Jencks, writing in the New Republic, concluded that the Coleman report 'makes a convincing though not a definite case for the view that student achievement depends largely on forces over which today's schools exercise little control (Freeman, 1969, p. 11).

Antithesis: Relevance

It could well have been expected that the remedies for the apparent dead end into which the educational enterprise had been maneuvered would come from outside the profession of education.[3] To the top of new and widespread discontent came the watchword "relevance." This was offered up as the new goal. It was to prove more mystery than panacea. It had good and bad influences like all social movements. Young people in colleges and schools (the latter is our primary concern) began in the mid-1960's to articulate demands for a curriculum which was relevant. Throughout the "relevance era," the primary but seldom acknowledged question was, "Relevance to what?" In retrospect, the simple answers were: personal relevance and social relevance (Bruner, 1971, 114).

As is often true of the *antithesis*, this was a shorter-lived movement than its predecessor. Some submitted that relevance was better because it could be used to demonstrate what wonderful things schools and colleges could do for any- and everybody.

[3]An interesting case can readily be made for the premise that significant contributions to education are not made by educationists. Witness the fact that curriculum changes in the 1960's were largely wrought by scientists.

Bruner (1971, p. 114) sagely calls the term *relevance* a "thumb-worn symbol in the modern debate about the relation of education to man and society." It seems that we must always have a one-word symbol.

It seems proper to digress from the thrust of these remarks to submit the notion that Bruner foresaw the trend toward accountability and career education. The following excerpts from his insightful article (1971) illustrate:

> First, education must no longer strike on the exclusive posture of neutrality and objectivity. Knowledge, we know as never before, is power (p. 115).
>
> Second, education must concentrate more on the unknown and the speculative, using the known and established as a basis for extrapolation (p. 116).
>
> I am no innocent to matters of schooling and the conduct of instructional enterprises. What I am proposing involves a vast change in our thinking about schools, about growth, about the assumption of responsibility in the technological world as we know it. I have wanted to highlight the role of intention and goal directedness in learning and the acquisition of knowledge, and the conversion of skill into the management of one's own enterprises. The objective is to produce skill in our citizens, skill in the achieving of goals of personal significance, and of assuring a society in which personal significance can still be possible (p. 117).

The Pendulum Swings

The appeal of relevance carried the pendulum far and wide. For some, relevance meant Black studies. Many traditional academic departments allegedly became relevant by offering new courses which were really old courses with the relevant word "Black" prefixing them. Others, spurred by societal problems and often responding to legislation-designed educational programs which would be relevant to inner-city, Spanish speaking, Indian American, Appalachian, rural disadvantaged, unemployed and out-of-school youth, and other disassociated peoples. Relevance came to mean concern for what previously had been the educational enterprise's least benefitted publics.

Social Relevance

One of the better arguments for social relevance was submitted by Holloway (1970). Schools should change to maximize the human resource. In large part, this can be accomplished by "... insuring full integration and participation of the poor and the ethnic groups into the mainstream of American society" (Holloway, 1970, p. 20). Holloway argues urgently for integration along every dimension, while disparaging ability grouping and other teacher-serving techniques which tend to perpetuate entry socioeconomic and learning levels.

Few would refute that much of what was said about and done to assure social relevance was good. This chapter is not an essay to disparage excellence or relevance. Aligning education with societal needs has always been and shall always be a laudable, if illusive goal.

Similarly, few would dispute that much of what was offered up as relevant education was nothing more than old remedies in new bottles. Journals in subject matter fields (say social science) and process-oriented fields (say guidance) was replete with terse and wordy treatises which were nothing more than shallow disguises for content which the authors had long since determined should be taught, no matter what. Too few professionals focused on learning rather than on teaching.

A ludicrous example was developed by Ohme (1970). Ohme alleges that an interest-centered English offering will be relevant if it permits students to select from an offering of short-term courses with titles such as "Sports in Literature," "Contemporary Scene," and "Advertising: The Miracle Worker." Obviously, these and any others that teachers might conjure up would be relevant to personal or social needs, depending upon timeliness and other well-established criteria. To offer them in short courses is no different than including them as units in a longer course. Smaller pigeon holes, alone, do not assure relevance or any other desired outcome.

For some, social relevance became cultural relevance. Under this guise, one could argue the case that any of the traditional subjects is relevant. Hocking (1970) attempted to show that Latin could be relevant if done with the most complete audio-visual materials available. Most of his argument is given over to an accurate and tear-jerking portrayal of the demise of Latin and foreign language study in general. Nowhere does the article tell which personal or social concerns might relate to the study of Latin. This is the failing of hundreds of articles which purport to depict relevant education.

Personal Relevance

In a very meaningful chapter "Education for Relevance," Beck, et al, (1968) point out that *ultimately it is the individual that determines what is relevant to his life.* As Burns and Brooks (1970) point out, educators must admit that most educational experiences are not relevant to the lives of students. They go on to show that it is easy to tell what is not relevant to very diverse students. For example, students in the Philippines would question the relevance of *Beowolf* or a study of travel in New York. Thus, it is easy to establish that curriculum builders should consider hunger, disease and sanitation, crime, drugs, job security, income, and other personal and social conditions. But, it "does not follow that all instruction must be confined to these problems, nor must instruction deal only with 'what is' rather than 'what should be'" (Burns & Brooks, 1970, p. 9). Education should begin where the youngster is and inspire him to the highest vocation and avocation possible.

The relevance era produced a lot of very meaningful books which dealt with humanistic approaches to various kinds of people. These are well worth the reader's time for general and specific understanding. Together, they illustrate the lasting good of the relevance era — that is, that American educational enterprises shall never again be permitted (1) complacency with the dualism of traditional college preparatory goals for those who achieve in spite of schools, and mediocre vocational education for those who do not achieve but choose to stay; (2) satisfaction with the spurious submission that the home and inner-city or penurious rural environments are to blame for nonlearners; (3) ignorance of the indulgences of unemployed young adults in alcohol, drugs, crime and other diversions; (4) forgetfulness of the fact that learning capacities and more essential features of human existence may be realized at levels beyond all imagination in schools which are relevant to the human condition; (5) ignorance of the successes which Cohen and Filipczak (1971), Dawson (1968), Silberman (1970), McLuhan and Leonard (1969), Glasser (1969), Leonard (1968), Postman and Weingartner (1971; 1969), and others reflect; or (6) assurance that other institutions will not assume the formal school's functions if it continues its traditional course.

Relevance Wanes

This reduces relevance to a mere platitude. Like all platitudes, relevance fell out of favor. It was shorter-lived than excellence because under its guise only the kinds of patients and, in some instances, the delivery method were changed. In the main, the pill (i.e., the content of instruction) was the same: traditional studies for those who could further their education, and, at best, out-of-date vocational or terribly watered general education for those who could not. By the late 1960's, astute speakers and authors (e.g., Wagner, 1969) were asking "relevance to what?"

The movement was not dismissed as an out-and-out sham because many of the changes it signalled were good. But learned analysts of the educational scene, such as Crabtree (1971) found the argument for relevance wanting. Crabtree examines the word in the fashion of a logical positivist, concluding that relevance means "solving my problems" and hastening to point out that each person solves his own problems. This leaves us with the same concern which ushered in the relevance era. *With what problems of what individuals should the educational enterprise be concerned?* The relevance argument is, after all, empty. It is not spurious at the level of example, but empty in its entirety.

Relevance was a good watchword for piecemeal analysis of localized curriculum issues, concerning homogeneous groups or as related to given individuals. But, it fell short of being a guidepost for the thrust of education in the 1970's.

Only a few, such as Feldman (1968) had argued that education should be relevant to modern technology and unemployment. Fewer still had Feldman's foresight to suggest massive improvement in the entire process of education. Far more, such as Blyth (1970), spoke of the value of irrelevance without proposing a replacement principle of content selection or matching.

After all, a lot of the affluent and as many as before of the so-called disadvantaged were not being assimilated psychologically, socially or economically into the mainstream of America. The pendulum had swung through its arc and would reverse along a new dimension. Relevance had righted educational conditions for some, but reflection showed that it did not adequately define education for particular peoples and places.

Legacy of Relevance

Relevance was never to be forgotten. It *did* teach educators the significance of social and personal relevance. In *Schools Without Failure* Glasser (1969) puts well the objection to determinism which was the life and bequeath of the relevance era. "I do not accept the rationalization of failure commonly accepted today, that young people are products of a social situation that precludes success. Blaming their failure upon their homes, their communities, their culture, their background, their race, or their poverty is a dead end for two reasons: (1) it removes personal responsibility for failure, and (2) it does not recognize that success is potentially open to all young people" (Glasser, 1969, pp. 4-5). For Glasser, success in school depends upon involvement, relevance, on a problem-solving approach. These are integral with good *education* of all kinds and career education especially.

Synthesis: Accountability

By 1970, a number of prominent people on the American educational scene had begun to use the synthesizing term *account-*

ability. Several major developments suggested that the public educational enterprise should heed the Webster's New World Dictionary definition: "the condition of being accountable, liable, or responsible." Soon it appeared that the more pointed American Heritage Dictionary definition: "noun, subject to having to report, explain, or *justify;* responsible, answerable," would prevail.

People who use the word "accountability" tend to subsume some of the features of excellence and relevance under the new term. Whereas in simplified form excellence tended to answer what, regardless of whom, and relevance tended to answer whom, regardless of what, *accountability* is an attempt to answer both the whom and what questions — *in that order.*

The new word is like most synthesizers. Synthesizing ideas incorporate the principles of multiple causality and are appreciative of the existence of pluralisms in society. Several of the antecedents of accountability were enumerated by Barro (1970, p. 196): "1) the new, federally stimulated emphasis on evaluation of school systems and their programs; 2) the growing tendency to look at educational enterprises in terms of cost effectiveness; 3) increasing concentration on education for the disadvantaged as a priority area of responsibility for schools; and 4) the movement to make school systems more directly responsible to their clientele and communities, either by establishing decentralized community control or by introducing consumer choice through a voucher scheme."[4]

Legislative Origin

Austin (1971) credits the late Senator Robert Kennedy with starting the accountability movement.[5] Senator Kennedy insisted on the evaluation features of the Elementary and Secondary Education Act of 1965. Since that time, legislation has tended to require clear measures of the benefits of funded programs. This trend was firmly established by the 1968 Amendments to the Vocational Education Act of 1963. This legislation required the establishment of independent advisory councils for vocational and technical education in each of the states and for the Nation. Annual reports in many states and especially for the Nation have been incisive and nearly damning of the educational establishment. The efforts of advisory councils have abetted the trend toward accountability in local schools and colleges.

[4]In the same issue of the Kappan, Lessinger and others point to these same forces.
[5]For an interesting description of "Accountability in Victorian England," see Small (1972).

Administrative Directive

By late 1970 the United States Office of Education was demanding credible and convincing evidence that monies from Title I and other appropriations were serving to effect significant educational gains. By this time, the demands were clearly for objective test results or other hard data. Whereas earlier programs had required only perfunctory evaluative procedures, we were by 1970 in an altogether different mood. This was made patently clear in President Nixon's education message of March 3, 1970. "School administrators and school teachers alike are responsible for their performance, and it is in this interest as well as in the interests of their pupils that they be held accountable" (Nixon, 1970, p. 4).

At the same time as funding agencies were increasing objectivity requirements, various segments of the public were examining educational enterprises in terms of cost/benefits. We began to look at education the way the Office of Management and Budgets looks at defense spending or the way industrialists look at value added in manufacturing and distribution enterprises.

During the 1960's schools had been rather adequately provided with funds on the premise that major education problems could be solved with money. But, by the late 1960's, bond issues and referenda were failing in most locales. Everywhere people were asking for evidence of the validity of proposed improvements and absolute values of previously effected improvements.

Primarily because of major discoveries which insightful researchers made during the conduct of specialized programs for disadvantaged peoples, the emphasis or orientation of education shifted, by the start of the 1970's, from *teaching* to *learning*. Lessinger (1970a) is perhaps more aware of the long-term implications of this tendency than any other. He submits that "the present and traditional methods of requesting resources for education as the principle bases for accrediting schools will undergo basic change. Instead of equating quality in terms of resources allocated, such as kinds and numbers of teachers, space available, materials for use and books in the library, the independent variable will become student accomplishment" (Lessinger, 1970a, p. 56).

Decentralization and Outside Review

During this same period there was a movement to decentralize control of large school systems. This was, in part, a response to the pressures of citizen groups which were concerned to foster the causes of civil rights and other social movements.

Decentralization is an approach to accountability. It places certain decision-making powers on the very people whose lives are most closely associated with the schools. Decentralization encourages citizen concern. In many places it raises incisive economic questions regarding the ratio of costs and benefits. This is the extension of the tradition of outside review in education. Now, more firmly than ever before, it is established that schools are accountable to the citizenry.

Alternative Deliveries

The movement toward new forms of accountability in education was fostered by experiments with new means for providing educational experiences.

(1) The voucher system was proposed by the Office of Economic Opportunity. One of the better sources of information regarding the voucher system is the September 1970, *Kappan*. Articles by Jencks (1970), Havinghurst (1970), and Clayton (1970) deal with the voucher system proposed by Christopher Jencks of Harvard University in a feasibility study done for the OEO. In sum, the voucher system would permit parents and guardians to send youngsters to the schools of their choice. There would be competition in schooling. Economics and government regulations would probably bring the level of competition to something between that of the utility and the appliance manufacturing industries. There would be special advantages for poor peoples; this is one of the intents of the plan.

For the present discussion it is important to note that voucher systems require kinds of accountability more like those in manufacturing corporations than in traditional government agencies. Parents and educational agencies in local and state government would have to be able to evaluate educational enterprises which compete in a more open market. This is not altogether a new development. There have always been private schools at all levels for liberal education and at secondary and higher levels for vocational education. The new feature is the voucher, which would permit individual shopping with tax dollars — thus to assure accountability for each educational transaction.

(2) Performance contracting is the other major alternative educational delivery system. The proponents of performance contracting submit that private contractors have greater opportunity to use modern motivational and instructional methods than existing school systems. The typical performance contract includes several rather standard procedures. These are clearly explained by Lessinger (1970b). First, the local school (or college) employs a management group which will be answerable to the central administration. This group works with school district personnel and community people to prepare a request for proposal (RFP). This document contains clear definitions of what is to be accomplished, time frames, resources to be invested, etc. The RFP is sent to interested agencies in keeping with local and state bidding requirements. Usually a pre-bidding conference is needed with those agencies which wish to submit formal bids. This conference results in information sharing, dispels misunderstandings and refines the RFP. Then formal RFP's are sent to those who indicate they will submit proposal-contracts. The governing board of the district selects the best bid and a performance contract is signed. This contract includes precise definitions of the accountability measures which shall be applied during and at the completion of the project period.

The major performance contracts have been undertaken at Texarkana, Arkansas, and Liberty-Eylan, Texas; Gary, Indiana; Gilroy, California; Norfolk, Virginia; and Grand Rapids, Michigan. These have been evaluated by Carpenter and Hall (1971) of the Rand Corporation. The study reports point up a number of advantages and pitfalls, concluding that performance contracting is especially useful for research and development purposes.

Advantages stem from the fact that an outside agency is freer to implement radical change than is any permanent part of the school system. Any number of valuable ideas can be tried, refined, and developed under performance contracts.

The major pitfalls of performance contracting are: (1) not having a responsible school officer assigned to the project and thoroughly committed to its success, (2) not assuring flexibility or maneuverability in the contract itself, (3) not defining the substance of the instruction carefully enough, (4) inadequate "selling" of features such as differentiated staffing to existing professionals, and (5) not specifying evaluative measures carefully enough before the fact.

Performance contracting has come under serious attack and may well fall from the American scene. This is partly the result of inadequate evaluative procedures and measures. Carpenter and Hall (1971) submit that standardized tests do not measure enough of the complexities of behavior which result from performance contracts. Counter to the fears of educationists, the individualized approach of most performance contracts has been humanizing for most students. Greater personal responsibility has been the key to this. In the main, the results of performance contracts have been disappointing to all parties concerned. Among other benefits of the few well-studied performance contracts which have been undertaken to date is the discovery that altogether new measures of cognitive gain will have to be developed. These will be designed to measure short-run gains against tight criteria.

Future of Accountability

Some oppose the movement which would make schooling more business-like and insist that schoolmen have all the say (Ratliff, 1971; Jordan, 1971). Others sagely forewarn schoolmen that accountability can be a wolf in sheep's clothing and show that only the word and the intensity of the movement is new; i.e., measurement has always been of some concern (Underwood 1970).

But no one can deny that education is going to be subjected to more and more careful scrutiny. Voucher systems; performance contracting; existence of the Office of Economic Opportunity, Manpower Development and Training Act, and other such programs; and proposed legislation which would establish new institutions for school-aged youth who do not succeed in extant educational enterprises suggest that accountability measures will become increasingly important. Forsberg (1971) identifies four groups which support the accountability movement in education: legislative and administrative people in government, corporations in the educational-industrial complex, inner-city school leadership, and minority and disadvantaged peoples. In the final analysis, education is simply too important — as are medicine, law, and other institutions — to be trusted to spurious self-regulation.

The concerns which spurred the accountability movement do not appear to be abating. In his book, *Every Kid a Winner: Accountability in Education,* Lessinger (1970c) states these as three basic rights: (1) Each child has a right to be taught what he needs to be a producing, participating member of society; (2) Taxpayers and their representatives have a right to examine educational results and costs; (3) Schools have a right to utilize a far larger array of resources such as technology and talent than they have heretofore.

In the future, accountability is certain to take several forms. People at different levels will be accountable to specified superiors for specified results. Alkin (1972) summarizes "Who is accountable to whom for what?" in Table 2-2.

The components of accountability are compatible with or, better put, are part and parcel of the two major present concerns

TABLE 2-2

ACCOUNTABILITY TYPES

	Who is Accountable	To Whom (Primary Responsibility)	For What
Goal Accountability	School Board	Public	Goal and objective selection
Program Accountability	School district management	School board	Development and/or selection of instructional programs appropriate for stated objectives
Outcome Accountability	Instructional manager (i.e., teacher)	School district management	Producing program outcomes consistent with preselected objectives at a performance standard appropriate for the instructional program

SOURCE: M. C. Alkin, "Accountability defined," *Evaluation Comment,* 1972, 3 (3), p. 4.

in education, i.e., career education (the principle concern of this book) and educational engineering.

Educational Engineering

Taken together with other developments which have enjoyed increasing success in corporate and governmental agencies since World War II, performance contracting may be called *educational engineering.* In the vernacular, this puts it *all together.* Again, Lessinger (1970b) is the best resource:

Since World War II several fields have been developed to enable managers of very complex enterprises to operate efficiently and effectively. These emerging fields of knowledge and practice are commonly known as systems analysis, management by objectives, contract engineering (including bids, warranties, penalities, and incentives), logistics, quality assurance, value engineering, and human factors engineering, to name a few of the more important. If to these are added instructional technology and modern educational management theory, a new and valuable interdisciplinary field emerges. This body of knowledge, skill, and procedure can be called educational engineering. It is the insights from education engineering that makes it possible for performance contracting to achieve accountability for results in education.

Why couple the term 'engineering' with education? Why more apparent dehumanization? It is not appropriate here to treat this question at great length. But I note that engineering has traditionally been a problem-solving activity and a profession dedicated to the application of technology to the resolution of real world difficulties and opportunities. While the teaching-learning environment differs from the world of business and industry, some rationalization of the two subcultures may be beneficial. A major objective of educational engineering may very well be to arm educational practitioners with both the technological competence of essential engineering generalizations, strategies, and tools and the professional practice of a successful instructor or educational manager. From this point of view, educational engineering can be a symbiotic art — a marriage of humanism and technology. It is this possible symbiosis that makes performance contracting for learning accomplishment feasible (Lessinger, 1970b, 218).

Summary

Accountability is certain to last longer than its antecedents. Synthesizers nearly always do because they utilize much of the good of previous movements. The excellence movement cried out for sterner assessments of education's product. Relevance cried out for concern for people. Accountability embraced this and business and industrial acumen as well. As Lieberman (1970) puts it, the issue is not whether accountability will remain a concern in American education, but what kind of accountability will prevail.

More important to our discussion is what accountability says about the function of schooling. Accountability takes cognizance of the fact that the educational enterprise cannot look to only one position on any dimension but must look to several positions on each of several dimensions for definitions of function. In short, *accountability* signifies education which is answerable to its clientele (relevance to all manner of students), to taxpayers and their evolving definition of the American life style (excellence for citizenship and worthy use of leisure), and to employers (excellence for work and continuing education necessary in an evolving, technological economy).

This latter is the glue which makes the thesis and antithesis over into a new and acceptable synthesis. Add to the older excellence and relevance the idea that people shall participate economically, i.e., shall work, and you get the new, tripartite accountability.

Suddenly it comes clear that a return to the more comfortable psychological, sociological, and economic conditions of the ephemeral "good old days" might — just might — be possible if schools somehow knit together individuals, the American dream, and employment. It dawns clear that what has been missing in too much of the American educational enterprise is occupational information, career guidance and occupational education. It is believed that domestic conditions may be better balanced if educational systems are designed to be at the same time adaptive to people, informative for nonutilitarian ends *and* career oriented. The psychological, sociological, and economic functions must not be compromised one for another. No two can be maximized without the other. If any one is more important than the others, it is the economic function because man derives his major satisfactions and status from his work.

In the mid-70's details of the new curriculum are not clear, but some features begin to come into focus:

1. Intensive study in specialized fields cannot be begun later than now. Schools and colleges are already too alien to the real world.
2. Children and youth deserve much more exposure to the social and behavioral sciences — better to understand themselves and groups they encounter in play, learning, and work.
3. Children and youth deserve general and, at some level on the educational ladder, specialized study about technology. Somehow the common school has to get handles on the major force of the age, i.e., technology.
4. Occupational awareness, orientation, exploration, and preparation for careers have to become *central rather than peripheral in the curriculum*. Regardless of school-leaving age, individuals should possess saleable entry skills and have the opportunity to return without stigma or penalty to the educational enterprise for instruction which will advance them on career ladders.
5. All aspects of prespecialized and much of specialized curriculum will be structured in other than traditional ways. The whims of professors and teachers must be satisfied outside the classroom. There are too many splinter disciplines, too many occupations, and too many mobility factors to permit still-camera thinking regarding

curricula. Movements now underway in universities presage what is sure to come in the secondary and elementary schools.

6. *Processes* will become more important than specific units of content. The emphasis will be upon learning how to learn, how to update for avocational and vocational purposes, how to move with the world rather than watch it go by. Learning resources centers — large libraries of taped materials for instance — differentiated staffing, and flexible modular scheduling which are already well-used features of the better schools and colleges will permit learners of all ages to come with purpose to prescribed content.

7. Detail regarding hardware, software and staff systems in the accountable educational enterprise are another, exciting story which shows that we will get more meaningful education for fewer dollars — that's the acid test of accountability.

BIBLIOGRAPHY

Alkin, M. C. Accountability defined. *Evaluation Comment,* 1972, 3(3), 1-5.

Austin, G. R. Educational accountability; hallmark of the 1970's. *Science Teacher,* 1971, 38, 26-28.

Barro, S. M. An approach to developing accountability measures for public schools. *Phi Delta Kappan,* 1970, 11(4), 196-205.

Beck, C. E. *et al. Education for relevance.* New York: Houghton Mifflin, 1968, 233-248.

Bell, D. *The reforming of general education.* New York: Columbia University Press, 1966.

Blyth, M. D. Case for irrelevance. *English Journal,* 1970, 59, 380-383.

Broudy, H. S., et. al., *Democracy and excellence in American secondary education.* Chicago: Rand McNally, 1964.

Broudy, R. W. Planning for excellence. In E. C. Short and G. D. Marconnit (eds.) *Contemporary thought on public school curriculum.* Dubuque, Iowa: Wm. C. Brown, 1968, 56-60.

Bruner, J. S. *The relevance of education.* New York: W. W. Norton, 1971.

Burns, R. W. and Brooks, G. D. The need for curriculum reform. *Educational Technology,* 1970, 10, 8-12.

Carpenter, P. and Hall, G. Case studies in educational performance contracting. Part 1. Conclusions and implications. Santa Monica, Cal.: Rand Corp., 1971. (ED 056-247).

Christine, E. R. What education is good? *Clearing House,* 1967, 42, 19-22.

Clayton, A. S. Vital questions, minimal responses: Education vouchers. *Phi Delta Kappan,* 1970, 52(1), 53-54.

Cohen, H. L. and Filipczak, J., *A new learning environment.* San Francisco: Jossey-Bass, 1971.

Crabtree, W. B. Age of irrelevancy. *Educational Theory,* 1971, 21, 33-41.

Dawson, H. *On the outskirts of hope.* New York: McGraw-Hill, 1968.

Durost, W. N. Accountability: The task, the tools, and the pitfalls. *The Reading Teacher,* 1971, 24, 291-304.

Ennis, R. H. Can philosophy of education be relevant? *Educational Theory,* 1970, 20, 337-344.

Feirer, J. L. Is industrial arts relevant? *Industrial Arts and Vocational Education,* 1970, 59, 29.

————. Relevancy and occupational education. *Industrial Arts and Vocational Education,* 1971, 60(2), 19.

Feldman, M. J. Making education relevant. In E. C. Short and G. D. Marconnit (eds.), *Contemporary thought on public school curriculum.* Dubuque, Iowa: Wm. C. Brown, 1968.

Forsberg, J. R. *Accountability and performance contracting.* Eugene, Oregon: ERIC Clearinghouse on Educational Management, 1971. (EA003 680).

Freeman, R. A. Dead end in American education. *Education Digest,* 1969, 34, 9-13.

Gardner, J. W. *Excellence.* New York: Harper & Row, 1961.

Glasser, W. *Schools without failure.* New York: Harper & Row, 1969.

Goble, F. *The third force — the psychology of Abraham Maslow.* New York: Grossman Publishers, 1970.

Goldman, H. Nature of curricular relevance. *Elementary Education Leader,* 1970, 27, 489.

Goodman, P. No processing whatever. In Beatrice and Ronald Gross (eds.), *Radical school reform.* New York: Simon & Schuster, 1969, 98-106.

Gordon, W. E. Relevance or revolt. *Perspectives on Education,* 1969, 3, 10-16.

Harlacher, E. L. and Roberts, E. Accountability for student learning. *Junior College Journal,* 1971, 41, 26-30.

Harmin, M. and Simon, S. B. Relevance and the kissing curriculum; satire. *National Elementary Principal,* 1970, 50, 40-43.

Havinghurst, R. L. The unknown good: Education vouchers. *Phi Delta Kappan,* 1970, 52(1), 52-53.

Hilton, A. M. *The evolving society.* New York: The Institute for Cybercultural Research, 1966.

Hocking, E. Culture, relevance and survival. *Modern Language Journal,* 1970, 54, 585-588.

Holloway, R. L. How relevant is equality? *Education Digest,* 1970, 35, 19-21.

Jencks, C. Giving parents money for schooling: Education vouchers. *Phi Delta Kappan,* 1970, 52(1), 49-52.

Jordan, B. Educational accountability: A crucial question. *Junior College Journal,* 1971, 41, 23-25.

Kaufman, R. A. Accountability, a system approach and the quantitative improvement of education — an attempted integration. *Educational Technology,* 1971, 11, 21-26.

Kranzberg, M. and Pursell, C. W. *Technology in western civilization, Vol. II.* New York: Oxford University Press, 1967.

Leonard, G. B. *Education and ecstacy.* New York: Delacorte Press, 1968.

Lessinger, L. M. Accountability and curriculum reform. *Educational Technology,* 1970, 10, 56-57. (a)

————. Accountability in education. *Educational Technology,* 1971, 11, 11-31.

————. Engineering accountability for results in public education. *Phi Delta Kappan,* 1970, 52(4), 217-225. (b)

————. *Every kid a winner: Accountability in education.* New York: Simon and Schuster, 1970. (c)

54   *Career Education*

Lieberman, M. An overview of accountability. *Phi Delta Kappan*, 1970, 52(4), 194-195.

Maslow, A. H. *The farther reaches of human nature*. New York: Viking Press, 1971.

McLuhan, M. and Leonard, G. Learning in the global village. In B. and R. Gross (eds.), *Radical school reform*. New York: Simon and Schuster, 1969, 106-115.

Metcalf, L. E. and Hunt, M. P. Relevance and the curriculum. *Phi Delta Kappan*, 1970, 5, 358-361.

Nelson, H. F. Upgrading the relevance of industrial arts. *School Shop*, 1970, 29, 95-97.

Nixon, R. M. Education message to congress. March 3, 1970.

Ohme, H. Steps toward relevance: An interest-centered curriculum. *Journal of Secondary Education*, 1970, 45, 299-304.

Parnell, D. State plan for applying relevancy to education. *American Vocational Journal*, 1969, 44, 14-17.

Postman, N. and Weingartner, C. *Teaching as a subversive activity*. New York: Dell Publishing, 1969. (a)

———. What's worth knowing? In B. and R. Gross (eds.) *Radical School Reform*. New York: Simon and Schuster, 1969, 161-178. (b)

———. *The self revolution*. New York: Delacorte Press, 1971.

Punke, H. H. Outlook for humanizing all vocational education. *American Vocational Journal*, 1968, 43, 19-20.

Ratliff, F. E. Accountability: At what cost? *English Journal*, 1971, 60, 485-490.

Reynolds, R. N. Toward relevancy, curriculum, and the social order. *School and Society*, 1971, 99, 29-30.

Robinson, D. W. Accountability for whom? *Phi Delta Kappan*, 1970, 52, 193.

Schon, D. *Technology and change*. New York: Delacorte Press, 1967.

Schure, A. Accountability and evaluation design for occupational education. *Educational Technology*, 1971, 11, 26-37.

Shields, J. J. Jr. Foundations of education: Relevance redefined. *Teachers College Record*, 1969, 71, 187-198.

Seckinger, S. Freedom and responsibility in education. *School and Society*, 1968, 96, 278-279.

Silberman, C. E., *Crisis in the Classroom*. New York: Random House, 1970.

Small, A. A. Accountability in Victorian England. *Phi Delta Kappan*, 1972, 53(7), 438-439.

Stadt, R. W. Excellence, relevance and accountability: Watchwords of the educational enterprise. *Illinois Vocational Progress*, 1970, 28(1), 32-35.

Stenner, J. Accountability by public demand. *American Vocational Journal*, 1971, 46, 33-37.

Stocker, J. and Wilson, D. F. Accountability and the classroom teacher. *Today's Education*, 1971, 23, 45-51.

Toffler, A. *Future shock*. New York: Random House, 1970.

Underwood, K. E. Before you decide to be accountable, make sure you know for what. *American School Board Journal*, 1970, 158, 32-33.

Wagschal, P. H. On the irrelevance of relevance. *Phi Delta Kappan*, 1970, 51, 51.

Wagner, R., Relevance and revolt. *Audiovisual instruction*, 1969, 14, 36-37.

Career Development Theory and Research

CHAPTER 3

Theories of Career Development
and Occupational Choice

Introduction

American public education is based on the very simple assumption that intervention (i.e., schooling) during the formative years of childhood and adolescence prepares individuals for adulthood and various and sundry roles in society. In Part I, it was demonstrated that the school has not served the majority of its students and that its curriculum is not designed to prepare youth for adulthood, but rather qualifies them only for more schooling. The school's responsibility for assisting individuals with career planning, decision-making and preparation for entrance into employment has been almost totally ignored. Many of the impediments to career education in the schools were likewise discussed in Part I. The rationale for this chapter is predicated on the belief that expansion of career education in the schools will require understanding on the part of teachers regarding the vocational development aspect of growth and learning.

That teachers must internalize some type of theoretical position relative to career development is made obvious by the requirements of good practice. For example, the systematic attempt to provide self-development experiences at the elementary school level implies a belief that self-concept development is important in career decision-making. Similarly, the decision to administer a particular type of interest inventory (or to reject the practice) is based on the belief that career decisions are influenced by the information which these instruments may provide. Teachers without a theoretical orientation will find it difficult to select from among the many available types of curriculum materials or to integrate such materials into an organized program of instruction. In this chapter, explanations and discussions of selected theories will help

57

the teacher (1) to see more clearly the beliefs implied in his own behavior, and (2) to question and modify many traditional practices and attitudes (Hoppock, 1967).

These professional needs are not the only reasons for learning more about vocational behavior. People have always been curious about themselves, i.e., about what makes them behave the way they do. Consequently, teachers may be motivated to study career development, not only because of professional responsibility, but also because of curiosity about themselves and how they came to be as they are (Hill, 1963).

The reader should understand at the outset that scientific attempts to develop theories to account for the phenomena of vocational behavior are in the infancy stage. While it is almost impossible to give a precise definition of what constitutes career development theory, there seems to be universal agreement that all theories of career development and occupational choice have been formulated to explain *how* individuals choose occupations and *why* they select and eventually enter different occupations (Crites, 1969).

Definition and Function of Theory

In the broadest sense, a theory is a systematic interpretation of the relationship believed to prevail in a comprehensive body of facts. There is a continuum among theories from those which describe to those which explain. A theory is more solidly supported by evidence than a general principle, but it is less firmly established than a law. Students of the physical sciences will be quick to note that theories in the behavioral sciences seldom approach the level of specificity and certainty as do theories in mathematics, for example.

The development of comprehensive theories to explain behavior is a continuous process of:
1. Collecting raw data;
2. Extrapolating theory from facts;
3. Testing hypotheses derived from that theory; and
4. Modifying, reconstructing, or adapting the theory in keeping with empirical data.

This outline of the research process is usually referred to as the *heuristic function* of a theory. An additional purpose of theory, and the one considered more important from this book's perspective, is its *operational adequacy*. Thus, theory should assist and guide the work of the practitioner. The functions of theory related to application in the work setting are listed by Zaccaria (1970, p. 3) as follows:

1. Keeps data in order.
2. Reduces complexities to manageable proportions.
3. Tells the practitioner what to look for, what to expect, and where to go.
4. Leads to the observation of relationships which might have been previously overlooked.
5. Defines operational truths.
6. Focuses attention on relevant data by telling what to look for.
7. Leads to the use of consistent terminology.
8. Helps to construct new methods of behaving.
9. Leads to useful generalizations.
10. Aids in seeing sense and meaning in other people's behavior.

Historical Perspectives: 1909-1951

The present theories of career development trace their roots to the beginning of the present century with the birth of the vocational guidance movement. Frank Parsons, director of the first vocational guidance center in the United States, provided the framework for the first theory of occupational choice. Parsons (1909) advocated a scientific approach to vocational counseling which he outlined in a three-phase approach: study and understanding of self; study of the requirements of occupations; and "true reasoning" about the relationships among the facts obtained.

The development of this approach was characterized by an emphasis on measureable attributes as predictors of educational and vocational success. Consequently, the psychology of individual differences, which underlies the method of determining occupational ability, became the basis of vocational psychology. Super (1954) and Pepinsky and Pepinsky (1954) have called this practice the "actuarial method." They define the underlying theory as the *trait theory of vocational guidance.* Katz (1963, p. 6) provides a concise description of this theory:

To oversimplify, this theory holds that first, the individual is in effect 'keyed' to one or a few 'correct' occupational positions; second, if left to his own devices, he would probably gravitate toward the right choice, but with some wasted motion and time and some possibility of missing the proper target altogether; third, the 'key' should therefore be learned — and can be learned — quite early in adolescence; fourth, all educational decisions should be determined by the requirements and characteristics imputed to this 'appropriate' vocation; fifth, the occupational goal should remain constant over a period of time and the final goal can be known early and can — and should — determine all preliminary decisions (for example, choice of high school curriculum and other educational alternatives) leading up to it.

One of the first applications of the psychology of individual differences was the emphasis on intelligence testing. Mental tests were first used to discover students' general level of intelligence for guidance purposes. Proctor (1920) ascertained that intelligence level could be used as a means of selecting school subjects and was a significant predictor of success in a particular subject. He concluded that "the best way in which to arrive at an estimate of a given pupil's probable success in a specific high school subject [was] to discover the general level of his intelligence" (Proctor, 1920, p. 381).

Use of the Army Alpha Intelligence Test with soldiers during World War I gave the intelligence testing movement the greatest stimulus it has ever had. There can be no doubt that the experience of the Army demonstrated the value of the various tests which were used. Some people were so impressed by the success of the Army tests that they believed a method had been found for classifying all human beings for all sorts of purposes (Super, 1957c).

The need for successful placement of men in the armed services resulted in studies designed to link intelligence levels with occupational classifications. On the basis of psychological examinations, one such study classified the Alpha grades of "literate white men" into fifty-five occupations. Each occupation was then ranked according to median intelligence scores. This ranking illustrated that there seemed to be four or five primary occupational levels. The researchers concluded that ". . . from the practical point of view . . . the table of occupational intelligence standards could be used in the Army with resulting increased efficiency in the placement of men" (Yerkes, 1921, p. 837).

The classification of occupations by intelligence levels resulted in attempts by vocational counselors to establish occupational-intelligence standards to assist in the process of vocational counseling and in the selection of personnel. Fryer (1922) established five occupational levels — Professional, Technical, Skilled, Semiskilled, and Unskilled — with intelligence as the basis for grouping. He then developed a table listing the occupational-intelligence standards for ninety-six occupational designations. The occupations were indexed according to the average intelligence scores of a few hundred cases. The intelligence mean for the occupation was presented as the "score average." The "score range" indicated the range of intelligence within which one could expect success in that occupation. Examples, with the score averages indicated, are as follows: Engineer 161; Clergyman 152; Teacher 122; and Fireman 27; Sheet metal worker 22; Fisherman 20. As incredible as it may seem, the classification of occupations according to required intelligence was for a long time the predominant technique of counselors who apprised individuals of their vocational potential.

The Extension of Trait Theory

During the 1920's a team of researchers at the University of Minnesota began to construct broad outlines for a scientific vocational testing and counseling program (Paterson, 1949). When the depression began in 1929, this group undertook to apply newly discovered techniques to the study of hundreds of cases of unemployed workers. The work was carried on by the Committee on Individual Diagnosis and Training of the Minnesota Employment Stabilization Research Institute. It was one of the first large-scale attempts to utilize a variety of psychological tests and measurements.

Throughout the five-year study, numerous independent studies were undertaken and completed. The program of individual diagnosis and training involved the principles and techniques of various related fields, including industrial social work, vocational psychology, industrial medicine, industrial education, and personnel administration and management. This approach to problems of unemployment may best be described as that of "human engineering." Out of this research came increased knowledge of the vocational significance of measures of standard intelligence, clerical aptitude, mechanical ability, manipulative dexterities, vocational interest, and personalities. Occupational ability profiles were developed so that individual psychographs could be interpreted in a limited way in terms of occupational requirements. The idea was itself a forerunner of the notion of job families as developed by the Occupational Research Program of the United States Employment Service. The Institute not only made significant contribution, but also set a pattern for studies of occupations which served as the foundation for nationwide occupational research, both civilian and military (Paterson, 1949; Paterson and Darley, 1936).

In the late 1930's, increasing attention was given to the measurement of basic psychological functions in aptitude tests and aptitude test batteries (Stuit, 1949). The United States Employment Service (USES), in 1933, launched a five-year study to develop a test battery through a process of job and worker analysis. The resultant USES General Aptitude Test Battery (GATB) was a combination of tests which measured a number of important aptitudes. The basic assumption underlying the GATB was that a large variety of tests could be boiled down to several factors, and that a large variety of occupations could be clustered into groups according to similarities in the abilities required (Dvorak, 1956).

The battery was standardized by first identifying jobs to serve as the basis for the selection of an experimental sample. Persons who were performing the same kind of job and who were regarded as proficient on that job (by foreman or supervisor) were included in the sample. This group was then administered fifteen subtests of the GATB, chosen as a result of factor analysis studies. Occupational Aptitude Patterns were established after analysis of test data and job analysis schedules showed that certain occupations required similar, minimum amounts of the same combination of aptitudes. The GATB could then be administered to a counselee to determine his Individual Aptitude Profile. The Individual Aptitude Profile was then compared with the twenty Occupational Aptitude Patterns to determine the fields of work that were most suitable for an individual's abilities (Dvorak, 1947).

The major purpose of the Occupational Research Program of the USES was to furnish public employment offices and other cooperating agencies with practical tools for counseling, classification and placement of workers. Thus, *this technique was a testimonial to the widespread acceptance of vocational counseling as a process of "matching" abilities and interests with occupational requirements and trends* (Crites, 1965; Stead and Shartle, 1940; Super, 1954).

A Changing Emphasis

During the years preceding World War I, the primary motive of test constructors appeared to be that of building tests which would measure specific psychological variables, regardless of the tests' predictive value. In the years between the two World Wars, the primary concern was to construct tests to predict success in particular areas of study or vocational activity. This approach, in other words, was empirical and not based on any formalized theory of aptitude or mental organization (Guilford, 1948; Stuit, 1949).

At the outbreak of World War II, the importance of problems of selection and classification accentuated a further development of the trait approach. Consistent with previous studies, the results of Army General Classification Test scores virtually duplicated the occupational hierarchies constructed from World War I Army Alpha scores (Stewart, 1947). There was a realization, however, of the possibility that the AGCT was a "measure of ability to manipulate words, numbers and space relations, . . . and those occupations with the lowest averages on the test [were] the occupations least concerned with words, numbers or space relations" (Harrell and Harrell, 1945, p. 239).

The second type of emphasis in occupational counseling was given to experimental and theoretical studies of the nature of abilities (Stuit, 1949). Work-sample tests were designed to present a task which resembled the features of a job or some elementary components of the job. An example of a work-sample test was the Army Air Force Classification battery which was designed to present a task analogous to that of a pilot operating an airplane in flight (Guilford, 1948). The Aviation Psychology Program of the Army Air Force utilized an array of aptitude tests for predicting success in a pilot selection program. Using multiple-regression techniques (a type of advanced statistical method) derived differentially from weighted combinations of test scores, assignments were made to pilot, navigator, or bombadier training (Katz, 1963).

The evolution of the trait-centered approach to vocational counseling culminated in the years following World War II. The early results of factor analysis studies indicated that there was considerable duplication in what was measured by different psychological tests. The number of functional units (factors) which accounted for variation in test scores was actually much smaller than the total number of tests. As the intercorrelational information regarding test and criteria grew, the basis for increasing use of factor analysis theory and practice was strengthened (Pepinsky and Pepinsky, 1954; Stuit, 1949; Guilford, 1948). Based on results of factor analysis studies, the emphasis approaching mid-century was primarily on the measurement of "pure factors" for the differential prediction and selection for civilian occupations. In regard to theory during this period:

> . . . the predominant conception of vocational choice was essentially a cross-sectional, nondevelopmental one . . . it emphasized the ahistorical, instantaneous, nondynamic elements in vocational decision making. Resolution of the problem of choosing an occupation, whether before or after entry into the world of work, was seen as a point-in-time event when the individual, more or less consciously and rationally, appraised his personal assets and liabilities, surveyed the employment opportunities open to him, and decided upon the one which offered him the greatest chances for job satisfaction and success (Crites, 1965, p. 1).

Concern for the Adequacy of Trait Theory

While guidance practices during this era were aimed at differential prediction through the application of trait-and-factor theory, there was growing concern that deficiencies existed in both theory and practice. Thorndike and Hagen (1959) conducted a study in 1955 of 10,000 men who had been given a battery of aptitude tests in 1943. Their investigation was based on tests administered to applicants for Aviation Cadet status in the Army Air Force in World War II. The analysis of aptitude test scores for these men was compared with information concerning their educational and vocational history.

Results showed that occupational groups differed with respect to personal background variables as well as aptitude test scores. The patterns were, in most cases, sensible and in accord with what might be expected. The authors reasoned that these differences should be "thought of as chance variables and ones that probably would not hold up in another sample" (p. 50).

With respect to the prediction of success within an occupation, however, their conclusions were quite different.

As far as we were able to determine from our data, there is no convincing evidence that aptitude tests or biographical information of the type that was available to us can predict degree of success within an occupation insofar as this is represented in the criterion measures that we were able to obtain. This would suggest that we should view the long-range prediction of occupational success by aptitude tests with a good deal of skepticism and take a very restrained view as to how much can be accomplished in this direction (p. 50).

. . .

In general, our conclusions must be that although the differentiation between occupations with respect to score on a group of tests is real, still this differentiation is less sharp than the test enthusiast would suggest, in this case when the occupations are all at approximately the same level and when the tests are limited to a battery of tests of abilities. We can hardly assert that the evidence presented in our results gives strong support for using tests to guide individuals into one or another of a set of occupations all at approximately the same level in the occupational hierarchy (p. 323).

In the final statement of their book, Thorndike and Hagen summarized their notions concerning the value of test batteries for predictive differentiation.

Individuals get into occupations for a great variety of reasons, many of which may be completely unrelated to their abilities or appropriateness for the occupation. Insofar as this is the case, we can hardly expect our tests to predict this event (p. 323).

Exposing the Myth

As concern grew about the appropriateness of trait-and-factor theory, methodology based on this approach continued to dictate vocational guidance practice. Barry and Wolfe (1962) refer to this method as the greatest myth in vocational guidance. "The repetition of the same theoretical position creates the myth that a single, universally accepted theory exists and the corollary myth that

vocational guidance practices have a sound theoretical basis"
(p. 3).

During the early 1950's, *alternative theories of vocational
behavior began to emerge.* These theories attempted to establish
generalizations and patterns that give knowledge about occupations
and the people in them. They were referred to by Barry and Wolfe
(1962) as "pattern" theories and were extremely important because they furnished the basis for the eventual destruction of antiquated methodological theory and practice.

The best-known theories are those dealing with "life stages."
Super (1954, 1960) credits two Austrians, Buehler and Lazarsfield,
with laying the groundwork for the modern theories. Lazarsfield
supplied research methods and forces for later pattern investigations and raised important issues about choices. Buehler's study
had a more direct influence on later American theories. She traced
the processes of development throughout the entire life span. Her
theory of life stages (growth, exploration, establishment, maintenance, and decline) was to serve as a framework for the organization of data concerning vocational choice and adjustment. A person's vocational development, as well as other aspects of his life,
was assumed to fit into this same developmental pattern.

The second half of the twentieth century marked the beginning
of a new era of career development theorizing. During the fifties
and sixties, dozens of authors, individually and collectively, offered
theories re the process of choosing a career. In the sections that
follow, the more prominent of these theories will be discussed.

Ginzberg's General Theory of Occupational Choice

In 1951, the research team of Ginzberg, Ginsburg, Axelrad,
and Herma (1951) published the first comprehensive theory of
vocational behavior — or what they called "a preliminary approach
to a general theory." This group was obviously influenced by
Buehler's study of life stages and is credited with introducing the
developmental approach to occupational selection theory. The
Ginzberg theory resulted from an empirical study in which interviews were conducted on sixty-four students at Horace Mann -
Lincoln School and Columbia University, both in New York City.
A cross-sectional sampling method was used to select a group
which they felt had maximum freedom in choosing an occupation.
All of the sample students were male, Protestant or Catholic, of
Anglo-Saxon background, and reared in an urban environment. The
researchers' purpose was to establish generalizations about the

types of occupational choices young people make before and after college. They concluded that the process of occupational decision-making could be analyzed in terms of three developmental periods. These periods can be differentiated by the way an individual "translates" his impulses and needs into an occupational choice.

The first stage they refer to as the *fantasy* period. During this time, ages six to eleven, a child thinks about an occupation in terms of his wish to be an adult and tries out a variety of adult situations by playing make-believe work roles — often the more stereotyped sex roles such as nurse, astronaut, cowboy, teacher, and doctor. The Ginzberg team coined the term "fantasy choice" to stress the nature of the choices (not the specific occupation) at this level. At this age, the child makes many types of choices and is usually unaware of any barriers which may stand in his way. He believes he can be whatever he wants to be. The primary criteria for selection of work activity is the pleasure function; i.e., the activity is selected because it is fun to do. The outstanding characteristic of the fantasy period is that the choices are arbitrary and are made without reference to reality, abilities, and potentials — three of the important ingredients which Ginzberg identified in the occupational choice process.

As the child continues to mature, he becomes increasingly concerned about the conditions of reality. The *tentative* period (ages eleven to seventeen) is characterized by the recognition of the problem of deciding on a future occupation. This period is further divided into four stages. The "interest stage," approximately ages eleven to twelve, is the time when the pre-adolescent begins to select activities primarily in terms of likes and interests. He is no longer satisfied with his old fantasy choices and often tends to regard them as "kid's stuff." During the "capacity stage," ages twelve to fourteen, the individual begins to evaluate his ability to function in areas in which he is interested. For the first time, he begins to become aware of external factors such as different occupations, different salaries, and different types of required education or training. In the "value stage," around ages fifteen and sixteen, the adolescent becomes aware of the range of factors which have to be taken into account in making an occupational choice. He must assess the whole range of factors related to a particular occupational preference and evaluate them in terms of his own goals and values. Finally, in the "transition stage," which is usually at the age of seventeen, the individual begins to shift from subjective factors — interests, capacities, and values — to reality conditions. The transition stage coincides with the end of high school and is a pivotal point in the individual's development. The turbulence of early adolescense is now gradually giving way to the calmer period of late adolescence.

The *realistic* period begins at about age eighteen and is composed of the stages of exploration, crystallization, and specification. During this time the individual recognizes that he must work out a compromise between what he wants and the opportunities which are available to him.

It is well to recall that the Ginzberg theory is based primarily on the study of a sample of students before and after college. Consequently, the description of the realistic period reflects this limitation. In the "exploration stage" the young adult tries to acquire the experience and education which he needs to resolve his occupational choice. An essential characteristic of the next stage, "crystallization," is that most individuals have now committed themselves to a vocational objective. The individual is finally able to synthesize the many forces, internal and external, that have relevance for his decision. The final stage in the realistic period is "specification." This stage represents a process of closure and involves specialization and planning within the area of choice.

The significance of the Ginzberg research and resultant general theory is the conclusion that occupational choice is not a single decision, but a developmental process which takes place over a minimum of six or seven years, and more typically, over ten or more years. This process can be differentiated by gross distinctions in behavior at different age levels.

From this primary finding, a second important generalization is stated: the process is largely irreversible. This is not to imply that the individual does not have control over the process of occupational decision-making, but rather to emphasize (1) that decisions cannot be repeated and (2) that later decisions are limited by previous decisions. Time cannot be relived. Early childhood experiences, educational exposures, and other factors can be experienced only once.

The final element of the Ginzberg theory states that the process of occupational choice ends in a compromise. During the years leading up to choice, the individual attempts to achieve a balance between a series of subjective elements — interests, capacities, values — and the opportunities and limitations in the real world.

After this chapter was drafted a restatement of Ginzberg's original theory appeared in the *Vocational Guidance Quarterly*. Ginzberg's (1972) reformulated theory has grown out of two decades of empirical research in manpower economics, much of which has been focused on the occupational problems of disadvantaged populations. Following is a summary of the three major elements of Ginzberg's original theory (1951, p. 169); his reformulated theory (1972, p. 172); and the authors' comments.

IA. "Occupational choice . . . is a decision-making *process* that extends from pre-puberty until the late teens or early 20's when the individual makes a definitive occupational commitment" (1951).

IB. "Occupational choice is a process that remains open as long as one makes and expects to make decisions about his work and career" (1972).

(Ginzberg now recognizes that the process is open-ended, that it can coexist with the individual's working life. For example, many men and women established in an occupation move on into related and occasionally into different types of work).

IIA. "Many educational and other preparatory and exploratory decisions along the way have the quality of irreversibility . . ." (1951).

IIB. "While the successive decisions that a young person makes during the preparatory period will have a shaping influence on his later career, so will the continuing changes that he undergoes in work and life" (1972).

(While Ginzberg still acknowledges that previous educational and occupational decisions have a cumulative effect on an individual's future occupational prospects, he now feels that it was wrong to see these decisions as having an irreversible impact. For example, an individual who joins a large company with training and promotional opportunities may have the key decisions about his career to follow. Previous occupational decisions will be of relatively little significance.)

IIIA. "Thirdly, the resolution of the choice process always ends in a *compromise*, since the individual seeks to find an optimal fit between his interests, capacities, and values and the world of work" (1951).

IIIB. "People make decisions about jobs and careers with an aim of optimizing their satisfactions by finding the best possible fit between their priority needs and desires and the opportunities and constraints that they confront in the world of work" (1972).

(Ginzberg still regards the concept of compromise valid since he believes that one never makes an occupational choice that satisfies all of his principal needs and desires. However, he believes a more relevant formulation is that of *optimization* since each career decision involves weighing the punative gains against the probable costs.)

Ginzberg's "new" theory, then, is not so much a radical departure from his previous one as it is a refinement of earlier principles. In particular his reformulated theory shows a greater sensitivity to reality factors of income, sex, and race. "Our greater sensitivity to reality factors in our present formulation of a theory of occupational choice does not obscure our conviction that the individual remains the prime mover in the decision-making process" (Ginzberg, 1972, p. 175).

Super's Developmental Self-Concept Theory

In 1953 Donald Super prepared an article which attempted to synthesize current knowledge and to begin formulation of a comprehensive theory of vocational development. He criticized Ginzberg's theory of occupational choice because it failed "to take into account the continuity of the development of preferences and of the differences in the stages, choices, entry and adjustment; it [should] explain the process through which interest, capacities, values, and opportunities are compromised" (Super, 1953, p. 187). He then sketched the main elements of a theory of vocational development as they appeared in the literature. According to Super, such a theory had a dozen elements: individual differences; occupational multi-potentiality of the individual; occupational ability patterns; identification with parents and the role of models; continuity of the adjustment process; life stages; career patterns; development that can be guided; development as the result of interaction; dynamics of career patterns; job satisfaction; and work as a way of life.

Following this enumeration of diverse elements, he organized the elements into a summary statement of a comprehensive theory. The statement entailed ten "propositions."

1. People differ in their abilities, interests, and personalities.
2. They are qualified, by virtue of these characteristics, each for a number of occupations.
3. This process may be summed up in a series of life stages . . .
4. The nature of the career pattern (that is, the occupational level attained and the sequence, frequency, and duration of trial and stable jobs) is determined by the individual's parental socioeconomic level, mental ability, and personality characteristics, and by the opportunities to which he is exposed.
5. Development through the life stages can be guided . . .
6. The process of vocational development is essentially that of developing and implementing a self-concept . . .
7. The process of compromise between individual and social factors, between self-concept and reality, is one of role playing . . .

8. Work satisfactions and life satisfactions depend upon the extent to which the individual finds adequate outlets for his abilities, interests, personality traits, and values . . . (1953, pp. 189-190).

In order to clarify and test his theoretical model, Super began in 1951 a long-term research project entitled the *Career Pattern Study*. The developmental approach was influenced by the developmental psychology of Buehler's life stages, and the variations suggested by Ginzberg *et al* (1951) and Miller and Form (1951). The research was a project of the Horace Mann - Lincoln Institute of School Experimentation, Teachers College, Columbia University, and utilized a sample of 142 eighth-grade and 143 ninth-grade boys (Super, 1954, 1955, 1957c).

In setting up a model for the Career Pattern Study, Super (1957c, pp. 40-41) synthesized previous generalizations of life stages into the following:

Growth Stage (Birth-14). Self-concept develops through identification with key figures in family and in school; needs and fantasy dominate early in this stage; interest and capacity become more important in this stage with increasing social participation and reality-testing. Substages of the growth stage are Fantasy (4-10), Interest (11-12), and Capacity (13-14).

Exploration Stage (Age 15-24). Self-examination, role tryout, and occupational exploration take place in school, leisure activities, and part-time work. Substages of the exploration stage are: Tentative (15-17), Transition (18-21), and Trial (22-24).

Establishment Stage (Age 25-44). Having found an appropriate field, effort is put forth to make a permanent place in it. There may be some trial early in this stage, with consequent shifting, but establishment may begin without trial, especially in the professions. Substages of the establishment stage are: Trial (25-30) and Stabilization (31-44).

Maintenance Stage (Age 45-64). Having made a place in the world of work, the concern is now to hold it. Little new ground is broken, but there is continuation along established lines.

Decline Stage (Age 65 on). As physical and mental powers decline, work activity changes and in due course ceases. New roles must be developed; first that of selective participant and then that of observer rather than participant. Substages of this stage are: Deceleration (65-70) and Retirement (71 on).

According to Super, this outline gives a description of the nature of vocational behavior which seems characteristic of each life stage and indicates the approximate age limit of the stages. The importance of this synthesis is that it furnishes a research base for two major concepts: that vocational development is "an ongoing, continuous, generally irreversible process," and that it is "an orderly, patterned process" (Super, 1957c; p. 42).

The concept of vocational development as used by Super (1957b, 1957c) led to a completely new set of behavioral definitions. The term "vocational choice," which was borrowed from differential psychology, conveyed a misleading notion of neatness and precision of time and of singleness and uniqueness in the life of the individual. "Choice is, in fact, a process rather than an event" (1957b, p. 184). For these reasons, a new term was adopted:

> Vocational development is conceived of as one aspect of individual development . . . Work, like social life and intellectual activity, is one specific medium through which the total personality can manifest itself. Like other aspects of development, vocational development may be conceived of as beginning early in life, and as proceeding along a curve until late in life . . . Just as general development can be broken down into major life stages placed sequentially on a continuum, each stage having characteristics which are peculiar to it and which justify singling it out, so the continuum of vocational development can be broken down into vocational life stages, each defined by its peculiar characteristics (1957b, p. 185).

The next revision of Super's vocational development theory occurred in the early 1960's. In a monograph consisting of five essays, he presented his model for explaining vocational behavior. Super (1963) views an individual's occupational preference as an attempt to implement a self-concept. He maintains that a person selects an occupation whose requirements provide a role consistent with his self-image.

The processes by which the self-concept is developed are identified as the processes of *formation, translation,* and *implementation.* The Formation stage further includes exploration of the world and of the self, self-differentiation, identification, role playing, and reality testing. Translation occurs in various ways: (1) Identification with an adult may make his particular occupation seem interesting, (2) Experience in a role in which one is cast may lead to the discovery of a vocational translation, and (3) Awareness that one has attributes which are important in a certain field may lead to an investigation of that occupation. The implementation of the self-concept is the end result of the process. In this stage, the person begins his professional training, completes his education, and ultimately enters the world of work. According to Super, the process of forming a concept of self begins in infancy. "This is essentially an exploratory process which goes on throughout the entire course of life . . ." (1963, p. 11).

A Conceptual Framework of Occupational Choice

Blau, Gustad, Jessor, Parnes, and Wilcock (1956) have proposed what they call a "conceptual framework" rather than a theory of occupational choice and selection. Theory, they explain, is concerned with the interconnection between direct and remote determinants, while the function of a conceptual model is to call attention to different kinds of antecedent factors, the exact relationship to be demonstrated through research. Regardless of this distinction, the approach makes a valuable contribution to the body of knowledge related to career development theory.

This model is based on the proposition that the *process of choice* as well as the *process of selection* must be taken into account in order to explain why people end up in different occupations. That is to say, there are certain factors which are related to an individual's choice, but there are also certain occupational factors which, in effect, select the individual. In Table 3-1, this twofold relationship is presented schematically. The left side of the table suggests examples of individual characteristics which may result in occupational choice. The right side of the table illustrates those factors which are beyond the control of the individual but which also may determine occupational choice.

A time dimension is represented on the table by a dotted line running horizontally between the second and third boxes. The upper part of the table represents the social and psychological conditions of choice and selection. The lower part indicates the factors that produce those conditions. Blau *et al* obviously agree with Ginzberg and Super on the important point that occupational choice is a developmental process which extends over many years.

The factors shown below the dotted line (Boxes 3 and III) are the antecedent conditions — personality development and historical change — which affect the intermediate (Boxes 2 and II) and immediate determinants of occupational choice (Boxes 1 and I). The lowermost boxes in the table represent the influence of heredity, social structure, and environment. The significance of these latter elements are recognized by the fact that an individual, within limits set by his native endowment, responds to the social structure within which he lives to form various behavioral patterns that collectively constitute his personality.

With respect to the immediate determinants of occupational choice, there are eight factors of entry which interact to produce hierarchies of individual preferences (Box 1) and of occupational expectations (Box I). The second level of boxes (Boxes 2 and II) represent additional factors which may influence individual careers. It is hypothesized, however, that the effect of these "second level" factors are traceable through the immediate determinants and do not directly account for occupational entry.

The actual process of occupational choice, as shown in the uppermost part of the table, is a compromise between an indi-

TABLE 3-1

RELATIONSHIP OF PROCESS OF CHOICE
AND PROCESS OF SELECTION

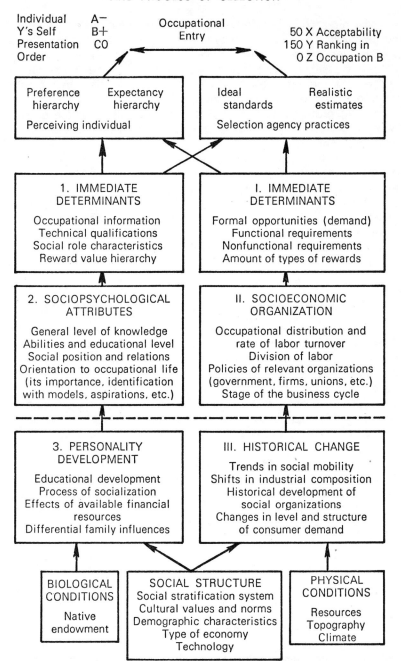

Individual A−
Y's Self B+
Presentation CO
Order

Occupational
Entry

50 X Acceptability
150 Y Ranking in
0 Z Occupation B

Preference Expectancy hierarchy hierarchy Perceiving individual	Ideal Realistic standards estimates Selection agency practices
1. IMMEDIATE DETERMINANTS Occupational information Technical qualifications Social role characteristics Reward value hierarchy	I. IMMEDIATE DETERMINANTS Formal opportunities (demand) Functional requirements Nonfunctional requirements Amount of types of rewards
2. SOCIOPSYCHOLOGICAL ATTRIBUTES General level of knowledge Abilities and educational level Social position and relations Orientation to occupational life (its importance, identification with models, aspirations, etc.)	II. SOCIOECONOMIC ORGANIZATION Occupational distribution and rate of labor turnover Division of labor Policies of relevant organizations (government, firms, unions, etc.) Stage of the business cycle
3. PERSONALITY DEVELOPMENT Educational development Process of socialization Effects of available financial resources Differential family influences	III. HISTORICAL CHANGE Trends in social mobility Shifts in industrial composition Historical development of social organizations Changes in level and structure of consumer demand

BIOLOGICAL CONDITIONS Native endowment	SOCIAL STRUCTURE Social stratification system Cultural values and norms Demographic characteristics Type of economy Technology	PHYSICAL CONDITIONS Resources Topography Climate

SOURCE: Peter M. Blau *et al.*, "Occupational Choice: a Conceptual Frame-work," *Industrial and Labor Relations Review*, 1956, 9(4), p. 534.

74   *Career Education*

vidual's hierarchy of preferences and his hierarchy of expectations. For example, an individual may prefer one occupation over another, but realizes there is little chance of entering the preferred occupation. Consequently, he must compromise between aspirations and reality and settle for a less preferred occupation. In the same way, occupational selection involves compromise between hierarchies of preferences and expectations. In selection, the occupation (rather than the individual) compromises between ideal and available workers. Although the process of choice is discussed above from the standpoints of individual selection and of actions of selectors, it is the combination of the two procedures which explains why people end up in different occupations. "Lest the complicated and extended developmental process that culminates in occupational choice be oversimplified, it is necessary to consider it as a series of interrelated decisions rather than a single choice" (Blau *et al*, 1956, p. 546).

Tiedeman's Model of Occupational Decision-Making

David Tiedeman, writing shortly after Super's *Psychology of Careers* appeared, offered a formal statement on the process of decisions within the broader framework of vocational development. According to Tiedeman, "The structure of decisions must be specified before investigation of the theory of vocational development can enter new phases . . . The set of decisions and the context of relevance for the anticipation and implementation of each constitutes the essence of vocational development" (1961, p. 15).

The process of vocational development is determined by each of several decisions with respect to school, work, and life which a person makes as he matures. The act of decision-making may be separated into two aspects, the Period of Anticipation and the Period of Implementation or Adjustment.

Anticipatory behavior may itself be analyzed into stages of exploration, crystallization, choice, and specification. "Exploration" is characterized by random acquisitive activities in which a number of possible goals are considered. Preliminary self-appraisals are conducted in relation to each alternative. The second stage of "crystallization" is one in which patterns begin to emerge in the form of alternatives and their consequences. An ordering of all relevant considerations, in relation to each alternative, takes place as choice becomes imminent. In "choice," the behavioral system of the individual is readied to act upon the decision. In the final stage, "specification," former doubts concerning the decision dissipates as the image of self in relationship to goal is perfected. With the making of an actual decision, the anticipation or preoccupational stage ends and the next major period is begun.

The period of Implementation or Adjustment is further divided into stages of induction, transition, and maintenance. During "induction," concerns only imagined come face to face with reality as the preferred occupation or educational preparation is attempted. The person is expected to meet the requirements of the office as well as the requirements of co-workers and supervisors. With the gaining of confidence that one has been successful, the "transition" stage is begun. Here a metamorphosis occurs; the individual becomes less responsive and more assertive in his role. As the assertive needs subside, the "maintenance" stage is initiated. Equilibrium is reestablished as the individual develops a successful component of the self-concept. The maintenance stage is not unalterable but is rather a condition of dynamic equilibrium. Forces externally or internally imposed may alter the status quo. For example, new members in one's group may increase individual aspirations. Such conditions may enhance vocational maturity or result in some level of disintegration.

The above sequence of exploration-crystallization-choice-specification-induction-transition-maintenance occurs each time a career-related choice must be made. The problem may be prevocational, such as planning a program of studies on the completion of junior high school, or it may involve the question of whether to leave a stable occupation to pursue better opportunities in another field of endeavor. New behaviors must be implemented each time a new decision is made. As the individual copes with the decision-making and adjustment tasks, a self-concept emerges and assumes a greater influence on subsequent decisions.

"Vocational development then is self-development viewed in relation with choice, entry and progress in educational and vocational pursuits" (Tiedeman, 1961, p. 18).

Tiedeman further describes the process of decision-making in relation to a developmental structure of man, school, and work. The characterization of vocational development in Table 3-2 is compatible with Super's (1957c) outline. It is obvious that not all decisions occur sequentially. At any given time an individual may be at several stages which require choices on related aspects of life. Thus, the career evolves in a time pattern in harmony with the evolution of other aspects of life.

TABLE 3-2

CHARACTERIZATION OF VOCATIONAL DEVELOPMENT

Age	Possible Grade for Age	Work	Education and Training	Physical and Psychological
12-	6			
13-	7			
14-	8		Selection of Junior High School Subjects	
15-	9		Selection of High School Subjects	
16-	10	Part-time employment	Selection of College / Selection of Coll. Prog.	Puberty
17-	11	First full-time position		
18-	12	Changes in full-time employment	Selection of Graduate School	Perception of "middle-age"
19-	13		Selection of Grad. Course Prog.	
20-	14			
21-	15		Selection of Armed Service	Marriage
22-	16		Selection of specialty in A. S.	Birth of first child
23-	17			
24-	18			Maturation of last child
25-	19			
26-	20			Menopause (in women)
27-				
28-				Perception of "old"
29-				
30-				
35-				
40-		Retirement		
45-				
50-				
60-				
65-				
Death-				

Key:
Solid Line (———) indicates time when a decision must be considered.
Broken Line (   ) indicates time when problem can and may exist.
Dotted Line (. . . .) indicates a period when problem can exist but usually does not.

SOURCE: David V. Tiedeman, "Decision and Vocational Development: a Paradigm and Its Implications," *Personnel and Guidance Journal*, 1961, 40(1), p. 20.

A Psychoanalytic Framework for Vocational Development

The process of career choice is described by Bordin, Nachmann, and Segal (1963) within a psychoanalytic framework. The basis for this point of view is that occupations are chosen to satisfy needs, to gratify impulses, and to reduce anxieties. Like Roe, Bordin and associates emphasize the importance of early childhood experiences which they believe influence the type of mode chosen for obtaining gratification. Their theoretical formulations of work and vocational choice are the result of three studies dealing with the analysis of selected occupations to identify what needs might be satisfied through participation in them (Segal, 1961; Nachman, 1960; Galinsky, 1962). The theory rests on several preliminary assumptions and considerations.

1. A continuity in development which links the earliest work of the organism in food getting and mastery of the body and coping with the stimulations of the environment to the most highly abstract and complex of intellectual and physical activities.
2. That the complex adult activities retain the same instinctual sources of gratification as the simple infantile ones.
3. That although the relative strengths and configurations of needs are subject to continual modification throughout the life span, their essential pattern is determined in the first six years of life. The seeking out of occupational outlets of increasingly precise appropriateness is the work of the school years, but the needs which will be the driving forces are largely set before that time (Bordin *et al.*, 1963, p. 110).

There are several *limitations* to this theory which the authors have not hesitated to point out. This is a theory of "vocational commitment" in the sense that those activities to which individuals have committed their energies are the only ones discussed. Consequently, persons who have little capacity to obtain gratifications from work are excluded. A further limitation is that the theory does not deal with people who are motivated or constrained to choose occupations based on economic, cultural, geographic, and other external forces. This theory applies only to people who have a fairly high degree of freedom in their choices.

The elaboration and refinement of Bordin's construct of work is carried out via a repeated weaving back and forth between job analysis, personality traits, and assumptions regarding childhood experiences. Ten dimensions of work activity, or impulse expression, were identified and described in terms of their physiological functions. An occupational counterpart identifies the gratifications that various types of work can offer. Table 3-3 summarizes these relationships. Consider the following example for illustration. The sensual dimension has to do with the use of the sense organs, not for gaining information, but for sensual pleasure — as the

TABLE 3-3

SUMMARY OF NEED-GRATIFYING ACTIVITIES

Dimension	Physiological Functions	Occupational Expression
1. Nurturant	feeding; protecting and promoting the growth of people, animals, plants	social work, nursing, teaching
2. Oral Aggressive	cutting, biting, chewing, devouring	manufacturing, construction, mining
3. Manipulative	physical power, influencing, persuading, threatening, seducing	computer operations, sales, advertising
4. Sensual	sight, touch, taste, sound	artistic and creative occupations
5. Anal	acquiring, timing and ordering, hoarding, smearing	accounting, book-keeping, painting
6. Genital	erection, penetration, impregnation, producing	architectural, deep sea diving, agricultural occupations
7. Exploratory	investigating, exploring, knowing the facts	fields of scientific investigation, e.g., mathmetician, chemist, physicist
8. Flowing and Quenching	urethral	plumbing, fire fighting, hydraulic engineering
9. Exhibiting	impulse to exhibit phallus or whole body	acting, law, advertising, the ministry
10. Rhythmic Movement	physiological rhythm (heartbeat, respiration)	musical, industrial craftsmanlike, and artistic occupations that involve bodily rhythm

infant looks, touches and tastes because things are pretty, feel good, and are sensually gratifying. This dimension may find expression most clearly in the artist whose senses are exquisitely developed and whose work is the giving of such pleasures to others.

The generality of this type of theory is obvious. The psychoanalytic theories of occupational choice assume that little difficulty is encountered in occupational selection for "normal" individuals. If problems do arise they are attributed to deeper psychological processes. Career development is usually regarded as a by-product of personality development and not considered to be worth attention based on its own merit.

Holland's Personality Theory of Vocational Choice

The theory by John Holland (1959) is an attempt to develop a theory of vocational choice which is comprehensive enough to integrate existing knowledge while also providing a framework to stimulate future research. Basically, the theory assumes that at the time of vocational choice, the person is the product of the interaction of his particular heredity with a variety of cultural and personal forces including peers, parents and significant adults, his social class, American culture, and the physical environment. Out of this experience, the person develops a hierarchy of preferred methods of dealing with environmental tasks, which he refers to as the individual's adjustive orientation. In the act of selecting a vocational choice, the individual in a sense "searches" for situations (occupational environments) which satisfy his hierarchy of adjustive orientations (i.e., modal personal orientations or simply personality).

To explain the theory, a parallel classification system was developed. Major classes of occupational environments and individual personal orientations are described along six dimensions. Table 3-4 summarizes these two primary constructs.

Holland uses the occupational environments as a framework for organizing and classifying knowledge about occupational choice. Though not exhaustive, the classification is assumed to include all the major kinds of American work environments. In addition, the six classifications serve to classify various data about self, e.g., interest, values, interpersonal skills. In choosing an occupation, the individual seeks an environment which will enable him to cope with work tasks which are in harmony with his major personal orientation.

TABLE 3-4

A SUMMARY OF HOLLAND'S (1959, 1966) PERSONALITY TYPES AND ENVIRONMENTAL MODELS

Personality Types * (Modal Personal Orientation)		Environmental Models * (Occupational Environments)	
Type	Description	Type	Typical Occupations
Realistic (Motoric) Investigative	Enjoys activities requiring physical strength; aggressive; good motor organization; lacks verbal and interpersonal skills; prefers concrete to abstract problems; unsociable; etc.	Realistic (Motoric)	Laborers, machine operators, aviators, farmers, truck drivers, carpenters, etc.
Intellectual Investigated	Task oriented, "thinks through" problems; attempts to organize and understand the world; enjoys ambiguous work tasks and intraceptive activities; abstract orientation; etc.	Intellectual Investigated	Physicist, anthropologist, chemist, mathematician, biologist, etc.
Social (Supportive)	Prefers teaching or therapeutic roles; likes a safe setting; possesses verbal and interpersonal skills; socially oriented; accepting of feminine impulses; etc.	Social (Supportive)	Clinical psychologist, counselor, foreign missionary, teacher, etc.
Conventional (Conforming)	Performs structured verbal and numerical activities and subordinate roles; achieves goals through conformity.	Conventional (Conforming)	Cashier, statistician, bookkeeper, administrative assistant, post office clerk, etc.
Enterprising (Persuasive)	Prefers verbal skills in situations which provide opportunities for dominating, selling, or leading others.	Enterprising (Persuasive)	Car salesman, auctioneer, politician, master of ceremonies, buyer, etc.
Artistic (Esthetic)	Prefers indirect personal relationships, prefers dealing with environmental problems through self-expression in artistic media.	Artistic (Esthetic)	Poet, novelist, musician, sculptor, playwright, composer, stage director, etc.

*Terms within parentheses denote earlier nomenclature.

SOURCE: J. Zaccaria, *Theories of Occupational Choice and Vocational-Development.* Boston: Houghton Mifflin, 1970. p. 44.

Roe's Early Determinants of Vocational Choice

A clinical psychologist, Anne Roe, has proposed a theory of occupational choice which grew out of her research on personality traits. In a series of studies on physical-biological and social scientists, Roe (1951a, 1951b; 1953) concluded that major personality differences between the two groups of scientists were primarily due to the type of interaction they have with people. She further concluded that the personality differences were partly the result of early parent-child relationships.

Several years following completion of the above research, Roe (1957) offered a theory to explain the relationship between childhood experiences and vocational behavior. According to Roe, the emotional climate in the home, i.e., the interaction between parent and child, is of three types: emotional concentration on the child, avoidance of the child, or acceptance of the child. This classification refers to the dominant pattern in the home, whether shown by one or both parents. Figure 3-1 illustrates these be-

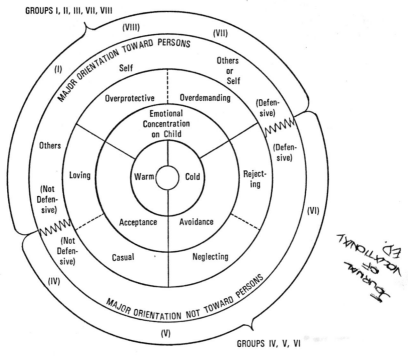

SOURCE: Anne Roe, "Early Determinants of Vocational Choice," *Journal of Counseling Psychology,* 1957, 4 (3), p. 216.

Fig. 3-1. Behavioral Variations and Their Relationships

havioral variations together with their relation to basically warm and cold attitudes of parents, and their relation to the outcome in the child in terms of his orientation with regard to persons. The exact division between persons or nonpersons is uncertain and is suggested by a jagged line. The other subdivisions in the figure were set arbitrarily.

Depending upon which of the three emotional climates is experienced, there will be developed basic attitudes, interests, and capacities. These will be given expression in the general pattern of the adult's life, in his personal relations, in his emotional reactions, in his activities, and in his vocational choice. The selection of an occupational goal usually reflects most clearly the coalescence of the genetic and experiential variables discussed previously.

Several examples serve to demonstrate the possible relationship between the types of parent-child interaction and orientation with respect to persons. Individuals brought up in warm, overprotective homes manifest a major orientation toward persons. Occupational Group VIII meets these needs. In the case where the parents are warm, loving, and accepting, the major orientation is toward persons and not defensive. These needs would be fulfilled by an occupation in Group I. The basic orientation is later evidenced in patterns of special interests and abilities. It is possible to relate these abilities directly to major occupational groups which are shown in Table 3-5.

The relationships between the eight occupational groups and early childhood experiences were suggested in Fig. 3-1. Occupations which are person-oriented are in the categories of service, business contact, organizations, general culture, and the arts and entertainment. Most person-oriented occupational areas include those of technology, outdoors, and science. For purpose of review, an individual whose childhood emotional climate was casual or neglecting is more likely to move toward technical or scientific occupations, while an individual whose family provided an accepting or protective environment is likely to enter an occupation concerned with service or business contact.

There are six levels of occupations within each of the groups. The level selected within any given occupational area is influenced by the intensity of the person's "needs." It is here that Roe has integrated Maslow's (1954) hierarchy of needs into her theory. The need intensity which an individual reflects, in turn, is a product of such elements as genetic factors and is limited by variables such as intelligence and socioeconomic background.

TABLE 3-5

CATEGORIES IN ROE CLASSIFICATION OF OCCUPATIONS

Groups	Levels
I. Service	1. Professional and managerial 1.
II. Business Contract	2. Professional and managerial 2.
III. Organizations	3. Semiprofessional, small business
IV. Technology	4. Skilled
V. Outdoor	5. Semiskilled
VI. Science	6. Unskilled
VII. General Cultural	
VIII. Arts and Entertainment	

SOURCE: Anne Roe, "Early Determinants of Vocational Choice, *Journal of Counseling Psychology*, 1957, 4 (3), p. 217.

In a recent essay, Roe (1972) acknowledges that the person or not-person orientation is less in importance than she originally believed. The person or not-person orientation is related to later major orientation, but does not by itself account for any large amount of the variance. In summarizing her essay, Roe (1972, p. 80) provides a series of statements which reflect the cumulative results of her research and related professional activities.

1. The life story of any man and many women, written in terms of or around the occupational history, can give the essence of the person more fully than can any other approach.
2. Situations relevant to this history begin with the birth of the individual into a particular family at a particular place and time, and continue throughout his life.
3. There may be differences in the relative weights carried by different factors, but the processes of vocational decision and behavior do not differ in essence from any others.
4. The extent to which vocational decisions and behaviors are under the voluntary control of the individual is variable, but it could be more than it sometimes seems to be. Deliberate consideration of the factors involved seems to be rare.
5. The occupational life affects all other aspects of the life pattern.
6. An appropriate and satisfying vocation can be a bulwark against neurotic ills or a refuge from them. An inappropriate or unsatisfying vocation can be sharply deleterious.
7. Since the goodness of life in any social group is compounded of and also determines that of its individual members, the efforts of any society to

maintain stability and at the same time advance in desired ways can perhaps be more usefully directed toward developing satisfying vocational situations for its members than any other. But unless the vocation is adequately integrated into the total life pattern, it cannot help much.

8. There is no single specific occupational slot which is a one-and-only perfect one for any individual. Conversely, there is no single person who is the only one for a particular occupational slot. Within any occupation, there is a considerable range in a number of variables specifying the requirements.

Hoppock's Composite Theory

In his book *Occupational Information,* Hoppock (1967) makes a very pragmatic assumption that years will elapse before enough empirical data will have been collected to validate theories of career development and occupational choice. He submits that in the meantime, practitioners (primarily counselors) need a broad base of knowledge to understand the behavior of students they serve. Hoppock presents his theory not as hypotheses to be tested but rather as a *series of speculations* about why people behave as they do when they are trying to reach an occupational decision. His theory is presented in the form of ten postulates:

1. Occupations are chosen to meet needs.
2. The occupation that we choose is the one that we believe will best meet the needs that most concern us.
3. Needs may be intellectually perceived, or they may be only vaguely felt as attractions which draw us in certain directions. In either case, they may influence choices.
4. Vocational development begins when we first become aware that an occupation can help to meet our needs.
5. Vocational development progresses and occupational choice improves as we become better able to anticipate how well a prospective occupation will meet our needs. Our capacity thus to anticipate depends upon our knowledge of ourselves, our knowledge of occupations, and our ability to think clearly.
6. Information about ourselves affects occupational choice by helping us to recognize what we want and by helping us to anticipate whether or not we will be successful in collecting what the contemplated occupation offers to us.
7. Information about occupations affects occupational choice by helping us to discover the occupations that may meet our needs and by helping us to anticipate how well satisfied we may hope to be in one occupation as compared with another.
8. Job satisfaction depends upon the extent to which the job that we hold meets the needs that we feel it should meet. The degree of satisfaction is determined by the ratio between what we have and what we want.
9. Satisfaction can result from a job which meets our needs today or from a job which promises to meet them in the future.
10. Occupational choice is always subject to change when we believe that a change will better meet our needs (Hoppock, 1967, pp. 111-112).

It is obvious that Hoppock has drawn from many of the previously described theories to arrive at his composite theory. He
uses the term *needs* in a very broad, general sense to describe the
"inner tensional states" that other writers have variously labeled
interests, motivations, values, self-impulses, etc. Hoppock's theory
seems to be based on the simple premise that the counselor must
have sufficient knowledge to identify the needs of a client and
assist him to resolve the situation, i.e., need. This observation is
suggested by the following statement:

> ... when occupations are being chosen to meet needs, as they will be, the
> more occupations we counselors know and the more we know about them, the
> better is the chance that we will be able to help our clients to find occupations
> that will meet their needs and in which they can also get and hold jobs
> (Hoppock, 1967, p. 121).

As a result of this particular orientation, Hoppock accords
primary importance to the role of occupational information in the
career development process. The counselor's role correspondingly
becomes that of resource person and dispenser of occupational
information.

Learning Theory and Career Development

O'Hara (1968) outlines a theoretical approach which views
career development as a learning process. He reasons that changes
in vocational behavior are the result of cognitive changes, i.e., boys
and girls *learn* how to be doctors, electricians, teachers, and
nurses. According to O'Hara, all vocational learning is a function
of motivation. The student acts to satisfy his vocational needs;
for example, the conscious choice of high school courses related
to a future occupational goal is a result of an understanding of the
intimate relationship between education and occupation.

In order for vocational learning to take place, a proper learning environment is required. The adolescent should be helped to
understand the relationship among variables involved in career
development such as interests, aptitudes, and values. The complex
nature of career development itself, e.g., vocational life stages,
irreversibility, and compromise, should be presented to the student
in a learning situation in such a way that he can comprehend it.
Similarly, a vocabulary of occupational terms, as well as various
pictorial and auditory symbols, can be presented to help the student vicariously explore the world of work. This approach does
not detract from the importance of affective and psychomotor

learning, but merely recognizes that a core of cognitive material is required to make intelligent occupational decisions.

The essence of O'Hara's theoretical approach is that the career development of students can be facilitated by involving them in various learning situations which have occupational implications. "If we teach the students to make increasingly more adequate vocational differentiations and integrations, then our theory says that the result will be more adequate vocational responses" (1968, p. 640).

Another attempt to relate learning theory to vocational behavior is proposed by Miller (1968). His theme is that a learning theory of vocational behavior can contribute to both understanding and to theory development in the area of vocational decisions. Miller begins with a discussion of the definition of vocational decisions and a description of the three functions of a theory. He defines a vocational decision "as any behavior that consistently and significantly relates to eventual participation in an occupation" (1968, p. 18). The functions of a theory he identifies as those of explanation, prediction, and control.

The explanatory element of the learning theory approach to vocational decisions is based on knowledge of the individual's past history, current stimulus situation, and present motivational status. Manipulation of the environment under the *control* of the teacher or parent thus becomes possible. As a result of increased understanding of the variables involved in decision-making, and control of the environment, more *predictable* changes in student behavior become possible. According to Miller, potential for control is the major advantage of a learning theory approach over other approaches.

Review of Major Viewpoints

In the preceding sections the major theories of career development and occupational choice were presented individually. Little attempt was made to compare or contrast them. This was done intentionally. It is reasoned that the reader will be better able to identify and understand their commonalities after having become familiar with the full range of theories.

It is fair to say, without being overly critical, that the "formal adequacy" of the theories leaves much to be desired. There seems to be a tendency for many theorists to propose entirely new conceptions rather than attempt to build on existing theories. However, the theories display major similarities. They emphasize the same kinds of critical agents and periods. The major differences between the theories are differences of emphases (Osipow, 1968). Following is an attempt to summarize the various theories according to their *primary* orientation. Naturally, an individual theory may contain elements of each of the six major groupings, i.e., trait factor, developmental, psychoanalytic, personality, motivational, and general approaches.

Trait and Factor Approaches

The trait and factor approach was the forerunner of all modern theories of occupational choice and still dictates much of the current practice of vocational guidance. The origin of trait and factor theory is traceable to Parson's (1909) three-step process of (1) a clear understanding of self; (2) a knowledge of the requirements and conditions of various occupations; and (3) "true reasoning" between the two sets of information. In other words, the individual compares his abilities with those demanded by the occupation and agrees on the one he "matches" best. The labeling of this method as trait and factor theory is related to two of its fundamental tenets: that the individual is organized in terms of unique patterns of capabilities and potentials (traits); and that occupations can be described in terms of homogeneous qualities (factors).

Historically, this approach has dictated much of the practice of vocational guidance because of its simplicity and ease of implementation. This was made obvious when the National Vocational Guidance Association (1937) defined the major components of vocational guidance as the study of individuals, the study of occupations, and counseling. The dangers of over-reliance on trait and factor methods are narrow perspectives on the study of individual occupations and the use of various types of aptitude, intelligence, interest, and personality tests to predict success in an occupation. The use of such tests in a counseling situation may provide useful data for a qualified counselor, but the prediction of an individual's future life work should not be based upon test results alone.

Developmental Approaches

While most theories of career development and occupational choice are concerned to some extent with the differentiation of vocational behavior over a period of time, the distinguishing feature of developmental theories is the recognition that decision-making behavior begins to develop in childhood and continues throughout adulthood. Conceptualizations of occupational choice as a developmental process have their origins in studies of "life stages" which were begun by two Europeans named Buehler and Lazarsfeld during the early 1930's (see Super, 1957b); in Carter's (1940) early work on the formation of interests; and Havighurst's (1953) concept of "developmental tasks."

Within a structure of stages or periods, developmental theories describe both the typical kinds of behavior for each period and the factors related to those behaviors. The Ginzberg, Ginsberg, Axelrad, and Herma (1951) theory, for example, classifies choice behaviors according to the Fantasy, Tentative, and Realistic periods. The choice behaviors within these periods are related to specific factors, e.g., fantasy choices are based on anticipatory pleasure while tentative choices rely more upon values and goals (Miller, 1968). "The truly developmental quality of Ginzberg's theory is clearly evident from the fact that vocational choice is seen as a process, that the process is systematic, that it is predictable, and that occupational choice culminates in an eventual decision to enter a specific occupation" (Zaccaria, 1970, p. 42).

Super bases the framework of his theory (1953, 1957a, 1957b, 1963) on the writings of Buehler and Ginzberg, but in addition synthesizes principles from differential psychology (the study of individual differences) and phenomenological psychology (self-concept theory), as well as to integrate the work of two sociologists, Miller and Form (1951). As a result of his systematic attempts to develop and revise his theory, and to test his formulations through longitudinal research, Super's theory is regarded as the most comprehensive and valid explanation of vocational behavior currently available.

Super places even more emphasis than Ginzberg upon vocational choice as a process. Consequently, he chose to change the wording from *vocational choice to vocational development*. He further introduced the concept of vocational maturity to denote the degree of development from childhood through retirement (Crites, 1969). The most basic theme of Super's theory, however, "is that the individual chooses occupations whose characteristics will allow him to function in a role that is consistent with his self-concept, and that the latter conception is a function of his developmental history" (Herr, 1970, p. 26).

Although written by representatives from the fields of psychology, economics, and sociology, the conceptual framework proposed by Blau, Gustad, Jessor, Parnes, and Wilcock (1956) clearly reflects a developmental orientation. They too see occupational choice as a series of interrelated decisions and not as a single choice. Actual entrance into an occupation they trace to the dual processes of (1) occupational choice and (2) occupational selection. The purpose of distinguishing between the two is to call attention to the fact that an individual's preferred choice must be balanced with the available opportunities in that occupational area. Their discussion of occupational selection is a very legitimate attempt to explain how a competitive job market, or surpluses in many occupations, results in individuals choosing a less preferred occupation. Thus, like Ginzberg, they see occupational decision-making as a process of compromise.

An excellent summary of the theory and research of Tiedeman (1961), and more recently Tiedeman and O'Hara (1963), is contained in a statement by Holland (1964, p. 267) "... it seems to consist in attacking a number of sub-problems on vocational behavior within the Ginzberg, Super, and Blau orientations." Like Super, Tiedeman sees career development as a process of evolving and of acting upon a conception of self. However, he emphasizes the formation of self in relation to educational experiences more than does Super. He also conceives of the self as the individual's evaluation rather than perceptions of himself (Crites, 1969).

The major contributions of Tiedeman and his associates have been in research methods rather than in model development. They have sought to clarify and specify the sequence of decisions within a context of stages and to develop sophisticated techniques to predict educational and occupational choice. In addition, Tiedeman has actively explored many practical applications for a knowledge of career development, for example, the development of a computerized *Information System for Vocational Decisions.*

Psychoanalytic Approaches

Psychoanalytic conceptions of vocational behavior must be understood within the broader context of psychoanalysis. "A central proposition in orthodox psychoanalysis is that the individual adjusts to social expectations and mores by sublimating the desires and impulses which he experiences as a result of his biological nature. He expresses libido in a socially acceptable form by participating in appropriate activities or by making responses which are conversion of psychic energy" (Crites, 1969, pp. 91-92). Brill (1949) in his book *Basic Principles of Psychoanalysis*, offers an explanation of work: "Every activity or vocation not directed to sex in the broadest sense, no matter under what guise, is a form of sublimation" (p. 266).

The most comprehensive application of psychoanalysis to occupational choice has been made by Bordin, Nachmann, and Segal (1963). The major contribution of Bordin and his associates has been to specify the aspects of work which satisfy various needs. It is obvious how this type of theory differs from trait and factor theory. Psychoanalytic theories of occupational choice emphasize the differential ability of various occupations to satisfy instinctual needs, to gratify impulses, and to reduce anxiety, whereas trait and factor theory emphasizes differential traits in people as requisites for success and satisfaction in various jobs. It is interesting that Bordin et al. have said that "Knowledge of occupations is an external factor which curtails freedom of choice" (1963, p. 110).

The scope of this type of theory is very limited. Psychoanalytic theorists are careful to say that their theories only apply to individuals who have maximum freedom of choice and to persons who obtain the largest part of their gratification from their work. This point of view increases the efficiency of the theory's predictiveness, at the expense of its generality.

Personality Approaches

A fourth orientation which was discussed in this chapter may be called the "personality approach to career development." The underlying assumption of this approach is that workers select their jobs because they see potential for the satisfaction of their basic personal orientation. A corollary assumption is that exposure to a job gradually modifies the personality characteristics of the individual so that his personality becomes very similar to those of individuals performing the same kind of work.

Holland's theory (1959, 1962, 1966), while explicitly developmental, emphasizes the factors that determine occupational choice. He has sought to expand the basic orientation of personality theory; i.e., career choice represents an extension of personality and an attempt to implement broad personal behavioral styles in the context of one's career. Holland's theory has evolved from a narrow attempt to explain occupational choice to a much more comprehensive theory of personality which applies to other behavioral phenomena.

According to Holland, in choosing an occupation the individual seeks an occupational environment which is in harmony with his major personal orientation for coping with those work tasks. He further assumes that at the time a person makes an occupational choice, he is a product of his heredity and environment. The process of occupational selection is very much affected by the amount and accuracy of the individual's self knowledge and occupational knowledge. Both contribute to the understanding of the range, levels, and adequacy of various potential occupational choices (Zaccaria, 1970).

The problem of translating occupational information into psychological terms, and the problem of describing the interaction of persons and environments is being resolved through an extensive series of longitudinal studies (Holland, 1969). One consequence of the research by Holland and his associates has been the development of an inventory of personality which he calls the *Vocational Preference Inventory.*

Need Theory Approaches

Need theories of occupational choice focus on desires and wants which stimulate individuals to prefer one occupation over another. The most prominent need theory is the one formulated by Roe (1956, 1957, 1964), although her theory admittedly contains elements of psychoanalytic, personality, and developmental theories.

Roe's use of a need structure may be understood in two ways: *organization* of need and *intensity* of need. She hypothesizes that early parent-child relationships shape the child's patterns for satisfying his needs, i.e., learning to satisfy his needs largely through interaction with other people or in activities not involving people. Once developed and utilized for meeting needs in general, this fundamental relationship to persons or nonpersons influences the choice of an occupational group, e.g., service, technology, or science. The level selected within any given occupational group is influenced by the person's need intensity. Need intensity, in turn, is composed of such elements as genetic factors and unconscious patterns of behavior (Zaccaria, 1970).

Crites (1970, p. 97) discusses an aspect of Roe's theory that is generally not recognized. She (Roe) points out how any occupation may serve to satisfy needs at a given level, instead of relating specific needs to specific occupations or groups of occupations. Thus, her theory pertains to the relationship between *levels* of needs and occupations, not between *kinds* of needs and occupations.

Hoppock's theory is a non-theory in the sense that he has synthesized a series of speculations rather than a set of researchable hypotheses. His composite theory is stated in the form of ten postulates which focus upon occupational choice as a means for satisfying needs. Hoppock's approach stems from the assumption that occupational activities are related to basic needs and that the adequacy of occupational choice improves as people are better able to identify their own needs and the potential need satisfaction offered by a particular occupation (Osipow, 1968). The impetus for his theory was to develop a functional approach that would

---

help the counselor to better understand complex human behavior. In practice, Hoppock's approach employs methods similar to those used by trait and factor devotees. He emphasizes that the counselor should: (1) provide every possible opportunity for the client to identify and to express his own needs; (2) help the client to discuss the occupations which may meet his needs; and (3) stay with his client through the process of placement (Hoppock, 1967, p. 122).

General Approaches

This final category has been included to permit brief discussion of a *potpourri* of emerging points of view. These seem to be the antecedents of future, major theories. Two attempts to relate learning theory to career development by Miller (1968) and by O'Hara (1968) were discussed in a previous section. The major assumption guiding the learning theory approach is that the determinants of occupational selection are not just random behavior — they are learned behaviors. The interested reader is referred to Zaccaria (1970, p. 74) for a description of other applications of learning theory.

Another type of theory referred to as *decision* theory is becoming increasingly apparent in the professional literature. Although previously confined to the area of economics, these models seem to have the potential for determining the "probability" of various courses of action, i.e., occupational decisions. Crites (1969, pp. 105-108) and Herr (1972, pp. 38-41) summarize briefly the work of prominent authors in this area.

Two additional general approaches are worthy of mention. Simons (1966) has attempted to point out that the literature of existential philosophy has produced a meaningful theory of career development. A central tenet of existential philosophy is that career choice is the key decision that will largely determine an individual's personality. A final, extremely important approach is that of career development for women. However, the authors have chosen to defer discussion of emerging theories of career development of women to Chapter 5.

Summary

The general process of occupational selection and entrance into employment has been presented in this chapter in terms of two historical periods: (1) Prior to 1951; and (2) 1951 to the present. The early history of vocational theorizing was the result of application of the psychology of individual differences. The underlying theory during this period came to be known as the trait and factor approach to occupational choice. The implementation of this method resulted in an emphasis in vocational guidance on the measurement of psychological traits and the prediction of an individual's probable success in a specific occupation. Thus, the approach to vocational phenomena was predominantly applied, not theoretical.

The contributions of Carter and Super during the 1940's notwithstanding, it was not until after Ginzberg's book appeared in 1951 that theory construction in vocational psychology reached any significant proportions. In the fifties, theorists became more concerned with explaining *why* and *how* persons choose one occupation over another, than determining *which* is the appropriate occupation for an individual. Theories during this period ranged from those which focused primarily upon the process of choosing an occupation and the factors influencing the occupational choice, e.g., psychoanalytic and personality approaches, to those which viewed career development as encompassing a series of occupationally-related choices at different life stages. Regardless of the relative emphasis that a theory ascribes to the processes of occupational choice and career development, all literature reviewed in this chapter suggests that there is an interdependence among (1) personality variables, (2) choice dimensions, and (3) environmental conditions.

It is well to conclude this chapter by reasserting that the present theories of vocational behavior are somewhat lacking when evaluated against rigorous criteria of formally adequate theories. Readers who are acquainted with theoretical models in the physical and natural sciences will have, by now, probably raised important questions about the status of vocational theorizing. In defense of the material presented in this chapter, the writers hold that the theories serve as a valuable orientation for the practitioner and offer a comprehensive consideration of the range of variables involved in occupational decision-making. The issue is not whether to accept the theories, but rather how to apply knowledge of the theories to the solution of classroom and guidance problems. In Chapter 11, it will be demonstrated how a curriculum framework can be developed from a synthesis of career development principles.

BIBLIOGRAPHY

Barry, R. and Wolfe, B. *Epitaph for vocational guidance.* New York: Teachers College Press, 1962.

Blau, P. M., Gustad, J. W., Jessor, R., Parnes, H. S., and Wilcock, R. C. Occupational choice: a conceptual framework. Industrial and Labor Relations Review. 1956, 9 (4)

Bordin, E. S., Nachmann, B., and Segal, S. J. An articulated framework for vocational development. *Journal of Counseling Psychology,* 1963, 10 (2), 107-117.

Brill, A. A. *Basic principles of psychoanalysis.* Garden City, New York: Doubleday, 1949.

Carter, H. D. The development of vocational attitudes. *Journal of Counseling Psychology,* 1940, 4, 185-191.

Crites, J. O. *Vocational psychology.* New York: McGraw-Hill, 1969.

———. Measurement of vocational maturity in adolescense: 1. Attitude test of the vocational development inventory. *Psychological Monographs,* 1965, 79 (1), 36.

Dvorak, B. The general aptitudes test battery. *Personnel and Guidance Journal,* 1956, 35, 145-152.

———. The new USES General Aptitude Test Battery. *Occupations,* 1947, 26, 42-44.

Fryer, D. Occupational intelligence standards. *School and Society,* 1922, 16, 273-277.

Galinsky, M. D. Personality development and vocational choice. *Journal of Counseling Psychology,* 1962, 9, 299.

Ginzberg, E., Ginsburg, S. W., Axelrad, S., Herma, J. L. *Occupational choice: an approach to a general theory.* New York: Columbia University Press, 1951.

Ginzberg, E. Toward a theory of occupational choice: a restatement. *Vocational Guidance Quarterly,* 1972, 20, 169-176.

Guilford, J. Factor analysis in a test development program. *Psychological Review,* 1948, 55, 79-94.

Harrell, T. and Harrell, M. AGCT scores for civilian occupations. *Educational and Psychological Measurement,* 1945, 5, 229-239.

Havighurst, R. J. *Human development and education.* New York: David McKay, 1953.

Herr, E. L. *Decision-making and vocational development.* Boston: Houghton Mifflin, 1970.

Herr, E. L. and Cramer, S. H. *Vocational guidance and career development in the schools:* toward a systems approach. Boston: Houghton Mifflin, 1972.

Hill, W. F. *Learning: a survey of psychological interpretations.* San Francisco: Chandler, 1963.

Holland, J. L. A theory of vocational choice. *Journal of Counseling Psychology,* 1959, 6, 35-44.

———. Some explorations of a theory of vocational choice: I. One- and two-year longitudinal studies. *Psychological Monographs,* 1962, 76 (26), (Whole No. 545).

———. Major programs of research on vocational behavior. In Henry Borow (ed.) *Man in a world of work.* Boston: Houghton Mifflin, 1964, 259-284.

———. *The psychology of vocational choice.* Waltham, Massachusetts: Blaisdell Press, 1966.

Hoppock, R. *Occupational information.* New York: McGraw-Hill, 1967.

Katz, M. *Decision and value.* New York: College Entrance Examination Board, 1963.

Maslow, A. H. *Motivation and personality.* New York: Harper, 1954.

Miller, A. W. Learning theory and vocational decisions. *Personnel and Guidance Journal,* 1968, 47, 18-23.

Miller, D. and Form, W. *Industrial sociology.* New York: Harper, 1951.

Nachmann, B. Childhood experience and vocational choice in law, dentistry, and social work. *Journal of Counseling Psychology,* 1960, 7, 243-250.

National Vocational Guidance Association, Principles and practices of vocational guidance. *Occupations,* 1937, 15, 772-778.

O'Hara, R. P. A theoretical foundation for the use of occupational information in guidance. *Personnel and Guidance Journal,* 1968, 46, 636-640.

Osipow, S. H. *Theories of career development.* New York: Appleton-Century-Crofts, 1968.

Parsons, F. *Choosing a vocation.* Boston: Houghton Mifflin, 1909.

Paterson, D. Developments in vocational counseling technique. In E. Williamson (ed.), *Trends in student personnel work.* Minneapolis: University of Minnesota Press, 1949, 80-96.

Paterson, D. and Darley, J. *Men, women, and jobs.* Minneapolis: University of Minnesota Press, 1936.

Pepinsky, P. and Pepinsky, H. *Counseling: theory and practice.* New York: Ronald Press, 1954.

Proctor, W. Psychological tests and guidance of high school pupils. *Journal of Educational Research Monographs,* 1920, 1 (5).

Roe, A. A psychological study of eminent biologists. *Psychological Monographs,* 1951, 65 (14), (a)

————. A psychological study of eminent physical scientists. *Genetic Psychological Monograph,* 1951, 43, 121-239, (b).

————. Early determinants of vocational choice. *Journal of Counseling Psychology,* 1957, 4 (3), 212-21.

————. *The psychology of occupations.* New York: John Wiley, 1956.

————. Perspectives on vocational development. In J. M. Whitely and A. Resnikoff (eds.), *Perspectives on vocational development.* Washington, D. C.: American Personnel and Guidance Association, 1972, 61-82.

Roe, A. and Siegelman, M. *The origin of interests.* Washington, D. C.: American Personnel and Guidance Association, 1964.

Segal, S. J. A psychoanalytic analysis of personality factors in vocational choice. *Journal of Counseling Psychology,* 1969, 8, 202-210.

Simons, Joseph B. An existential view of vocational development. *Personnel and Guidance Journal,* 1966, 44, 604-610.

Stead, W. and Shartle, C. *Occupational counseling techniques.* New York: American Book, 1940.

Stewart, N. AGCT scores of army personnel grouped by occupations. *Occupations,* 1947, 26, 5-41.

Stuit, D. Significant trends in aptitude testing. In E. Williamson (ed.), *Trends in student personnel work.* Minneapolis: University of Minnesota Press, 1949, 62-79.

Super, D. A theory of vocational development. *American Psychologist,* 1953, 8, 185-190.

————. Career patterns as a basis for vocational counseling. *Journal of Counseling Psychology,* 1954, 1, 12-20.

————. Dimensions and measurement of vocational maturity. *Teachers College Record,* 1955, 5, 151-163.

Super, D. E. and Bachrach, P. B. *Scientific careers and vocational development theory.* New York: Teachers College Press, 1957. (a)

Super, D. E. *The psychology of careers.* New York: Harper & Brothers, 1957. (b)

Super, D. E. *et. al., Vocational development: A framework for research.* New York: Teachers College Press, 1957. (c)

Super, D. and Overstreet, P. *The vocational maturity of ninth-grade boys.* New York: Teachers College Press, 1960.

Super, D. E., Starishevsky, R., Matlin, N., and Jordaan, J. P. *Career development: self-concept theory.* Princeton, New Jersey: College Entrance Examination Board, 1963.

Thorndike, R. and Hagen, E. *10,000 careers.* New York: John Wiley, 1959.

Tiedeman, D. V. Decision and vocational development: a paradigm and its implications. *Personnel and Guidance Journal,* 1961, 40, 15-21.

Tiedeman, D. V. and O'Hara, R. P. *Career development: choice and integration.* New York: College Entrance Examination Board, 1963.

Yerkes, R. (ed.), Psychological examining in the U. S. Army. *Memoirs of the National Academy of Science.* Washington, D. C.: Government Printing Office, 1921, 15, 819-837.

Zaccaria, J. *Theories of occupational choice and vocational development.* Boston: Houghton Mifflin, 1970.

Factors Affecting
Career Development

Introduction

The previous chapter has provided an overview of the more prominent theories which have been advanced to explain the *process* which leads to the formation and implementation of an occupational choice. In this chapter, attention is turned to the *factors* which influence an individual's selection of an occupation. Chapter 4 is comprised of three major parts. The first discusses the concept of *vocational maturity* to illustrate the range and complexity of factors involved in career development. The next two sections deal with *environmental and psychological factors* respectively.

Because of space limitations, only selected research studies have been reported. Only studies which deal with elementary and secondary school age groups have been included. The number of studies which exemplify major research findings and trends was also somewhat comprised by the space restriction. Although the studies presented are not exhaustive, they are representative of empirical data which characterize the determinants of career choice.

In describing the research, the authors have repeatedly used such phrases as "positively correlated" or "associated with" to describe the relationship between and among variables. The reader should remember that significant correlations or associations do not imply cause-effect relationships. To say that variable A is correlated or associated with variable B is not to say that variable A caused the specific response or outcome manifest in variable B or that B caused A.

Concepts, Constructs, and Variables

The discussion of research in this chapter does not presuppose previous background in educational research. Therefore, it will be helpful to define several terms which the reader may be encountering for the first time (at least in their present context). The following definitions have been synthesized from Kerlinger's (1967, pp. 31-33) book on *Foundations of Behavioral Research*.

- A *concept* is a term that expresses an abstraction formed by generalization from observed behavior. For example, "achievement" is an abstraction formed from the observation of behaviors associated with the learning of school tasks — reading words, doing arithmetic problems, writing themes, and so on. Thus, various observed behaviors are put together and expressed as a concept, i.e., "achievement."

- A *construct* is a concept that has the added meaning of having been deliberately and consciously invented or adopted for a specific scientific purpose. A concept becomes a construct once researchers begin to systematically describe and measure it.

- The properties or values which are used to symbolize constructs are called *variables*. Examples of important variables in career development are: social status, sex, ability and interests. It is important to keep in mind that a variable is often influenced by a multiplicity of other variables.

The above three terms have been singled out for definition because of the regularity in which they appear in the text. Additional terms which might be foreign to the reader will be defined as they are introduced.[1]

The Concept of Vocational Maturity

The shift in orientation from "occupational choice" to "vocational development" during the early 1950's resulted in a realization that new descriptors and measurement techniques were required to assess developmental vocational behavior. Dysinger (1950, p. 198) appears to be among the first to indicate the need for a term ". . . to express the vocational implication of maturation." Following is a summary of resultant theory and research.

[1]See Crites (1969, pp. 570-578) for a summary of career development concepts, constructs, and variables.

A Definition of Vocational Maturity

The previous chapter revealed that the major theories of career development view occupational choice as a process which takes place over a period of several years and encompasses many related occupational decisions. "Consistent with this emphasis upon the longitudinal nature of vocational decision-making is the concept of vocational maturity which has been introduced to refer to the various behavioral dimensions along which vocational development proceeds" (Westbrook and Cunningham, 1970, p. 171).

Super (1955) was the first to attempt an operational definition of vocational maturity. Having described vocational development as a continuum, beginning early in life and proceeding along a curve until late in life, he found it necessary to construct a "yardstick" with which to measure career development. Super's definition is as follows:

The term vocational maturity is now used to denote the degree of development, the place reached on the continuum of vocational development from exploration to decline. Vocational maturity may be thought of as vocational age, conceptually similar to mental age . . . The place reached on the vocational development continuum may be described not only in terms of the gross units which constitute the life stages but also in terms of much smaller and more refined units (1955, p. 153).

Dimensions of Vocational Maturity

To test his theory of vocational development, and the concepts of vocational maturity and vocational adjustment, Super began in 1951 a longitudinal research project entitled the Career Pattern Study (CPS). Subjects consisted of 142 eighth-grade and 134 ninth-grade boys in Middletown, New York.

Following characterization of vocational maturity as a point on the career development continuum, Super attempted a specification of the dimensions of vocational maturity which is reported in the first Career Pattern Study Monograph (Super, *et. al.*, 1957) By analyzing Ginzberg and associates' (1951) description of vocational behavior during the exploration stage, Super postulated five dimensions of vocational maturity: (1) Orientation to Vocational Choice, (2) Information and Planning about Preferred Occupations, (3) Consistency of Vocational Preferences, (4) Crystallization of Traits, and (5) Wisdom of Vocational Preference. The theoretical dimensions proposed by Super were logically derived from what was then known about adolescent vocational behavior, and were generally consistent with Baldwin's (1955) three basic characteristics of mature behavior: cognition, goal selection, and goal-directed behavior.

In 1960, a second CPS monograph appeared. In it Super elaborated on the concept of vocational maturity. The five original dimensions were extended to include twenty indices believed to measure them. Following is his list of dimensions and indices (Super and Overstreet, 1960, pp. 33-34):

Dimension I. Orientation to Vocational Choice
    a. Concern with choice
    b. Use of resources in orientation

Dimension II. Information and Planning about the Preferred Occupation
    a. Specificity of information about the preferred occupation
    b. Specificity of planning for the preferred occupation
    c. Extent of planning activity

Dimension III. Consistency of Vocational Preferences
    a. Consistency of vocational preferences within fields
    b. Consistency of vocational preferences within levels
    c. Consistency of vocational preferences within families (fields and levels)

Dimension IV. Crystallization of Traits
    a. Degree of patterning of measured interests
    b. Interest maturity
    c. Liking for work
    d. Degree of patterning of work values
    e. Extent of discussion of rewards of work
    f. Acceptance of responsibility for choice and planning
    g. Vocational independence

Dimension V. Wisdom of Vocational Preferences
    a. Agreement between ability and preference
    b. Agreement between measured interests and preference
    c. Agreement between measured interests and fantasy preference
    d. Agreement between occupational level of measured interests and level of preference
    e. Socioeconomic accessibility of preference

These behaviors are strictly hypothetical and were proposed so they might be tried out. The attempted validation of these formulations via the CPS are reported in a series of three monographs. Monograph two, *The Vocational Maturity of Ninth-Grade Boys* (Super and Overstreet, 1960) describes the analysis of data for the base year of 1951-52. Monograph three (Heyde and Jordaan, in press) deals with vocational development during the high school years. It reports on data collected when the study subjects were high school seniors. The fourth monograph (Super, Kowalski, and Gorkin, in press) contains data collected in 1962 and 1963 when the subjects were 25 years old.

An additional report in the CPS series entitled *Emerging Careers* is actually an independent study done by Gribbons and Lohnes (1968) to replicate the early stages of Super's research. A sample of fifty-seven boys and fifty-four girls were monitored from eighth grade to two years beyond high school. A vocational maturity measure labeled *Readiness for Vocational Planning* (RVP) was modified from the lengthy interview schedule used for the CPS. The RVP consists of the following eight dimensions and measures:

Variable I: Factors in Curriculum Choice. Awareness of relevant factors, including one's abilities, interests, and values and their relation to curriculum choice; curricula available; courses within curricula; the relation of curricula choice to occupational choice.

Variable II: Factors in Occupational Choice. Awareness of relevant factors, including abilities, interests, values; educational requirements for choice; relation of specific high school courses to choice, accuracy of description of occupation.

Variable III: Verbalized Strengths and Weaknesses. Ability to verbalize appropriately the relation of personal strengths and weaknesses to educational and vocational choices.

Variable IV: Accuracy of Self-Appraisal. Comparisons of subject's estimates of his general scholastic ability, verbal ability, and quantitative ability with his actual attainments on scholastic aptitude tests, English grades, and mathematics grades.

Variable V: Evidence for Self-Rating. Quality of evidence cited by subject in defense of his appraisal of his own abilities.

Variable VI: Interests. Awareness of interests and their relation to occupational choices.

Variable VII: Values. Awareness of values and their relation to occupational choices.

Variable VIII: Independence of choice. Extent of subject's willingness to take personal responsibility for his choices.

Subjects in the study were interviewed using the RVP instrument in the eighth, tenth, and twelfth grades and two years after graduation. The study revealed small increases in RVP scores (i.e., vocational maturity) from grade eight to grade ten. These were not as great as the researchers wished to have established. Nonetheless, the study tends to corroborate major aspects of Super's vocational maturity theory. Gribbons and Lohnes (1968, p. 103) summarize their contributions as follows: "We agree that vocational maturity is a most meaningful developmental concept, that it is emergent with the passage of time, that it is persistent over time, and that it is differentiated into a multidimensional syndrome of traits, the kernel of which is informed planfulness."

In a recent monograph, Crites (1965) elaborates on Super's concept of vocational maturity. (See Fig. 4-1.) Crites retains Super's Dimensions III and V, but synthesizes the other three into what he calls "Vocational Choice Competencies" and "Vocational Choice Attitudes." Choice competencies refer to cognitive processes such as vocational problem-solving and planning, while choice attitudes are considered to fall within the affective domain. He hypothesizes that each of the four group factors (i.e., dimensions) are moderately correlated with the others. Further, the dimensions are comprised of certain specific *variables* which reflect moderate interactions between groups and fairly high associations within groups. Thus, like Super, and Gribbons and Lohnes, Crites assumes that the construct of vocational maturity is multidimensional, with each dimension composed in turn of various vocational behavior variables.

Implications

The purpose of the preceding discussion has been to provide the reader with a framework for understanding the review and synthesis of research which will be discussed in the remainder of this chapter. The definition of vocational maturity and the dimensions offered by Super, Gribbons and Lohnes, and Crites clearly indicate that the construct of vocational maturity is different from career development and more comprehensive than occupational choice.

Research related to the measurement of vocational maturity tends to support Super's general theory but fails to adequately validate its major dimensions. As a result, the writers have chosen not to discuss the various vocational maturity studies, but refer the interested reader to the previously mentioned research and to a promising new study being conducted by Westbrook (Norton, 1970).

The fact that the exceedingly complex dimensions of vocational maturity have yet to be isolated and validated does not mean that little is known about vocational behavior. On the contrary, a considerable body of research exists describing the variables of vocational maturity. However, until such time as a comprehensive,

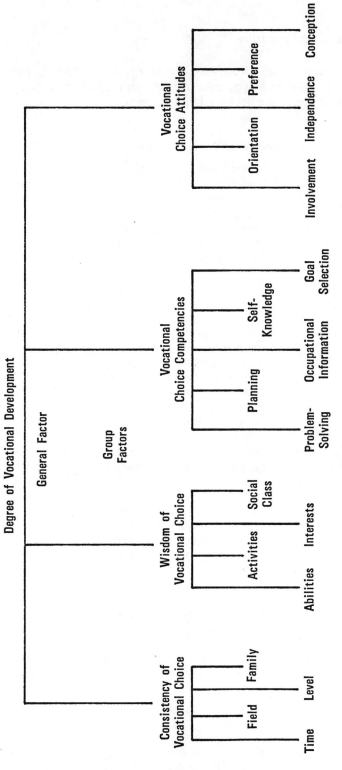

Fig. 4-1. The Construct of Vocational Maturity as Derived from Theories of Vocational Development

SOURCE: J. O. Crites, "Measurement of Vocational Maturity in Adolescence: I— Attitudes Test of the Vocational Development Inventory," *Psychological Monographs*, 1965. p. 5.

empirically derived model of vocational maturity is developed, the practitioner must rely on a synthesis of research findings to understand and assist the students they hope to serve.

Personal and Social Factors

This section discusses personal and social variables which are related to career choice. They include: (1) subculture, (2) sex, and (3) age. The criteria for the inclusion of these variables are that they are largely constant, e.g., parental educational and occupational level, and are predetermined as in the case of sex, race, and age. Contrast this with the psychological variables which are much more dynamic and much less observable and measurable.

Subculture

According to Lipsett (1962, p. 433), "Probably the broadest and most significant social factor affecting human behavior is social class identification." The validity of this assumption as it relates to career development will be the subject of this section. Closely related familial influences of parent's occupation and education, place of residence, and race will also be discussed.

Family and Social Class. As part of a larger study, Jenson and Kirchner (1955) attempted to answer the question, "Do sons follow their fathers' occupation?" Data were collected in 1951 on a nationwide basis from interviews with over 8,000 heads of households. The findings reported here deal only with a comparison of the frequency of fathers and sons in various occupational groups.

Analysis of the data revealed the following facts. In five of the ten occupational groups — professional and technical; manager, officials, and proprietors; clerical; craftsman and foreman; and operators — more sons followed their father's occupation than any other. For the remaining groups, at four occupational levels — sales; service and household; farm laborers and foreman; and other laborers — sons tended to enter occupations at levels *above* those of their fathers. The only major trend toward downward mobility was at the level of farmers and farm managers. This finding, however, seems to be explainable by the decrease in the number of farmers over the years.

The overall evidence from this study reveals that sons *do* tend to follow the general type and level of their fathers' occupations. When they do not, sons tend to make a jump up the occupational ladder.

Sampson and Stefflre (1952) attempted to measure the relationship of parental occupation level to the occupational choice of high school seniors. Students in the study were first submitted to a routine of 10-12 hours of vocational advisement. Following a series of tests, interviews, and study in the vocational library, students were again interviewed to determine their occupational aspirations and the occupations of their fathers.

The most obvious overall trend indicated by the data was for students to aspire to occupations at a higher level than those of their parents, e.g., professional and semiprofessional. Statistical analyses were then conducted to determine the relationship between father's occupational level and student's stated preference. Results showed a direct relationship between the level selected by the student and the level occupied by his father.

An extensive questionnaire was administered by Youmans (1954) to 1,279 twelfth grade boys to determine the relationship of "social stratification" to the work attitudes and interests of youth. Father's occupational level was used as the index of social stratification. The three levels were (1) white collar workers, (2) manual workers, and (3) farm owners and tenants.

The study revealed that work attitudes and stated interests were related to numerous social factors. Only selected findings can be reported here. Social stratification, based on father's occupational level, was the most important social factor in senior boy's occupational expectations. The majority of boys evidenced considerable "upward striving," but there was a strong tendency for them to actually expect to enter a job in the same social stratum as that of their fathers. With respect to boys' work experience, they tended to assimilate the values of the group with which they associated. In other words, boys with white collar work experience adopted the values of white collar workers, while boys with manual work experience manifest values more similar to manual workers. In the school situation, it was also found that boys tended to assimilate the values of the groups with which they associate. The data suggest that in relation to college preparatory courses, extra class activities, and in the use made of vocational guidance facilities, the secondary schools tend to reinforce and manifest the values of the American white collar class.

A second study, involving a sample of high school seniors, was conducted by Sewell, Haller, and Straus (1957) to test the association of youth's level of educational and occupational aspiration with social status of their families. A one-sixth random sample of nonfarm seniors in public and private high schools in Wisconsin were included. Rather than use occupational level as was done in the previous study, Sewell, Haller, and Straus converted parents' occupation to an "occupational prestige scale," i.e., social status.

The relationship of level of occupational aspiration to educational aspiration was analyzed with sex and intelligence controlled. Results showed that both boys and girls from high status families, as determined from fathers' occupations, more frequently chose higher level occupations than did students from lower status families. Similarly, there were significant, positive relationships between high level educational aspirations or college plans and parental social status.

Moser (1952) studied the effect of level of parents' education upon vocational preferences of high school students. Student vocational preferences were (1) determined by administration of the *Kuder Preference Record* and (2) ranked in descending order as follows: literary, computational, social service, artistic, scientific, persuasive, clerical, musical, and mechanical. Parents' educational level was treated in terms of the proportion who had attended college and the proportion who had attended high school.

A comparison of the two sets of data revealed a high positive correlation. That is, students whose parents had the highest percentage of college attendance preferred occupational areas with high cultural status. To help explain this finding, Moser tested a corollary hypothesis: that the number of books and magazines in the home is related to students' preference. The nine occupational areas were arranged in a descending order of reading material in the home. It was found that the former preference ranking based on parents' educational level and the aitered ranking based on amount of reading material was correlated at .80. According to Moser ". . . this data seems to indicate that the cultural atmosphere of the home, the parental background and hence parental example and training play an important part in influencing young people in their vocational preferences and selections" (p. 526).

Hyman (1956) conducted a study to test the hypothesis that social status affects vocational interests. Data were collected on 137 male high school seniors. The criteria for social status was equated with the six level Bureau of Census Classification as follows:

     Class 1. Professional
     Class 2. Proprietors, Managers, and Officials
     Class 3. Clerical and Kindred Workers
     Class 4. Skilled Workers and Foremen
     Class 5. Semiskilled Workers
     Class 6. Unskilled Workers

School records were examined for information on parental occupation, which was then converted to one of the above six classes. Students were administered the *Kuder Preference Record, Form BB,* to determine generalized occupational interests.

A comparison was made between the nine Kuder interest areas — mechanical, computational, scientific, persuasive, artistic, literary, musical, social service, and clerical — and the six social status classifications. Simple inspection of the data suggested slight differences in various interest areas for different social status groups. However, when a statistical analysis was performed, no significant differences were found. Thus, the hypothesis that differences in social status are significantly related to vocational interests was not sustained. Although social status has been associated, in previous studies reported here, with student's stated preference, occupational and educational aspirations, work attitudes and interests, Hyman found no relationship between social status and measured vocational interests.

Rural-Urban Background. Middleton and Grigg (1959) designed a study to measure and compare the occupational and educational aspirations of twelfth grade students from rural and urban backgrounds. Occupational aspirations were determined by asking each subject, "In what occupation do you think that you will most likely be working ten years from now?" Educational aspirations were classified as "planning to attend college" and "not planning to attend college."

Sixty-four percent of the rural residents and 77 percent of the urban residents aspired to "white-collar" occupations. Similar statistically significant rural-urban differences were found in educational aspirations. Thirty-five percent of the rural residents and 56 percent of the urban residents planned to attend college. These findings suggest that students from urban environments verbalize greater occupational and educational aspirations at the completion of high school than do rural residents.

The anaylsis was refined by introducing sex as a control variable. Rural-urban differences which were found for the total group remained stable for boys in relationship to both occupational and educational aspirations, and for girls on educational aspirations. However, though the occupational aspirations of girls were uniformly high, no significant differences were found between urban and rural girls for this variable. This is interpreted to mean that girls from both environments reflect the same fairly homogeneous aspirations for occupations at approximately the same level in the occupational hierarchy.

Studies of the type conducted by Middleton and Grigg usually reveal gross differences in educational and occupational aspirations between students from urban and rural environments. Burchinal (1961) also found that farm residence is negatively correlated with levels of occupational and educational aspiration. To explain these differences, he attempted to isolate and measure factors unique to farm family socialization which tend to depress the level of aspiration.

The hypothesis that farm parents are not as frequently involved in their sons' occupational planning as urban parents was tested by asking, "What does your father think of your present occupational plans?" The question was also repeated by substituting "mother" in the question where "father" appears. The percentages for the noninvolvement responses support the hypothesis. It was unexpectedly revealed, however, that fathers were less involved in son's occupational planning than mothers.

A similar hypothesis regarding parental expectations was tested by asking, "How does your father (mother) feel about your educational plans?" An analysis of response patterns clearly revealed that rural boys less often received encouragement from parents to continue their education beyond high school. Once again, it was surprising to find that mothers were more supportive of their sons' aspirations than fathers. These two sets of data with respect to parental involvement in occupational and educational planning illustrate the importance of family influences on students' aspirational levels.

Straus (1969) restricted his study to ninety-eight farmers' sons in the eleventh and twelfth grades to investigate factors which underlie the disadvantaged position of farm-reared youth when they enter the urban labor force. Comparisons were made between this sample and three previous studies using similar groups. Although the study examined the social psychological characteristics of farm boys, their occupational choices, personality, and other variables, only selected findings related to educational and occupational aspirations will be reported here. Like Burchinal's, this study revealed major differences in the extent of parents' support for their sons' aspirations. Only two percent of rural boys, as compared to 22 percent of urban boys, perceived their parents as wanting them to attend college. Straus concluded: "The fact that a smaller proportion of the parents in the sample wanted their sons to attend college than were actually planning to attend is undoubtedly one of the factors accounting for the low levels of educational and occupational achievement of the farm population." (1969, p. 419)

Stevic and Uhlig (1967) compared the occupational aspirations of rural Appalachian youth with two groups of urban high school youth: (1) urban "natives" and (2) urban "migrants" from Appalachia. Like previous studies, the mean occupational aspiration level for rural youth was found to be significantly lower than the mean of the migrant and native groups. Further, the Appalachian youth identified different personal role models and characteristics for success than did students who had migrated from the Appalachian area.

The major, significant finding of this study, however, was that the group of urban migrants did not seem to be a great deal different from the native urban youth. The authors conclude that one of the major problems in raising the occupational aspirations of rural Appalachian students appears to be lack of information and opportunity rather than lack of ability.

Studies reported thus far demonstrate lower occupational and educational aspirations for rural high school students. In a recent study, Asbury (1968) found that younger students do not possess the lower occupational aspirations which are more prevalent among students in the upper grades. He compared the occupational aspirations of rural Appalachian Kentucky eighth grade boys with a sample of junior high school boys in Mason, Wisconsin. No significant differences were found. A possible explanation for these data is that the aspirations of rural disadvantaged youth (and perhaps rural youth in general) drop after the eighth grade. Asbury concluded that "Perhaps boys growing up in Appalachia begin to realize during the high school years that occupational opportunities are scarce in their home counties, causing their vocational self-concepts and aspirations to drop. The lack of part-time jobs and their recognition of lack of post-high school educational opportunities, due to financial difficulties and distance to colleges, might also result in lower aspirations" (1968, p. 111).

Race. This section on subcultural variables has previously dealt with family and social class, and geography of residence as factors affecting career development. The part which follows begins by relating rural-urban differences to ethnic background, and then discusses racial differences in career development.

The study of Middleton and Grigg (1959) found significant differences between the occupational and educational aspirations of rural and urban twelfth grade boys. However, when a comparison was made with respect to race, no differences were found between the occupational and educational aspirations of rural and urban Blacks who remain in the school through the twelfth grade.

Kuvlesky and Ohlendorf (1968) have extended the former study to explore rural-urban differences among Black youth only with respect to occupational aspirations and expectations. Data were obtained for students at the sophomore level of high school.

Although the majority of rural and urban Black youth generally reflected high occupational aspirations and expectations, significant differences were observed. Urban boys had higher aspirations and expectations than did rural boys. These finding are in agreement with previous studies of rural-urban differences, but contradict the Middleton and Grigg data for Black students. Kuvlesky and Ohlendorf explain that in their judgment the Middleton-Grigg study was actually measuring "expectations." Interpreted in this way, the findings of the two studies are compatible, i.e., significant rural-urban differences in occupational aspirations hold true for both Black and white boys.

Social class membership, occupation of parents, family influences, and geography of residence have been shown to be associated with differences in vocational behavior. Since Black families, on the average, maintain a lower socioeconomic level than whites, it would be expected that Black children might differ from white children in various aspects of career development.

In an early study by Witty, Garfield, and Brink (1941) students were asked to list in order of interest the occupations which they would like to enter. Data were obtained for boys and girls enrolled in racially segregated high schools.

Unique differences were found regarding the occupational preferences of boys. In the white high school, 25 percent of the boys expressed a preference for engineering, 21 percent showed interest in aviation. In the Black school, postal work was the most popular choice with 22 percent, and music was second with 15 percent. An unexpected finding was that medicine, law, and teaching were more popular for Black boys than for white boys. For girls, the predominant occupational preferences were virtually the same for both races. Three occupational fields — stenographic and office work, teaching, and nursing — were indicated by 97 percent of the white and 99 percent of the Black girls.

With respect to educational ambitions, practically all of the students in both schools expected to graduate from high school. In response to the question, "Do you intend to go to college?," the responses were again unexpected. It was revealed that 49 percent of white and 65 percent of the Black pupils expected to attend college. This finding is all the more dramatic in light of the fact that the study was conducted during the 1940's.

A study conducted several years later by Gray (1944) reported similar findings for subjects in the first six grades of school. The data collected revealed that Black boys and girls choose occupations, on a five-point scale, about one point higher than white children. Typical of the findings was the fact that Black boys demonstrate more interest in professional level occupations, particularly the occupation of physician. The apparent conclusion from these studies is that Black children manifest educational and occupational aspirations, with larger components of unrealism, than do white children.

A more recent study by Antonovsky and Lerner (1959) corroborates the findings of other studies of this type. A sample of Black and white youth of similar low economic status showed that Black students have a higher level of occupational aspiration than white students. It is significant that in this study, as contrasted to previous research, socioeconomic status was held constant by using youth of the same general background.

How then to explain the logically unexpected responses of Black youth? Antonovsky and Lerner interpret these findings as a manifestation of several factors. First, the traditional stress within the Black community on successful Black men (e.g., Paul Lawrence Dunbar, Ralph Bunche, Martin Luther King) may have resulted in a belief that there are only two kinds of Blacks: the exceptional and the mass, with nothing in between. Thus, to succeed for a Black person may only mean to achieve a high status. Second, Blacks are well-acquainted with discrimination in middle level occupations in the skilled trades, retail businesses and corporate offices. Education for the professions is thus one of the most readily available routes to upward mobility. Third, acute lack of self-esteem, which is typical of minority group members, may result in overcompensation in the form of success drive. Finally, Black families often lack successful adult role models for children to emulate. Rather than being content to rise one step above his father's occupation as are many lower class white students, the Black youth often aspires to much higher occupational levels.

Due to his high level of aspiration, the Black person often encounters serious psychological crises when his aspirations are tempered. The reader should be cautioned at this point to avoid the inference that Black youth should be counseled toward lower status occupations. On the contrary, the implications are that a dynamic program of intervention (i.e., education and guidance) is required to assist Black youth with early identification of talents, greater self-understanding, and competencies development which will allow achievement of stated levels of aspiration.

Sex Differences

It will be recalled from Chapter 3 that the major theories of career development and occupational choice do not provide alternate conceptualizations for men and for women. Yet, observation of the American labor force reveals widespread differences in the relative proportion of men and women workers in various occupations. Are the differences for occupations due to the obvious biological differences, or are other phenomenon more important determinants? The research studies in the section which follows have been selected to help answer this question.

One of the earliest studies of sex differences in vocational behavior was conducted by Lehman and Witty (1936). The *Lehman Vocational Attitude Quiz,* consisting of a list of 200 occupations, was administered to over 26 thousand boys and girls during the late 1920's. The purpose of the study was to simply determine the occupations in which boys and girls respectively manifest interest. No inferences were made regarding *why* students selected various occupations.

Responses for each of the 200 occupations were grouped into four categories: (S) sedentary nature, (T) requiring travel, (A) aesthetic appreciation, and (V) vigorous physical activity. Among these gross categories, it was observed that fully 90 percent of preferred occupations for girls were sedentary, and over 50 percent required some degree of aesthetic appreciation or interest. Boys preferred occupations which require travel (45 percent versus 15 percent for girls), and occupations which demand vigorous physical activity and some physical danger. The data from this study have served to provide empirical support for the obvious; i.e., boys and girls are not equally interested in the various occupations. The implications of this study will be discussed in the summary of this section.

Singer and Stefflre (1954) compared the job values and desires of 17- and 18-year-old white males and females. Students were handed a card upon which were listed ten different value preferences. They were then asked: "If you had a choice of one of these kinds of jobs which would you choose?" Examples of the value statements are: A job where you could be a leader; a very interesting job; a job where you could be boss.

Statistically significant differences were observed between boys and girls on five categories. Boys were more prone to select those categories dealing with a desire for a job offering power, profit, and independence, while girls were more inclined to select job values characterized by interesting experience and public service. The implications are that boys and girls have learned their sex stereotypes very well. Variations in job value preferences, for these students, reflect traditional cultural expectations of "maleness" and "femaleness."

Edmiston and Starr (1948) derived twenty-seven factors affecting the choice of an occupation through an examination of five books on vocational guidance. The factors were presented to students in questionnaire form. Each student indicated those factors which were the most important consideration in making an occupational choice. Questionnaires were completed by 443 boys and 575 girls in grades seven through twelve.

Differences between the indices of boys and girls indicated that girls were more eager to enter white-collar occupations; preferred positions involved in meeting people; were more conscious of healthful working conditions; would accept lower salaries; and were more anxious for a shorter work week. Boys, on the other hand, were more willing to travel; preferred more adventurous occupations; and demanded more independence. As expected, boys rated job requirements of mechanical and general ability more desirable than did girls. Thus, like Singer and Steffle, Edmiston and Starr found that boys and girls typically reflect the more dominant cultural expectations and sex roles.

The former studies were all conducted prior to 1954. A more recent study by Powell and Bloom (1962) investigated the reasons for occupational choice of adolescents through the high-school years. Like the previously reported studies, Powell and Bloom also found differences in occupational preferences associated with sex. Girls, for example, indicated their most preferred occupations to be office work (22 percent), teacher (15 percent), nursing (14 percent), and airline hostess (4 percent). Specific occupations selected by boys were engineering (23 percent), medicine and automobile mechanic (each 6 percent), scientific research (4 percent), and aviation and business (each 3 percent). Although these data reflect sex differences in occupational choice, Powell and Bloom point out that youth are frustrated in the intelligent selection of an occupation because of the lack of knowledge about occupations. "The goals as specified by the student are not mature in outlook nor do they represent an understanding of adult culture" (Powell and Bloom, 1962, p. 130).

It is possible to deduce several interpretations of the occupationally-related sex differences cited in the previous studies. The hypothesis that certain aspects of physical growth and development are associated with differences in career development seems logical and plausible. The research findings presented here, however, appear to be explainable by an alternate hypothesis; i.e., sex differences are more attributable to mores, sex role expectations, and limited student awareness of available occupational options. The case could be argued that these descriptive studies did not employ appropriate research designs or adequate psychometric instruments. Extraneous variables may have had more influence on findings than they should.

A more sophisticated research study was conducted by Crites (1965) to develop and validate the *Vocational Development Inventory*. Comparisons of test data were made between age, grade, sex, and school variables. With respect to sex differences, Crites (1965, p. 23) observed that "About the most that can be concluded now is that the available data indicate only a few differences between males and females in the vocational attitudes and concepts which they endorse as self-descriptive. Evidently, sex is not a very significant factor in the maturation of these verbal aspects of vocational development." It is significant to note that the Crites study suggests that when more objective and rigorous research methodologies and statistical procedures are employed, differences which *may be* attributed to the socialization process do not become manifest.

The early studies which dealt with sex differences seemed to intimate that boys are more vocationally mature than girls. As social customs change and equal guidance, education and training, and employment opportunities are extended to women, it may be revealed that girls are more vocationally mature than boys. The Davis, Hagan, and Strouf (1962) study (discussed in more detail in the following section) shows that more mature choices among sixth grade students are correlated positively with the female sex. O'Hara (1962) also found that understanding of future careers was more realistic for girls than for boys. A recent study by Smith and Herr (1972) extends the Crites research in an investigation of vocational attitudes among adolescents. They conclude that females possess more maturity in terms of their attitudes toward work and career planning than do males in the eighth and tenth grades.

In summary, research findings regarding sex differences in career development are conflicting and incomplete. The older studies which reported differences in male and female attitudes, values, and preferences seem to reflect sex roles which are the result of the process of socialization. More recent studies reveal either no differences in vocational maturity or differences which tend to be more positively associated with the female sex.

Age Factors in Career Development

Almost all of the theories of career development and occupational choice provide descriptions for vocational behavior at various age levels. It is generally hypothesized that realism in occupational decision-making increases with advancing age. The findings of the studies which follow provide better understanding of the relationship of vocational behavior and differences in age.

The purpose of a study by Davis, Hagan, and Strouf (1962) was to investigate the validity of an aspect of Ginzberg's theory of occupational choice. The Ginzberg team theorized that the process of occupational choice could be analyzed with respect to three periods: *fantasy* (prior to age eleven), *tentative* (between eleven and seventeen), and *realistic* (between seventeen and young adulthood). The research question was: Do twelve-year-olds make more tentative choices than fantasy choices?

A sample of 116 sixth grade elementary school students were asked to write paragraphs telling what they would like to do when they grow up and why they had made that particular choice. The papers were evaluated by two judges and classified according to Ginzberg's definitions. Fantasy choices were defined as translations of simple needs and impulses into occupational goals. Tentative choices, however, indicated decisions based upon capacities, interests, and values of the individual. Analysis of the data revealed that 60 percent of the 116 twelve-year-old students made tentative choices. Thus, it was demonstrated that maturity of occupational choice is a function of age.

A second study to investigate Ginzberg's theory is reported by O'Hara (1962). The purpose of the study was to determine whether the three substages of the tentative period — interest (ages eleven and twelve), capacity (thirteen and fourteen), and value (fifteen and sixteen) — might in fact occur at earlier ages.

O'Hara asked 829 boys and 750 girls in grades four to six two questions: (1) "What sort of person do you want to become?" and (2) "Why do you want to be that kind of person?" The statements were collected and classified into the five categories of interest, value, family, capacity, and others. The major finding related to maturation is that choices become more "realistic" with increasing age. For boys, interests are the dominant basis for choice by the sixth grade, but values are the dominant basis for girls. Data for both boys and girls reveal a decline in family influence with increasing age. Consistent with Ginzberg's theory, capacity does not seem to be a factor affecting choices at any of these grade levels.

Montesano and Geist (1964) designed a study to investigate differences in occupational choice between ninth and twelfth grade boys. Thirty boys each in grades nine and twelve were equated for reading stability and fathers' socioeconomic status to control for differences in reading achievement and economic background. Students were administered the *Geist Picture Interest Inventory* to collect responses regarding why given choices were made. The responses to the inventory were then grouped into eight categories, e.g., identified interests, personal need satisfaction, assessment of abilities, assessment of opportunities.

Statistically significant differences were found between the two groups of students for each of the eight categories of responses. The categories most often used by ninth grade students were interest and personal-need satisfaction. Assessment of abilities was the least used category. Twelfth grade students, however, were much less concerned about personal interests and needs and more concerned about conditions in the occupational world. In addition to *different* reasons for choice, older boys take into account *more* factors related to choice, specifically their abilities, occupational requirements, conditions of work, and opportunities related to an occupation. The results of the study provide support for the assumption that occupational decision-making results from and is interwoven with a maturation process.

Nelson (1963) used students in grades three, five, seven, nine, and eleven in an effort to determine how various age groups compared in their occupational knowledge. Colored slides of workers in sixteen occupations were presented to students followed by a questionnaire which determined both knowledge of and interest in the occupation. Four major areas about each job were explored: (1) title of job, (2) description of job, (3) interest in job, and (4) with respect to interest, why he responds favorably, unfavorably, or neutrally.

For areas one and two, older children exceeded younger children significantly in naming occupations and in describing jobs accurately. Differences in interest, i.e., reactions toward the sixteen occupations were also noted between grade levels. However, it was observed that as age increases, children respond positively less often to the occupations. This finding suggests that the process of occupational elimination starts early in the elementary grades. The final area of study, reasons for responding positively or negatively, remains relatively similar from grade to grade. O'Hara saw this as an indication that these children reacted toward the occupations in much the same way that adults might be expected to react.

That occupational decision-making is intimately related to the general process of maturation seems valid in light of the studies reported here. Significant differences have been observed between youngsters of various age groups. As youth mature, occupationally-related decisions progress from fantasy to realism and involve judgments based more and more on interests, capacities, values, and personality factors.

Whereas considerable empirical data are available to support the theory that occupational choice is a developmental process, a number of writers contend that the process begins much earlier than most theorists believe. Nelson's (1963) study which was reported previously challenges the assumption that children in the third and fifth grades are in a fantasy stage of career development. In a preference ranking of occupations, he found that the correlations between grades three, five, seven, nine, and eleven were remarkably similar. In addition, O'Hara's (1962) data showed that a large proportion of students base their "tentative" occupational choices on interest and values as early as grade four.

McDaniels (1968) contends that children are not too young to make choices, but only too poorly prepared to do so. He rejects the assumption that the decision-making process must proceed at its own pace and cannot be affected by outside forces. According to Herr (1970) current theories of career development seem to be descriptive of what happens when no purposeful intervention to facilitate choice-making behavior is introduced by the schools. Career development theories, especially those of Super and Ginzberg, are observational and descriptive. They report on the nature of vocational behavior if left to develop on its own.

It must be emphasized that students at an early age *do* make choices. Many of these choices serve as referents with which later-encountered occupations are compared. The realities of biological factors (youth are more highly developed physically and intellectually today than any comparable group in recorded history), failures of education (high rates of youth unemployment), and professional considerations (researchers have demonstrated that elementary grade children possess greater "occupational readiness" than theorists acknowledge) suggest that youth can and must be prepared to choose. This is not to advocate that children make specific occupational choices. On the contrary, the purpose of this discussion is to point out to the practitioner the need for a systematic curriculum program for career development to safeguard the individual's right to make free choices (McDaniels, 1968).

Psychological Factors

The three most prominent psychological variables are interests, mental abilities, and work values. Unlike personal and social factors, psychological variables may be more directly assessed by the use of some type of psychometric instrument. As a result, vocational tests and inventories have been widely used by counselors to help "predict" a student's chances of success in a specific occupation. Although responsible counselors no longer use these tests for prediction purposes, tests are generally acknowledged to yield valuable data for self-appraisal and career guidance.

Interests

When used as variables in occupational decision-making, interests are the manifestation of liking or preference for certain types of activities. Occupational interests are of two major types: *expressed* and *inventoried*. The former term refers simply to a verbal profession of interest in an activity, task, or occupation. Inventoried interests, however, are inferred from recorded responses to items on some type of measurement instrument, e.g., the *Ohio Vocational Interest Survey, Vocational Interest Blank,* or the *Kuder Preference Record.* Crites (1969, p. 254) notes ". . . that expressed and inventoried interests are not highly enough interrelated to be considered interchangeable." Thus, both types of interests will be discussed in relationship to vocational behavior.

Nelson's (1971) study is an example of the type of research which lends support to the conclusion that expressed and inventoried interests are low to moderately correlated. A sample of eleventh grade boys was administered the *Kuder DD Occupational Interest Survey* and the *Occupational Choices Questionnaire.* The analysis of data consisted of a comparison of each student's expressed interests as indicated by his first and second occupational choices on the questionnaire with his inventoried interests as expressed on the *Kuder.* For 65 percent of the group, it was found that inventoried interests were closely related to expressed interests. For the remaining 35 percent, there was a discrepancy between expressed and measured preference. The practical implications of these findings are that for a thorough analysis of a student's occupational interests, both the expressed choice and the inventoried approach should be used to assist the student in more accurate self-appraisal.

It should be properly acknowledged that many studies which have investigated students' occupational choices, preferences, and aspirations could be subsumed here under the category of "expressed interests." As Super and Crites (1962) have pointed out, ". . . some questions concerning vocational preferences are so put as to elicit information concerning expectations, some so as to ascertain preferences, and some to evoke fantasies. The degree of realism of preferences varies with the question asked." The relationship of social and personal variables to expressed and inventoried interests has been dealt with previously and will be reviewed in the next several pages.

Interests have been shown to be related to numerous personal and social factors. In general, expressed occupational and educational aspirations (which presumably reflect interests) are greater for students from higher social status backgrounds and for students who reside in urban areas. The inference is that certain social environments encourage the development and expression of certain kinds of interests which are typical of that environment. The major exception is that Blacks consistently aspire to educational and occupational levels considerably above their social status level.

Studies which report the relationship between measured interests and social status are not entirely consistent. Moser (1952) determined that students whose parents had higher levels of education preferred *Kuder* interest areas which ranked high in cultural status. Hyman (1956), however, found no relationship between *Kuder* interest areas and social status. The seemingly contradictory findings may be due to the fact that the former study used parents' educational level as a criterion of social status while the latter used occupational level. When Hyman took students' intelligence into consideration, interests were found to be related to social status. For example, bright boys of upper middle-class status were more interested in "social service" than equally bright boys of middle-class background.

Several studies have shown that interests vary with age. Davis, Hagan, and Strouf (1962) and O'Hara (1962) indicate that interests are the dominant basis for the occupational preference of young children. As individuals mature, other factors such as abilities and values begin to assume more significance. Sometime during the period between age fifteen and twenty-five interests seem to crystallize, remaining relatively stable thereafter (Cottle, 1968).

Research of the type conducted by Lehman and Witty (1936), Edmiston and Starr (1948), and Powell and Bloom (1962) reveal differences in occupational interests associated with sex. Super and Crites (1962) have summarized studies on interests which show that men tend to be more interested in physical activity, mechanical and scientific matters, politics, and selling. Interest in art, music, literature, people, clerical work, teaching, and social work is more characteristic of women. As pointed out earlier, however, cultural expectations probably affect occupational interests of men and women to a greater degree than physical or biological constitution.

Tyler (1964) points out what may be the most important generalization to be drawn from several decades of research, i.e., interests measure the *direction* rather than the *strength* of a person's interests. This is evidenced in cases where a legitimate interest in an occupational area has little effect on grades earned in the subjects which lead to that occupation. At present there is no known technique except observation of behavior for assessing how strong a person's drive is in the direction he wishes to go.

It should also be remembered that interests depend as much on "dislikes" as "likes." For example, Nelson (1963) and Tyler (1955) found that the process of occupational elimination starts early in the elementary grades. Since interests provide information about an individual's characteristic pattern of choice and rejection, they constitute one means of assessing individuality and for providing resultant self-understanding.

It is often difficult for practitioners to derive meaningful implications from research findings. Implications for practice and an appropriate summary for this treatment of interests are given in an article by Gerken (1964). Gerken suggests ways in which interests may be used to help students develop greater self-understanding. His suggestions are presented in the form of six "guidelines," which are summarized as follows:

- *Guideline 1.* It is important to differentiate between "lay" interests and "career" interests. Many people are universally interested in space exploration, sports, automobiles and music. Students should be encouraged to understand, however, that lay interests are not sufficiently adequate to serve as bases for career decisions.
- *Guideline 2.* Students should be counseled to accept the fact that changes of interests based upon new experiences or education is normal and usually desirable.
- *Guideline 3.* Closely related to number two, is that students should realize that interests may change even after they have committed themselves to a particular pattern of specialized training. A shift in goals is not necessarily an indication of indecisiveness.

- *Guideline 4.* For some students it may help to emphasize that interests may develop while working on the job, rather than only as a function of prior experiences.
- *Guideline 5.* Students should be encouraged to explore the values and life styles of people in various occupational fields in addition to interests. Interests must be classified in relation to non-task aspects of occupations.
- *Guideline 6.* When interests are used as a point of departure for educational and career planning, it would be helpful to insert an action-verb between the words "interested in" and the object specified by the student. For example, an interest in engineering is incomplete without knowledge of action-verbs such as "reading about," "studying," "earning high grades in courses leading to" and so forth. Use of this procedure would encourage a student to define personal needs in relation to the occupation in which he has expressed interest. .

Students should fully understand the importance of looking beyond the somewhat naive way in which the word "interest" is used. If students are helped to explore many related aspects of their claimed interest, the likelihood of self-understanding will be considerably enhanced.

Mental Ability

The relationship of mental ability to vocational plans and vocational preferences was investigated by Porter (1954). A group of 100 senior high schools boys were presented with a questionnaire which included queries asking them to list the occupation they would prefer to be doing at age twenty-five, and the occupation they actually planned to pursue at age twenty-five. The former occupation was referred to by Porter as indicating a "vocational preference" and the latter a "vocational plan." Mental ability was measured by the *Adaptability Test*.

To allow statistical comparisons to be made, a scale was developed to rank in order occupations in terms of "prestige value." An example of a high prestige level occupation is "engineer," while "truck driver" is an example of a low prestige level occupation.

The two variables, preference and plan, were found to be correlated at the .88 level. Intercorrelations among variables revealed that mental ability was significantly related to both vocational plan (.40) and vocational preference (.36). In other words, boys with higher mental ability tend to select occupations with a higher prestige level ranking. In addition to the moderate relationship obtained when compared with mental ability, vocational plans and preferences were correlated with fathers' occupation at the .44 and .42 levels respectively.

Perrone (1964) also studied the relationship between high school seniors' occupational preference and mental ability. He used an occupational preference questionnaire which listed ten occupations under each of Roe's eight occupational groups: service, business contact, outdoor, science, organization, technology, general culture, and arts and entertainment. Pupils were asked to select the occupation that was most like the one they would wish to enter. Mental ability was measured by both a verbal and a nonverbal test of intelligence. Comparisons were then made between the students' mean IQ and occupational preference, grouped under one of the eight categories. Separate analyses were conducted for boys and girls.

Results for boys indicated significant differences between the eight occupational preference categories for both verbal and nonverbal IQ. For girls, significant differences were only obtained between verbal IQ and occupational preference. Next, a more specific analysis was performed. When results were analyzed in terms of "low" and "high" IQ, it was found that boys with lower mean intelligence more consistently selected occupations in the service category. Boys with higher mean intelligence tended to select science occupations more often than any other group. Girls with lower intelligence scores more often selected organizations occupations (more specifically secretarial), while girls with higher intelligence scores indicated a preference for the general cultural group (identified quite specifically as teaching).

Since the study by Perrone did not employ the same type of design as Porter's, no direct comparisons are possible. However, it can be said that gross relationships tend to exist between mental ability and preference for certain occupational groups and levels.

The purpose of a study by Holden (1961) was to determine the relationship between intelligence and persistence of the level of career choice. He postulated that students of high ability would make more "appropriate" occupational choices than the low IQ group.

A study group consisting of 109 members was tested and interviewed in the eighth grade and again when they were in the eleventh grade. At both grade levels, students were asked if they planned to pursue post-high school education, and if so, what type of institution they expected to attend. The level of occupational choice was represented by the number of years of post-high school education expressed. Two IQ tests were administered and the mean of two scores was used to represent the IQ of each student.

A distribution of career choice levels revealed that in the eighth grade, 61.5 percent of the students were considering an occupation that required four or more years of college and 91 percent expected to go into an occupation requiring some post-high school education. No differences in expectations were associated with different levels of IQ. Thus, lower ability students' expectations were unrealistically high. Comparisons of eleventh grade expectations with eighth grade responses were different. Students in the higher IQ group had made no major change in the level of occupational choice. The data for the lower IQ group, however, indicated that they had lowered sights considerably toward jobs requiring less formal education. This supported the hypothesis that students in the lower range of IQ are more likely to change the level of occupational preference between grades eight and eleven than are students in the upper range of the IQ continuum.

As part of their research to measure *Readiness for Vocational Planning*, Gribbons and Lohnes (1966) reported on the relationship of occupational preference to measured intelligence. Personal interviews were conducted with each of 111 students in the eighth, tenth, and twelfth grades. At each grade level, students were asked to state three occupational preferences. These were then classified according to the *Occupational Outlook Handbook* classification system. Mental ability was tested and classified into three groups: (1) IQ 115 and over, (2) IQ from 105 to 114, and (3) students with IQ below 105.

Like Holden's, this study suggests that students at the grade eight level were aspiring to occupational levels out of proportion with the number which will be able to enter such occupations. Most revealing was the finding that over 50 percent of grade eight students below 105 IQ preferred occupations at the professional level. At all three grade levels, the preferences of students with IQ's of 115 and over were relatively consistent. Unlike Holden, however, Gribbons and Lohnes found that students in the lower IQ ranges persist in their preferences for occupations which require greater levels of educational preparation than they may reasonably be expected to attain.

Values

The previous two factors, interests and abilities, are generally well-defined and well-understood variables. Interests take the form of liking or disliking an object or an activity. Ability usually refers to learned qualities or skills principally confined to the cognitive realm of human behavior. The variable to be dealt with in the following section, values, is more difficult to define and measure.

Zytowski (1970) uses *work values* as a term which describes the internal state or motivating force of a person, i.e., needs. An individual attracted to the occupation of farming, for example, probably manifests a valuing (need) for autonomy. Katz (1969) likewise uses values to refer to the characteristic outer expressions and culturally influenced manifestations of needs. "More specifically, values represent feelings about outcomes or results, such as the importance, purpose, or worth of an activity" (Katz, 1969, p. 461).

Values are similar to interests in that both encompass a range of descriptors for various types of work activity. The number of units of work values, however, are probably more limited than the number of distinct interests. One way of comparing the relationship of values and interests in occupational decision-making is to think of interests as affecting the orientation or direction of a choice while values affect the degree to which the occupation (or the preference for an occupation) may be important or satisfying to the individual. The studies which follow are reports of research conducted in an attempt to identify how work values may be associated with various vocational behaviors.

Schwarzweller (1960) conducted a study of senior high school boys and girls to determine what values are related to their occupational plans. Twelve value variables were selected for the study: achievement, material comfort, security, hard work, mental work, creative work, work with people, service to society, individualism, familism, external conformity, and friendship. Students' occupational choices were obtained by questionnaire and classified according to status dimension. For analysis, occupational choices were coded as "high" status (professional, semiprofessional, and managerial) and "low" status (clerks, skilled, semiskilled, and unskilled).

In the case of boys, values on creative work, work with people, and service to society are positively related to high status occupations. Low status occupations were significantly associated with material comfort, hard work, and external conformity. For girls, values on mental work, work with people, and service to society were positively related to high status occupations. A negative relationship, for girls, was observed between low status occupations and material comfort, security, hard work, and familism.

Boys and girls who value material comfort, which emphasizes the desirability of being able to buy many things, and value hard work which emphasizes physical labor as a means to success, are less likely to choose high status jobs. Both boys and girls associate work with people, and service to society, with high status occupations. No significant associations were found between occupational status of choice for the values of individualism, friendship, and achievement. Thus, the findings from this study lend general support to the influence of values in occupational selection.

A study by Singer and Stefflre (1954), which was previously discussed in relation to sex differences, compared the job values and desires of high school seniors. They used the *Job Values and Desires Card* which contains the value categories of leadership, interesting experience, esteem, power, security, self-expression, profit, fame, social service, and independence. Comparisons were made between male and female responses for each category.

Significant differences were obtained for five of the ten categories. A desire for a job offering power, profit, and independence is more characteristic of boys than it is of girls. Occupational values characterized by interesting experience and social service were more often selected by girls than by boys. Based on this sample, it is possible to conclude that specific job values and desires are related to the sex of the respondent.

In a second study Singer and Stefflre (1954b) also used the *Job Values and Desires Checklist*. Again, a sample of male and female high school seniors were used. The purpose of this study, however, was to compare job values with level of vocational aspirations. More specifically, the study was designed to test how students in the upper quartile and the lower quartile of level of aspiration compared in relation to job values, i.e., how students aspiring to high level jobs and students with low levels of aspiration compare in job values.

An analysis between the ten value categories and the upper and lower quartiles of students, for the combined sample of boys and girls, indicated significant differences for two categories. Students with high levels of vocational aspirations are more concerned with job values dealing with leadership and self-expression. When an analysis was performed using only the male sample, two significant differences were also obtained. Upper quartile boys often selected the category of self-expression, while lower quartile boys often selected the category of job independence. For girls, there appeared to be no significant relationship between aspiration levels and job values.

The authors interpreted these findings by comparing them to Centers' (1949) studies of socioeconomic differences in job values. Centers noted a tendency for values to be related to social class status. According to Singer and Stefflre, "It is possible that the adolescent with a high level of vocational aspiration identifies himself with the middle class and hence views job values in the manner of adult middle class members while the adolescent with a low level of vocational aspiration may identify himself with the working class" (1954, p. 422).

Interaction Among Variables

A developmental approach to career development suggests that an occupational decision is a function of a combination of variables which interact and are modified over time. Why then have researchers tended to study only the relationship between a limited number of variables? Until recently, statistical methods and data processing technology have not been generally available. Widespread availability of computers now makes possible analysis of large quantities of data. Comparisons among many different variables can be made in minimal time. The two studies which follow are examples of recent attempts to study the interaction among a combination of occupational determinants.

Mierzwa (1963) selected five representative types of data — abilities, interests, environmental information, temperament, and personality — to study the relationship among multiple variables. The study sample consisted of 192 boys all above average in intelligence. A type of statistical analysis which permits comparisons among all five variables was used. The results indicated that the most important predictor of occupational choice was interests, followed by environment, ability, temperament, and personality.

Even though the study was restricted to high-ability boys, the results provide empirical support for the concept of multi-determinants of career choice. The implication is that it is necessary to use various systems of data in combination, or at least simultaneously, in order to understand and predict career choice.

Madaus and O'Hara (1967) report research in which they also used high-ability high school boys to investigate the relationship among measures of general values, work values, aptitudes, and interests. Results obtained indicate that interests, as measured by the *Kuder*, are more important determinants of stated occupational choice than personality, values, or aptitude dimensions. "Vocational interests once again emerged as the best system of data in differentiating between occupational choices made during high school" (1967, p. 112).

These studies are examples of the type of research which is required to provide the empirical data to validate theories of career development and to identify the major dimensions of the construct of vocational maturity. In the meantime, the practitioner must rely on collective findings and research generalizations such as have been provided here.

Summary

A review of related literature and research of the type presented in this chapter is usually summarized by a synthesis of major *conclusions.* The authors prefer to be less specific to avoid attaching more importance to the research findings than may be legitimately deserved. This chapter is intended to *extend the reader's comprehension of career development theory* by identifying and describing the factors which seem to influence occupational plans and decisions. A reliable body of data exists describing *what* these factors are, but the *exact relationship* among the factors has yet to be demonstrated. The following "generalizations" are offered to help teachers and guidance workers diagnose and abet individual career development.

1. Consistent with career development theory, research indicates that a wide range of individual, social, and psychological variables influence or are related to career decision-making. However, at the moment there is little conclusive data regarding how the variables interact and which are the more important ones that are generalizable to the total population.
2. The process of occupational choice appears to extend over a considerable period of time and can be differentiated into gross stages. Again the data are not complete; specific variables seem to exert more influence during one developmental period than another. For example, more so than students in grade nine, students in grade twelve take abilities into consideration.
3. As a corollary to the previous generalization, manifestations of occupational choice begin to appear in children at a relatively young age. Several studies have shown remarkably mature behavior exhibited by children in the primary grades.
4. Formulation of an occupational choice consists of a dual process of narrowing the field of preferred occupations while at the same time eliminating others from considera-

tion. In fact, the "exclusion" process may precede the more positive selection process.

5. Cultural and socioeconomic factors are potent affectors in educational and occupational aspirations. Of equal significance is the fact that a "positive" change in environment is often associated with more mature and more realistic behavior.

6. The same social values and norms which have traditionally defined the role of women are revealed in their occupational choices and aspirations. It is logical and plausible that differences in male and female interests and values exist. But, that they are as extreme as studies to date indicate is questionable.

7. Because career-planning and decision-making involves a cognitive process, it is to be expected that psychological factors would be instrumental as occupational determinants. Interests, abilities, and values have been shown to have low to moderate relationships with occupational plans and decisions. Several studies have revealed that, of the three, interests emerge as the more important predictor of occupational choice for students in the high school years.

This chapter has dealt primarily with a description of relationships between individual variables. In closing, it should be reasserted that a *combination* of factors influence the ultimate direction of a career. The implication for curriculum and guidance is that a variety of experiences for personal awareness and exploration are required for the individual to discover these factors and to test them in relationship to a variety of occupational alternatives. "There remains plenty of latitude in various occupations for diverse persons, and a great number of unaccounted-for factors in the path to each" (Zytowski, 1970, p. 88).

BIBLIOGRAPHY

Antonovsky, A. and Lerner, M. J. Occupational aspirations of lower class negro and white youth. *Social Problems*, 1959, 7 (4), 132-138.

Asbury, F. A. Vocational development of rural disadvantaged eighth-grade boys. *Vocational Guidance Quarterly*, 1968, 17, 109-113.

Baldwin, A. L. *Behavior and development in childhood.* New York: Dryden, 1955

Burchinal, L. G. Differences in educational and occupational aspirations of farm, small-town, and city boys. *Rural Sociology*, 1961, 26, 107-121.

Centers, R. *Psychology of social class.* Princeton, New Jersey: Princeton University Press, 1949.

Cottle, W. C. *Interest and personality inventories.* Boston: Houghton Mifflin, 1968.

Crites, J. O. *Vocational psychology.* New York: McGraw-Hill, 1969.

———. Measurement of vocational maturity in adolescence: Attitude test of the vocational development inventory. *Psychological Monographs,* 1965, 79(2), 1-36.

Davis, D. A., Hagan, N. and Strouf, J. Occupational choice of twelve-year-olds. *Personnel and Guidance Journal,* 1962, 40, 628-629.

Dysinger, W. S. Maturation and vocational guidance. *Occupations,* 1950, 29, 198-201.

Edmiston, R. W. and Starr, C. H. Youth's attitudes toward occupations. *Occupations,* 1948, 26, 213-220.

Gerken, C. Interests: some questions we haven't asked. *Vocational Guidance Quarterly,* 1964, 13, 280-284.

Ginzberg, E., Ginsburg, S. W., Axelrad, S., and Herma, J. L. *Occupational choice: an approach to a general theory.* New York: Columbia University Press, 1951.

Gribbons, W. D. and Lohnes, P. R. Occupational preferences and measured intelligence. *Vocational Guidance Quarterly,* 1966, 15, 211-214.

———. *Career Development.* Weston, Massachusetts: Regis College, 1966.

———. *Emerging Careers.* New York: Teachers College Press, 1968.

Gray, S. The vocational preference of negro school children. *Journal of Genetic Psychology,* 1944, 64, 239-247.

Herr, E. L. *Decision-making and vocational development.* Boston: Houghton Mifflin, 1970.

Heyde, M. B. and Jordaan, J. P. *The high school years.* Career Pattern Study: Monograph III, in press.

Holden, G. S. Scholastic aptitude and the relative persistence of vocational choice. *Personnel and Guidance Journal,* 1961, 40, 36-41.

Hyman, H. The relationship of social status and vocational interests. *Journal of Counseling Psychology,* 1956, 3(1), 12-16.

Jenson, P. G., and Kirchner, W. K. A national answer to the question, "Do sons follow their fathers' occupations?" *Journal of Applied Psychology,* 1955, 39, 419-421.

Katz, M. Interests and values: a comment. *Journal of Counseling Psychology,* 1969, 16, 460-462.

Kerlinger, F. N. *Foundations of behavioral research.* New York: Holt, Rinehart and Winston, 1967.

Kulvesky, W. P. and Ohlendorf, G. W. *Rural Sociology,* 1968, 33, 141-152.

Lehman, H. C. and Witty, P. A. Sex differences in vocational attitudes. *Journal of Applied Psychology,* 1936, 20, 576-585.

Lipsett, L. Social factors in vocational development. *Personnel and Guidance Journal,* 1962, 40, 432-437.

Madaus, G. F. and O'Hara, R. F. Vocational interest patterns of high school boys: a multivariate approach. *Journal of Counseling Psychology,* 1967, 14, 106-112.

McDaniels, C. Youth: Too young to choose? *Vocational Guidance Quarterly,* 1968, 16, 242-249.

Middleton, R. and Grigg, C. M. Rural-urban differences in aspirations. *Rural Sociology,* 1959, 24, 347-354.

Mierzwa, J. A. Comparison of systems of data for predicting career choice. *Personnel and Guidance Journal,* 1963, 42, 29-34.

Montesano, N. and Geist, H. Differences in occupational choice between ninth and twelfth grade boys. *Personnel and Guidance Journal*, 1964, 43, 150-159.

Moser, W. B. The influence of certain cultural factors upon the selection of vocational preferences by high school students. *Journal of Educational Research*, 1952, 45, 523-526.

Nelson, A. G. Discrepancy between expressed and inventoried vocational interests. *Vocational Guidance Quarterly*, 1971, 20, 21-24.

Nelson, R. C. Knowledge and interests concerning sixteen occupations among elementary and secondary school students. *Educational Psychological Measurement*, 1963, 23, 741-754.

Norton, J. L. Current status of the measurement of vocational maturity. *Vocational Guidance Quarterly*, 1970, 18, 165-170.

O'Hara, R. P. The roots of careers. *The Elementary School Journal*, 1962, 62, 277-280.

Perrone, D. A. Factors influencing high school seniors' occupational preferences. *Personnel and Guidance Journal*, 1964, 42, 976-980.

Porter, J. Predicting vocational plans of high school senior boys. *Personnel and Guidance Journal*, 1954, 33, 215-218.

Powell, M. and Bloom, V. Development of and reasons for vocational choice of adolescents through the high-school years. *Journal of Educational Research*, 1962, 56(3), 126-133.

Sampson, R. and Stefflre, B., Like father . . . like son? *Personnel and Guidance Journal*, 1952, 31, 35-39.

Schwarzweller, H. K. Values and occupational choice. *Social Forces*, 1960, 30, 126-135.

Sewell, W. H., Haller, A. O., and Strauss, M. A. Social status and educational and occupational aspiration. *American Sociological Review*, 1957, 22, (1), 67-73.

Singer, S. L. and Stefflre, B. Age differences in job values and desires. *Journal of Counseling Psychology*, 1954, 2, 89-91.

————. The relationship of job values and desires to vocational aspirations of adolescents. *Journal of Applied Psychology*, 1954, 38, 419-422.

————. Sex differences in job values and desires. *Personnel and Guidance Journal*, 1954, 32, 483-484.

Smith, E. D. and Herr, E. L. Sex differences in the maturation of vocational attitudes among adolescents. *Vocational Guidance Quarterly*, 1972, 20, 177-181.

Stevic, R. and Uhlig, G. Occupational aspirations of selected Appalachian youth. *Personnel and Guidance Journal*, 1967, 45, 435-439.

Straus, M. A. Societal needs and personal characteristics in the choice of farm, blue collar, and white collar occupations by farmers' sons. *Rural Sociology*, 1964, 29, 408-425.

Super, D. E. The dimensions and measurement of vocational maturity. *Teachers College Record*, 1955, 57, 151-163.

Super, D. E. and Crites, J. O. *Appraising vocational fitness.* New York: Harper & Row, 1962.

Super, D. E. et. al. *Vocational development: A framework for research.* New York: Teachers College Press, 1957.

Super, D. E., Kowalski, R. S. and Gotkin, E. H. *Floundering and trial after high school.* Career Pattern Study: Monograph IV, in press.

Super, D. E. and Overstreet, P. L. *The vocational maturity of ninth grade boys.* New York: Teachers College Press, 1960.

Tyler, L. E. The development of "vocational interests": The organization of likes and dislikes in ten-year-old children. *Journal of Genetic Psychology,* 1955, 86, 33-44.
————. The antecedents of two varieties of interest pattern. *Genetic Psychology Monographs,* 1964, 70, 177-227.
Westbrook, B. W., and Cunningham, J. W. The development and application of vocational maturity measures. *Vocational Guidance Quarterly,* 1970, 18, 171-175.
Witty, P., Garfield, S. and Brink, W. A comparison of the vocational interests of negro and white high-school students. *Journal of Educational Psychology,* 1941, 32, 124-132.
Youmans, E. G. Social factors in the work attitudes and interests of twelfth grade Michigan boys. *Journal of Educational Sociology,* 1954, 28 (2), 35-48.
Zytowski, D. G. *Psychological influences on vocational development.* Boston: Houghton Mifflin, 1970.
————. The concept of work values. *Vocational Guidance Quarterly,* 1970, 18, 176-185.

5 CHAPTER

Career Development Needs
of Special Groups: Women
and the Culturally Disadvantaged

Introduction

The career development needs of two subgroups in the population, women and the culturally disadvantaged, are significant enough to warrant special consideration. The first half of the chapter deals with women and the second half deals with the culturally disadvantaged. Together they reveal the educational and occupational discrimination which results from attitudes and practices of sexism, racisim and lack of concern for the conditions of the poor. Although the "war on poverty" and the passage of antidiscrimination legislation in the sixties marked a significant turning point, not enough ground has been gained. Thus, many youth continue to make educational and occupational plans in keeping with knowledge and aspirations which are depressed by discrimination and social stereotyping.

According to Ginzberg (1971), the need to devote special attention to females and the culturally disadvantaged (the majority of whom are members of ethnic minorities) follows directly from the theory and practice of career guidance: (1) These are the two groups that are most likely to be misinformed about options; (2) They lack adequate models; (3) Their informal informational systems are likely to be deficient. These shortcomings reflect dramatic and substantial changes in the paths that have opened up and the opportunities that lie ahead. An important role for education, guidance and counseling is to reduce the time lag between the new reality and the awareness and response to it, particularly among the present generation of young who are making plans for the future.

132

Women in the Labor Force

In present day society the term "revolution" is often used to describe social, technological, educational, or ideological change. During this century there have been revolutions in conceptions of the social, economic, and political rights of individuals; in the means of producing goods; in the kinds of services available to people and methods for providing such services; in systems of transportation; and in avenues of communication (Westervelt, 1965). Another extremely dramatic change has also occurred, but with little fanfare or recognition. This situation is characterized by changing patterns of employment for women and has been referred to by Drews (1965) as a "silent revolution."

Growth in Labor Force Participation

The actual growth in the number of women in the labor force has been phenomenal. The U. S. Department of Labor (1969, 1971b) reports that in 1970, 31.6 million women were in the labor force, over twice as many as before World War II; 43.4 percent of women 16 years of age and over were working. Since 1940, American women have been responsible for more than 60 percent of the total increase in the labor force and their representation in the labor force has risen from 25.4 percent to 36.7 percent of all workers. Within the population of working-age women, the percentage of employed women advanced from 28.9 percent in 1940 to 43.4 percent in 1970. (See Table 5-1.)

TABLE 5-1

WOMEN IN THE LABOR FORCE, SELECTED YEARS,
1890-1970

(Women 16 Years of Age and Older)

Date	Number in Thousands	As Percent of all Workers	As Percent of Women Population
1970	31,560	36.7	43.4
1960	23,272	33.3	37.8
1950	18,412	29.2	33.9
1940	13,783	25.4	28.9
1930	10,396	21.9	23.6
1920	8,229	20.4	22.7
1900	4,999	18.1	20.0
1890	3,704	17.0	18.2

SOURCE: U S. Department of Labor, *1969 Handbook on Women Workers,* 1969. p. 10. U. S. Department of Labor, *Manpower Report of the President,* April, 1971, pp. 204-205.

The important advances made by women since World War II are more dramatic when compared with those of men for a similar period. During the years 1947-70, the number of women in the civilian labor force increased by 89 percent (from 16.7 to 31.6 million), while the number of men rose only 23 percent (from 44.3 to 54.3 million). It seems likely that the rate of women entering the work force will continue to increase during the next decade.

In addition to greater labor force participation by women, there has also been a shift in the age group showing the greatest increase. Since 1964, increases in rates of labor force participation have not been quite as rapid for women aged forty-five and over, while the group aged twenty to twenty-four has been expanding its work role very energetically. In the period 1964 to 1970, the rate for women twenty to twenty-four has not only overtaken but has surpassed that of older women and is now the highest for any age group. In 1970, 57.8 percent of all women twenty to twenty-four years old were working, compared with less than 50 percent in 1964. The increased rate of participation for this age group, from 50 to 57.8 percent in six years, amounts to more than 1,600,000 additional workers.

Reasons for Increased Employment

The remarkable rise in the number and proportion of women in the labor force is due to a combination of demographic, economic and social developments. One of these elements is longevity. The same factors that have extended the lifespan have reduced the incidence of disease and have given women greater vitality for fuller enjoyment of their added years. For a woman born in 1920 life expectancy was fifty-five years, but for a woman born in 1968 life expectancy is seventy-four years. Women are marrying young today and consequently bear their children earlier. Half of all women marry by age twenty-one and more marry at eighteen than at any other age. By the time the majority of women reach their mid-thirties their children are in school, and they can anticipate at least another thirty to thirty-five years of active life to fill with enriching experiences.

Financial reasons are given by women as being the strongest motivator for working. The majority of women in the labor force are married and work to supplement inadequate family income, to raise the family's general standard of living, or to pay for special items such as a better house or children's education. Financial remuneration is, however, not the sole reason why so many women seek employment. An evolution in social attitudes and values has encouraged women to develop their abilities and talents to the fullest. It is significant that the more education a woman acquires the more likely she is to seek paid employment. The educated woman desires to contribute her skills and talents thus to reap the psychic rewards which come from achievement and recognition and service to society (U. S. Department of Labor, 1969; U. S. Department of Commerce, 1971).

According to Ginzberg (1966), the "womanpower" revolution is also due to a change in the characteristic of the American manpower scene. The United States is now characterized as a service economy. Two out of every three workers are employed in service occupations as compared to goods-producing occupations. The relevant point is that the service field has a high proportion of women workers.

Underutilization of Women Workers

Womanpower is one of the nation's greatest resources. It is being used more fully and more creatively than ever before. Yet, it is still a long way to the satisfactory realization of women's potential contributions. Despite the great increase in the number of employed women, they are becoming increasingly concentrated in the relatively less skilled, less rewarded, and less rewarding fields of work (Keyserling, 1965).

Data from the Department of Labor (1969) and Department of Commerce (1971) indicate that the rise in women's representation among all workers from 25.4 percent in 1940 to 36.7 percent in 1970 was not spread equally among the major occupational groups. A large gain occurred among clerical workers (from 53 to 73 percent) and among sales workers (from 28 percent to 40 percent). On the other hand, there was a significant decline (from 45 percent to 39 percent) in the proportion of women among all professional and technical workers. Even in the teaching profession, where women have traditionally been a large majority, the proportion of men has increased slightly in recent years. Moreover, many of the new professional positions which have opened up since 1940 have been in science and engineering, fields in which women constitute only a small minority. Since it is not genetically determined that 99 percent of the country's engineers, 99 percent of its federal judges, 97 percent of its lawyers, 93 percent of its doctors, 91 percent of its scientists, or 81 percent of its college faculties, should be men, we have to look to other courses or influences that create these disparities (Taylor, 1970).

The differences between men and women with respect to salaries are also a matter for deep concern. It is not unexpected that women receive a smaller average annual income than do men when total wage or salary incomes are compared, since a much smaller proportion of women than men work full time the year round. However, a comparison of median wage or salary incomes of full-time, year-round women and men workers reveals not only that the incomes of women are considerably less than those of men but also that the gap has widened in recent years. In 1960, for example, among full-time, year-round wage or salary workers, women's median income of $3,257 was 61 percent of the $5,368 received by men. Women's median wage or salary income rose to $4,977 in 1969, while men's rose to $8,455. Both sexes had significant increases in income; but because women's income increased at a slower rate, their median income in 1969 was only 59 percent that of men (U. S. Department of Commerce, 1971).

The real meaning of the wage gap is not merely that women receive unequal pay for equal work; it is also that women are more likely to be employed in lower-skilled, lower-paying jobs. In 1970 approximately one-fifth of working women who had completed four years of college were employed in clerical, sales, service, or other semiskilled occupations. In addition, unemployment is significantly greater for women — particularly among minority teenage girls. In 1970, nearly one out of three Black girls between the ages of sixteen and twenty-one was out of school and out of work.

Summary
Many of the impediments to acceptance of women in the labor force result from lack of information and understanding. Following is a condensation of the major "emotional" issues (U. S. Department of Labor, 1971a).

The Myth	The Reality
A woman's place is in the home.	Homemaking is no longer a full-time job. Goods and services formerly produced in the home are now commercially available; laborsaving devices have lightened or eliminated much work around the home.
Women are not seriously attached to the labor force; they work only for "pin money."	Of the 31 million women in the labor force in March 1970, nearly half were working because of pressing economic need. They were either single,

widowed, divorced, or separated or had husbands whose incomes were less than $3,000 a year. Another 5.7 million were married and had husbands with incomes between $3,000 and $7,000.

Women are out ill more than male workers; they cost the company more.

A recent Public Health Service study shows little difference in the absentee rate due to illness or injury: 5.9 days a year for women compared to 5.2 for men.

Women do not work as long or as regularly as their male co-workers; their training is costly — and largely wasted.

While it is true that many women leave work for marriage and children, this absence is only temporary for the majority of them. They return when the children are in school. Despite this break in employment, the average woman worker has a worklife expectancy of twenty-five years as compared with forty-three years for the average male worker. The single woman averages forty-five years in the labor force.

Women take jobs away from men; in fact, they ought to quit those jobs they now hold.

There were 31.5 million women in the labor force on the average in 1970. The number of unemployed men was 2.2 million. If all the women stayed home and the unemployed men were placed in the jobs held by women, there would be 29.3 million unfilled jobs.

Women should stick to "women's jobs" and should not compete for "men's jobs."

Jobs, with extremely rare exceptions, are sexless. Tradition rather than job content has led to labeling certain jobs as women's and others as men's. For example, although few women work as engineers, studies show that two-thirds as many girls as boys have an aptitude for this kind of work.

Women do not want responsibility on the job; they do not want promotions or job changes which add to their load.

Relatively few women have been offered positions of responsibility. But when given these opportunities, women, like men, do cope with job responsibilities in addition to personal or family responsibilities.

The employment of mothers leads to juvenile delinquency.

Studies show that many factors must be considered when seeking the causes of juvenile delinquency. Whether or not a mother is employed does not appear to be a determining factor.

These studies indicate that it is the quality of a mother's care rather than the time consumed in such care which is of major significance.

Men do not like to work for women supervisors.

Most men who complain about women supervisors have never worked for a woman.

Toward Equal Employment of Women

Many of the inequities relating to women's employment which were manifest in the previous section have resulted in part from various State and Federal laws. Many of the laws which were originally well-intended to "protect" women against discrimination, now appear needlessly discriminatory (Simpson, 1971). Following is a brief summary of recent Federal legislation and policies which have all but eliminated discrimination in employment "under the law" (U. S. Department of Labor, 1969).

- Equal Pay Act of 1963, prohibits employers from discriminating on the basis of sex in the payment of wages for equal work on jobs requiring equal skill, effort, and responsibility and which are performed under similar working conditions.

- Title VII of the Civil Rights Act of 1964, prohibits discrimination in private employment based on sex as well as on race, color, religion, and national origin in industries affecting commerce.
- Executive Order 11246 (September 29, 1965), forbids discrimination by federal contractors on the basis of race, color, religion, or national origin.
- Executive Order 11375 (October 13, 1967), amended E. O. 11246 to explicitly prohibit discrimination on the basis of sex.
- Executive Order 11478 (August 8, 1969), took additional steps to strengthen and assure equal employment opportunities. Personnel policies and practices were extended to include not only employment, but also recruitment, development, and advancement of all Federal Government employees.
- "Order No. 4," issued by former Secretary of Labor George P. Schultz on February 5, 1970, required Federal contractors to establish affirmative action programs relating to the employment of minorities and women. Supplemental guidelines relating to sex discrimination were published in the *Federal Register* on June 9, 1970.
- "Revised Order No. 4" was published in the *Federal Register* on December 4, 1971. The order outlines new requirements to correct the "underutilization" of women. Efforts are required to correct any and all deficiencies in the employment of women at all levels and in all segments of the workforce.

Decades of struggle by women's groups and sympathizers culminated in Senate passage of The Equal Rights Amendment to the United States Constitution on March 22, 1972 (Olson, 1972). The major paragraph states: "Equality of rights under the law shall not be denied or abridged by the United States or any state on account of sex." The proposal now goes to the individual states for consideration.

The rationale for passage of the amendment is to provide constitutional protection against laws and official practices which treat men and women differently. The mechanism to afford equality of rights for men and women is already embodied in the Fifth and Fourteenth Amendments. However, the Supreme Court has never ruled favorably to extend the "due process" provision of the Fifth Amendment or the "equal protection" concept of the Fourteenth Amendment to protection against sexual discrimination. If ratified by the states, the equal rights amendment would assure the rights of all persons to *equal treatment under the law* without distinction according to sex. Though passage is not guaranteed and equal employment opportunities will not be spontaneous, the amendment would most certainly help to eliminate inequalities in salary, occupational group membership, and opportunity for advancement.

Relevant Factors in Women's Career Development

Adequate approaches to preparing women to take advantage of expanded opportunities in the work world must be grounded in understanding of the nature and characteristics of their vocational behavior. As demonstrated in the previous two chapters, however, major theoretical formulations have not distinguished between sexes, and empirical tests of these theories have been limited almost entirely to boys and men. Only a few studies have approached female vocational behavior from the standpoint of any of the currently accepted theories.

Based on interview data from only ten Barnard College women, Ginzberg, et. al. (1951) concluded that his theory could explain the career behavior of girls throughout most of the tentative period — that is, until they are on the threshold of college. At this point marriage considerations assume dominance.

Citing the limited size of Ginzberg's sample of girls, McKenzie (1957) conducted a study to test the validity of the major findings of Ginzberg regarding young women and to extend the implications of his work. Utilizing a sample of intellectually superior high school girls, she established that these girls were much more marriage-oriented than work-oriented. Likewise, she concluded that they emerge through the stages of occupational choice as described by Ginzberg. There was a tendency, however, for these girls to regard career as an interim between formal education and marriage and possibly as continuing until they start their families.

Another study designed to test Ginzberg's theory was conducted by Davis, et al. (1962). Their purpose was to determine if twelve-year-olds made more "tentative" occupational choices than "fantasy" ones. Tentative choices were indicated by decisions based on capacities, interests, and values of the individual. It was found that more mature choices seemed to correlate positively with intelligence and the feminine sex.

The most experienced vocational development researcher, Donald Super, has shunned women almost entirely. However, he did suggest a system for classifying the career patterns of women. According to Super (1957), it should be possible to study women's career development by organizing their work histories into the following types:

1. *The stable homemaking career pattern;* includes all women who marry while in or very shortly after leaving school or college.
2. *The conventional career pattern;* working followed by homemaking.
3. *The stable working career pattern;* entering the work force on leaving school, college, or professional school and embarking upon a career which becomes the woman's life work.
4. *The double-track career pattern;* pattern of the woman who goes to work after completing her education, marries, and continues with a double career of working and home-making. She may take occasional time out for child-bearing.
5. *The interrupted career pattern;* sequence is one of work-ing, homemaking, and working while or instead of home-making.
6. *The unstable career pattern;* consists of working, home-making, working again, returning to full-time homemaking, etc.
7. *The multiple-trial career pattern;* consists of a succession of unrelated jobs, with stability in none, resulting in the individual having no genuine life work.

Two sociologists, Theodore Caplow and Lowell Carr, were among the first to point out the necessity for studying the voca-tional development of women apart from that of men. According to Caplow (1954, p. 234), "occupational inequality is guaranteed by customs and folkways [and] differentiates the career of women apart from those of men." He lists several "special conditions" which should be considered in examinations of female employment:

1. The occupational careers of women are not normally continuous.
2. Most employed men support the family group to which they belong, but most employed women are secondary breadwinners.
3. Women tend to be residentially immobile.
4. In any woman's occupation, a considerable proportion of the qualified workers in a given area will be out of the labor force at a given moment.
5. Women are everywhere confronted with a vast network of special statutes, rules, and regulations (pp. 234-236).

Carr (1955), utilizing data about the careers of housewives, attempted to distinguish periods in women's careers somewhat analogous to the work periods noted by Miller and Form (1951). His eight designations were: the preparatory period; the transitional and mixed period; the period of marriage and establishment of a home; the period of marital adjustment; the period of settled domesticity; the period of divided interests; the period of increasing biological risk; and, the period of retirement or widowhood.

Another major figure in career development theory and research, David Tiedeman, concluded that a separate theory of development was needed for men and women. This judgment was based upon a number of propositions which were summarized in Matthews (1960, p. 15).

1. Men and women differ biologically and these biological differences give rise to differentiated qualifications for employment.
2. Women are taught to be women; men are taught to be men.
3. Women are expected to live with their parents as long as necessary, but in this case must satisfy their special wants by themselves provided the family income is modest or less.
4. Women are expected to marry.
5. Education is frequently considered of questionable value to a woman; education is the road to professional employment for women.
6. The husband is the "breadwinner"; the wife is the "homemaker."

Tiedeman decided, however, to concentrate his research efforts to develop a theory for men. Although he did not personally investigate women's career development, two of his students — Ester Matthews and Mary Mulvey — had different ideas.

The precise focus of Matthews' study (1960) was the marriage-career conflict in the development of girls and young women. She posited that the crux of the differences between men's and women's career development might lie in the definition, derivation, development, and implications of the marriage-career conflict. She considered female attitudes toward marriage and career in relation to developmental stages (i.e., age), educational expression of self (i.e., curriculum), and life plan. Her data revealed that attitudes toward marriage and career change as a girl ages; attitudes toward marriage and career vary according to the life plan girls express; and the majority of girls and young women shift from career-directed goals to marriage-directed goals in late adolescence. To a lesser degree, the hypothesis was confirmed that attitudes toward marriage and career will vary according to the high school curriculum that girls elect or have elected in the past.

Using Super's classification as a guide, Mulvey (1961, 1963) specified career patterns in terms of an acceptance of work as a "primary" or "secondary" mode of validating identity. Her categories resemble Super's seven category system except that she omitted his seventh and added two categories which he had not considered. Utilizing a sample of women in their middle years, she found that marital status was the most influential factor in a woman's decision to change her present life style. It is the center of the common core of factors interacting with career patterns. Level of education was concluded to be the most important determinant of the career pattern, with level of aspiration equally influential. Intelligence level was found to be unrelated to either of these two factors. She noted specifically that women's career patterns seemed to be uninfluenced by and unrelated to three factors in their adolescent lives: socioeconomic background of parents; scholastic achievement; and personality rating.

The most recent addition to women's career development theory has been made by Zytowski (1969). He has offered a series of nine postulates in an attempt to characterize the distinctive differences of the work life of men and women, the developmental stages unique to women, their patterns of vocational participation, and the determinants of these patterns. However, his postulates are in large part combinations and refinements of what already exists, with a few new observations about the characteristics and behavior of women.

Theories of career development for women, like their more global counterparts, do not provide all the answers required by curriculum specialists, teachers and counselors. The theories and research, however, have helped to focus more clearly on those factors which require additional consideration for girls and women, e.g., identity, sex role, types of educational-occupational choices, personal values, and career patterns. The following section discusses these factors and suggests ways of eliminating barriers to the career development of women.

The Need for Total Life Planning

The fundamental implication of the labor force participation of women, and of theories of occupational decision-making, is that young women need to prepare for *multiple roles* during different periods in their lives. A shift has been made from the traditionally organized family where the husband was the sole breadwinner and the wife was the sole homemaker, to multiple-role families in which both partners share responsibilities for household tasks and for earning (U. S. Department of Labor, 1966). Whereas at first multiple-role families were usually established in response to economic necessity, now more and more of these families are developed by *choice.*

Inevitable results of women's search for identity and for their rightful place in society are conflicts in values, needs, feelings and situations. Figure 5-1 depicts the components which give rise to role conflicts. It is obvious that occupational decision-making for women is not a simple choice among occupational alternatives, but rather choices for "total life plan." Total life planning cannot be completed in a short chat with a counselor during the last year of high school. Planning must be done with keen awareness of the many possibilities the years to come will bring. Following are ways in which education can aid and abet this process.

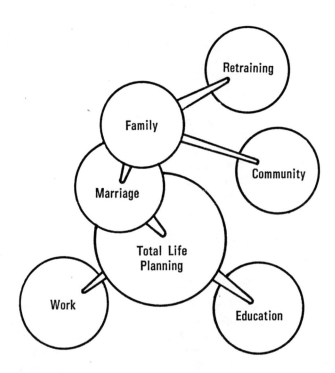

SOURCE: U. S. Department of Labor, *Counseling Girls and Women: Awareness, Analysis, Action.* Washington, D. C.: Government Printing Office, 1966, p. 7.

Fig. 5-1. Components of Total Life Planning

Multiple Choices and Career Patterns

It is readily apparent that women are required to make a greater number of educational, occupational, and personal decisions than men. The choice is not simply between marriage and career, but between various patternings of school, work, and marriage. Compounding the situation is the fact that choice points come much faster for a contemporary girl than they did for her mother and grandmother. "During the age period from 15 to 20 most girls take the steps and make the decisions that determine their career pattern" (Havighurst, 1965, p. 154).

The initial choice which a young woman makes is a significant factor in affecting her ultimate career pattern. For example, girls who marry upon leaving or graduating from high school (these two groups encompass approximately 35 percent of all women) who do not obtain additional education and/or work experience are almost automatically relegated to the lower paying, lower status jobs if they choose later to work. The role of education and guidance is not to dictate personal decisions or values, but to assist girls to prepare for the dual careers of homemaking and wage earning and for interruptions in education and work. A realistic approach which does not compartmentalize girls' views of life goals is necessary. To ensure that girls have requisite employment skills when they choose to enter the labor force, it is paramount that they be prepared *before* they leave the secondary school environment.

Identity and Sex-Role

The identity issue for males is primarily an occupational question, but for girls self-definition depends more on marriage and sex role, i.e., "whose wife will I be, what kind of family will we have?" Men have to be educated as working members of society. The social role expectations for girls, however, are not so clearly defined (Neuman, 1963). Thus, women must make career choices on bases other than social approbation. Farmer (1971) points out that the source of this conflict is not the fact that more than one role is open to women (home and career) but that a cultural lag exists between social opportunity and social sanction.

That society holds different definitions for the roles of men and women is abundantly clear in the research literature discussed in Chapter 4 and in the earlier part of this chapter on labor force participation. Education as a part of the larger society has also done its part. Taylor (1970) cites examples of subtle educational practices which perpetuate sex-role bias. The brainwashing many girls and women receive includes: (1) encouragement to avoid science and mathematics courses in high school; (2) almost no opportunities to choose occupational courses commonly thought of as suitable for boys; (3) advisement to lower ambitions or reconsider "unsuitable" career choices, such as engineering, veterinary medicine, or business administration; (4) evaluation against higher standards of criteria for entrance into graduate school; and (5) discrimination in the awarding of fellowships and scholarships.

To change sex-role stereotypes which are as deeply ingrained as these is no easy matter (Eyde, 1970). However, two areas of attack appear especially fruitful. The first is to expose myths about women's place in society. It can best be achieved by exploding the fallacy of deficiencies which are ascribed to women. For example, it is easy to illustrate that job turnover and absenteeism do not differ appreciably for men and women. The best single source of data about women is a 1971 publication entitled *Women: A Bibliography on Their Education and Careers* (Astin, et al., 1971). The annotated bibliography includes more than 350 abstracts of recent books and articles. This publication provides adequate ammunition for those who wish to assist the "movement."

The second area of attack is expansion of educational programs and services to help girls and women become aware of the broader opportunities open to them. Educators would do well to emulate many of the techniques of the feminist movement. Of particular relevance is the popular and successful "consciousness-raising" groups (Gardner, 1971). Recognition of the fact that many of women's problems are universal and not individual helps significantly to accelerate individual discovery and self-development.

Educational Opportunity

Successful participation in individual, dual, and interrupted career patterns is well within the capacity of most women. However, successful combinations of education, marriage and work have been difficult for women to achieve, given the present nature of education and the employment prerequisites of most jobs. Since women are not lacking for abilities and capacities, and since their contributions to society are as needed as are their contributions to families, the problem may be what Neuman (1963) describes as a question of "educational timing." In simple fact, educational curricula are not set up to suit the restrictive life patterns of many women. While there are many for whom a conventional pattern of education works, there are many for whom it doesn't. The need for occupational preparation at the secondary school level for all women, including intensive guidance and counseling, has been suggested previously. In addition, there must be accompanying adjustments in post-secondary education to permit and encourage women to continue education as times, needs, and interests permit.

Educational programs and practices designed for adolescents and young adults have proven inadequate and frustrating in many ways to more mature women who wish to continue their education. Many such women are married and have family responsibilities; many have been out of school for 10 to 20 years. A continuing education program for these women should contain the following minimum characteristics (U. S. Department of Labor, 1969): (1) less rigid interpretation of entrance requirements, e.g., substituting equivalency tests for credit earned too long ago to be considered eligible, (2) scheduling to permit part-time attendance at hours convenient for those with young children, (3) special counseling services re both educational and occupational opportunities, (4) financial aid for those on part-time schedules, (5) and, finally, course material and teaching methods especially designed for mature women with broader backgrounds of life experience such as employment and volunteer work.

A Matter of Simple Justice

Discussion of women's rights runs the risk of becoming emotion-charged. Stereotypes of bra-burning, man-hating females are brought to consciousness by mention of Women's Liberation. Major movements for political, religious, or social justice are spurred by vocal, radical elements which frighten and alienate many people. The situation with respect to women's rights is typical. Overaction by proponents and overreaction by opponents tend to shroud the movement's focus on its two most fundamental issues (Astin, 1971, p. 1):

- The bind that women are in because of early role stereotyping which continues to be reinforced throughout their lives, preventing them from searching for alternate and/or multiple roles and from engaging in a variety of tasks.
- Discrimination against women in education and work.

The authors have attempted in the first half of this chapter to sensitize its audience to the career development needs of girls and women. Although treatment of the subject has been brief, the situation is clear: Sexism in education and work exists and must be eliminated. Put another way, equal educational and occupational opportunities for women is *a matter of simple justice* (President's Task Force . . . , 1970).

Understanding the Culturally Disadvantaged

Future historians will have available a choice of terms for describing the decade of the 1960's, ranging from "The Era of Assassination" to the "Age of Space." For the educational historian, the choice will hardly be a difficult one. The 1960's were assuredly the decade of the disadvantaged child. Caldwell (1970) traces the short history of this period from *enthusiasm and optimism*, to *skepticism*, then *disillusionment*, and finally to a period of *consolidation* at the beginning of the seventies. The following pages retrace the beginning of this era, synthesize the literature about culturally disadvantaged individuals, and outline issues and future courses of action.

The currently popular label, culturally disadvantaged, which is used to describe a subgroup in the population, is denounced by some as technically inaccurate and by some as derogatory. The authors share the observation by Frost and Hawkes (1970, p. 1) that much of the debate about labels of this nature is mere prattling. "It is obvious even to the novice that all people have a culture, that no social group can be explained in one phrase. So let us build our poverty skirmish into a real war and systematically attack not the jargon but the problems that are denying large segments of humanity the right to literacy and decency."

There is a well-accepted axiom that is particularly appropriate for introducing this section: There are more differences *within* any group of human beings than *between* groups. It is extremely difficult to generalize about the culturally disadvantaged because this grouping includes diverse peoples, such as American Indians, Blacks, Spanish-speaking Americans, and the rural poor. However, certain characteristics which have particular relevance for career development are generally evident in all of these groups (Menacker, 1971). While it is recognized that not all individuals from ethnic minorities or persons from lower socioeconomic backgrounds are disadvantaged, there is no question that such persons compose the major proportion of those categorized as culturally disadvantaged. The overemphasis in this section on Blacks, in comparison to other groups, is a reflection of the fact that a greater body of literature and research is available for Blacks and that they constitute the largest single subgroup in the population.

The Concept of Cultural Deprivation

The notion of cultural deprivation was apparently developed in the mid-1950's by psychologists and educators, principally within the New York City school system (Friedman, 1967). A major event in the chronology of the development of this concept was the presidential address to the School Psychology division at the 1955 annual meeting of the American Psychological Association. The president, a psychologist of the Board of Education in New York City, made reference to "deprived homes" and "deprived areas" in describing an experimental study of lower-class school children. The researcher had noted an attitude syndrome of "cultural deprivation" manifest by low self-conceptions, guilt and shame feelings, distrust, and family problems. He concluded that these behaviors and conditions adversely affect a child's motivation and functioning in school and even impair school adjustment before entry (Krugman, 1956).

During the period 1956 to 1962, New York City became a pioneer in various experimental efforts to provide education for the so-called culturally deprived. As a result, special guidance programs and curriculum innovations, e.g., the Demonstration Guidance Project and the Higher Horizons Program, became models which were variously duplicated in many other cities.

As experimental projects and approaches multiplied, the body of literature and research expanded. In July 1961, the classification *cultural deprivation* was added to *The Education Index* with twenty-one entries. During the first third of the 1960's, observers of cultural deprivation maintained that cognitive and linguistic handicaps were brought about by poverty, meagerness of intellectual resources in the home and surroundings, and by the incapacity, illiteracy, or indifference of elders in the entire community (Friedman, 1967; Brooks, 1966).

In June 8-12, 1964, The Research Conference on Education and Cultural Deprivation was held at the University of Chicago to review what was known about the problems of education and cultural deprivation, to make recommendations about what might be done to solve some of these problems, and to suggest critical problems for further research. The published results of the conference, *Compensatory Education for Cultural Deprivation* (Bloom, et al., 1956), represented a consensus of a group of prominent scholars on the nature, causes, characteristics, and remedial measures for culturally deprived students. What emerged from the conference was a theoretical concept described as follows:

In the present educational system in the U.S. (and elsewhere) we find a substantial group of students who do not make normal progress in their school learning . . . We will refer to this group as culturally disadvantaged or culturally deprived because we believe the roots of their problem may in large part be traced to their experiences in homes which do not transmit the cultural patterns necessary for the types of learning characteristic of the schools and the larger society . . . A large proportion of the youth come from homes in which the adults have a minimal level of education. Many of them come from homes where poverty, large family size, broken homes, discrimination, and slum conditions further complicate the picture (1965, p. 4-5).

The fashioning of the cultural deprivation concept by psychologists and educators in the early 1960's paralleled a growing public and political concern for the education of lower class children. Conant's (1961) *Slums and Suburbs* published in 1961 and Riessman's (1962) *The Culturally Deprived Child* published a year later did much to reinforce and broaden use of the term. The idea's image was spurred by the civil rights movement and the "war on poverty" which was initiated during the Kennedy-Johnson administrations. The major manifestation of the war on poverty was the Economic Opportunity Act of 1964 which sought to assist the plight of culturally deprived students through such programs as Operation Head Start, Project Upward Bound, and the Job Corps. In addition, the *Vocational Education Act of 1963* and the *Elementary and Secondary Education Act of 1965* authorized large sums of money for special services to disadvantaged students.

Thus, it is clear that the concept of cultural deprivation was introduced by well-meaning educators and psychologists in response to identifiable social problems. The movement was heralded by a broad spectrum of persons and publics. However, because of several potentially false assumptions and explanatory inadequacies, solutions were destined to be less than fully adequate. Before extending discussion to a treatment and evaluation of what has come to be called *compensatory education*, it will be well to consider the conditions and characteristics of the "culture of poverty."

The Consequences of Deprivation

Whereas prescriptions for dealing with problems of the disadvantaged should be considered tentative and in need of revision in light of new evidence, there is no need to qualify the fact that the compensatory education movement was a response to social and economic conditions which *do* exist. This section examines the conditions of deprivation and the nature of affected individuals during three periods: preschool, childhood and adolescence, and young adulthood.

Preschool: The Early Years

The home environment and child-rearing practices have been the focus of much of the research and literature on cultural deprivation. The large body of empirical literature supports the assumption that the home is the single most important influence on the intellectual and emotional development of children in the preschool years (Bloom, et al., 1965). Circumstances in the home and interaction between children and parents can raise or curtail a child's ability to adopt the role of pupil and adapt to the formality of the classroom. Comprehensive reviews of the effects of environmental improverishment reveal at least four areas in which the disadvantaged exhibit deficiencies: (1) language development, (2) general learning skills, (3) motivation, and (4) self-image (Bloom, et al., 1965; Karnes, et al., 1971; Passow, 1970).

Language Development: The language of children from disadvantaged homes is frequently markedly different from that used in school. It tends to be more motorial and concrete; limited in vocabulary; and characterized by short sentences, diverse syntactial structure, idiomatic expressions, and limited use of conjunctions, adjectives, and adverbs. English is often a second language. Put another way the language of the disadvantaged is not nearly so eloquent as the language of schools.

General Learning Skills: Inadequacies in general learning skills have long been considered to be characteristic of the disadvantaged. Deutsch (1963) found such children to have inferior auditory discrimination, visual discrimination, judgment concerning time, number skills and other basic skills. These inferiorities are not due to physical defects of eyes, ears, or brain, but to inferior "habits" of hearing and seeing and thinking.

Motivation: In addition, disadvantaged children usually do not internalize motivation to achieve academic goals which are established by schools. They often are apathetic and detached from formal educational goals and processes. Their orientation to life includes seeking gratification in the here-and-now rather than learning to study and work for delayed gratification and rewards.

Self-image: The final generalization that is characteristic of disadvantaged children is low self-image. Low self-image denigrates both potential for individuality and potential for learning. Some of the manifestations associated with a negative self-image are: extremely high or extremely low level of aspiration, fear of failure, external focus of control, low academic motivation, and withdrawal.

It should be reasserted that culturally disadvantaged is a *relative term.* That is, a child can be said to be disadvantaged only with respect to another individual. More specifically, the term means disadvantaged for living competently in an urban, industrial, and democratic society (Havighurst, 1964b). The term is also relative in the sense that not all individuals who are classified as disadvantaged exhibit the general characteristics described above. Every social group and ethnic group, every man-made organization is subject to disadvantages (Frost and Hawkes, 1970). However, there is one common denominator of all the people for whom compensatory education is designed. The stark reality behind preferred euphemisms, such as culturally deprived and culturally disadvantaged, is that they refer to populations of *children of the poor.*

Childhood and Adolescence: The Disadvantaged Pupil

The consequences of certain inadequacies in language development, perceptual skills, motivation, and general habits of learning are accentuated when a disadvantaged child enters school. The first day of school begins a self-perpetuating cycle of failure and frustration which is known as the phenomenon of "cumulative academic retardation" (Passow, 1970). The nature of this process is vicious. Lower than desired abilities produce lower achievement. Lower achievement induces a diminished self-concept, which in turn feeds back upon achievement, and so on.

The longer disadvantaged students are exposed to the traditional school curriculum, the more their academic performance tends to fall behind established achievement norms. By the eighth grade, these children are, on the average, three years behind grade norms in reading and arithmetic and usually all other subjects as well (Bloom, et al., 1965). One of the consequences of this cumulative deficit is that students drop out as soon as age permits — though most drop out psychologically long before that. Moreover, progressively lagging achievement tends to be paralleled by growing alienation, often expressed in dramatic and disruptive behavior.

That the school itself is much to blame for these conditions cannot be denied. Ausubel (1963, p. 454) describes the inappropriateness of the school environment for the disadvantaged child:

His cumulative intellectual deficit, therefore, almost invariably reflects, in part, the cumulative impact of a continuing and consistently deficient learning environment as well as his emotional and motivational reaction to this environment. Thus, much of the lower-class child's alienation from the school is not so much a reflection of discrimination or rejecting attitudes on the part of teachers and other school personnel — although the importance of this factor should not be underestimated; it is in greater measure a reflection of the cumulative effects of a curriculum that is too demanding of him, and of the resulting load of frustration, confusion, demoralization, and impaired self-confidence that he must bear.

Young Adulthood: Out-of-School Youth

This section deals with the educational and employment conditions of disadvantaged youth who have (a) completed high school or (b) dropped out before graduation. While improvements have been made in bringing the educational level of minority[1] group members up to that of whites, there continues to be a large gap. In both cities and suburbs, the average educational attainment of Blacks is much lower than that of whites (see Fig. 5-2). Not re-

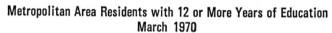

Metropolitan Area Residents with 12 or More Years of Education
March 1970

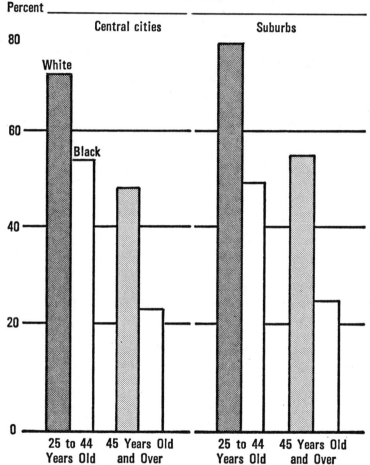

SOURCE: *Manpower Report of the President.* U. S. Department of Labor, 1971, p. 92.

Fig. 5-2. Educational Gap between Whites and Blacks Persists in Younger Age Groups and Is Wider in Suburbs Than in Central Cities

[1]The problem of terminology becomes especially apparent here. The Department of Labor and the Bureau of Census often deliberately use Blacks to mean "Blacks and other minorities" because Blacks make up 92 percent of the larger group.

vealed directly in Fig. 5-2 is the fact that in the sixteen—seventeen age group, Blacks were almost one and a half times as likely to drop out of school as were their white counterparts. For the eighteen to twenty-one age group, the ratio was approximately two to one (U. S. Bureau of the Census, 1969).

Other comparative educational indicators are standards of academic achievement. Using average scores of whites in metropolitan areas of the Northeast as a standard for verbal ability, reading achievement, and mathematical achievement, Kacser (1971) reports that Blacks are two grade levels behind the criterion at the sixth grade and four years behind at the twelfth grade. Thus, the disparity between educational attainment of minorities and whites is all the more dramatic when levels of achievement are taken into consideration.

Disadvantaged students and particularly members of minority groups, who fare badly in educational establishments, experience the same difficulties in the labor market. The average unemployment rate for Blacks was about double the rate for whites in 1969 and 1970. Furthermore, this ratio has worsened in the past decade for minority teenagers, especially younger males. For the sixteen to nineteen age group, the unemployment rate in October 1970 was 15.3 percent for whites and 32.9 percent for Blacks (Kacser, 1971). The essence of high youth unemployment is reflected in the paradox of the following propositions (U. S. Department of Labor, 1968, p. 111).

- The United States keeps larger proportions of its children in school longer than does any other nation to insure their preparation for lifetime activity.
- Yet the unemployment rate among youth is far higher here than in any other industrialized nation and has been rising steadily.

The obvious implication is that American schools have not considered preparation for employment as preparation for lifetime activity. Put another way, the problem of "bridging the gap" between school and work is how to make real, the unfulfilled promise of American educational opportunity.

Smooth transition from school to work, retention of drop-out prone youth, and assistance to those who have already left school require many fundamental changes in educational enterprises. Some of these have been accomplished in a few places. Programs of the type described in *Vocational Education: Innovations Revolutionize Career Training* (Smoker, 1971) suggest that substantial improvements in curriculum and more linkages to the reality of the work world will help substantially to improve the occupational preparation of youth. As many academically-oriented educators continue to argue with those who want to expand occupationally-related content throughout the curriculum, agreement grows on several points:

1. Existing subject matter can generally be enriched by materials and experiences drawn from real work situations.
2. All students should be exposed to a systematic program of career education and guidance and much earlier than is now the practice.
3. Occupational programs at the secondary level should offer opportunities for students of a very wide range of interests and abilities to try out occupationally-oriented curricula and go on to jobs or to post-high school education or training — directly or after periods of employment.

The paramount goal of the educational system should be to assure that all youth who receive a high school diploma are equipped to find and keep meaningful jobs (U. S. Department of Labor, 1968).

Perspectives on Compensatory Education

Compensatory education is a term which has come into use to describe special programs which are directed at overcoming or circumventing assumed deficiencies in the background, functioning, and current experiences of children from economically deprived, culturally isolated, and/or ethnically segregated families (Gordon and Jablonsky, 1968). Special programs are diverse, reaching young people at all levels from preschool to college. An overview of major programs is presented in Table 5-2. The programs differ in nature and scope from enrichment efforts in a single classroom to multimillion dollar Job Corps centers which provide basic educational development and occupational training for thousands of young adults. Efforts appear to be concentrated at (1) the preschool and early elementary levels and (2) at the secondary level where potential drop-outs are found. It is significant that educational innovations at these two points entail minimal alterations of the "regular" school programs (Wilkerson, 1970a).

A wide variety of techniques has been employed in attempts to achieve stated goals (Gordon and Jablonsky, 1968, Wilkerson, 1970a).

1. The most notable curricular emphasis is on reading and language arts. Considerable attention is given to diagnosis and remediation of individual learning difficulties.

TABLE 5-2

SUMMARY OF MAJOR, SELECTED
COMPENSATORY EDUCATION PROGRAMS

Preschool

Operation Head Start, largest and probably the best-known compensatory education program. Designed to better prepare children for elementary school through a broad based program of educational, medical, and social services.

Elementary and Secondary Education

Title I, Elementary and Secondary Education Act of 1965, provides financial assistance to local educational agencies for programs and projects which will meet the educational needs of educationally deprived children in school attendance areas in a district having high concentrations of children from low-income families.

Title III, Elementary and Secondary Education Act of 1965, grants for planning and establishment of programs designed to provide supplemental educational services and activities, e.g., persons who are or have been otherwise isolated from normal educational opportunities.

Out of School and Drop-Out Prone Youth

Neighborhood Youth Corps, encourages disadvantaged youth of high school age (14 to 21) to continue in or return to school by providing paid work experience. Emphasis shifting to job preparation, especially in an out-of-school program.

Job Corps, assists low-income disadvantaged youth 16 to 21 years of age, who require a change of environment to profit from training, to become more responsible, employable, and productive citizens through a residential program of intensive education, skill training, and related services.

Higher Education

Project Upward Bound, supported remedial education and counseling for severely disadvantaged youngsters to help them gain admission to college. Primary focus is on developing interest in higher education among tenth and eleventh grade pupils from poor families.

2. Enrichment and modification of the curriculum are basic. They include expanded use of audio-visual instructional aids, e.g., television, films, tape recorders, language laboratories. "Doing" is stressed as opposed to mere "listening." Many trade books are used to supplement basal readers. Emphasis is also given to the selection and preparation of instructional materials relating to the history and culture of Blacks and other ethnic minorities.
3. Guidance services and individual counseling are increased to assist self-concept development and to promote positive attitudes and motivation toward school.
4. Extended reciprocal involvement of school and community is accomplished via field trips into the community and through the use of adult models as resource persons in the classroom. Home visitations by teachers and parental participation in school affairs are stressed.
5. Alternate staffing practices such as the use of several types of paraprofessionals and other supporting personnel are common. Inservice education and special workshops are held to equip personnel with insights, attitudes, and techniques which are deemed essential to effective work with the disadvantaged.

The following observation about the Chicago schools by Havighurst (1964a, p. 63) is particularly appropriate for describing the developments and characteristics of compensatory education. "There probably is not a single suggestion made anywhere in the country for improvement of the educational program for such children that is not being tried out, within the limits of available resources, in some Chicago school."

Issues in Compensatory Education

Compensatory education may be a fraud perpetuated upon a poor and unsuspecting citizenry which has traditionally looked to education to lead it out of bondage . . . Because compensatory education has resulted in a rising tide of expectations among the poor, the Black, and the disadvantaged, its failure to achieve a noble end presents a danger to the very fabric of American education that cannot long be ignored. It is for this reason that the 'National Debate on Compensatory Education' has been set in motion (Winschel, 1970, p. 3).

The compensatory education movement, which resulted from the civil rights movement and the war on poverty, has produced a vast number of Federal programs and an equally vast amount of literature and research. Yet, there is little substantial data to document that the academic performance of disadvantaged children has been improved. (For example see White, 1970.) Both theorists and practitioners are divided. Many subscribe to disparate views on the bases of emotion and concern rather than hard data. At the beginning of the seventies there is little agreement; unresolved issues abound. The issue of *etiology* is probably the most fundamental unanswered question (Wilkerson 1970a, 1970b). More specifically:

- Why do disadvantaged children tend to perform poorly in school?
- Are disadvantaged children really capable of effective learning? Are they genetically inferior?
- Are inept and dysfunctional school practices the cause?
- What is the role of busing?
- Is racial discrimination at the heart of the problem?
- Does it matter?

All of these etiological questions remain unresolved. The authors do not pretend to have definitive answers to any one of them. Certainly, even cursory treatment of these questions is beyond the scope of this book. Rather, the following pages are addressed to concerns over which career education and guidance professionals may have some control. Although the suggested modifications for testing and curriculum are not adequate in themselves, they are important steps toward assurance of equality of educational opportunity.

The Assessment of Culturally Disadvantaged

The use of paper-and-pencil tests for the purpose of assessing the abilities, aptitudes, interests, and personality dimensions of children and youth is a subject of considerable controversy. Its two major "myths" are discussed by Barry and Wolfe (1962, p. 26-27).

. . . first, that various facets of human personality can be accurately and definitively expressed in terms of numbers; and second, that those numbers have implications for the individual's success in various educational and vocational enterprises . . . Tests are being used for purposes that were never intended, with groups for whom they are unsuitable, and in ways that are antagonistic to the best principles of measurement. Currently many testing experts are inveighing against these abuses and warning that tests are useful tools only so long as their users recognize their limitations as well as their advantages.

Testing culturally different individuals appears to have disadvantages which outweigh advantages. "A test should be considered for what it is — a single, isolated sample of behavior, which outside of the Latin-American's cultural context can be of little value in and of itself" (Pollack & Menacher, 1971, p. 59).

In short, disadvantaged youngsters do poorly on tests in large part because their socioeconomic conditions and/or subcultures have not prepared them to take tests. They may not read well enough to understand the test items, and/or they may perceive the matter of testing as irrelevant to their lives (Vontress, 1971). To avoid belaboring the point, suffice it to say that the literature is replete with research data which demonstrate that culturally different students perform less well than most WASP children. This being true, there is little reason for continuing to administer tests to such persons.

It is imperative that individuals who persist in believing that tests may provide important diagnostic information answer two questions prior to administering tests: "What information is needed to assist the child in school experiences or preparation in making an occupational choice?" and "What evaluation methods can I use to gather such data?" (Cappelluzzo, 1971).

It is probable that the type of data required for career-planning and decision-making can be gleaned from sources other than normative-based tests. The important principles to keep in mind with respect to assessment are (1) that the measurement process should take into account as many possible aspects of a child's background and current characteristics as possible, (2) that it should provide him with maximum opportunity to demonstrate his abilities, and (3) that it should guard against premature labeling or categorization which tend to result from overemphasis on test scores (Goslin, 1967). Ebel (1970, p. 233) offers four principles which should be applied to school testing programs. They are equally appropriate for career guidance.

1. Emphasize the use of tests to improve status and deemphasize their use to determine status.
2. Broaden the base of achievements tested in order to recognize and develop the wide variety of talents needed in our society.
3. Share test results openly with the persons most directly concerned. Include all that the tests have revealed about students' abilities and prospects.
4. Decrease the use of tests to impose decisions on others and, instead, increase their use as a basis for better personal decision-making.

Reordering Priorities

In addition to understanding the cultural and personal characteristics of the disadvantaged and modifying testing practices, teachers and counsellors must question the validity of traditional academic goals for all students. Because disadvantaged youth are socially out of step with the traditional school program, significant changes must be made in the school scene to meet their needs. The first ingredient of academic achievement is social and emotional adjustment.[2] According to Karnes, Zehrbach, and Jones (1971, p. 76), "School personnel from the superintendent to the custodian must recognize that a priority system for the disadvantaged may rate social development first, cultural development second, emotional development third, physical development fourth, and academic development fifth." Teachers who are willing to lessen emphasis on spelling, writing, mathematics, and manipulation of abstract ideas will in all probability find that academic achievement increases in the long run. Revision of educational priorities not only allows for greater student success but also provides professionals with feelings of accomplishment which they are often denied when working with disadvantaged students.

That academic development may be less important than social and emotional development for disadvantaged persons is evidenced by research. In a pilot study conducted for the Department of Labor, Glaser and Ross (1970) attempted to differentiate disadvantaged individuals who have escaped the ghetto from those who have not. A selective review of literature on the disadvantaged revealed that the following life factors are often evidenced by those who have risen successfully out of disadvantaged backgrounds:

1. *Identity:* Having a strong sense of self, pride, worth.

2. *Alienation:* Experiencing some degree of alienation, often externally imposed, from the ghetto culture.

3. *Freedom from Conditioning:* Escaping the routine ghetto brainwashing that would normally produce a sense of guilt, inferiority, limited perspective, absence of hope, dysfunctional standards, pacifying illusions about life.

4. *Physical Removal:* Breaking dependency ties, social norm pressure, and identity definition as a result of moving, imprisonment, military service, illness, etc.

5. *Luck:* Benefiting from chance occurrences which help him avoid trouble or find constructive outlets and relationships.

6. *Supportive, Inspiring Relationships:* Receiving help from special people who believe in him, guide him, and stand for a new set of standards.

[2]This principle has been known by successful professionals since ancient times. It appears to require periodic rediscovery.

7. *Identification Models:* Identifying with "folk heroes," "big shots," and even ordinary people who symbolize identities other than disadvantaged.

8. *Questioning Orientation:* Asking at critical points in formative years, "Who am I?" or "Where am I going?"

9. *Awareness of Alternative Paths:* Discovering that there are other routes than being a slave or hustler. Such goals as self-determination, money, creativity, or status must come to seem attractive to him, and actions such as hard work or studying must be seen as steps which pay off.

10. *New Perception of Self:* Seeing himself as someone not locked into one fixed negative or limited identity; envisioning himself as having potential for being a person different from what he is now.

11. *Existential Crises:* Dramatic encountering of clear-cut choices and new ways. There must be a buildup of tension, a conflict escalation, in which the person openly faces the cost of his old ways, the high stakes involved, and the attractiveness of gambling on a new way of life. An existential crisis must be confronted head-on and resolved through a higher form of self-and-world-affirmation.

12. *Risk-Taking Capacity:* Being willing and able to endure the anxiety, suspense, disappointment, and humiliation of experimenting with new behavior.

13. *Channeling of Rage:* Learning to direct the rage over being disadvantaged into strategic actions effectively designed to fight one's way out of the ghetto; avoiding burying one's anger beneath defenses of passivity and self-deprecation, or firing it out at the world impulsively in ways that merely provoke punishment.

14. *Rewards for Change:* Receiving support and acceptance for new behavior and identity from key individuals, new peer group, or internalized ideal images.

This study is a significant pioneering effort to identify relevant factors of successful individuals who lived their early childhood in a deprived environment. If these variables are, indeed, major contributors to success, it follows that curriculum specialists should begin systematic development of experiences and activities which will enable students to acquire these behaviors. For example, self-concept development, decision-making skills, and awareness of available options should become *central* in the curriculum rather than peripheral.

Toward a More Effective Curriculum

Without getting involved in extremely controversial philosophical and moral questions surrounding compensatory education, it is safe to state that the major thrust of such programs was to prop up education *as it was*. There were few attempts to hold education up to a mirror to show it for *what it is* — an outdated system. If professional educators had heeded the following words of former Commissioner of Education Francis Keppel (1967), the situation might have been different.

- All American children are educationally disadvantaged.
- Despite the avalanche of educational activity and the surge of additional money, we are still in the business of repairing an anachronistic machine.
- We are laboring to serve the needs of academic subjects, not the needs of children.
- There is less wrong with the learner (the product of education) than with the process and institutions by which he is taught.

Thus far, the target of most attempts to improve the education of the disadvantaged has been the learner himself rather than the educational process. One means of attending to the needs of learners is to orient the curriculum around what Fantini and Weinstein (1967) call the four major "career concerns" of each individual. The career concerns are: *work world, parent, citizen,* and *personal development.* That these four "careers" include the full range of individual needs could be questioned, but suffice it to say that the essence of what is being advocated is a shift from a subject matter-oriented curriculum to one which is based on an analysis of adult roles in the social and economic order. A primary assumption of this approach is that education becomes more relevant as students are able to see relationships between schooling and later life.

Historically, schools have been variously involved in education for careers, home and family living, citizenship education, and individual development. Yet, many educators fear career education as an intrusion on the teaching of academic subjects. Much of the remainder of this book is devoted to exposing this myth. For now, the following conclusions from Fantini and Weinstein (1967, p. 111) are adequate counter argument.

Indeed career-oriented education is really the most humanistic education if we acknowledge that education in a free society should enable an individual to pursue these satisfying, effective careers in the world of work, as a parent, and as a citizen, and to sense that he is something of value, that he is growing positively, and that he is cultivating — and being helped by society to cultivate — his potential.

BIBLIOGRAPHY

Astin, H. S., Suniewick, N., and Dweck, S. *Women: a bibliography on their education and careers.* Washington, D. C.: Human Service Press, 1971.

Ausubel, D. P. A teaching strategy for culturally deprived pupils: cognitive and motivational considerations. *School Review*, 1963, 71, 454-463.

Barry, R. and Wolf, B. *An epitaph for vocational guidance.* New York: Teachers College Press, 1962.

Bloom, B. S., Davis, A. and Hess, R. *Compensatory education for cultural deprivation.* New York: Holt, Rinehart and Winston, 1965.

Brooks, C. K. Some approaches to teaching English as a second language: In S. W. Webster (ed.) *The disadvantaged learner.* San Francisco: Chandler, 1966, 515-523.

Caldwell, B. M. Introduction: Period of consolidation. In J. Hellmuth (ed.), *Compensatory education; a national debate.* New York: Brunner/Mazel, 1970, v - vii.

Caplow, T. *The sociology of work.* Minneapolis: University of Minnesota Press, 1954.

Cappelluzzo, E. M. *Guidance and the migrant child.* Boston: Houghton Mifflin, 1971.

Carr, L. J. *Analytical sociology.* New York: Harper Brothers, 1955.

Conant, J. B. *Slums and suburbs: a commentary on schools in metropolitan areas.* New York: McGraw-Hill, 1961.

Davis, D., et. al Occupational choice of twelve-year olds. *Personnel and Guidance Journal*, 1962, 40, 628-29.

Deutsch, M. P. The disadvantaged child and the learning process. In A. H. Passow (ed.), *Education in depressed areas.* New York: Bureau of Publications, Teachers College, Columbia University, 1963.

Drews, E. M. Counseling for self-actualization in gifted girls and young women. *Journal of Counseling Psychology*, 1965, 12, 167-175.

Ebel, R. L. The social consequences of testing. In B. Shertzer and S. C. Stone (eds.), *Introduction to guidance.* Boston: Houghton Mifflin, 1970, 226-234.

Eyde, L. D. Eliminating barriers to career development of women. *Personnel and Guidance Journal*, 1970, 49, 24-28.

Fantini, M. D. and Weinstein, G. Taking advantage of the disadvantaged. *Teachers College Record*, 1967, 69(2), 103-112.

Farmer, H. S. Helping women to resolve the home-career conflict. *Personnel and Guidance Journal*, 1971, 49, 795-801.

Friedman, N. L. Cultural deprivation: a commentary in the sociology of knowledge. *The Journal of Educational Thought*, 1967, 1, 88-99.

Frost, J. L. and Hawkes, G. R. (eds.), *The disadvantaged child*. Boston: Houghton Mifflin, 1970.

Gardner, J. Sexist counseling must stop. *Personnel and Guidance Journal*, 1971, 49, 705-714.

Ginzberg, E. *Career guidance: Who needs it. Who provides it, who can improve it.* New York: McGraw-Hill, 1971.

————. Manpower in a service economy. In U. S. Department of Labor and Department of Health, Education, and Welfare. *Training health service workers: the critical challenge.* Washington: Government Printing Office, 1966, 16-20.

Ginzberg, E., et al. *Occupational choice: an approach to a general theory.* New York: Columbia University Press, 1951.

Glaser, E. M. and Ross, H. L. A study of successful persons from seriously disadvantaged backgrounds. Final Report, March 31, 1970, Contract No. 82-05-68-03, Office of Special Manpower Programs, Department of Labor, Washington, D. C.

Gordon, E. W. and Jablonsky, A. Compensatory education in the equalization of educational opportunity. *Journal of Negro Education*, 1968, 37(3), 268-279.

Goslin, D. A. *Teachers and testing*. New York: Russell Sage Foundation, 1967.

Havighurst, R. J. Counseling adolescent girls in the 1960's. *Vocational Guidance Quarterly*, 1965, 13, 153-160.

————. The public schools of Chicago: a survey. Chicago: The Board of Education of the City of Chicago, 1964.

————. Who are the socially disadvantaged? *Journal of Negro Education*, 1964, 33, 210-217.

Kacser, P. H. Background paper on minority children and youth for the 1970 White House Conference on Children and Youth. In *Government research on the problems of children and youth.* Washington, D. C.: Government Printing Office, 1971.

Karnes, M. B., Zehrbach, R. R., and Jones, G. R. *The culturally disadvantaged student and guidance.* Boston: Houghton Mifflin, 1971.

Keppel, F. Target for education. Quoted in M. D. Fantini and G. Weinstein, Taking advantage of the disadvantaged. *Teachers College Record*, 1967, 69 (2), 104.

Keyserling, M. D. Facing facts about women's lives today. In *New approaches to counseling girls in the 1960's.* A report of the Midwest Regional Pilot Conference. University of Chicago, 1965, 2-10.

Krugman, J. L. Cultural deprivation and child development. *High Points*, 1956, 38, 5-20.

McKenzie, F. W. Life plans of intellectually superior twelfth grade girls. Unpublished doctoral dissertation. Yale University, 1957.

Matthews, E. The marriage-career conflict in the career development of girls and young women. Unpublished doctoral dissertation. Harvard Graduate School of Education, 1960.

Menacker, J. *Urban poor students and guidance.* Boston: Houghton Mifflin, 1971.

Miller, D. C. and Form, W. H. *Industrial sociology.* New York: Harper Brothers, 1951.

Mulvey, M. C. Psychological and sociological factors in prediction of career patterns of women. Unpublished doctoral dissertation. Harvard Graduate School of Education, 1961.

——. Psychological and sociological factors in prediction of career patterns of women. *Genetic Psychological Monograph,* 1963, 68, 309-386.

Neuman, R. R. When will the educational needs of women be met? Some questions for the counselor. *Journal of Counseling Psychology,* 1963, 10, 378-383.

Olson, C. T. The U. S. challenges discrimination against women. *Junior College Journal,* 1972, 42(9), 13-16.

Passow, A. H. Early childhood and compensatory education. In A. H. Passow (ed.), *Reaching the disadvantaged learner.* New York: Teachers College Press, 1970, 33-56.

Pollack, E. and Menacker, J. *Spanish-speaking students and guidance.* Boston: Houghton Mifflin, 1971.

The Report of the President's Task Force on Women's Rights and Responsibilities. *A Matter of simple justice.* Washington, D. C.: Government Printing Office, 1970.

Riessman, F. *The culturally deprived child.* New York: Harper and Row, 1962.

Simpson, E. J. The new womanhood: education for viable alternatives. In R. C. Pucinski and S. P. Hirsch (eds.), *The courage to change: new directions for career education.* Englewood Cliffs, New Jersey: Prentice-Hall, 1971, 59-81.

Smoker, D. S. *Vocational education: innovations revolutionize career training.* Washington, D. C.: National School Public Relations Associates, 1971.

Super, D. E. *The psychology of careers.* New York: Harper & Brothers, 1957.

Taylor, E. The women's movement: What it's all about. *American Vocational Journal,* 1970, 45 (9), 16-17.

U. S. Bureau of the Census. School enrollment: October 1969. In current populations reports, Series p. 20, No. 206.

U. S. Department of Commerce. *Pocket data book, USA 1971.* Washington, D. C.: Government Printing Office, 1971.

U. S. Department of Labor. *Counseling girls and women.* Washington, D. C.: Government Printing Office, 1966.

U. S. Department of Labor. *The myth and the reality.* Washington, D. C.: Government Printing Office, 1971. (a)

——. *Manpower report of the President.* Washington, D. C.: Government Printing Office, 1971. (b)

——. *Manpower report of the President.* Washington, D. C.: Government Printing Office, 1968.

——. *1969 Handbook on Woman Workers.* Washington, D. C.: Government Printing Office, 1969.

Vontress, C. E. *Counseling Negroes.* Boston: Houghton Mifflin, 1971.

Westervelt, E. M. Counseling today's girls for tomorrow's womanhood. In *New approaches to counseling girls in the 1960's.* A report of the Midwest Regional Pilot Conference, University of Chicago, 1965. pp. 11-33.

White, S. H. The national impact study of Head Start. In J. Hellmuth (ed.), *Compensatory education: a national debate.* New York: Brunner/Mazel, 1970, pp. 163-184.

Wilkerson, D. A. Compensatory programs across the nation: a critique. In A. H. Passow (ed.), *Reaching the disadvantaged learner.* New York: Teachers College Press, 1970. (a)

————. Compensatory education: defining the issues. In J. Hellmuth (ed.), *Compensatory education: a national debate.* New York: Brunner/Mazel, 1970. (b)

Winschel, J. F. In the dark . . . reflections on compensatory education: 1960-1970. In J. Hellmuth (ed.), *Compensatory education: a national debate.* New York: Brunner/Mazel, 1970, 3-23.

Zytowski, D. G. Toward a theory of career development for women. *Personnel and Guidance Journal,* 1969, 47, 660-664.

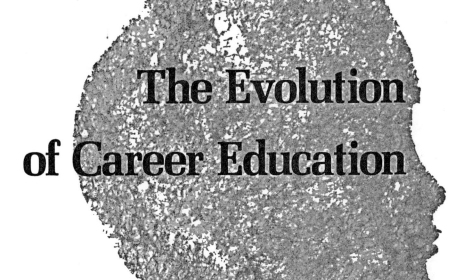

The Evolution of Career Education

CHAPTER 6

Historical Perspectives:
Vocational Education to 1962

Introduction

The history of vocational education is relatively unknown to most educators and is essential to understanding the circumstances which lead up to contemporary concerns to reorient schooling around the career development process. For present purposes, a history of vocational education must be brief. Only highlights in this fascinating story can be described. Only major events and thinking can be treated. The student of educational history should read Bennett (1926, 1937), Hawkins, Prosser and Wright (1951), Butts (1955), and other book-length treatments of man's attempts to improve his lot via vocational instruction.

Imitation
(from 50,000 B. C.)

Vocational education is as old as man. All other features of the formal school, such as classical studies, are obviously much newer than vocational education. It is not difficult to conceive of the kind of vocational instruction which prehistoric peoples employed in the rearing of young. The process of learning was *unconscious imitation* of the skills of providing food, shelter, clothing, protection from animals and the elements, and protection from unseen powers via worship. The crude skills of hunting, cooking, and farming and the more refined skills of making pottery, implements, clothing, and domiciles were passed on by simple imitation. For many centuries, the young learned elementary tasks from their elders and made almost no technological improvements.

169

When man learned to control fire, he became less nomadic and over long periods of time, developed handicrafts, arts, and eventually writing. Early historic man could cook, shape rather refined implements, and melt metals. These skills made possible a simplified division of labor, and from this came guilds which began to control entry into specialities. In this era, the process of instruction was *conscious imitation*, and the content was refined skills of accomplished workmen and artisans. Workmen in ancient Egypt and elsewhere were skilled in their trades, and culture came to be based somewhat on scientific knowledge. Great monuments, which survive in good form to this day, could not have been built by slovenly workmen using ill-conceived designs.

Apprenticeship

Mays (1948) submits that indentured apprenticeship was introduced in ancient Egypt. Certainly informal apprenticeship was the principle method of vocational instruction for many centuries. The first written reference to organized apprenticeship is made in the Babylonian Code of Hammurabi: "If an artisan take a son for adoption and teach him his handicraft, one may not bring claim against him. If he does not teach him his handicraft, the adopted son may return to his father's house" (1948, p. 6). Even after the Greeks organized the liberal arts, informal apprenticeship continued to be the primary method of vocational instruction.[1] Apprenticeship became more formalized as tradesmen and workers formed into guilds or associations. Requirements for entrance into a guild were carefully defined to assure that only the qualified were admitted. Thus evolved the *apprentice, journeyman,* and *master* titles. The master agreed to reveal all of the skills of a craft in return for the services of the apprentice for a specified span of years. This varied from craft to craft and from locale to locale, but it could be for as long as twelve years. Apprenticeship was a means of social mobility for many of the impoverished.

Apprenticeship has been variously praised and buried. It is a very viable means of occupational education. It is much more prominent in Canada and other parts of the Western world than in the United States of America. In the USA, formal apprenticeships are nearly always fostered cooperatively by union and employer

[1]Butts (1955, p. 50) makes the very interesting point that the liberal arts achieved preeminence because practical arts were not organized and written. "The weight of written materials in a field of human activity is undeniably enormous in commanding respect in the academic and educational world."

associations. Such arrangements are more prominent in the larger population centers and in the building construction, printing, metal-working, barbering, and a few other service trades. It is the hope of many manpower development specialists that apprenticeship will be extended to at least as many skilled occupations as are covered by apprenticeship laws in the Provinces of Canada. Consumer concern for quality and safety in goods and services may spur the expansion of apprenticeship. Good relationships with the managers of apprenticeship programs are very important to local, public vocational education programs. For example, the local school or college often contracts to conduct the classroom part of apprentice training for local apprenticeship councils which consist of representatives of employer and labor groups.

Formal Instruction

In early historic times, several vocations came to merit special instruction. For example, the Assyrians and the Persians, like many warring peoples to follow, took great care in the preparation of foot soldiers, artillery, and cavalry.[2] The privileged classes of ancient Greece and Rome used education as a means of assuring that vocations associated with ruling and lawmaking were preserved for the elite. In many parts of the world in prehistoric and historic times, the priestly class was the first to be educated. Special skills relating to religious rites were taught by imitation and more formal methods. Military, political, and religious occupational education have held prominent places in nearly all cultures to modern times. As the length of preparation for these and the academic occupations has increased, preparation for technical, skilled, and unskilled occupations has become more formalized, lengthy, and respected.

The history of formal schooling is replete with attempts to foster vocational education. Students of educational history would be well-advised to read accounts of developments during the seventeenth, eighteenth, and nineteenth centuries in England, Germany, France, and the United States of America. The literature which describes the contributions of people such as Locke and Owen in England; Comenius, Salzmann, Froebel, Pestalozzi and Goetze in Germany; and Rabelais and Rousseau in France reveals

---

[2]To this day, much of the very best technical and vocational education is done in the armed services. Many public school and college vocational educators judiciously emulate military instruction. Furthermore, many advancements in audio-visual techniques were first made in the military.

(1) a rather widespread concern for the practical education of working men and their children, (2) a relatively continuous development of content and methodology for manual training and other forms of handwork for the schools, (3) a developing controversy between those who would teach meaningful skills for the general education of all and those who would teach for vocations, and (4) the development of the fore-runners of public day schools, public evening schools, church-related vocational schools, private vocational and technical schools, and corporate or factory schools. Few modern ideas and practices in education are altogether new. It would be much easier to argue that they are altogether old. For example, the arguments for and against vocational education are very old. Even approaches to serving disadvantaged, handicapped, displaced and other people with special needs are not without antecedents. That is, *history is one of the important foundations of schooling for and about occupations.*

Until the latter half of the nineteenth century, schooling about and for vocations in the United States was largely transplanted from Europe. For example, in the 1630's Franciscan monks in the Southwest incorporated many kinds of practical arts in curricula for Indian and white children. In 1685, Thomas Budd, a Quaker, submitted that public schools should teach useful trades together with other subjects. Butts (1955) states that Budd's ideas did not catch on because of the strength of humanistic and sectarian religious traditions. In 1745, the Morovian sect opened an industrial school near Philadelphia. Dr. Benjamin Rush, a signer of the Declaration of Independence and a physician in Philadelphia, applauded a number of practical schools of his era (1745-1813) and is credited with influencing Dr. John de la Howe of Abbeville, South Carolina, who in 1797 bequeathed a large tract of land for an agricultural school, making stipulations regarding subject matter for both boys and girls (Bennett, 1926). This school was variously operated for the good of students and for its management until 1919, when it became part of the higher education system of the State of South Carolina. It is alleged to be the oldest agricultural school in the United States. Its history is typical of many schools which have emphasized practical studies divorced neither from occupations nor from academic subjects.

During the early 1800's, many schools were opened for poor and pauper children. Most of these attempted to teach children a trade. In 1825, Robert Owen introduced manual arts in New Harmony, Indiana. During this same period, several penal institutions began to teach trades, hoping to prepare prisoners to earn legitimate livelihoods after their release. (This is not to be confused with *prison industries,* which are primarily designed to use prison labor to produce clothing, furniture and other objects for state and federal institutions.)

Private and Public
Agricultural and Mechanical Schools

During the last half of the nineteenth century, and prior to 1906, vocational education was fostered by individuals and trade associations. Many private and public agricultural and industrial or mechanical schools were founded by large cities, universities, and technical institutes. Many of these schools failed, but some have survived to this day. They were often the brain children of prominent people in medicine, state education agencies, or university administration. The relationships between skilled manpower and the economic and sociopsychological well-being of society were clearly stated by men such as Calvin M. Woodward, Dean of the Polytechnic School of Washington University, and John D. Runkle, president of the Massachusetts Institute of Technology.

These and other leaders of their time were greatly influenced by the Russian system of training mechanics. This system was developed by Victor Della Vos of the Imperial Technical School, Moscow. Della Vos perfected a system of analyzing and teaching trades in the late 1860's and displayed it at an exposition in Vienna in 1873 and at the Centennial Exposition in Philadelphia in 1876.

Victor Della Vos' system was widely accepted because it had several admirable features: (1) it involved careful analysis of specific trades and the ordering of tasks from simple to complex; (2) it facilitated a much larger student-teacher ratio than had theretofore been practicable; (3) it recognized the values of group, small group, and individual instruction; (4) it recognized the value of application and immediate knowledge of results; (5) it established the value of teachers who are expert in their occupation and in pedagogy; and (6) it had a military-like regimen which was compatible with the thinking of many schoolmen and the temperament of youth of the era. This system and its influence in several countries are well documented by Bennett (1937).

In the United States of America, a large number of cities built specialized manual training high schools for boys and girls, and many elementary schools introduced manual training in the upper grades. Manual training was interpreted by what came to be two rather disparate camps.

The first camp of teacher educators and public school leaders was aligned with the mental discipline psychology of the era. This camp fostered the notion that manual training developed certain faculties such as hand-eye coordination and was thus a general education subject. This group was influenced by *sloyd*, more so than was the second camp. Sloyd is the Swedish word for hand-work which was practiced in the home to occupy winter hours and produce useful objects, mostly of wood. With the introduction of factories, home sloyd declined in Scandinavia and school sloyd flourished. This development was fostered by Uno Cygnaeus of Finland and, in turn, by Otto Soloman of Sweden (Bennett, 1937). Educational sloyd was contrasted to manual training primarily in that it was for purposes of general education. Manual training was invented by a government engineer for special and peculiar utilitarian education purposes and sloyd was developed for the schools by educators to enrich study for all children. In the United States of America, sloyd's most widely known advocate was Gustav Larson, who came to Boston in 1888. Sloyd had great influence on both camps, but primarily on this camp which was called *manual arts* after the turn of the century and, in time, *industrial arts*. This camp's champion is the American Industrial Arts Association, an NEA affiliate, which has a long history of (1) allegiance to general education; (2) a struggle to be accepted in general education; (3) a struggle to be differentiated from vocational education, especially when Federal appropriations for vocational education are increased; and (4) an abhorance of vocational education, especially among its more influential members.

The second camp of educators makes more accurate interpretations of Della Vos. These are vocational educators. As was indicated above, prior to 1906, vocational education was fostered by laymen and trade associations. Men of means and/or stature, who understood the pedagogical efficiencies and economic advantages of formalized instruction, fostered schools which employed manual training methods. The story of how these ideas affected public education follows.

Impetuses to Public Vocational Education

According to Bennett (1937), the public vocational education movement began in 1906. Two very significant events occurred in that year:

Massachusetts Commission

The first event was the report of a Massachusetts Commission, appointed by Governor William L. Douglas and chaired by

Caroll D. Wright, former U. S. Commissioner of Labor.[3] The findings of the Commission were not unlike the findings of subsequent state and national studies. Its two recommendations would require little adjustment to contemporary nomenclature and conditions to be applicable in the 1970's.

The first recommendation was that elementary education for boys and girls include instruction and practice in the elements of productive industry, including agriculture and the mechanic and domestic arts, and that instruction in other subjects show application in industrial life.

The second recommendation was that high schools offer elective courses in agricultural, mechanical, and domestic arts and that instruction in mathematics, the sciences, and drawing show application and use, especially to local industries. The commission recognized the importance of day, part-time, and evening schools. A second, administrative commission fostered legislation and the establishment of industrial[4] schools. Initially, these were separate from the public school system; but in a few years, vocational education was incorporated into comprehensive schools.[5]

National Society for the Promotion of Industrial Education

The second significant event of 1906 was the formation of the National Society for the Promotion of Industrial Education. Dr. James P. Haney, Director of Art and Manual Training in New York City, and Charles R. Richards, Professor of Manual Training at Teacher's College, Columbia University, were the impetus for this organization (Bennett, 1937). This organization moved quickly to issue descriptive bulletins, secure the support of labor leaders such as Samuel Gompers, and deal with matters such as management-labor differences, the reticence of public school leaders, apprenticeship patterns, trade education for girls, and state and federal legislation. At its meeting in 1918, the society changed its name to National Society for Vocational Education. In 1926, this association joined with the Vocational Education Association of the Middlewest to form the American Vocational Association. The

---

[3]The reader would do well to note (1) that vocational education has often been spurred to new programming by administrative and legislative commissions and (2) that the responsibilities of government departments of labor and education in manpower development are sometimes overlapping.

[4]Early in the century, educators used the term *industry* to connote any branch of productive endeavor.

[5]Please note that whether to have comprehensive high schools or a dual system of (1) college preparatory and (2) vocational schools is a controversy which has raged hot and cold over the decades. The final sections of Chapter 8 deal with this matter.

AVA has flourished and has often had positive influence on legislation and the United States Office of Education.

Federal Legislation to 1962

Federal legislation for vocational education below the baccalaureate was not accomplished easily. Starting in 1862 with the Morrill Act, or land-grant colleges act, the Federal Government aided and abetted the development of collegiate level education in agricultural and mechanic arts. Four additional acts, ending with the Nelson Amendment in 1907, expanded Federal support and the scope of these colleges before legislation for vocational education was considered.

During the period 1906 to 1914, the Congress debated the merits of increased funding for land-grant colleges and of support for secondary vocational instruction. The Smith-Lever bill provided federal aid for extension training of farm people in agriculture and for industrial, agricultural and home economics education *in secondary schools*. As Hawkins, et. al. (1951, p. 81) put so well, both bills were democratizing and did not compete for students, programs, or appropriations. For reasons which are hard to define and variously interpreted, the Congress failed repeatedly to pass either bill. In January of 1914, Senator Smith, with the support of the National Society for the Promotion of Industrial Education (NSPIE), laid ground for breaking the deadlock. In short, the bargain was to adopt the Smith-Lever Bill and establish a Presidential commission to study issues identified by the Page-Wilson Bill.[6]

The Commission on National Aid to Vocational Education reported, proposing legislation in less than six months. The bill was referred to Senator Hoke Smith and Congressman Dudley M. Hughes, chairmen of the respective education committees. Working closely with the NSPIE and a special legislative committee, these men gained great support for the bill. Delays were caused by controversy over the makeup of a federal board of vocational education, illness which caused Congressman Hughes to be absent, and the election of 1917. Finally, after a third presidential appeal for passage, which was prompted by the results of a national referendum conducted by the Chamber of Commerce of the United States, and after compromises made in conference, the bill became law in 1917. *Vocational education, i.e., public education for occupations which require less than the baccalaureate, was born.*

[6]A much more thorough account of the commission and events during the delay of June 1, 1914 to February 23, 1917 is given by Hawkins, et. al. (1951, pp. 82-89).

The story of vocational education from 1917 to 1960 is closely associated with the provisions of the Smith-Hughes law and related legislation. Only the major provisions of these acts, let alone the several other aspects of this period in the history of vocational education, can be recounted here. Size of appropriations, basis for alloting funds by kinds of populations, and specific regulations have been omitted.

Smith-Hughes Act: Public Law No. 347, 64th Congress

The major purposes of this act were (1) the promotion of vocational education, (2) cooperation with the states in the promotion of education in agriculture, trades and industries, (3) cooperation with the states in the preparation of vocational teachers, and (4) regulation of funding for these activities. The act was a continuous authorization, i.e., it provided for annual appropriations by the Congress. Funds were available for paying salaries of teachers, supervisors, and directors of vocational programs in agriculture, trades and industries, and home economics subjects. Only a few amendments were made to this bill. The most significant amendment abolished the Federal Board for Vocational Education[7] in 1946.

To receive funds, states had to comply with several provisions of the act. Each state had to (1) create or designate a board of not less than three members for vocational education, (2) prepare a state plan, describing programs which would be conducted, (3) make an annual report to the Federal Board of Vocational Education, (4) provide a program, only in public schools, for students fourteen years of age or older and of lesser than baccalaureate grade, (5) provide plant and equipment with state or local funds, and (6) gear programs to occupational entry.

George-Reed Act: Public Law No. 702, 70th Congress

This act was effective from 1929 to 1934. It (1) provided for further development of vocational agriculture and home economics in states and territories and (2) removed home economics from the trade and industrial service area, making it subject to some features of the appropriations for agriculture.

---

[7]Another fascinating story for the serious student of educational history concerns the makeup, administrative position, and function of this board (see Hawkins, et. al., 1951, pp. 135-164). This chapter of the history of public vocational education contrasts and compares with the contemporary relationships of the Department of Labor and the Office of Education in the totality of human resource development. This matter is illustrative of the foundational value of knowledge of past practice.

George-Ellzey Act: Public Law No. 245, 72nd Congress
This act was effective from 1934 to 1937. It made modifications in the regulations affecting home economics, part-time classes in trades and industries, and funds for attendance at professional meetings.

George-Deen Act: Public Law No. 673, 74th Congress
This act was a continuous authorization, effective from fiscal year 1937. It made two major changes in existing regulations: (1) It provided for matching Federal funds on a graduated scale. States could begin by matching 50 percent and increase over ten years to matching 100 percent of their federal allotment. (2) Distributive education was added as a full partner (excepting that the authorization level was lower) in the vocational education family.

George-Barden Act: Public Law No. 586, 79th Congress
This act amended the George-Deen Act and was continuous from fiscal year 1946. It allowed increased authorization levels and provided for greater flexibility in the administration of state and local programs. It permitted expenditures for salaries of vocational counsellors, occupational information and data collection, training and work experience for out-of-school youth, apprentice training, purchase or rental of equipment, purchase of instructional supplies, support of a second youth organization in agriculture, pre-employment schools and classes for school leavers over eighteen years of age, and professional travel for staff not previously approved. It limited support for distributive education to part-time and evening courses for employed workers.

George-Barden Act: Title II, Health Amendments Act of 1956 and 1961 Public Law No. 911, 84th Congress and Public Law No. 87-22, 87th Congress
These amendments provided funds for practical nurse training through 1965. For the first two years, Federal funds were furnished on a three-for-one basis. Then the rates became the usual one-for-one.

George-Barden Act: Amendment to Title I, Fishery Training Act, Public Law 1027, 84th Congress
This act was a continuous authorization from fiscal year 1957. Unlike other vocational education acts, this legislation provided for allotments according to the extent of the fishing industry in a state or territory and for universities and colleges to prepare scientists and technicians needed in commercial fishing.

George-Barden Act: Title III, National Defense Education Act, Title VIII, Public Law 85-864, 85th Congress and Public Law 87-344, 87th Congress

This act provided for the training of highly skilled technicians for the five-year period 1958-1962. It permitted much of the flexibilities of the original act for the level of vocational education which is commonly called "technical." It also provided funds for transporting students or for distribution to students who transport themselves to temporary housing. The act made the first mention of using guidance funds to maximize retention. It required that state plans (1) demonstrate need in the employment market for those trained, (2) demonstrate that curricula were developed by specialized analyses, (3) show that background general education was available to students, (4) show that technical courses were of sufficient duration to provide the background necessary to employment, (5) show that classrooms, laboratories, and instructional equipment and supplies would be available, (6) demonstrate that instructors and supervisors would have appropriate technical and professional preparation, and (7) show that students would be selected on the basis of previous educational and work experience, aptitudes and interests. Programs had to be for technical as contrasted to manual occupations. The act permitted the use of extension courses for employed persons and/or pre-employment trainees for technical or scientific occupations — not skilled trades. Programs were required to have appropriate advisory committees.

Area Redevelopment Act: Public Law 87-27, 87th Congress [8]

The purpose of this act was to alleviate substantial and persistent unemployment and underemployment. It authorized funds

---

[8]This act and the next are, like so many, only *related* to public vocational education. Most of the programs established under these acts as amended are administered by public educational agencies. The significance of these acts to the common welfare and to the individuals served is obvious. Less obvious is the fact that these acts are an indictment of public education — not so much of public vocational education but, more so, of the general education track. Evans (1971, p. 80) states that 88 percent of MDTA students come from the general track. This is an understandable and a shocking disclosure of (1) the lack of readily available and viable secondary, public vocational education programs and (2) the inevitable failing of so-called general education which prepares people neither for further study or for employment beyond the second paycheck.

Note that these acts were evidence of only the beginnings of the U.S. Department of Labor's attempt to establish educational agencies to do what the common schools cannot or will not do. Space in future sections of this book will not permit description of this continuing debate in the Federal administration and legislature. Suffice it to say that public school people should pay heed to the clamor for a prepared work force.

from 1961-1965. It provided vocational education services and facilities for training and retraining of unemployed and under-employed in areas designated by the Department of Commerce as redevelopment areas. The Secretary of Labor was empowered to identify and refer those eligible for training. The Secretary of Health, Education, and Welfare was empowered to contract with public or private educational enterprises for services not available from state and local vocational education agencies. Vocational education was only a small feature of this act. (This is illustrative of the many Federal acts which have provisions for vocational education.)

Manpower Development and Training Act: Public Law 87-415, 87th Congress and Public Law 88-214, 88th Congress, and others

The purpose of this act was to alleviate the hardships of unemployment, reduce the costs of unemployment compensation and public assistance, and maximize utilization of resources in the space age. Somewhat like the previous act, the Secretary of Labor was empowered to determine skill requirements, develop policies, and encourage diversified programs. The Secretary of Health, Education and Welfare was empowered to provide training to people referred by the Secretary of Labor. Of course, the actual referrals and training were done by state and local agency people at the local level. Again, the states were to contract with private educational or training agencies for services if they could not be provided by public institutions or agencies.

As amended, this act has provided for special training since 1962. Programs are restricted to training for skills which are required in the immediate locale. The programs are usually of rather short duration and emphasize entry-level employment. Together with Job Corps and the lesser known special vocational education programs, MDTA programs emphasize one side of the dual versus comprehensive controversy which is treated in the final sections of Chapter 8.

Summary

The reader should appreciate that vocational education was a major improvement to public education. Although much of the following commentary is negative, it is important to recall that during the period 1917-1962 vocational education assured livelihoods for many tens of thousands of people. Much of it was good.

Appropriations increased and, especially with the George-Barden Act and its amendments, many innovative and viable programs served an ever larger public. But there were shortcomings.

The first of these was that, from inception, the focus was on rather specific occupations. Within the service areas, the tendency was to restrict programs to a very limited list of occupations. In agriculture, too many programs were for production agriculture and not enough were for occupations in agri-business and marketing. In trades and industries, by the 1950's, and even more so by the 1970's, too much effort was devoted to woodworking and drafting occupations and too little was devoted to emerging occupations in the electrical, manufacturing, and construction industries. In no small part because they subconsciously emulated the liberal arts and sciences content model, vocational educators too often analyzed occupations and then got set in their ways, using laboratories and texts until they were long out of date. In large part because of costs, curricula and laboratories were not rebuilt for modern employment needs.

The second shortcoming was probably state planning. It is true that many state plans changed but little over even a ten-year period. Most incorporated new provisions in keeping with new acts. But change was very slow. Because of the legislation there was a tendency to have too many regulations. *The Statement of Policies for the Administration of Vocational Education* (commonly called Bulletin No. 1) of the U. S. Office of Education was revised at least as often as there were major legislative changes. But it was generally more restrictive than the acts required. In turn, state plans added regulations. At the next level, documents with titles such as "Essentials of Trade and Industrial Education" in the states could be restrictive. By the 1950's, most of the "chiefs" of the service areas in state agencies were well-along in years and rather set in their ways. Vocational education was in the doldrums, repeating itself year-by-year. Restrictiveness was sometimes amplified by local vocational directors. Fortunately, some people in leadership positions and many teachers knew how to avoid or get around inappropriate regulations.

Funding procedures were surely a shortcoming. Under most of the acts, states received a specified allotment for each service area according to total or a specified kind (for example, rural) of population. Initially all, and until 1963 nearly all, funds had to be used to reimburse salaries. (In most states, this was fifty percent of nine months, excepting fifty percent of eleven months for agriculture and twelve months for directors.) The allocation was never large enough to pay half of the salaries of teachers in several service areas in all of the high schools of a state. Therefore, large cities and towns and/or cites and towns with political clout or *pork barrelesse* had many approved vocational programs, smaller centers had approved programs only in production agriculture and/ or homemaking, and the smallest schools had no vocational programs at all.

These conditions were fostered by strong lobbying by pressure groups representing agriculture and, to a much lesser degree, home economics. Lobbying tended to maintain authorization and appropriation levels across the service areas rather than shift monies to trades and industries and distributive education as population shifted from rural to urban centers. Furthermore, business and office occupations education had to wait until 1963 to be reimbursable.[9] The emphasis was simply too much on more of the same and not enough on the process of adjusting programs to student and social needs.

[9]Yet business education was a better deal for girls (and too few boys) than was most of vocational education for either sex by 1950.

BIBLIOGRAPHY

Bennett, C. A. *History of manual and industrial education to 1870.* Peoria: Charles A. Bennett, 1926.
————. *History of manual and industrial education 1870-1917.* Peoria: Charles A. Bennett, 1937.
Butts, R. F. *A cultural history of western education.* New York: McGraw-Hill, 1955.
Evans, R. N. *Foundations of vocational education.* Columbus, Ohio: Charles E. Merrill, 1971.
Hawkins, L. S., Prosser, C. A., and Wright, J. C. *Development of federal legislation for vocational education.* Chicago: Amercian Technical Society, 1951.
Mays, A. B. *Principles and practices of vocational education.* New York: McGraw-Hill, 1948.

CHAPTER 7

Foundations of
Vocational Education

Introduction

Vocational education is part and parcel of all societies. Because it is basic, widespread, and multidimensional, it is poorly understood even by those who associate closely with it. It is so important to advanced societies that it cannot be left to professionals alone. It is rooted broadly and deeply in *technology, educational theory, economics, psychology,* and *sociology.*[1] This chapter describes the larger contributions which these fields or areas of concern make to the foundation of vocational education in schools and colleges. Major issues and questions are identified and explored. Conclusions are drawn only when need and evidence are clear for all to see. In some instances, relationships between fields, i.e., the kind of communication links which must be open and functioning, are defined in terms of how problems may be approached. In many cases, questions are left undefined or delimited. In the main, the chapter illustrates the closeness of society, the behavioral sciences, education, and vocational education specifically.

It will be observed in this chapter that the authors use the terms "vocational education" and "career education" in various contexts. This does not assume that the two are synonymous and interchangeable. Career education is the more global term, while vocational education is an important and integral component *of* career education. Many of the foundations which are discussed have implications for the whole of career education. Other founda-

---

[1]In "systems" terms, these are the *inputs* to curriculum design, which result in the *process* of education, i.e., the learning experiences which children, youth, and adults undergo. *Outputs* (better called "outcomes") are the play, learning or work-related competencies possessed by individuals.

tions relate more directly to just vocational education. In all cases, the reader is urged to consider vocational and career education in their broader connotations.

Technological Foundations

Just as invention is the mother of science, so is technology a major impetus to educational change. Obviously, the whole of education — formal and informal — and schooling is affected by technological and scientific advance. Institutions of higher learning not only monitor technology to plan curricular changes but also contribute to technological advance via research and invention. All common educational enterprises are inextricably related to technology.

The qualities of vocational or career education depend upon keeping pace with technology. Leaders and practitioners in career education must monitor the industrial-science-technology milieu to establish new functions, time lines, and program and smaller experience components. Moreso than those who are responsible for supporting components of the curriculum and ancillary services, career education personnel must monitor major and minor, long- and short-range, and distant and nearby technological change and industrial advance.

Technological Horizons

The impacts of the following on career education at several levels are certain to be great.

1. The future of oceans: Will we harness the power of tides, desalinate water for irrigation and drinking, raise crops for foods and fiber, commercialize fish farming on a much larger scale, manufacture on the sea floor, and live full or part-time on the ocean floor or afloat? Surely the difficulty of many of these questions is only accuracy of timing and degree. We will do many of these things at some time and to some degree. In fact, economy of scale requires that many of them be done in large measure or not at all.

2. The future of recreation and leisure industries: Will we continue to establish second and third domiciles, acquire more mobile homes, increase intercontinental travel, develop huge outdoor vacation complexes, journey to satellites and planets for amusement, adopt new performing art forms, and commercialize new participation sports? The answers are the same.

3. The future of environment: Will we continue and expand programs to control gaseous and solid waste emissions from extracting and manufacturing enterprises, improve safety conditions everywhere we play or work, assure judicious recycling of water and wastes, retain large regions in their natural state, return other regions to near-natural conditions, exercise judicious control over the balance of nature in the plant and animal kingdoms to benefit ecological cycles and endangered species, and institutionalize preventative environmental maintenance programs? The answers are the same.

4. The future of human biological restraint and control: Will we establish legal requirements for family planning, improve the technology of birth control to near-perfect reliability and for maximum flexibility of decision, improve the technology of organ transplantation and prosthesis, increase control over birth defects, improve intelligence and other characteristics genetically, produce people with different physical and mental characteristics by genetic control, and automate more fully medical and psychological diagnosis and prescription? The answers are the same with underscored moral and ethical qualifications.

5. The future of transportation and communication: Will we change domestic air travel drastically, travel on the ocean floor; employ new communications media for commercial and amusement purposes; solve urban and intercity transportation problems with integrated surface, subterranean, public, private, wheeled, and other systems; transport messages and things on totally new media; and develop reliable language translators? The answers are the same.

6. The future of warfare: Will we continue to design offensive and defensive weapons systems for intercontinental and spatial warfare, for naval warfare, for land wars, for computer-simulated wars? Regrettably, the answers are the same.

7. The future of weather forecasting and control: Will we expand land, sea, air and space-based meteorological data collection facilities; improve predictive power and computerize forecasting procedures; and regularize weather control procedures as they are developed and tested? The answers are the same.

The gravity of these matters is witnessed more fully when one realizes their one-world nature. Ecology is a prime example of world-wide concern (Purpel and Belanger, 1972). Very few human problems are parochial problems. The implications of technology are far-reaching and deep, especially for formal education.

Summary of Technological Foundations:
Implications for Education

The impact of these and other scientific and technological developments on educational enterprises will be great. Three categories of implications are obvious. First, the educational program must be more relevant to the occupational milieu of changing jobs and highly mobile and adaptable people. Second, science and related components of the curriculum must be thought of as extensions of primary understandings of numbers and things, which all youngsters can accomplish in good measure in their own time — for the broad self-concept satisfaction and the specific or career-fulfillment functions of individualized education. Third, educational methodology will keep pace with the whole of technology to integrate home, employer, and school responsibilities for the rearing of young and for continuing education and counseling. Media complexes will weld several institutions into new cooperative partnerships in human resource development. Hopefully, barriers to human interchange across institutions at the community level will come down as rapidly as they come down between given types of institutions at local, regional, national, and international levels. Perhaps, "Schools in the forms we have known will virtually disappear. Instead education will take place via combined systems of machines and human assistants located in homes, neighborhood centers, and specialized learning centers, museums, *and industrial and business locations*"[2] (Purpel and Belanger, 1972, p. 17).

Theoretical Foundations

In most writings of this type, this section would be called *philosophical* foundations. Philosophy is a word with many meanings. Many career education people use the term in the lay sense, meaning the process of demonstrating foundations for career or vocational education by rational analysis of issues. Some use the term to describe the work of members of departments of educational foundations in colleges of education. Still others use the term to connote only the work of formal philosophy.

This section is called *Theoretical* Foundations for several reasons: (1) It is technically correct to reserve use of the term "philosophy" to describe only formal philosophy. (2) It is well to

[2]Emphasis added.

emphasize the facts (a) that very few formal philosophers address themselves to education, let alone career education, directly, and (b) that major issues in education must be resolved by educators as issues in education not as issues in philosophy for, after all, educators cannot play Superman in other domains. Put another way, few philosophers have anything to say about educational issues and educators cannot resolve controversies (the essence of philosophy) in other fields. (3) It is well to consider the work of full-time educational theorists, school and college administrators, government agency people, leaders in professional associations, and others when dealing with issues in career education. Statements of various and sundry people fit more comfortably under the term *theory* than they do under the term *philosophy*.

Typical Statements Re the Function of Schooling

The important issue which educational theory can attempt to resolve is, "What is the function of the formal school?" There are a number of common answers to this question.

Transmits Culture. A large variety of people maintain that the function of formal schooling is to transmit the assimilated culture of the civilization. This is probably the most widely used statement of function for schools. But, it is too sweeping. Many aspects of the assimilated culture are not trusted to schools for transmission because they are too essential. Basic common sense knowledge of how to get along in the world of many kinds of people and places with names and numbers and patterns for coming and going, being spoken to and speaking to others, simple buying and selling, and other conventions — these things are too important to wait for schooling. Many other essentials are learned out of school. Furthermore, refined and detailed knowledge of the past, such as the content of museums and archives, is stored and transmitted by other institutions. Finally, all institutions transmit culture, i.e., engage in some form of instruction. Witness the roles of commercial and educational television, other media, industry, government, and other agencies in education.

Transmits Organized Disciplines. A more refined definition of the function of the formal school is espoused by liberal arts and science professors and a great many professors of education, practicing professionals, and government educational agency people. Perhaps the largest group of theorists says: Yes, the function of the school is to transmit culture, but only the organized disciplines part of culture. This camp cannot be completely dismissed because, after all, much of what is known about the world around us is deposited in organized disciplines. Much of the content of school is taken from organized disciplines. The problems with this definition of the function of the formal school are (1) that it is difficult to decide what is and is not a discipline and (2) that there are too many disciplines. These difficulties make for a lot of bickering. Having no valid basis for selecting disciplines, schools and colleges teach those which are required for entry to the next level, and/or those which are advocated by people in various positions of authority, and/or those which can be taught by available staff, and/or those which can be afforded over and above the basics — which are algebra, physics, chemistry, biology and several others. Schools also attempt various kinds of core or integrated curricula because of the diversity of disciplines. Furthermore, this definition is inadequate because even those who espouse it advocate the teaching of other than disciplines — reading, writing, and arithmetic for example.

Teaches What Is No Longer Taught Elsewhere. Many theorists recognize that schools cannot be everything to everybody and argue that the school should do what other institutions do not do. This is much more noteworthy than the two theories described above. Another name for this theory is *residual* theory. It is an attempt to explain the historic origin of the schools. Residual theorists submit that schools should teach what used to be taught elsewhere, but is no longer taught there. But, in actual fact, schools have never taught what used to be taught elsewhere. Rather, schools and classroom subjects came into being to organize and present in a structured way what has become too complex to be trusted to casual instructional methods and/or what people are not able to learn because it is hidden, for one reason or another, from them in the out-of-school world. For example, the first schools[3] arose in the age of Pericles because free men and slaves who fought valorously for the right of citizenship had not learned by imitation how to dress, speak, and in other ways conduct themselves in polite society. These things had never been *taught* elsewhere. Slowly, teachers systematized grammar and the other liberal arts. Historically, and in modern times, much of what is taught in schools has been organized especially for instruction and has never been taught elsewhere.

Residual theorists are prone to crisis mentality. They say that people face a crisis and propose a corrective component for the

---

[3]Teachers in these schools were called "sophists" and were hired by the neophyte citizens from among poor citizens. Ever since, teaching has been a means of economic and social mobility for many in its ranks.

curriculum.[4] Driver education is introduced to reduce traffic deaths and injuries. Marriage and family living are introduced to reduce divorce, improper child rearing, and the like. Similarly, the evils of alcohol, narcotics, nicotine, and other things are introduced to reduce crime and delinquency.[5] In effect, these moves call for the creation of culture. That is, the school assumes that problems in the culture arise from the absence of values, ideas, and mores which could be found in older cultures. It is said that the old ways have been given up and must be instilled in the young. In fact, it is impossible for school people to create a universally acceptable set of principles about right and wrong. Much of recent student unrest is evidence of the unacceptability of school-based decisions regarding modes of action and thought, e.g., dress, sex, speech.

Some residual theorists support vocational education. They say that because of industrialization and urbanization, the farm and apprenticeship no longer prepare enough people for employment. Therefore, the school should prepare people for work. These theorists are right, of course. But for the same wrong reason. Just as other teachers do not teach what used to be taught by other institutions, vocational teachers (public and private) organize material which has not been taught in a formal and organized way. At best, it has been learned by unconscious or conscious imitation. In large part, vocational instruction concerns occupations which cannot be understood or even observed by youth and laymen. Thus, residual theory is an inadequate foundation for career education.

Meets Needs of Children and Youth. Especially in the 1950's, it was fashionable to say that the purpose of education was to meet the needs of children and youth. Educational psychologists and many secondary school curriculum people espoused this theory. This theory can mean one of two things. (1) It can mean all needs, including food, shelter, clothing, culture and derived needs, such as color television. Obviously, this is inane. After all, economic institutions meet many of these needs and no one seriously submits that the school should be concerned with them. Granted, meals and other necessities are supplied by some schools, but such things are done only to maximize learning, i.e., are only indirectly related to the function of schooling. (2) It can mean the needs of children and youth for education. This is even more obviously inane. It is

---

[4]Note that in each case material that has not been taught before is organized for formal instruction.

[5]Some residual theorists are properly called "life-adjustment educators." But, all are not. Witness the fact that many laymen who advocate rigorous regulations and instruction regarding the evils of narcotics and alcohol, deride *life-adjustors* who advocate sex education.

empty talk, begging the question, a mere play on words. Need theory doesn't work. The question remains: "What educational needs shall be met?" Need theory is not wrong. It is well to focus on people rather than content, but the focus itself does not suggest which kinds of educational experiences are right and which are wrong.

Reconstructs Society. Perhaps the largest number of educational theorists in departments of educational foundations are social reconstructionists. Such theorists assume (1) that society is in tremendous crisis, (2) that the school should be used as a social force or change agent, and (3) that children can be used as a positive force to improve society. These theorists represent an evangelistic crusade to return society to a less critical state. The basic problem with this camp is that of finding an uncritical condition in the past or of defining homeostasis hypothetically. Needless to say, achieving such a state would be much more difficult than defining it. Both the definition and the design of corrective actions require supermen in the social and behavioral sciences. Major issues in political economics, government, sociology, and other fields have to be resolved in such super planning. Schoolmen are not such supermen. Furthermore, to say that the way out of crisis is to restore unity is to say that people should be more alike in thought, action, and values. This imposes ideology instead of trusting human intelligence, respecting freedom, and letting individuals decide controversies for themselves.

Social reconstructionists tend to prescribe major doses of the social sciences and are to be commended for offsetting those who oversell the exact sciences. Somehow reconstructionists fail to promote vocational education. Their effect is to modify the recommendations of liberal arts and science people by emphasizing the newcomers in the curriculum, i.e., the social and behavioral sciences.

The Literature of Curriculum. Some would argue that the literature of curriculum, which is produced by people in university departments of curriculum and instruction or secondary and elementary education and by practicing curriculum directors, is educational theory. In fact, it is not even derived from educational theory. But, it does have more impact on the conduct of schooling than does educational theory and should not be dismissed lightly.

Texts on curriculum and principles and practices of secondary or elementary schooling are anthologies — anthologies of ideas and possibilities if not anthologies of writings *per se.* They describe a great many features of diverse curricula but, in the main, do not

.offer criteria for priority setting. That is, they say something about everything and prescribe nothing. The literature of curriculum mirrors the history and current state of curricular affairs. If vocational subjects and career information are mentioned at all, they are usually treated in small sections in a thin chapter on incidentals or curricular also-rans and tack-ons.

Most of the people who generate the literature of curriculum are, after all, not familiar with historic or modern developments in vocational education. Furthermore, they look on vocational education as an add-on. That is, they suggest that after schools have assured the welfare of the college bound, they should (1) offer general subjects for those who do poorly in the traditional courses and (2) offer vocational subjects for those who also do poorly in general courses.[6] In the schools, youngsters come to vocational education by the process of elimination. Potential "push-outs" who are no longer comfortable on the glory road, i.e., college preparation, go first to general education and then to vocational education.[7] The literature of curriculum does not propose these processes; it condones them by default. That is, it approves of the "cafeteria curriculum" and offers no principle for removing courses as new ones are added.

Summary of Theoretical Foundations:
Implications for Vocational Education

The several kinds of educational theorists do not give much place to preparation for employability or to occupational information. At best, they submit that preparation for work should be reserved for post-secondary public and private education. In sum, theorists advocate a college preparatory curriculum. By different routes, they attempt to justify the study of organized disciplines in the secondary school. Purposes for studying these and the number and kinds of experiences which should be available to those who fail to keep pace with the established curriculum vary, but, in the main, theorists advocate preparation for college entrance for all who can (or will) do the prescribed curriculum. The several kinds of theorists do not say drastically different things about the real stuff of the curriculum.

Those who get down to the matter of prescribing an ideal secondary curriculum are (perhaps unknowingly) elitist. They

[6]The language of curriculum is never so direct. But stripped of decoration, the literature of curriculum and secondary education is an attempt to rationalize what is actually done in the schools.

[7]Needless to say, many drop out or "blast out" because general and vocational education in many schools are no better suited to reality and need than is the college preparatory track.

advocate a rather narrow curriculum common for all. This is, of course, impossible in the world of practice. Thus, the curriculum is a hodgepodge, resulting from (a) pressures of various and sundry groups balanced by (b) tradition and reluctance to take out as new material is put in.

The hodgepodge is condoned with varying, minor qualifications by the literature of the comprehensive high school which, after all, would have the school be all things to all people. In the end, the major influences on curriculum are the software and hardware producers, publishers and equipment suppliers. Fortunately, this influence is primarily positive because, educational theory aside, schools try to buy what works with young people.

It is clear that the implications of educational theory and the literature of curriculum for vocational education are sparse indeed. Vocational education has the same mother as does invention, i.e., necessity. The great men and women in vocational education have been aware of this and have not been troubled by lack of support in educational theory and curriculum. The literatures of educational theory and curriculum demonstrate that vocational and career education professionals will have to provide their own theoretical bases. Fortunately, they have strong and influential allies who know that schooling is at a turn-around. Richard B. Ogilvie (1972), former governor of Illinois, put the matter well during the dedication of a new school:

> The Rockford Area Vocational Center is both a reflection of a profound shift in our thinking about career education, and an agent for effecting that long-overdue change. To understand this shift in attitude, we should be cognizant of the concept of vocational education as it has been practiced in the past.
>
> Every large community had its 'technical high school,' a forbidding fortress filled with machines and other devices, which commanded little respect from the community at large. For most people, the vocational high school was little more than a mechanized day care center for shiftless students who had neither the interest nor the intelligence to pursue a more 'respectable' academic career.
>
> This was the stigma of vocational education, and for years it has imposed an incredible obstacle to developing a quality vocational system — quality of programs offered, and quality of student served. In its place, we developed a mythology about college education which only recently has begun to come to grips with the reality of misallocated educational resources.
>
> We have all heard the myth. It goes like this: 'If you want to amount to anything in life, you have to go to college.' According to this notion, a university degree somehow becomes a magic key which guarantees entry into a world of economic well-being and endows the holder with a cloak of respectability otherwise unattainable.
>
> The long period of economic boom nurtured the myth for many years, but it has been rudely shattered on the rocks of an economic downturn and the simple law of supply and demand. We have more history teachers than our schools can absorb, but we haven't enough nurses to care for the sick. Nuclear

physicists are out of work, but we have trouble finding a competent mechanic to repair the mysterious rattle in the family car.

Our school system is preparing our young people to enter college, but for the majority of high school students who entertain no college ambitions, graduation too often is a dead end.

Americans have been slow to recognize the deficiency, but things are rapidly changing (1972, pp. 13-14).

Economic Foundations

There has been far too little collaboration of educators and economists. Public educational enterprises have until recent times not been subjected to the kinds of scrutiny which economists regularly give other institutions. (Elements of the public sector, generally have not been subjected to economic analyses as have segments of the private sector). Presently, there is a great deal of discussion about the kinds of assistance economists can give to educators. That education will be subjected to economic evaluations is obvious. That evaluations at all levels will contribute to judicious decisions regarding curricula and methodology is less clear. It behooves educators to know what economists can and cannot do for schools.

Economic Value of Vocational Education

From inception, public vocational education has had economic objectives. Like many other public projects, vocational education has been promoted, in part, on the principle that it makes positive economic contributions to the larger society, communities, and individuals. This principle has been emphasized from time to time throughout the history of vocational education. But, for several reasons, it was not tested rigorously until the 1960's. On the one hand, economists had little previous experience in the evaluation of public enterprises. Economic evaluations of education came after similar evaluations of other public projects, such as defense and flood control.

On the other hand, educators (and other public administrators) were privileged to function on the "more" principle. That is, educators were permitted to define the role and function of schools without serious public scrutiny, asking respective government agencies for more and more funds to meet increasing needs. Economists point out that many educators emphasize the consumptive good as contrasted to the investment good of education. If education is pursued for its liberalizing and intellectually enriching values as an end in itself, it is treated as consumptive good by economists. If education is pursued for contribution to future occupational opportunity and earnings, it is treated as an investment good by economists. Consumption goods are for immediate value or enjoyment. Investment goods are utilized as resources to increase future productivity. In recent years, economists have paid more attention to the investment feature of education than to the consumptive feature. There is a large literature which deals with the economic value of education at several levels, but treatment here must be limited to vocational or vocational-technical education.

Evaluation of the investment good of vocational education was spurred by the Report of the Panel of Consultants on Vocational Education, *Education for a Changing World of Work* (1963, p. 207).

Lack of data and tangible evidence, it must be admitted, make it difficult for laymen and professionals to fully evaluate the national program of vocational education . . . Objectives and standards are quite valueless if, as criteria of appraisal, they cannot be compared with data that indicate whether, or how efficiently, purposes are being achieved.

As concern to evaluate the investment good of vocational education grew during the 1960's, developments in other parts of the public sector presaged changes in both budgeting and economic evaluation in education. The *first* development was program planning and budgeting, which originated in the Department of Defense in 1961. Program planning and budgeting is an accounting technique which aligns costs with specified project objectives. Applied to public education, program planning and budgeting categorizes costs by programs and function rather than by traditional budget components such as salaries, commodities, and transportation. Thus, cost of guidance, adult basic education, athletics, custodial services, the college preparatory track, the general track, the vocational track, and other functions and subfunctions can be known. Program planning and budgeting has two important features. (1) It focuses on objectives. Costs are reported against end purposes or objectives. (2) It focuses on planning over time and shows future need for resources. Clear statements of objectives and knowledge of resource allocation requirements are obviously necessary to people who decide how much of what kinds of instructional and ancillary programs to provide children and youth.

The *second* development added analysis of benefits to analysis of costs. The results, cost-benefit and cost-effectiveness analysis, have extremely significant implications for education and for vocational and career education specifically. The most respected expert on economic evaluation of vocational education is Jacob J. Kaufman, Professor of Economics and Director of the Institute for

Research on Human Resources at Pennsylvania State University. The following sections draw heavily on his writings (1967, 1971) and his associates Hu, Lee, and Stromsdorfer (1969, 1971).

Cost-Benefit Analysis

Whereas it is relatively easy for economists to tell corporate managers what dollar returns are likely to accrue from investments in plant, equipment, and human resources, it is difficult for economists to tell agency administrators what community or societal benefits are likely to accrue from public investment projects. Cost-benefit analysis has overcome this difficulty in limited segments of federal agencies, e.g., health, urban renewal, defense, and education.

Cost-benefit analysis is a tool for presenting information to decision makers (including taxpayers and voters) in government. This tool was developed by economists to do for certain natural resource utilization projects what techniques such as operations research and profitability accounting do for economic activity in the private sector. It quantifies the input/output ratio of public projects. It is an *evaluative* technique which "relates the total value of benefits of a program to the total costs of the program" (Warmbrod, 1971, p. 364). Above all, the function of cost-benefit analysis is to aid decisions regarding optimum resource allocation. It comprises three steps (Hu, 1969). The first is identification of costs and benefits. Economists are quick to point out (a) that this is a very difficult matter, (b) that costs include foregone earnings of students, and (c) that readily available data do not permit rigorous economic analysis. Table 7-1, from Hu, et al. (1971, p. 17) describes social and private elements of costs and benefits.

The second step is to quantify benefits and costs. Quantities are usually expressed in monetary form. In many instances, quantification is impossible and in all cases, it is extremely difficult. (Primarily for this reason, economists propose cost-effectiveness analysis which is treated in the next section.)

If the economist can quantify cost and benefit information, he can calculate the ratio. It is generally assumed that if the ratio of benefits/costs is greater than one, the program — say cosmetology — is economically better than programs with lower ratios. Ratios for a number of vocational, academic, and general education programs would, of course, be of great value to decision makers in schools and colleges. If variables such as age, time, sex, marital status, and military status, which affect employability and earnings, can be controlled statistically, two or more vocational programs can be compared. Decisions to expand, modify, relocate, or

TABLE 7-1

THE DEFINITIONS AND ELEMENTS OF COSTS
AND BENEFITS OF EDUCATION

Social	Private
Costs Definition: Opportunity costs to the society at large (welfare foregone to the society as a result of expending resources on education rather than on other goods or services). Elements: 1. Schools' direct expenses incurred due to providing educational services (e.g., operation expenses and capital expenses). 2. Opportunity costs of non-school system inputs (e.g., PTA donations to school, foregone earnings of students).	**Costs** Definition: Opportunity costs to the individual (welfare foregone of the individual as a result of expending resources on education rather than on other goods or services). Elements: 1. Students' direct expenses incurred due to attending school (e.g., tuition, books, transportation). 2. Foregone earnings of students.
Benefits Definition: Welfare gained by the society at large as a result of education. Elements: 1. A greater rate of economic growth (e.g., increased productivity of associated workers). 2. Good citizenship and reduction of crime. 3. Continuation and exploration of knowledge and culture.	**Benefits** Definition: Welfare gained by the individual as a result of education. Elements: 1. Students' additional earnings due to education. 2. A broader appreciation of one's environment. 3. The acquisition of knowledge for its own sake.

SOURCE: T. Hu, M. L. Lee, and E. W. Stromsdorfer, "Economic Returns to Vocational and Comprehensive High School Graduates," *Journal of Human Resources*, 1971, p. 17.

discontinue programs can be made in light of cost-benefit ratios —
as long as the ratios are valid and reliable. Theoretically, the
optimum allocation of resources across several vocational-technical
and academic programs could be determined.

But, as has been indicated above, economists have trouble
applying cost-benefit analysis to education. The difficulty stems
from the facts (1) that benefits of education are difficult to quantify and (2) that costs such as foregone earnings are not easily
used in precise formulae.[8] The present state of the art suggests a
different kind of evaluation. Because there are (1) almost insur-
mountable difficulties in defining some of the costs and benefits
and (2) practical constraints on quantifying data, economists
recommend cost-effectiveness analysis.

Cost-Effectiveness Analysis

Because of differences in the nature of investment in education as contrasted to other public projects, Hu, et al. (1969) submit
that vocational programs "can be effectively evaluated with a
slightly modified version of cost-benefit analysis, known as cost-
effectiveness analysis" (1969, p. 31).

Unlike cost-benefit analysis, which attempts to quantify benefits of a project in money terms, cost-effectiveness analysis utilizes
output variables in nonmonetary forms to serve as indices for benefits of specific programs. The output variables are specified by
various goals of a specific program, such as numbers of persons
trained in a given skill, employment, voting behavior, or level of
proficiency on a standard test.

Research Findings. There have not been many studies of the
benefits of vocational education. The findings of two early studies
and a monumental study directed by Kaufman are contrasting.

Corazzini (1966) tried to compare the benefits of vocational
schools and "regular" high schools. Using cost-benefit analysis
techniques, he found that vocational education was expensive and
suggested that alternative delivery systems, involving on-the-job
training, be considered. Taussig (1968) found that the results of
vocational education were meager relative to social investment in
the programs and indicated that evidence to support vocational
education was lacking.

These disconcerting findings are offset by a study directed
by Kaufman. Hu *et al.* (1969) report a great many findings which
resulted from utilization of the cost-effectiveness technique to

---

[8]For a clear and precise discussion of the problems involved in defining and
quantifying costs and benefits, see Hu, et al. (1969, pp. 21-27).

compare such things as the six-year labor market performance of vocational graduates with that of noncollege-attending academic graduates. Some of the findings of this study are:

> During the first six months after graduation, vocational graduates earned $3,456 more than nonvocational graduates and were employed 4.3 months more than nonvocational graduates. By the sixth year, differences in earning between curricula were slight.
>   . . . investment in the vocational technical curriculum is an economically efficient investment . . . given this sample of graduates, funds should be shifted from the curricula in the comprehensive senior high school toward the vocational-technical curriculum in the vocational-technical high school. (1969, p. 182)
>   Over the six-year period, vocational curricula dropouts were employed 11.6 months more than nonvocational dropouts.
>   Vocational-technical dropouts in the study sample fare better than dropouts from the other four curricula. (1969, p. 202)
>   . . . with respect to the noneconomic indices of benefit and performance, curriculum is not a statistically significant variable . . . Differential voting behavior presents a mixed picture . . . there is clearly no difference with respect to aspiration level. (1969, p. 202)
>   Serious conceptual issues remain unresolved in the discussion of whether or not vocational-technical senior high schools provide net advantages . . . as lures to industry location. . . . for employees who do provide some form of training for new employers vocational technical graduates or employees who have had some vocational-technical training, benefit relative to those new employees who had no such training. (1969, p. 222)

The work which has been directed by Kaufman is corroborated by Kraft (1969) and others. Furthermore, as Warmbrod (1971, p. 370) suggests, if cost-benefit and cost-effectiveness studies of other training programs, such as MDTA programs, are considered in an overall judgment, the evidence weighs heavily that occupational education is a sound investment in human resources.

Conclusions about the future of economic evaluation of vocational education are widely held among economists and are generally optimistic. The obvious and pervasive conclusions are (1) that the effectiveness of expenditures on education will be assessed in some way and (2) that conceptual and practical considerations are far from resolved. Classification and measurement techniques must be refined. The human, social, and practical nature of education requires special analytic skills which other public enterprises do not. Data collection, maintenance and treatment systems must be different in many ways from what is currently available.

Astute authors are quick to point out that whereas there is certain to be a great deal more analysis of the investment good of vocational education, sight should not be lost of the consumptive good of vocational education. The authors recall that Rupert Evans of the University of Illinois has put an aspect of this matter clearly (and do not know whether he has put it in print). Dr. Evans has remarked that vocational education courses might be the best general education that a college preparatory student can experience. It would be interesting, indeed, to pursue this statement rigorously. Consider, for example, the shock waves education would experience if it is widely demonstrated that nonvocational students who have some exposure to vocational education do better against noneconomic objectives than do students with no vocational education experiences.

A great many more studies must be done in greater detail. The occupational education community and its public need information from evaluations of programs (1) at all levels of schooling through adult, (2) in the many kinds of secondary, post-secondary, and extra-secondary institutions, (3) by program type, such as allied health and personal service, and (4) by specific program, such as dental laboratory technology, cosmetology, and turf management, and (5) perhaps more important than all other variables, by student characteristics, e.g., ethnic, socioeconomic, age, sex, marital status, military status. This is a lot to ask. It will cost a great deal. A society which values the human condition will value scientific approaches to studying its economic and social development.

Finally, it is obvious that educators of several ilks and economists, guided by the advice and council of a wide range of employers, should work together to refine evaluative techniques. The planning and conduct of programs can only be judicious if costs and economic and other benefits are known. The skills of psychologists and sociologists should also be used to refine instruments and interpret noneconomic data.

The Future of Cost-Effectiveness Analysis. It appears that cost-effectiveness analysis is an accepted and useful tool for educators. It will undoubtedly be widely used to evaluate many kinds of professional enterprises. There are many objections to its use, but most of these are based on misconception and myths which are readily allayed by knowledge and the admonition that cost-effectiveness analysis is not a panacea. Rather, it is a method of managing information for incorporation into a larger decision making process. It can supply only parts of the data which leaders in occupational and career education must have. The future of cost-effectiveness analysis is best described in sketch form by categories of questions which are suggested by the literature and current professional events.

Delivery Systems

It is obvious to leading practitioners, government agency personnel, and legislators with special concerns for career education that a large number of alternative delivery systems must be evaluated. At this juncture no one professes to know all the alternatives, let alone all appropriate research questions. The major questions are clear.

1. For specified occupations and families of occupations, what are the relative costs and benefits of school-based, employer-based, and community-based training? What kinds of cooperative efforts will maximize individual and social effects? What specialized tasks are best learned on the job? What generalizable tasks are best learned in school? What jobs do specified kinds of industries look upon as entry points for people who will progress in the internal labor market?

2. What are the costs and effects of proprietary preparation relative to public schooling and on-the-job instruction? How should public and private resources be coupled?

3. What are the costs and effects of various kinds of secondary school delivery systems, e.g., comprehensive high schools, area vocational centers, residential schools, schools without walls (as variously defined) and specialized vocational schools?[9]

4. What are the costs and effects of remediation projects such as Manpower and Job Corps relative to potential dropout and/or delinquency identification, counseling, and preparatory programs which might be conducted by various combinations of agencies before serious social problems develop?

5. What are the costs and effects of various "sandwiches" of education and experience, i.e., various combinations, over time, of schooling, work, military service, and other experiences relative to employability and earnings in

[9]Questions of this sort require economists to examine the closely related matter of economics of scale. Occupational preparation is subject to the same principles of internal efficiency as are manufacturing enterprises. Limited evidence suggests that a secondary school of approximately 3000 students is the most efficient for vocational education purposes. Of course, matters such as population density, physical geography, area manpower needs and many other variables affect the economics of scale in a given instance. It is established that secondary schools of less than five hundred students can, at best, conduct marginally beneficial in-school occupational programs.

various and sundry endeavors? Assuming availability of continuing education experiences for citizenship and other objectives of consumptive education, how early should what kinds of people be permitted or encouraged to undertake occupational preparation? What kinds of programs will maximize benefits of military occupational experiences in the private sector? In the nonmilitary public sector?

Learner-Worker Characteristics

Even a free society must face up to conditions of the market. Student and community interests can only be served by knowledge and judicious decisions. On the one hand, students deserve to know what kinds of occupational possibilities are open (to what degree) to people with certain characteristics. This is only informative and humane. On the other hand, institutional decision makers need to serve community interests by assuring that monies are not expended unwisely, e.g., to attempt to prepare people for occupations they cannot master and/or enter. Imagine the wealth of questions which the following major questions suggest.

1. Given knowledge of costs and benefits relative to various delivery systems, what are the costs and benefits relative to learner characteristics? What are the costs and benefits of preparing people at various positions on a number of variables for specified kinds of employment? What are the effects of social class, levels of motivation and aspiration, attention span, primary and special abilities, marital status, ethnic origin, military experience, geographic history, sex, employment history, physical characteristics, including obvious handicaps, etc.?

2. Given knowledge regarding costs and benefits of delivery systems relative to learner characteristics, what are the costs and benefits of *hiring practices*? What levels of basic education are appropriate for what kinds of occupations? What should be the minimum level of schooling for what jobs? What occupational competency must be mastered before responsibility is assumed in skilled occupations? Semiprofessional occupations? Licensed occupations? What are the benefits of compensating employers who modify hiring practices to accommodate available personnel? What are the benefits of establishing enterprises primarily to employ certain kinds of peoples, e.g., disadvantaged, mentally retarded, mentally disturbed, physically handicapped?

Obviously, economic analysis of educational effort is in its infancy. Many of the above questions have not been defined and delineated any more fully than they have been here. In a very real sense, the entire world of adult employment and preparatory experience is being held up for analysis. Certainly only pieces of it can be researched at one time. There will be a great deal of cost-effectiveness research. Much that results will support earlier contentions regarding the value of formal vocational education. Some results will be shocking. On the whole, findings are sure to indicate that only the form and not the function of formalized preparation, updating, and upgrading, for employment must be questioned. In the main, economic analysis is certain to become a very significant if not the key foundation for much more viable vocational and career education schema.

Professional Manpower and Competence

There have been virtually no effectiveness studies of different kinds of staffing and professional development patterns in occupational education. Many of the questions have been debated from time-to-time, but they have not been researched widely or thoroughly.

1. What are the relative costs and effects of making occupational teachers out of other kinds of teachers or high school graduates as compared to making occupational teachers out of experienced workers in specified occupations and occupational families?
2. What are the relative costs and effects of various schemes of instructor updating, e.g., summer work, part-time work, instructor exchange, university based instruction, instructor-worker exchange?
3. What are the relative costs and effects of various components of university professional development programs, e.g., internships, classroom courses of specified kinds, correspondence and independent study, extension courses, industrial tours?
4. What are the relative costs and effects of various schemes for differentiated staffing? What kinds of paraprofessionals reduce costs and increase learning benefits?

Manpower Forecasting and Vocational Education

Surprisingly even to some old hands in vocational education, manpower forecasting has been more talked about than practiced. The need to fit vocational education practice to manpower needs was underscored in the Vocational Education Act of 1963. State plans for vocational and technical education must demonstrate (1) that local programs are adapted to current and projected manpower needs and (2) that local education agencies will cooperate with public employment offices to utilize what is known about employment trends in planning and guidance functions. There is no more appropriate place in the profession of vocational education to interject the saying, "easier said than done."

Kidder (1972) lists five questions which require forecasting:

1. How many students should be admitted to each specialty?
2. What will be the impact on vocational education programs resulting from changed patterns of participation by previously excluded groups such as Blacks, Puerto Ricans, American Indians, and women?
3. What is the appropriate design for a given curriculum?
4. What are the employers' alternative sources of supply in an occupation for which vocational education is being provided?
5. From what sources will teachers and administrators come and how will this supply change with changes in labor market conditions? (1972, pp. 3-4).

Several major difficulties make utilization of manpower forecasting a tenuous undertaking. Not the least of these is the sparcity of manpower data. The Employment Service of The United States Department of Labor is charged to publish manpower forecasts. This is done regularly in the form of the *Occupational Outlook Handbook* and the *Occupational Outlook Quarterly.* The handbook is published every two years. It forecasts moderate or sharp changes in demands for approximately seven hundred occupational fields.

The USDL also makes labor forecasts for each decade. The forecast for the 1970's is reported by Hodgson (1971). These forecasts usually take score on the previous forecast. Some of the rights and wrongs of the forecast for the 1960's are: slightly high on prediction of population growth, slightly low on prediction of large increase in women in the labor force, too large a prediction on construction workers and other occupations. Some of the major forecasts for the 1970's are: high employment levels; continuing high productivity; an increase of 15 million in the labor force, half of it accounted for by the twenty-five to thirty-four age bracket; sharp decline in growth of teenage and early twenties in the labor force; continued rise in employment of teenage Blacks; continued gains in education and level of employment for Blacks; more equitable employment of women; occupational shifts to white-collar, government, and service jobs; and other shifts, such as more jobs in construction and fewer in teaching.

Difficulties and Successes. It is generally agreed that USDL forecasts are helpful to vocational-technical education planners but that they do not go far enough. For example, it is difficult to translate demand information into training decisions when it is not known how many workers of various kinds might be readily retrained to shift into a high or moderate demand occupation. Knowing the projected increase or decrease together with the replacement or attrition rate, i.e., the number who will retire, die, and for other reasons leave an occupation, is one thing. But, knowing the number of people with similar skills who may have been raising families, serving in the armed services, or working in a related occupation and are prepared to re-enter the occupation is another thing. Furthermore, knowing the geography of demand and supply is an altogether different thing.[10]

Whereas national labor trends are of some help, local education agencies have to relate to area trends. There are many examples of judicious planning. The authors know of a number of regions in the Middlewest where state licensing agencies cooperate with hospitals and other employers to (1) project demands in occupations such as licensed practical nursing and (2) assist local education agencies in the planning and conduct of programs which will supply necessary numbers of competent people. But such instances are isolated. It is relatively simple to cooperate in such planning re licensed occupations which are performed in a limited number of establishments. Skilled occupations which are performed in a limited number of establishments are another matter (and of primary concern to vocational education).

State labor department and local employment agency projections vary a great deal. Some local employment agencies work hand-in-hand with vocational education agencies. The USDL published a *Guide to Local Occupational Information.*[11] This covers information from *ad hoc* area skill surveys. Area surveys are helpful to vocational education, but not enough surveys are done regularly. Everywhere cooperative planning, job placement, and data gathering functions must be improved. This may require new institutional forms. It is sure to require new kinds of professionals in employment agencies and vocational educational establishments—people who can conduct manpower analyses and interpret them to vocational education.

[10]This seems like an appropriate place to interject countercharges to the 1984 syndrome. Manpower forecasting is often challenged as an extremely socialist technique. The authors submit, simply that it is a set of techniques which must be projected in the interest of free and intelligent movement in the labor market. Individuals cannot move freely in a market which neither they nor vocational educators understand.

[11]For bibliographic information on this and other relevant government publications, see Kidder (1972).

An important feature of any forecasting model further complicates the difficulty of this fledgling science. Kidder (1972) calls this feature the "sociopolitical process." Consider the effects of reduced government spending or of major shifts in spending, such as from space and defense to domestic programs for poor and aged. Other sociopolitical decisions have more subtle effects. Increased or decreased efforts in occupational safety, crime prevention, consumer protection, drug traffic control and myriad other programs alter the accuracy of forecasting.

Before describing a new kind of institution, it is well to consider one other difficulty. This is the difficulty of defining an employment area or what economists call a *local labor market.* From the charge that local education agencies must relate to employment trends in the community and elsewhere, it follows that the first step is to define the local labor market which students enter or from which people enroll in continuing educational experiences. There are few local labor markets with less than fuzzy edges. The more readily defined markets would be industrialized centers which are themselves remote geographically. A town with a number of large employers, situated in mountains or a desert several hundred miles from other productive centers would obviously be *a* local labor market. Add mining, resort industries, farming, or whatever within commuter distance and the market becomes fuzzy.

Nevertheless, many local education agencies are using followup and employment agency information to define the labor market they can service with vocational programs. Aspects of such markets are ever changing. Thus, to make reasonable decisions about programs, enrollments, and the like, planners must have the best data, the best forecasts for local employment market(s) and for state and national markets moment-to-moment.

A New Institution. The writers submit that local forecasting and planning can be better done in a new institution, incorporating functions of agencies which exist in limited form in most locales. The new agency might be housed in and managed by community colleges, public technical institutes, or regional state government offices. They would serve several functions. They would do in refined and coordinated ways what state employment agencies and school and college student personnel units do already. (1) They would conduct regular manpower and skills surveys and forecasts. This would include information regarding people who are prepared to return to or move elsewhere in the job milieu. (2) They would serve the placement function for all secondary, post-secondary, and extra secondary occupational programs in the area. Private schools would be encouraged to participate on the same free basis as public schools and colleges. Depending on such variables as geography, the individual institutions might have branch offices. But the central office would coordinate vacancy information, interviews, and placement records. Drop-outs, or better, interrupters would be served the same as graduates. (3) They would conduct follow-up studies of graduates and nongraduates. This would yield information of value for program planning and redesign, enrollment increases and decreases, and the design of sundry continuing education offerings in the area. Above all, the agencies would be information gatherers, processors, and disseminators. Local agencies and individuals would make of the information what they would. Consider the advantages to guidance services, elementary career development, cooperative education, and the interface between private and public schools.

A long-lived difficulty assures the livelihood of forecasters no matter where they are employed. The work of forecasting shall never be done if for no other reason than that "it is often extremely difficult to identify jobs that are comparable across firms even in the same town and in the same industry" (Bowman, 1967, p. 75). No matter how the economy is sliced, no matter whether the forecaster uses occupations, skills, or some other categorical systems, shifts in technology and differences between establishments make projections difficult. It appears that surveys and forecasts should be done both by occupation and by skill or task. At first blush, it appears that in the case of licensure or otherwise well-defined occupations, the occupation approach would be adequate. But, skills change within well-defined occupations as much and perhaps more than they do within less well-defined job titles such as might be found in durable goods manufacturing, for example. That is, at a given moment, there may be more skill changes in occupations such as dental hygiene than in assembly jobs in appliance or furniture manufacturing. Vocational education designers must know trends in occupations and skills alike. Such forecasts, coupled with knowledge of hiring practices (including labor contract stipulations, apprenticeship practices and the like) permit better decisions on questions such as:

1. For what licensed and apprenticeable occupations should programs be designed?
2. What skills should be incorporated or excluded in these programs?
3. What kinds of programs should focus on skills rather than occupations?

4. How can such programs help people to move comfortably within a changing labor market in sales, marketing, personal service, public service, manufacturing, and repair establishments?
5. What are the continuing education needs of various segments of the manpower resource from laborer to supervisor and across all manner of establishment?

Summary of Economic Foundations

Economics and vocational education are, by nature, bedfellows. However, there has been all too little cooperative effort by these two professions. Primary and secondary decisions regarding vocational technical education programming must rely more and more heavily upon knowledge which economists can supply through cost-effectiveness analysis and labor market forecasting. The two techniques are certain to be used in concert to evaluate and refine decision-making in occupational education. Questions regarding internal manpower demands and training in occupational education are answerable through these same techniques. Finally, the very substance of career education should be shaped by parameters of the economy and by content reflective of the world of work.

Sociological Foundations

Fortunately, it is oftentimes difficult to differentiate contributions of the behavioral sciences. That is, sociologists, psychologists, and others tend to overlap in their concerns to understand individuals and groups — if not by design, at least because people and the organizations they create cannot be analyzed meaningfully in isolation by scientists who are motivated to respect the artificial boundaries of a "discipline," a variety of behavioral scientists study occupations, work, industry, and the like. Insofar as possible and reasonable the contributions of sociology, the examination of groups, and the contributions of psychology, the examination of individuals are treated separately in this and the next section of the chapter. This separation adds some clarity to the concepts which will be developed but it should be understood as a method of organizing material rather than as a division which exists in the real world.

It is likewise difficult to identify the part of sociology which contributes foundation material for vocational education. Terms such as organizational sociology, industrial sociology, occupational sociology, and the sociology of work are used rather interchangeably in the literature. The authors prefer to think of the sociology of work because this broader orientation permits second-level focus on occupations, jobs, tasks, etc. The sociology of work contributes many basic definitions to, and suggests a great many avenues of approach for vocational education. The reader is admonished to appreciate that the following material is only introductory and illustrative, not exhaustive or thorough in scope or depth.

The Meanings of Work

If vocational education is to prepare people for work roles, it follows that educators must understand work. This may seem trite, but consider the fact that most people of all ilks are unable to explain what work means to them. The meanings of work are extremely varied and complex. Especially when vocational educators are serving a special population, such as Blacks, Indians, Saudi Arabs, upper middle-class married women, or teen-age males, it is important to know (1) how work is viewed by management and employees, (2) where that population is or will be employed, and (3) what adjustments respective parties can be expected to make in the interest of human relations and productivity. The following is only a sketch of some of the meanings of work. The meanings of work have a long history of change, an exciting present, and an intriguing future.

Work Equals Sorrow. In ancient times, Western man considered work to be a curse. The Greek word for work, *ponos*, has the same roots as the Latin word for sorrow, *poena* (Tilgher, 1962). The Greeks abhorred work and believed that the gods had condemned men to drudgery out of hatred.

Work Equals Punishment and Expiation. The Hebrews looked on work negatively but added the concept that it was punishment for and a way of expiating the original sin of their forefathers. Workers (but not work) were to be respected. It was a means to a glorious end, i.e., a return to the grand conditions of harmony and light which existed in the earthly Eden before sin.

Work Equals Charity. The early Christians retained the Hebrew attitudes toward work and added a positive value to it. They added the function of charity (Tilgher, 1962). Given charity, wealth is not related to wickedness; work is a means of sharing with the needy. Christians also believed that all people should work to avoid the evils of idleness. Tilgher maintains that the early Christians were the first to give dignity, albeit spiritual and not intrinsic dignity, to work. It is interesting to trace the history of meanings of work in Catholicism but our purposes do not permit. Suffice it to quote

Tilgher once more ". . . work for its own sake, is an idea the church cannot allow, because of the same inner logic which makes it unable to allow the idea of life for life's sake" (1962, p. 17).

Work Equals Station. The Renaissance, Reformation and New World developed what has usually been called "the Protestant ethic" or "the work ethic." Evans (1971) calls this "the untaught curriculum." The work ethic begins with Luther. To the penal, educational, and charitable values of work, Luther added the concept that work is the basis of society. Each person should earn his living in the trade and in the social class where God put him. To use work and wealth for social mobility is wrong. Each to his own station. Luther also defined work as the best way of serving God. All wholesome work is necessary; worldliness and piety are not separate; work is divine; profession and vocation and calling are one; economic life (sans usury) is essential.

Work Equals Mobility and Freedom. Calvinism added a new feeling toward work. "All men, even the rich, must work, because to work is the will of God" (Tilgher, 1962, p. 18). Calvinism was a real spur to capitalism. On the one hand, it suggested that individuals should choose vocations and pursue them ardently with religious conviction. On the other hand, it suggested a worthy use of profit, i.e., reinvestment. Wealth, worldly goods, and the easy life are bad. Men must work not for these but to establish God's kingdom. Imagine the changes in man. Though living a reserved and severe existence, man becomes aggressive and progressive. Counter to Luther, the followers of Calvin believed that individuals should strive to better their vocation and social class. This would benefit both individual and society. Tilgher says "Work is thus freed from hampering ideas of caste and is endowed with the greatest possible initiative. It becomes mobile, fluid, man-made rather than man-molding, rationalized" (1962, p. 20). This change had great impact on owners, supervisors and workers. Coupled with industrialization, the work ethic reshaped the Western world.

Work Means Progress. In the United States of America these attitudes toward work were almost universally adopted. The pioneering attitude, abundant natural resources, and lack of Old World traditions and inhibitions, coupled with compatible religious and work ethics, fostered industrialization. Many circular relationships between institutions fostered the work ideal.

This was an excellent seedbed for vocational education. Some of the founding fathers and many of the early nineteenth century industrialists did more than think about inevitable linkages between industry[12] and formal (including public) vocational education. The previous chapter on historical foundations illustrated some of this development.

Until well into the twentieth century, nearly everyone extolled the values of work. Philosophers gave work a higher place than religion had given it. Public schools, being primarily Protestant-dominated, fostered the work ethic. In part, this was done by design. The values of work were illustrated in texts and in Protestant religious literature. In part, it was done unknowingly. Most teachers were Protestant and often unconsciously reflected the Protestant ethic. Government and business supported the concepts of hard work. The importance of work to individuals and society was so widely and deeply accepted that work became a religion of sorts, the work ethic. It was proper to be "lost" in one's work.

Work Means Establishment and Is Bad. There is more than scattered evidence of the failing of the work ethic. Perhaps because of certain successes and evils of advanced industrialization, many people are neo-hedonistic and/or anti-establishment. Affluence, leisure, and longevity are, at face value, great benefits and illustrative of the successes of industrialization. Sustained and highly mechanized wars pictured almost instantly in livingrooms, shrinking natural resources, and dirty air and water are illustrative of the evils of technological advance. These and other successes and failures appear to have fostered two new cults. Both of these are anti-work.

Many of the middle aged who have "made it" appear to worship physical and sexual well-being. This cult may be called *neo-hedonism.* Installment buying, vacation homes, and many forms of amusements, travel, cleanliness and ease add to their pleasure seeking with the least possible amount of work. The extreme members of this cult are perhaps exemplified by the *Playboy* syndrome — plush living and open and frank recreational sex. Especially in the older age brackets some of the symptoms are cosmetic surgery, diet fads, and health spas.

A significant number of adolescents and young adults are vocally anti-work. This second cult may be called *anti-establishment.* Perhaps because they do not know how hard-fought were industrialization, the world wars, and the depression; surely because they reflect negatively on the results of excessive adult play, e.g., divorce, alcoholism, trashy landscapes; surely because they reflect negatively on the Viet Nam war; and surely because many of them know the anomoly between what social science knows is

[12]Broad connotation.

possible and the actual human condition, many young people are anti-establishment. That is, anti whatever institutions appear to them to be party to, or condoning of, the inconsistencies between what could be done to assure equality and justice for all peoples and what are the facts of hunger, disease, oppression and other inhumane conditions. The extreme members of this cult are more inventive in their withdrawals. Drugs, communal living, demonstrations, shabby dress, nonhygiene, and a general disavowal of hangups, are only some of the forms which the anti-establishment cult takes. It is odd that whereas affluent hedonists and anti-establishment youth share the desire for least work, they fail to communicate. Perhaps the "generation gap" could be bridged by common concern about the negative values of work.

Work Can Mean the Human Condition. The future of work seems illusive to some. To the authors, it is more clear. Two features of the technological scene are at the base of a proposition which will be laid out shortly. (1) It is fact that automation has not advanced at anywhere near the rate predicted by social scientists in the fifties. Granted that (a) many people are displaced by technology, (b) employment growth is mostly in white collar and in service and sales occupations, (c) occupations generally require more brainpower and less muscle power, and (d) workweeks are shrinking. Nevertheless, (2) it is fact that (a) few computers work on durable goods production floors, (b) employment opportunities abound for skilled and semiprofessional workers, (c) leisure pursuits more than offset nonemployment by increasing employment in the leisure industries and in design, construction and operational phases of segments of the economy such as transportation-related industries and food establishments, and (d) new employment opportunities appear endless in health, environmental control and maintenance, social-psychological welfare, and safety-related occupations. Whereas some have observed that we have it made and are moving to a post-industrial state, much remains to be done.[13] Many diseases and other health problems remain to be conquered. The technologies of waste removal and several kinds of salvage are in their infancies. These and established technologies are readily taxed by expansion in emerging nations, space, and the oceans. Rather than a plateau, technology appears to be on the threshold of contributions to the human condition at altogether new magnitudes.

[13]The authors concur with those who submit that two cars for every driver, two domiciles and a mobile home for every family, and other forms of affluence are inane and indicative of advanced technology. What is challenged here are post-industrial and leisure-based descriptions of the society of the future.

If there is much to be done, if there are challenges to tax people of varying intellect, if changes in occupations and jobs and hours of work are evolutionary, if work is long to be a significant aspect of the lives of many, if work is essential to introducing the deprived to the human condition, if work is essential to maintaining and improving the human condition where it is already well-established, it follows that *work should be dignified and respected rather than degraded.*

Work Means Dignity. Fortunately, good proportions of the middle aged and the young do not belong to either of the cults described above. Many people have balanced work and leisurely experiences. Furthermore, many utilize leisure to do good works. Some of the idle rich "work" long and hard at charitable tasks. So do many of the middle aged in all socioeconomic groups. So do many of the young who are leisurely because they have yet to enter full-time employment. In sum, much of what is often called "middle America" appears to see dignity in labor and is not nearly as interested in nonproductive leisure or withdrawal as are members of the neo-hedonism or anti-establishment cults. Sociologists and vocational educators should (1) look to people who are motivated by the work ethic to better define and understand dignity of labor and (2) plan career education programs for the schools.[14]

Evans (1971) probably overestimates the omnipresence of the Protestant ethic, but he makes a cogent argument for the case that whereas society values work, the schools do not prepare many of the young for such a society. Schools should be busy about the task of developing free and intelligent understandings of the values of work to the human condition, i.e., to dignity.

This is a major undertaking, crucial to the success of a peacetime economy with goals that are not at first as compelling as

[14]There is a sizeable body of literature which deals with worker attitudes toward jobs and occupations. This and new research is part of the sociological foundation this section defines. Dignity of labor is a very important and illusive concept. It is characteristic of the world of work that even in economic recessions jobs go begging, some for want of qualified people and many for want of people who are not repulsed by unattractive jobs. How to alter unattractive jobs so that they will be dignifying is a challenging aspect of the work of industrial social scientists. A number of techniques are applicable to some but not all occupations. Among these techniques are: (a) formalizing preparation for the occupation, (b) excluding unprepared applicants, (c) devising a specialized uniform, (d) increasing benefits, (e) publicizing benefits to society, (f) expanding menial jobs to include more functions and add thought processes to the skill repertory. The matter of dignities of labor is especially important when opportunities for minority group members are primarily in occupations to which they attach little status. The present trend toward safer working conditions is sure to enhance many occupations. Career educators must work with social scientists to understand worker and job status and other aspects of dignity.

Westward expansion, defense, and standard of living, measured quantitatively. To understand the relationship of work to the quality of life, people need to understand the values which different kinds of people attach to work. Friedman and Havighurst (1962) submit that income, regulation of life-activity, identification, association, and meaningful life-experience are the meanings or functions which different people attach to their work. What combinations of these five meanings various workers attach to their jobs is a fascinating but only a small part of the sociology of work which should be known to career education planners and/or incorporated into instructional programs. How work varies from situation to situation across industry, trade, business, government, commerce, and along many other dimensions is an area of study which has only been scratched by sociologists, has foundational implications for educational programming, and has substance for the content of instruction.

Groups and the Employment Milieu

Sociologists know a great deal (and have a lot more to learn) about the interaction of various groups of people and the employability milieu. Career educators must know a great deal more than is currently known of these fascinating aspects of Americana, e.g., the interface of women and of minority groups with the world of employment. This kind of knowledge must be extended along each of its dimensions for each of many groups. A thorough discussion of what is known of these dimensions would be many times larger than this book. Only glimpses along these dimensions may be given here.

The variables of concern here are best dealt with under three headings, Table 7-2. It is important to note that this table is a first

TABLE 7-2

VARIABLES IN EMPLOYMENT

Characteristics of Groups	Employability Milieu	Impact on Groups and Individuals
Social class	Jobs, occupation, and careers	Job entrance
Ethnic origin	Mechanization	Income
Age	Vertical mobility	Other benefits
Sex	Horizontal mobility	Employability
Emotions and personalities credentials	Organized labor	Unemployability
		Socio-psychological rewards
		Retirement
		Second careers

attempt to categorize variables. This is not a description of their relationships. But, the table does facilitate the phrasing of questions which are important to general and specific career education situations. These are questions on the order of: given "X" group and "Y" conditions in the world of work, what are apt to be the characteristics of entrance possibilities and rewards, i.e., "Z"?

Try to calculate the number of variables which are depicted here. For example, there are more than fifty thousand occupations, at least six socioeconomic classes, many sizeable ethnic groups, all manner of occupational mobility patterns, and thousands of pay and fringe benefit patterns. The work of sociologists who study employment will never be done. It can and does result in judicious decision-making in career education when it focuses very intently upon small segments of a few of the variables, e.g., the advancement of Black males in building construction unions, the longevity of employment of school-leavers in durable goods manufacturing, the success potential of given kinds of veterans in specified occupational clusters, the job satisfaction of evening school technical students, cyclical and seasonal employment patterns in agri-business occupations in New England, barriers and gateways to union membership in resort and construction industries, employment barriers and gateways which result from the associate of technology degree.

The kinds of decisions which existing and new knowledge from occupational sociology can help are, in the main, new kinds of decisions for education. They are inextricably wrapped up in the problems and goals commonly subsumed under the phrase *societal need*. Consider, for example, decisions in career education for antipoverty. Riessman (1967) proposes that the *new careers* approach can be very effective. Given a reorganization and redefinition of jobs and career education, people who have experienced poverty can be moved to employment benefits and rewards in new occupations, which are necessary to the progress of poor peoples. That is, given sociological analysis, career education can effect change toward stated goals. That poor people can better help poor people is analogous to the concept that if all else fails another student can usually convey the desired instructional message.

Consider, for another example, career education decisions for programming for returning Indian or Black veterans. Like many other problems in career education, this is a *second career* problem. The question becomes: Given specific military training and experience, what kinds of skilled and semiprofessional opportunities are realizable for the population? This is the kind of question which occupational sociologists and career education people can attack. Many kinds of knowledge are needed. Some of them are: the history of minority employment in a variety of jobs at several levels in the employment region; the effects of organized labor and other forces in the employment milieu upon job entry and advancement; the expansion and development of government agencies and other employers, the characteristics of the returning veterans; *and* existing and potential counseling, training, and placement services — public and private — in the locale. These are the major kinds of information which programmers must have to design and conduct programs which serve both people and employers.

The Future of Work

The role of work in decades to come is presaged in several ways. Three such views are presented by Denis F. Johnston (1972). Dr. Johnston, senior demographic statistician of the Bureau of Labor Statistics, calls the three simplified "ideal type" societies "green," "blue," and "turquoise."

In the "green" society, the displacement of workers by automation is assumed to extend rapidly from basic activities of production and distribution into white-collar and service occupations as well. An increasing proportion of the population of working age is unable to find employment. Economic concern is no longer a significant motivation for work. The supply of goods is ensured by increasingly automated processes. And distribution of goods is ensured by a variety of social mechanisms. Desire for material affluence is gradually displaced by concern for psychic and social enrichment in nonwork. An underlying assumption here is, of course, a nearly complete separation of work and rewards.

The essential characteristics of the "blue" society are a full employment economy and progressive removal of remaining barriers to the employment of those groups whose employment has been frustrated by a variety of handicaps and discriminations. Two assumptions differentiate the "blue" and "green" societies. (1) The pace and direction of technology is changed and directed by the introduction of measures to sustain high demand for workers. (2) This demand is met by a supply of trained persons willing to work.

The "turquoise" society assumes continued progress in mechanization. It differs from "green" society in regard to life styles. Economic security and material wealth are accompanied by sustained demand for work in four areas: (1) highly trained technicians and engineers to maintain and improve the machinery of production and distribution, and ombudsmen to provide feedback to direct machinery in accord with societal needs; (2) workers in public and personal services; (3) craftsmen and artisans whose handiwork continues to be valued because it is individualistic and stylistic; and (4) employees in the "experience" industries, i.e., recreational and educational packages to appeal to the interests of increasingly affluent and educated people with greater amounts of leisure. In the "turquoise" society, work retains conventional significance. Unlike the "blue" society, it entails a major transformation in the relative importance of economic and noneconomic work.

Summary of Sociological Foundations

In a sense, career education *is* informing young and old about the variables which are depicted in Table 7-2, preparing people to move in the employability milieu, affecting variables at least as much as they are affected; and updating understandings and/or changing employability continuously. These functions cannot be served without gross amounts of sociological information. To be meaningful to decisions, such information must be current and situational. Thus, professionals with sociological training are required in career education. Career education is action sociology — and other things. The two major contributions of sociology are (1) the meaning of work along several dimensions in the world of work and (2) understandings of the interaction of characteristics of groups, conditions in the employment milieu, and benefits and potentialities which impinge on the worker.

Psychological Foundations

It is especially ambitious to undertake a succinct description of the psychological base of vocational education. On the one hand, much of psychology is as applicable to vocational as to general education. On the other hand, not a great deal of effort has been devoted to studying the special learning, motivational, and other psychological problems of vocational education. Furthermore, as was the case with economic, sociological, and technological foundations the scope of this book does not entail thorough treatment of this matter. Rather, the intent of this section is to treat briefly each of several significant footings which are supplied by psychology, indicating the nature of their support and identifying some of the more powerful sources for the reader who is motivated to pursue issues more thoroughly than can be done here.

Intelligence, Categorical Systems, and Content Organization

The material in this subsection is adapted from earlier work by Stadt (1965) which was germane to all of education. In its present form, it is more applicable to vocational education. All education is concerned in some way to improve individual intellectual facility. Everywhere in education, content should be organized in manners which expedite this end. Defining education in this way emphasizes the idea that success depends in large measure upon how well we understand intellectual development and the related problems of content organization and presentation — no matter what we would accomplish specifically. It is important to examine (1) the nature of intelligence, (2) the nature of categorical systems and (3) the major implications of these statements for the organization and presentation of subject matter content.

Intelligence is a derivative of heredity and experience which is evidenced by the facility to categorize and integrate objects and events. To explain in detail what is meant by this statement, one should begin with a discussion of the effects of hereditary and environmental variables upon the formation of intelligence. However, such an undertaking is not fitting here and has been well done elsewhere.[15] Furthermore, an understanding of the relative effects of nature and nurture upon the development of intelligence is not important to vocational educators. Pragmatically, educators must help people to make the most of what they have.

All that vocational educators need to assume about the nature-nurture controversy is that the significance of environmental variables justifies the belief that intelligence is changeable.[16] (Without this assumption, discourse about education would be meaningless.) This idea is adequately supported by contemporary psychology. Indeed, it appears that the nature side of the controversy is losing ground at an increasing rate. Reference to heredity and experience is included in the above definition because the importance of these two categories of variables has not been established and because few psychologists argue that one or the other is the sole determinant of intelligence.

Categorization. The latter part of the above definition is important to vocational education. The words "categorize and integrate objects and events" are of major importance. To categorize means to classify, to label things according to established groupings (or, as is sometimes the case, to modify old groupings or

[15]Perhaps the most thorough and insightful examination of the nature-nurture controversy is J. McV. Hunt's *Intelligence and Experience.* New York: Ronald Press, 1961. See also Donald O. Hebb, *The Organization of Behavior.* New York: John Wiley and Sons, Inc., 1949, pp. 294-296.

[16]Some biologists submit that the critical issue is not the relative importance of heredity and environment, but rather how each may be controlled to maximize intellectual development. This thinking also suggests that intelligence is changeable.

design new categories)[17], to put things in their respective pigeon-holes, so to speak. One who is adept at categorization readily identifies things as this and/or that.

As one becomes more intelligent, one's distinctions become more sophisticated. An automobile is no longer just a car. It is either American or foreign; standard, sport or compact; Oldsmobile, Chrysler . . . Mercury; etc. Put another way, one aspect of the scale of intelligence is the scale of explicitness regarding classification. As classification becomes more accurate, precise, explicit, timely — many adjectives are appropriate —, intelligence is maximized.

Integration. To integrate means to put back together again, to form into a whole. Once what one perceives has been analyzed and put into classes of things, the units must be related meaningfully (always in the mind and sometimes in the environment) with themselves and with elements from other times and places. If one can only say that given objects are chairs, he is not very intelligent.[18] The intelligent person considers chairs in their temporal and spatial relationships. A statement such as "This pedestal chair is the one Mr. Smith uses each evening while reading his newspaper in the living room" is more indicative of intelligence regarding chairs than is the simple "This is a chair."

Peculiar circumstances require the intelligent person, the person who understands the world around him, to make many kinds of connections between chairs and other objects and events. When and how it became possible to produce a chair at a price most people could afford, the history of a particular chair, how chairs will fare in light of changing interior design, whether a given design meets minimum safety and health requirements, and many other connections may concern vocational students. Put another way, a second aspect of the scale of intelligence is the scale of number and complexity of integrations. When integrations are compound and complex, intelligence is maximized.

Thus far it has been argued that level of intelligence depends upon quantity and quality of categorizations and integrations. These are the major processes of thought. It remains to be said about categorization and integration that they are not discrete, especially not in time. It is sometimes difficult to say that a given act of

[17]Creativity involves the establishment of new categories and/or integrations and can thus be classed as a specific kind of intelligence.

[18]There are situations in which the most intelligent act is to simply call a chair a chair and to think no more about it. Sophisticated action involves selective recall of previous categorizations and integrations.

The above discussion describes potential to deal with chairs in many situations, not complete acts of thought in specific situations.

thought is categorization and not integration, because categorization often involves comparison and contrast, and these are special and very useful methods of showing relationships. Even if the processes of categorization and integration are, for the most part, different in kind, they often occur very close together in time.

What happens when one encounters a "What's going on here?" picture quiz exemplifies categorization and integration in combination. Sometimes categorizations of the separate elements in the picture are possible before attempts to examine the action are made. But often the elements cannot be identified separately; i.e., they can be categorized only when they are considered in relation one to another. In most cases, categorization is not complete until integrations are made. When integration occurs, objects are no longer classed in isolation — the chair is no longer just a chair but rather a chair to be repaired or arranged with other furniture in a restaurant, etc. Put another way, classification is incomplete until spatial integrations are made with other objects and/or events.[19] Categorization may be defined as a simple beginning of description or identification, and integration may be defined as higher level, continuing description. But they are inseparable and convergent. Categorization establishes simple awareness which is concomitant with (or followed very closely by) the process of integration; together they establish higher levels of intelligibility.

The major stuff of thought, the material that is processed, what is thought about, is *objects and events.*[20] Little more need be said to explain the meaning of these two words in the above definition of intelligence. Thought deals with things in terms of times and places, with "What's going on in the world?" kinds of questions — past, present, and future; here, there, and yon. Objects are connected, related, integrated with times and places, i.e., with events and other objects. Put another way, spatial and temporal descriptions are the stuff of thought. Spatial and temporal descriptions are inseparable; they aid and abet each other. They are the essence of all description, i.e., of categorizations and integrations.

Categorical Systems

If vocational education is to facilitate development to the full potential and if intellectual development depends upon one's ability

---

[19]Neither process is ever complete. There are always more possible connections, i.e., always more to be known about objects, times and places. Higher level description is always possible, though often difficult. Fortunately, in vocational pursuits, externally supplied functions specify purposes and aid focus.

[20]Thought is a special kind of event — the kind psychologists, neurophysiologists, and others try to categorize and integrate.

to categorize and integrate objects and events, people who organize materials for vocational instruction should understand the nature of categorical systems. Understanding the processes of categorization and integration is not enough. To assure that students use these processes intelligently as they organize ideas in their minds and/or to organize instructional materials, educators must also understand the products of these processes, i.e., categorical systems themselves. Several major characteristics of categorical systems can be more fully defined.

Multiplicity. Perhaps the most important characteristic of categorical systems is their multiplicity. Objects and events that occur with reasonable frequency can be classed in many ways. For example, major aspects of productive society, important segments of the world of work, can be categorized: (1) according to size of organization from the small, local firm which employs a limited number of workers to the large corporate enterprise which employs thousands of workers and operates at the international level; (2) according to degree of mechanization from the organization which produces custom goods or services to the organization which mass produces goods on continuous, highly automated production lines and seldom redesigns products; (3) according to type of institution, e.g., financial, governmental, religious, educational, recreational; (4) according to degree of vertical integration with reference to primary, secondary, and tertiary operations; (5) according to degree of horizontal integration with reference to diversity of goods and/or services produced; (6) according to major materials, e.g., rubber, metals, plastics; (7) according to major processes, e.g., mining, data processing, communication, casting, repair; (8) according to major products, e.g., automobiles, appliances, toys, missiles. These are only a few of the ways organizations which produce goods and services may be classified. Vocational educators devise many useful systems of classifying firms and other elements of the economy.

These and many other categorical systems, singly or in combination, are useful tools of analysis for the sundry purposes vocational educators analyze productive society. There are many ways to categorize occupations. Vocational educators in a given locale will use categorical systems which fit their needs for description, instruction, recruitment and the like.

Artificiality. A second characteristic of categorical systems is artificiality. Categorical systems can be said to be artificial simply because they are man-made. It is difficult to identify dichotomies and other systems of discrete categories which occur in nature.[21] Dichotomies in particular have suffered severely at the hands of philosophers, e.g., John Dewey. Many theoreticians have submitted that one or another dualism is false. One of the most interesting attempts to win the point that categorical systems are artificial is an argument developed by Karl Pearson, prominent mathematician and early statistician. In developing formulae for the tetrachoric correlation coefficient, Pearson argues that many variables commonly thought to be dichotomous are actually continuous — even sex. He submits that if one considers the totality of sex characteristics rather than simple physiological equipment — the physiological sex boundary has been crossed by a few individuals — one finds that most people display both masculine and feminine characteristics in nearly equal quantities, i.e., that most people fall near the midpoint of the composite sex variables, and further that only a few people are so extremely masculine or feminine that they fall several standard deviations from the midpoint. In other words, one finds that sex is a normally distributed variable.

Especially since enactment of the Vocational Educational Act of 1963, vocational educators have appreciated the artificiality of older categories of occupations and have tried a large variety of approaches to organizing specific programs within regional or State programs. In many instances, older labels have been found to be meaningless and newer labels have been established. This is most evident in the many kinds of occupational clustering systems which have been tried for categorizing exploratory experiences.

Mutability. A related and very significant characteristic of categorical systems is mutability. They do not always fit actual objects and events[22]; i.e., they are changeable. When, as is often the case, we are unable to classify certain things, we are forced to establish new categorical systems or to modify existing ones. For example, when we find it difficult to classify an object as either fruit or vegetable, we establish a "half and half" kind of category. We are often forced to recognize that our categorical systems do not suit natural occurrences.[23]

For the most part, fundamental classification of the animal, vegetable, or mineral order are well-suited. However, lower-level

[21]Many of the categorical systems used by statisticians consist of mutually exclusive and exhaustive categories. However, these are usually established by statisticians to facilitate investigation.
[22]When categorical systems "fit" all objects and events, we will have exhausted the possibilities for intellectual growth, i.e., will have learned to categorize and integrate everything — an impossibility.
[23]Because of their greater variability, man-made objects and events are often more difficult to classify than are natural objects and events.

classifications nearly always require finer distinctions and are thus more difficult. If birds are feathered vertebrates, we have one thing; but if we add the characteristic "flying," we make modifications to accommodate grounded species such as ostriches. The wealth of controversy regarding classifications in biology (and many other disciplines) is evidence of the artificiality and inevitable fallability of categorical systems. When the variety of forms is great, it is difficult to establish division points which do not make classification of certain new-found or man-made forms difficult.

Classification above the animal, vegetable, mineral level is also often difficult. Some of mankind's most controversial issues are found in the discourse which deals with the nature of things. Whether ours is a world which was created by a supreme being or not, whether the universe was formed by explosive or other forces, whether the universe is an expanding one or not — these kinds of classifications and the kind which deal with the nature of things generally at the molecular and atomic levels, e.g., questions regarding the classification of particles in nuclei, are very difficult. Generally accepted, well-demonstrated categorical systems at these levels of understanding are few and very mutable.

Vocational educators modify categorical systems in several ways to serve people and manpower demands. (1) Program offerings and components are modified as clientele change. People who have more (or less) of the prerequisites to competence in specified categories cause shifts in experiences. (2) Changes in the market cause program shifts toward preparation for entry into jobs which are plentiful and away from preparation for jobs with declining potential. (3) Changes in technology, safety and sanitation regulations, product design, and the like cause adjustments of many kinds. Viable vocational education is flexing education, i.e., education managed by people who can adjust experience categories and their relationship, frequently to assure people-market matches.

Importance. Perhaps the paramount characteristic of categorical systems is their importance. Categorical systems are important insofar as their relationship to the processes of thought and the development of intelligence is as direct and universal as it was described above. Secondly, they are important insofar as they give organization or structure to, and thus facilitate understanding of, bodies of information. It is for this reason that we value the organization which Euclid gave to geometry.[24] Similarly, we value what

[24]The existence of non-Euclidian geometries supports the idea that there are multiplicities of categorical systems.

Newton and his followers did for physics, Einstein's more fundamental and larger structure (of which Newtonian physics was just a part), and organizations in which Einstein's ideas share a similar relationship.

The search for larger and more meaningful systems of categorizing what we already know about the world and the results of contemporary investigations is of primary concern to vocational educators. The search for sets of common denominators, i.e., logical categorical systems which give meaning to families of occupational tasks which are transferable to many occupations, human relations patterns which are evident in many enterprises, and skills necessary to advancement in a changing job milieu, is at the core of professional endeavor.

Content Organization

The foregoing suggests no specific procedures for organizing and presenting units of content. How to sequence elements in given classroom or laboratory experiences is too large a concern for present purposes. However, several interrelated, general implications for content organization can be drawn.

It follows from what has been said that the content of instruction cannot always be structured logically. For vocational education purposes, *content must be organized in several ways.* Experiences which have occupational orientation purposes should be organized according to sound psychological principles. Experiences which lead to entry-level competence in specified work tasks — say carburetor overhaul — must be organized in disassembly-assembly sequence, according to manufacturer's maintenance specifications. Instructional material which updates workers should probably be organized according to degree of learner understanding, seasonal job demands and other considerations which define applicability in established job settings. Compared to the structure of organized disciplines studied for their own sake, vocational education experiences must be structurable in sundry ways to assure effectiveness against stated goals.

Because schooling is somewhat alien to the working world, content organization in vocational education will depend upon pedagogical and administrative decisions and may thus differ from content as it exists in the workaday world itself. However, unless these differences can be understandable and small, the preparation of specialists will be nominally effective.

Regardless of their purposes, *students should be told why the content presented to them has been organized in a certain way* and should furthermore be shown how it could be organized in other ways for immediate or future purposes. Students should learn the structure of the large and small units of content they are learning. This procedure expedites learning of a given body of content. When the procedure is extended, when students are shown other ways the material could be organized, broadened viewpoints, extensions, and related understandings in many dimensions are facilitated.

An example may clarify what is meant here. Suppose that the desire to develop a given understanding and certain practical limitations suggest that some content from economics, psychology and sociology should be presented. If the material is organized as it is found in sociology and what is said about the same issues in economics and psychology is tacked on, so to speak, students should be shown how the material might have appeared if economics or psychology had been used as the major thread and if material from other fields had been introduced. The warp and woof of the cloth should always[25] be made meaningful, and related materials that have been excluded because of time and other practical considerations should be made known to students to assure that learning can be continuous, i.e., that future learning is not restricted because of limitations placed on present learning. If people are not fully informed about the organization of what they learn in school, they get mistaken ideas, such as the attitude that they know all there is to know. Students should know where the material they are learning comes from, how it is valued by experts in fields that study similar phenomena, how it may fare in light of contemporary developments, etc. Textbooks and teachers should not give youngsters interpretations which are over-simplified or finalized in any way. Especially, in vocational programs which assist people to progress along career ladders, students should know what may be forgotten and what will have to be learned at steps along the way. As a later subsection illustrates, students should be helped to understand what skills are transferable to new job categories.

If the *content* of education is to improve individual intellectual facility, it follows that it *should be organized and presented in ways which foster understanding of modes of thought.* If students are to understand the several ways sundry specialists examine phenomena and solve problems, they must study those methods. Put it another way, students should learn to categorize and integrate modes of investigation and thought. If students are to understand methods of investigation which are peculiar to occupations,

[25]Granted qualifications if, for example, the population is educable mentally handicapped.

it behooves educators to organize and present materials which make major problem-solving methods meaningful.

Intelligence, categorical systems, and content organization are closely related. Insofar as the content of instruction creates awareness and understanding of multiplicities of important, mutable, and artificial categorical systems, intelligence will be maximized.

Learning, Individual Differences, and Quality of Instruction

From the early years of the century, psychology and education have shared concerns regarding the mental development of individual human beings. During the past several decades, the literature of educational psychology has ballooned. But, the literature is still replete with information about how animals learn, how people learn nonsense syllables, and how college and some high school students learn academic material. There is not a sizeable and widely used literature of the psychology of learning vocational attitudes, knowledges, and skills.

Gagné is highly respected among learning theorists and contributes a good deal to the psychology of vocational education. He defines learnings as " *a change in human disposition or capability, which can be retained, and which is not simply ascribable to the process of growth*" (1965, p. 5). It follows that learning is observable in terms of what behavior can be exhibited after given experiences. The elements of any learning event are the learner with his senses, central nervous system, and muscles; the stimulus situation; and performances (1965).

From this simplified model of learning, it follows that vocational educators (and others) are on good ground with the behavioral objective approach to learning. The following sequence is good pedagogy. (1) Establish learning goals and state them in measurable terms with temporal and spatial descriptors. (2) Design and provide experiences which past practice indicates will bring learners to the desired performance standards. (3) Provide for individualized experience with full knowledge of results, personal pacing and other known learning benefactors. (4) Assess learning outcomes. (5) Adjust future situations for the learner(s) according to new objectives and readjust the given situation for new students. This analysis of schooling stresses the facts that teachers can only provide the conditions of learning, that learning is individual, that instruction should be as individualized as possible, and that conditions should be continuously redesigned, according to measured results.

Successful vocational education is a good model of learning. Stimulus situations (or lessons) are begun with clear statements of objectives in measureable behavioral terms. These are readily relatable to adult, paid work — a powerful motivation, indeed. New material is presented with media which appeal to several senses. Learning includes establishing sequences of mental and often manual tasks. These procedures are applied by individual learners. And performances are evaluated by students and instructional personnel (often including employers) so that they may be corrected and done again until the pre-established proficiency level is achieved.

One way to describe the vocational education process is to call it four-step teaching. The four steps are: (1) *prepare* the learner, (2) *present* the material, (3) enable learners to *apply* the material, and (4) *test* performance. This paradigm fits programmed instruction as well as it fits vocational instruction. Good learning is good learning. Vocational education is programmed learning. Individual pacing, individual pathways in a "library" of materials and experiences, opportunity for application, and immediate and full knowledge of results are principles of learning with broad applicability.

Gagné (1965) devotes a major portion of his book to description of eight varieties of learning. His summary (1965, pp. 57-59) is paraphrased below with implications for vocational education added.

Pending further research evidence, it seems proper to categorize human learning into eight varieties. These eight varieties are:

Type 1: Signal Learning. The individual makes a general, diffuse response to a signal. Pavlov's classical conditioned response is signal learning.

Type 2: Stimulus-Response Learning. The individual learns precise responses to discriminated stimuli. This is the kind of learning described as connectionism or as operant conditioning.

Type 3: Chaining. The learner acquires a chain of two or more stimulus-response connections.

Type 4: Verbal Association. This is learning of chains which are verbal. Conditions resemble conditions of motor chains. But, language permits human beings to select responses from a previously learned repertoire.

Type 5: Multiple Discrimination. The individual learns to make a number of different responses to as many different stimuli. These may be easy or difficult to distinguish.

Type 6: Concept Learning. The learner makes a common response to a class of stimuli which may differ a good deal in physical appearance.

Type 7: Principle Learning. Principles are chains of concepts. They control behavior so that it takes the form of the verbalized rule.

Type 8: Problem Solving. This is the kind of learning which requires thinking. Two or more previously acquired principles are combined. This results in a new capability. Gagné (1965) maintains that higher order learning, such as problem solving, requires as prerequisites each of the lower level learnings, with the possible exception of signal learning.

Individuals and Career Performance. Although vocational educators and psychologists have not collaborated on enough research into vocational learning, some generalizations can be drawn from what is known of human learning. For example, it is appropriate to infer that some people will be more proficient with peculiar varieties of learning and performance than others. This is not to say simply that some people work better with their hands than with their heads. All learning and performance above the signal learning level involves the central nervous system. Furthermore, nearly all occupations involve some problem solving, some thinking. The factors to consider are (1) the relative amount of performance at the several levels in given occupations and (2) the peculiar kind(s) of problem solving in given occupations. That is, occupations can be described in terms of required kinds of problem solving performances and in terms of how much of the total performance is at each of the levels of learning. Classifications could be made at each of the levels. For instance, gas station attendents, tourist information center workers, and department store floor walkers must have facility with people and geography at the problem-solving level and high facility for reciting a chain of verbal directions, consisting of steps in the process of getting to a destination.

Motor chains (Type 3) are important only to the first of these three occupations. Obviously, psychomotor skills are important to many jobs. But, professionals must be extremely cautious about classifying jobs as primarily psychomotor. It is proper to think of repetitive jobs, such as operating a punch press which processes plumbing supplies, as consisting primarily of Type 4 performances. But, all too often, jobs which appear to be primarily motor chains are similarly classed. Maintenance plumbing, for example, should not be so classified. This occupation requires high facility for identifying problems, considering alternative solutions, procuring materials and tools, and realizing the physical solution with minimum disruption of service, and other undesired results.

Quality of Instruction. The psychology of learning says over and over again that first learning must be as successful as possible. Bad habits are as easy to learn as good habits. It is more difficult to "unlearn" than to learn. First learning is especially important in vocational education. In a very real sense vocational education is learning problem-solving procedures. Mental and manual processes in proven and proper sequence are the essence of vocational performance. Mental and manual procedures, once established, are difficult to change. Verbal associations and manual chains are long lasting. Thus, performances which might be applied in jobs months or years later should be learned well. Problems should be presented as they are encountered in the world of work. Simulations should be as real as possible. Experiences which provide samplings of job clusters along career ladders should be realistic. Learning should be in keeping with job performance and should not be haphazard or slovenly. Performance in classrooms and laboratories will affect job performance years later. Vocational knowledges, skills, and attitudes, especially those involving much motor chaining are long lived. Vocational performance cannot be delayed for perfection after schooling. Because it is inevitable that much of education about and for occupations and careers will involve sample work tasks, these must be performed properly, lest impioper procedures hinder employment later. (Of course, learning experiences must also be carefully done for other educational purposes such as accuracy of understanding and safety.)

From the assumption that higher level teaching depends upon facility with lower level performances, it follows that schooling should entail a lot of activity in the third dimension. Vocational and practical arts educators have long extolled the values of laboratory learning. Learning theory is replete with statements regarding the effectiveness of multimedia approaches to student performance. Yet, far and away too often, schooling is verbal, with only audiovisual appeals. In all subjects, people learn better if they are involved physically. More than eyes and ears are involved in maximal learning. Because problem solving and conceptualization depend on verbal association and motor chaining as prerequisites, education should entail much more touch, smell, and taste. It has far too little see and hear and all too little kinesthetic involvement. High-quality vocational education capitalizes on this principle. Education cannot be high quality unless it involves the kinds of experience which vocational education has always entailed.

There is great need for research which will permit occupational and career information programs to apprise young and old of kinds of performances which are required in various segments of the world of work. Teachers and counselors need to make a great deal of this kind of knowledge available to people who are learning about work and about themselves, ultimately to decide on an appropriate match(es). This research will affect career development theory (Part II) and practice (Part IV).

Occupational Adaptability

Vocational educators have always assumed that students should be able to make adaptations necessary to become workers. They have also assumed that once in the labor market, workers should be able to adapt to changing requirement of jobs and of jobs along a career ladder. Recently, vocational educators have added the further assumption that workers should be able to adapt from one job to another in a job cluster or from one occupation to another not in the same cluster. Thus, occupational adaptability has become an important part of the psychological foundation of vocational education.

Sjogren's (1971) review of the state of the art in research into occupational adaptability is evidence of the sparsity of knowledge and the need to know a great deal more about successful movement within job clusters and across occupational families. Especially because of the intent of the 1963 and 1968 legislation (see Chapters 6 and 8) for vocational education, it is important to design programs which will enable people to "adapt in the dynamic world of work" Sjogren (1971, p. 4).

There is a rather extensive psychological rationale for empirical studies of occupational adaptability. Connectionists and associationists in psychology have supplied models for classifying cognitive and psychomotor behaviors. Models of affective behavior are less well developed. But, there are systems for categorizing different kinds of job performances. These have been used with some success but much more must be known about the movement of people in the labor force.

Sjogren (1971) identifies four kinds of studies which are essential to vocational education. (1) More must be known about adaptability from job to job. Case studies and normative studies must be used to develop understanding of barriers and gateways to transferability. (2) Sjogren (1971) submits that job analysis is a well-developed technique for establishing statements about the requirements of jobs. The authors are not as optimistic. Analysis techniques must be perfected and results must be continuously updated. (3) Vocational educators have to undertake a lot of development and evaluation to determine the feasibility of the job cluster approach to curriculum. A lot is known already about the commonalities of such things as mathematical skills across technical occupations. Not so much is known regarding general job skills and knowledges across jobs in the several kinds of clusters which have been established by federal and state curriculum planners. Experimentation and refinement of curricula which will assure adaptability is certain to involve vocational educators and psychologists for a long time. (4) Work adjustment studies are also important to vocational education. Work adjustment has three aspects: performing the work satisfactorily, deriving satisfaction from the work, and adapting to the neighborhood and community (Sjogren 1971). Knowledge of these three aspects of work adjustment is especially important to those who are responsible for vocational education programs which serve disadvantaged, geographically displaced, and those people from sparsely populated areas and others who will relocate to be employed. Obviously, this same kind of knowledge is important to programs about and for work which are as concerned with attitudes as they are with skill and knowledge development.

Motivation

The psychology of motivation is an essential foundation for program which would move young (and old) to economic responsibility. Indeed, the matter of moving disadvantaged and other unemployed peoples to employment has been identified as a problem in motivation. People need first to be motivated to assure a role in the world of work and second to be motivated to prepare for that role.

The literature of motivation is very large and refined. The reader who wishes thorough treatment of human motivation should begin by reading Maslow (1954) for general treatment, Gellerman (1968) for understanding the role of motivation in management and supervision, and Stadt, et al. (1973, pp. 75-95) for understanding motivation and morale in educational enterprises.

Maslow (1954, p. 80) describes a hierarchy of needs. This feature of his theory of motivation is probably the most cited feature of modern human development theory. It is useful to vocational education. In much the same way as Gagné (1965) describes the prerequisite nature of lower varieties of learning, Maslow submits that lower level needs must be satisfied before higher level needs can function to motivate learning. He lists needs from high to low: (1) physiological, (2) safety, (3) belongingness and love,

(4) importance, respect, self-esteem, and independence, and (5) information, understanding, beauty, and self-actualization.

What motivational psychologists know of needs alone tells vocational educators a great deal about programming and ancillary services. Many people are quick to jump to the conclusion that other institutions satisfy most needs and that schools need only be concerned with select ones of the fifth category of needs. In fact, schooling cannot be effective unless the degree of satisfaction of all categories of needs is assessed and serious voids are filled. Physiological needs must be satisfied through instructional and ancilliary personnel who are attuned to personality types, stress indicators, and myriad human relations techniques. Only after people have been reasonably satisfied *generally and for the moment* at the first four levels of need can they be on with the stuff of education.

The satisfaction of needs at all levels takes on special significance with vocational education populations with special needs. Disadvantaged, handicapped, displaced, and other peoples require more attention to lower level needs than do so-called normal people. Furthermore, individuals from such groups may have very peculiar definitions of what is satisfying and what is not. Vocational education cannot be effective if people (1) define satisfactory physical health as being able to avoid medical doctors and dentists (2) define satisfactory eating habits out of keeping with principles of nutrition, or (3) define satisfactory social conditions as possible only upon return to a distant home environment and as impossible in a specialized vocational education environment. Vocational education cannot be concerned with satisfying informational man alone. At least some of man's lower level needs must be satisfied moment-to-moment in the vocational education setting. Fortunately, planned classroom, laboratory, and work station experiences rather naturally satisfy a great many physiological and psychological needs. But even vocational education cannot rest on its laurels. Humans are important. As the previous section indicated, much more must be known about satisfactions which are derived from specified job clusters and jobs. Vocational education must become better and better at motivating people to prepare for places in the world of work.

Motivation depends upon degrees of novelty and success. Healthy people want to encounter novel situations which require learning and which result in success. Vocational education can, with little difficulty, assure that people move from success to success. That is, motivation theory says that the nature of vocational education, e.g., relation to the workaday world and full participation of learners, has distinct advantages. Vocational education capitalizes on principles of motivation; it involves people in realistic and satisfying situations which build on each other and "go somewhere."

Summary of Psychological Foundations: Implications for Further Research

The psychology of human development has much to contribute to the design and conduct of vocational education programs. What is known about the nature and development of intelligence, learning, motivation, and adaptability of human beings speaks loudly for the kind of experiences which vocational education provides. This knowledge is likewise essential to the conduct of vocational programs.

Much more research is needed, the better to describe occupations, to help individuals understand personal characteristics relative to kinds of employment, and to help individuals match self to occupations. The relationships (1) of personal characteristics such as sex, physical attributes, interests, aptitudes, academic achievement and (2) of employment factors such as job characteristics and occupational adaptability must be much better known as education evolves from preparation for specified jobs to preparation for success in a changing career.

BIBLIOGRAPHY

Barlow, M. L. Foundations of vocational education. *American Vocational Journal*, 1967, 42, 16-19.

Barro, S. M. An approach to developing accountability measures for public schools. *Phi Delta Kappan*, 1970, 52(4), 196-205.

Bell, D. *The reforming of general education.* New York: Columbia University Press, 1966.

Bowman, M. J. Decisions for vocational education: an economist's view. In Schafer, Carl J., and Kaufman, Jacob J., (eds.) *Vocational-technical education: a prospectus for change.* Advisory Council on Education, The Commonwealth of Massachusetts, 1967, 81-101.

Broudy, H. S., Smith, B. O., and Burnett, J. R. *Democracy and excellence in American secondary education.* Chicago: Rand McNally, 1964.

Clayton, A. S. Vital questions, minimal responses: Education vouchers. *Phi Delta Kappan*, 1970, 52 (1), 53-54.

Corazzini, A. J. *Vocational education. A study of benefits and costs: A case study of Worchester, Massachusetts.* Princeton, New Jersey: Industrial Relations Section, Princeton University, 1966.

Dewey, J. *Democracy and education.* New York: MacMillan, 1916.

Dittrick, A. R. New directions in vocational education. *National Association of Secondary School Principles Bulletin,* 1965, 49(301), 47-53.

Evans, R. N. *Foundations of vocational education.* Columbus, Ohio: Charles E. Merrill, 1971.

Friedman, E. A., and Havighurst, R. J. Work and retirement. In Nosow, Sigmund, and Form, William H., (eds.) *Man, Work and Society: A Reader in the Sociology of Occupations.* New York: Basic Books, 1962, 41-55.

Gagné, R. M. *The conditions of learning.* New York: Holt, Rinehart and Winston, 1965.

Gellerman, S. W. *Management by motivation.* New York: American Management Association, 1968.

Havinghurst, R. L. The unknown good: Education vouchers. *Phi Delta Kappan,* 1970, 52(1), 52-53.

Hebb, D. O. *The organization of behavior.* New York: John Wiley and Sons, 1949.

Hilton, A. M. *The evolving society.* New York: The Institute for Cybercultural Research, 1966.

Hodgson, J. D. Manpower patterns of the 70's. *Manpower,* 1971, 3(2), 3-6.

Hu, T., Lee, M. L., Stromsdorfer, E. W., and Kaufman, J. J. *A cost effectiveness study of vocational education: a comparison of vocational and non-vocational education in secondary schools.* University Park, Pennsylvania: Institute for Research in Human Resources, The Pennsylvania State University, March 1969.

Hu, T., Lee, M. L., and Stromsdorfer, E. W. Economic returns to vocational and comprehensive high school graduates. *Journal of Human Resources,* 1971, 6, 25-50.

Jencks, C. Giving parents money for schooling: Education vouchers. *Phi Delta Kappan,* 1970, 52(1), 49-52.

Johnston, Denis F. The future of work: three possible alternatives. *Monthly Labor Review,* 1972, 95, 3-11.

Jordon, B. Educational accountability: a crucial question. *Junior College Journal,* 1971, 41, 23-25.

Kaufman, J. J. Cost-effectiveness analysis and evaluation. In Gordon F. Law (ed.) *Contemporary concepts in vocational education.* Washington, D. C.: American Vocational Association, 1971, 386-395.

Kaufman, J. J. and Lewis, M. V. *The potential of vocational education: observations and conclusions.* University Park, Pennsylvania: Institute for Research in Human Resources, The Pennsylvania State University, May 1968.

Kaufman, J. J., Stromsdorfer, E. W., Hu, T. and Lee, M. L. *An analysis of the comparative costs and benefits of vocational versus academic education in secondary schools.* University Park, Pennsylvania: Institute for Research in Human Resources, The Pennsylvania State University, October 1967.

Kidder, D. E. *Review and synthesis of research on manpower forecasting for vocational technical education.* Columbus, Ohio: The Center for Vocational and Technical Education, The Ohio State University, February 1972.

Kraft, R. H. P. *Cost-effectiveness analysis of vocational-technical education programs.* Tallahassee, Florida: Florida State Department of Education, 1969, (VT 009 690).

Kranzberg, M. and Pursell, C. W. *Technology in western civilization,* Vol. II. New York: Oxford University Press, 1967.

Leonard, G. B. *Education and ecstasy.* New York: Delacorte Press, 1968.

Lieberman, M. An overview of accountability. *Phi Delta Kappan,* 1970, 52(4), 194-195.

Maslow, A. H. *Motivation and personality.* New York: Harper and Row, 1954.

Mays, A. B. 50 years of progress in vocational and practical arts education. *American Vocational Journal,* 1956, 31 (9), 29-38; 105.

Mumford, L. From erenow to nowhere. *New Yorker,* 1960, 36(34), 180-197.

Ogilvie, R. B. Vocational training. *Illinois Career Education Journal,* 1972, 29 (4), 12-14.

Purpel, D. E. and Belanger, M. *Curriculum and the cultural revolution.* Berkeley, California: McCutchan Publishing, 1972.

Riessman, F. The new careers concept. *American Child,* 1967, 49(1), 2-8.

Schon, D. *Technology and change.* New York: Delacorte Press, 1967.

Sjogren, D. *Review and synthesis of research on occupational adaptability.* Coulmbus, Ohio: ERIC Clearinghouse on Vocational and Technical Education, The Center for Vocational and Technical Education, The Ohio State University, 1971.

Stadt, R. W., Bittle, R. E., Kenneke, L. and Nystrom, D. C. *Managing career education programs.* New York: Prentice Hall, 1973.

Stadt, R. W. Intelligence, categorical systems, and content organization. *Educational Theory,* 1965, 25(2), 121-129.

Sussman, M. B. Sociological perspectives and vocational-technical education. In Schaefer, Carl J. and Kaufman, Jacob J. (eds.), *Vocational-technical education: a prospectus for change.* Advisory Council on Education, The Commonwealth of Massachusetts, 1967.

Taussig, M. K. An economic analysis of vocational education in the New York City high schools. *Vocational education,* supplement to, *Journal of Human Resources,* 1968, 3, 59-87.

Tilgher, A. Work through the ages. In Nosow, Sigmund, and Form, William H. (eds.) *Man, work and society: A reader in the sociology of occupations.* New York: Basic Books, 1962.

U. S. Department of Health, Education, and Welfare, Office of Education. *Education for a changing world of work.* Washington, D. C.: U. S. Government Printing Office, 1963.

Venn, G. Vocational education for all. *National Association of Secondary School Principal Bulletin,* 1967, 51(34), 32-40.

Vocational education for the 1970's: Conference discussion paper. Division of Vocational and Technical Education, USOE, March 2, 1971, (mimeographed).

Warmbrod, J. R. Economics of vocational-technical education. In Law, Gordon F. (ed.) *Contemporary concepts in vocational education.* Washington, D. C.: American Vocational Association, 1971.

————. *Review and synthesis of research on the economics of vocational-technical education.* Columbus, Ohio: The Center for Vocational and Technical Education, The Ohio State University, November, 1968.

CHAPTER 8

The Emergence
of Career Education

Introduction

This chapter describes several factors which have contributed to the emergence of career education thought and action. Insofar as possible, these are treated in chronological order. But, the reader is cautioned to appreciate that the several factors overlap in time and thus have interaction. The effects of commissions and councils, legislation, professionals and public officials on the evolution of career education as it is viewed in the United States Office of Education and elsewhere are, on the surface, easy to understand. However, the evolution is not as simple as cursory examination indicates. Several individuals and groups have affected this major shift in thinking regarding the function, the forms, and the substance of education. These people have had impact on each other and, in the authors' views, have had more to do with the shaping of sound educational thought than all who preceded them. This is not to distract from previous contributions such as the literature of educational theory, but only to argue that much progress has been made in very recent times to align educational thought and practice with societal need.

The National Manpower Council

The National Manpower Council was established under a grant from the Ford Foundation at Columbia University in 1951. Its two purposes were (1) to study important manpower problems and (2) to contribute to the development and utilization of manpower resources. The Council was a body of private citizens who shared concern for the state of manpower resources and conviction that

235

the nation's most critical resource is people. In the 1950's the concepts of manpower in a post-industrial state were espoused by only a few.

From its inception in 1951 to its termination in 1964, the council published eleven book-length reports of research studies, reports of conferences, and policy statements. These were descriptions of the state of the art and projections for the future. In many instances, they were a springboard for federal and state action and study of specified manpower problems.

A list of these publications illustrates the scope and basic wisdom of the Council's efforts.

1952 Student Deferment and National Manpower Policy

1953 A Policy for Scientific and Professional Manpower

1954 Proceedings of a Conference on the Utilization of Scientific and Professional Manpower

1954 A Policy for Skilled Manpower

1955 Improving the Work Skills of the Nation: Proceedings of a Conference on Skilled Manpower

1957 Womanpower

1958 Work in the Lives of Married Women: Proceedings of a Conference on Womanpower

1960 Education and Manpower

1964 Government and Manpower

1964 Public Policies and Manpower Resources: Proceedings of a Conference on Government and Manpower.

1965 Manpower Policies for a Democratic Society

Several of these publications dealt very directly with public school vocational education, guidance, and related matters. Three chapters in *A Policy for Skilled Manpower* (National Manpower Council, 1954) were titled "Secondary Education," "Issues in Vocational Education," and "Types of Vocational Schooling." Most of the proposals made in these chapters would be acceptable to vocational education leaders in the 1970's. Issues such as preparing for jobs vs. preparing for later training, and preparing in the secondary school vs. preparing in the community college or technical institute, were addressed as well as they can be today. The following summary of recommendations from *A Policy for Skilled Manpower* would be a very challenging statement of purpose for a state plan for vocational and technical education (1954):

> Five major long-range objectives must be pursued if we are to strengthen the nation's resources of skilled workers and technicians. These are:
>> To strengthen the contributions made by secondary education to the acquisition of skill
>> To develop a more effective program for vocational guidance

To provide more equal opportunities for all individuals to acquire skill

To improve the facilities and methods used to train skilled and technical manpower

To increase knowledge about our manpower resources.

These objectives can be achieved only through a continuing and many-sided effort sustained by an informed public opinion and requiring the cooperation of the schools, employers, labor organizations, voluntary groups, the armed services, and local, state, and Federal government.

With respect to strengthening the contributions made by secondary education to the acquisition of skill, the National Manpower Council recommends that:

1. Local and state governments encourage men and women of ability to enter and remain in the teaching profession by establishing more desirable conditions of employment, including salaries commensurate with their training and responsibilities.

2. Boards of education and school officials concentrate on achieving the key purposes of secondary education — to prepare the individual for citizenship, for a worthwhile life, and for work — by insuring that all students, excepting the small minority unable to profit from it, pursue a common program at least through the second year of high school which concentrates on teaching them to communicate effectively in writing and speech, to handle elementary mathematical operations, and to apply their knowledge to solving the problems they will encounter in life and work.

3. Boards of education and school officials insure that students are permitted 'to specialize intensively in vocational subjects only after they have completed two years of high school, and that able and interested vocational students also are provided with the opportunity to qualify for college entrance.

4. Local and state educational officials, in cooperation with special advisory committees comprising employer and labor representatives, critically reappraise existing vocational education programs in order to insure their effectiveness in the light of current changes in technology, employment standards, and on-the-job training practices; the growth of junior and community colleges and technical institutes; and the training programs of the armed services.

5. The Congress review existing Federal legislation providing grants-in-aid for vocational education purposes in order to ascertain whether the objectives, scale, and methods of allocation of funds are enabling the Federal government to make the most effective contribution to the development of the nation's resources of skilled manpower.

With respect to developing a more effective program for vocational guidance, the National Manpower Council recommends that:

1. State and local governments and boards of education recognize that the provision of essential education and vocational guidance services is a major responsibility of secondary education by increasing substantially and rapidly the funds and staff available for guidance and counseling purposes.

2. School officials use their guidance and counseling staff primarily for vocational guidance purposes and, when expanded resources of staff and funds permit, also for counseling students with personal adjustment problems.

3. School officials make vocational guidance available no later than the ninth year and have it continue throughout the high school course, and that they assign to the classroom teacher major responsibility for helping the student to make sound educational and occupational decisions.
4. School officials take the lead in their communities to assure a vigorous cooperative effort, in which industry, business, labor, government, the armed services, and civic groups participate, to provide occupational information and other types of assistance essential for effective vocational guidance.

With respect to providing more equal opportunities for all individuals to acquire skill, the National Manpower Council recommends that:
1. All employers hire and promote employees and all unions admit individuals to membership without regard to their race, creed, color, national origin, or sex.
2. Employers and unions and the Joint Apprenticeship Councils and Committees eliminate the practice, wherever it exists, of barring individuals from admission to apprenticeship programs because of their race or national origin.
3. The President insure that the heads of Federal departments and agencies eliminate discrimination based on race, creed, color, national origin, or sex wherever it remains in Federal employment; and that the full authority of the Federal government be used to prevent such discrimination in all work performed for it under contract.

With respect to improving the facilities and methods used to train skilled and technical manpower, the National Manpower Council recommends that:
1. Unions and employers and the Joint Apprenticeship Councils and Committees review regularly the content and length of training time of apprenticeship programs in order to insure their efficiency and effectiveness.
2. Employers seek to provide greater opportunities for their employees to acquire increased skills through a planned system of varied job assignments, broader training on and off the job, and increasing the competence of their supervisory staffs.
3. State and city governments undertake comprehensive surveys to determine whether existing training facilities are adequate to meet the requirements for skilled and technical manpower.
4. The Congress, by adjusting pay and other service benefits, enable the armed forces to reduce excesssive turnover and to encourage re-enlistment, so as to retain a larger core group of qualified technicians, specialists, and noncommissioned officers.
5. The Secretary of Defense direct the Secretaries of the Army, Navy, and Air Force to utilize, wherever appropriate, the facilities and personnel available in the civilian community in meeting the training requirements of the services.

With respect to increasing knowledge about our manpower resources, the National Manpower Council recommends that:
1. The universities and foundations encourage and support research to increase our knowledge about manpower resources with particular reference to the complex process of occupational choice; the types of information essential for effective vocational guidance; the role of skilled and technical manpower in economic development; the impact of governmental policies upon the supply of skilled manpower re-

sources; and the relation between how people are trained and their subsequent work performance.

2. The Secretary of Defense direct the Secretaries of the Army, Navy, and Air Force to evaluate the varied experiences of the services with training and make their new methods available for civilian use.

3. The President direct the appropriate agencies of the government to provide periodic and comprehensive appraisals of the country's available resources of skilled and technical workers and to seek improvements in the methods of estimating future manpower requirements (1954, pp. 3-7).

Part two, Secondary Education and the Development of Skill, of *Improving the Work Skills of the Nation* (National Manpower Council, 1955) introduces many concepts which vocational educators maintain and foster in the 1970's. Some of these are: The need to equip vocational laboratories with modern machines; the value of continuous vocational education; the importance of education as contrasted to training; stimulating governing bodies to support vocational education; encouraging school officials to use guidance and counseling staff primarily for vocational guidance; assuring that vocational guidance be made available no later than the ninth grade; stimulating teachers to help students make sound educational and occupational decisions; and working with public employment services and other agencies to provide occupational information.

The manpower challenges of the present and future are made clear in *Government and Manpower* (National Manpower Council, 1964):

. . . problems of manpower scarcities and surpluses promise to confront and challenge the nation. Manpower policies, both public and private, will have to respond with determination, imagination, and vigor to both sets of problems (1964, p. 73).

Effective response to the dual challenge of manpower scarcities and surpluses can be made through purposeful decisions to invest more heavily in the people of the United States in their health, their education and training, their capacities and skills (1964, p. 75).

. . . two broad and interdependent purposes: to enhance the abilities, skills, and competences of the population as a whole and to minimize both needless loss and waste of potential and actual ability . . .

These two purposes can be realized in large part through the broadening of opportunities for all individuals without regards to race, religion, ethnic origin, sex, or age — to develop their potentialities and to make use of their abilities and skills (1964, p. 76).

The last paragraph of the Council's final publication, *Manpower Policies for a Democratic Society* (1965) speaks well for vocational education.

Wise and enhanced investment in people and achievement of the ideal of equality of opportunity for all are not only the foundation stones of round manpower policies. They are also means for realizing the American Dream (1965, p. 115).

The Panel of Consultants on Vocational Education

On February 20, 1961, President John F. Kennedy addressed the Congress on American education. He spoke directly to the matter of vocational education. He was concerned with vocational education because of information which the Manpower Council. and other informed groups and individuals had brought to the attention of leaders in industry and government, manpower data from the U. S. Department of Labor, Sputnik and the race for space, the beginnings of the cry for excellence in education (see Chapter 2), and national concern for the education of all peoples.

The National Vocational Education Acts, first enacted by the Congress in 1917 and subsequently amended, have provided a program of training for industry, agriculture, and other occupational areas. The basic purpose of our vocational education effort is sound and sufficiently broad to provide a basis for meeting future needs. However, the technological changes which have occurred in all occupations call for a review and re-evaluation of these acts, with a view toward their modernization.

To that end, I am requesting the Secretary of Health, Education, and Welfare to convene an advisory body drawn from the educational profession, labor-industry, and agriculture, as well as the lay public, together with representation from the Departments of Agriculture and Labor, to be charged with the responsibility of reviewing and evaluating the current National Vocational Education Acts, and making recommendations for improving and redirecting the program (Panel . . . . 1963b, p. i).

The White House announced that the Secretary of Health, Education, and Welfare had appointed a Panel of Consultants on Vocational Education on October 5, 1961. The panel utilized various consultants and commissioned special studies in addition to the ones which were conducted by its staff. The Council also conducted a number of conferences. The full report of the Panel of Consultants was published under the title *Education for a Changing World of Work* (1963a) and four appendices (1963, b - e) which dealt with related matters such as technical education and socioeconomic background of vocational education. These documents continue to be appropriate reading for the noviciate.

According to Mobley and Barlow (1965), the Panel of Consultants on Vocational Education was to the Vocational Education Act of 1963 as the Commission on National Aid to Vocational Education was to the Smith-Hughes Act of 1917.

In their deliberations, the Consultants concluded that vocational education had not been responding to social and economic change, had been largely insensitive to labor market conditions, and had failed to serve diverse populations. The Consultants' conclusions were nearly all negative. For example: availability of vocational education varies inordinately from state to state, the typical high school program is narrow in relation to needs, only one-fifth attend schools with trade and industrial programs, there is general dissatisfaction with results in vocational guidance, research is far from adequate to information needs, vocational education is not sensitive enough to supply and demand in the labor force, opportunity for choice is greatly limited, schools do not have enough kinds of occupational programs, placement is seldom provided on an organized basis, service to the urban population and to special needs people everywhere is meager, instruction is all too often limited to single occupations, planning is short- rather than long-range. The Report identified limitations of the national program for vocational education. Several years later another advisory body summarized these in its publication, *Vocational Education: The Bridge Between Man and His Work,* Publication I:

Compared with existing and projected needs of the labor force, enrollments of in-school and out-of-school youths and adults were too small.

Service to the urban population, with an enrollment rate of 18 percent in the high schools of the large cities, was grossly insufficient.

Most schools did not provide efficient placement services, and few schools had organized programs for systematic follow-up of students after graduation or placement.

Programs for high school youths were limited in scope and availability: about one-half of the high schools offering trade and industrial education had four or fewer programs, most of which involved a narrow range of occupations; high schools failed to provide training programs for groups or families of occupations.

Research and evaluation programs were neglected.

Adequate vocational education programs for youth with special needs were lacking; in many respects, vocational education had become as selective as academic education with regard to accepting students.

In many states, youths and adults did not have significant opportunities for post secondary vocational instruction; curriculums tended to concentrate on the 'popular' technologies, particularly electronics; insufficient funds and restrictive Federal legislation inhibited the development of certain types of programs, such as office occupations.

There was a lack of initiative and imagination in exploring new occupational fields. Severe limitations existed in regard to related training for apprentices, such as adequate classrooms and appropriate instructional equipment; craftsmen used as teachers for related training and skill training of apprentices and journeymen were not afforded adequate opportunities to learn modern instructional methods.

Many school districts were too small to provide diversified curriculums or proper supervision of vocational teaching activities.

Curriculum and instructional materials had not been developed for many of the new occupations (1968 a, pp. 11-12).

Agenda for Action

The Consultants proposed an agenda for action to make people more productive and versatile and to build a stronger and better America:

IN A CHANGING WORLD OF WORK, VOCATIONAL EDUCATION MUST:

Offer training opportunities to the 21 million non-college graduates who will enter the labor market in the 1960's.

Provide training or retraining for the millions of workers whose jobs will disappear due to automation or economic change.

Meet the critical need for highly skilled craftsmen and technicians through education and training beyond the high school.

Expand vocational and technical training programs consistent with employment possibilities and national economic needs.

Make education and training opportunities equally available to all, regardless of race, sex, or place of residence.

VOCATIONAL AND TECHNICAL EDUCATION
A LOCAL-STATE-FEDERAL PARTNERSHIP

The Federal Government must continue to work with States and Local communities to develop and improve the skills of our citizens.

The Local-State-Federal partnership must increase its support of vocational or technical education for

I Youth in high school who are preparing to enter the labor market or to become homemakers.

II High school youth with academic, socioeconomic or other handicaps that prevent them from succeeding in the regular vocational education program.

III Youth and adults who have completed or left high school and are full-time students, preparing to enter the labor market.

IV Youth and adults unemployed or at work who need training or retraining to achieve employment stability.

V Services and facilities required to assure quality in all vocational and technical education programs.

OCCUPATIONAL PREPARATION IS A TASK
OF EVERY AMERICAN HIGH SCHOOL

The world of work requires many more young people well-trained to enter employment in agriculture, the skilled trades, business, industry, merchandising, service occupations, and the technical and health fields, as well as homemaking. Since our population is highly mobile, responsibility for occupational preparation must be shared by every high school, but vocational and technical education is especially important in our urban centers, which offer the most employment opportunities.

I For Youth in High School Who Are Preparing to Enter the Labor Market Or to Become Homemakers

Present vocational education programs should expand:

TRAINING FOR OFFICE OCCUPATIONS should be included among federally reimbursed vocational education programs.

PRE-EMPLOYMENT TRAINING FOR THE DISTRIBUTIVE OCCUPATIONS should be eligible for Federal support as well as the present cooperative work-school programs.

THE VOCATIONAL AGRICULTURE PROGRAM, under Federal reimbursement, should be broadened to include instruction and increased emphasis on management, finance, farm mechanization, conservation, forestry, transportation, processing, marketing the products of the farm and other similar topics.

II For High School Youth with Academic, Socioeconomic Or Other Handicaps That Prevent Them from Succeeding in the Regular Vocational Education Program:

INSTRUCTION should be highly individualized to meet the unique needs of these students for employment. Specially qualified and highly motivated teachers with occupational competence, who understand the needs of disadvantaged youth, should be employed for this purpose.

OCCUPATIONAL INFORMATION of practical significance and expert vocational counseling must be made available to these youth.

DIVERSITY AND FLEXIBILITY must characterize these programs. Experimental or pilot projects should be fully supported by Federal funds to develop effective instruction.

III For Youth and Adults Who Have Completed or Left High School and Are Full-Time Students, Preparing to Enter the Labor Market:

OUR ADVANCING TECHNOLOGY demands more skilled craftsmen and highly skilled technicians in occupations requiring scientific knowledge. Vocational and technical education must prepare many more technicians and skilled craftsmen for employment in industry, agriculture and the health fields.

THE AREA VOCATIONAL SCHOOL and the specialized vocational school in large urban centers both provide a diversity of occupational training programs to large numbers without the usual restrictive residence requirement. Many more of these schools are needed, especially for training highly skilled craftsmen and technicians.

TECHNICIAN TRAINING is also available in community or junior colleges, agricultural and technical institutes and vocational-technical schools. To expand their output — a national need of urgent importance — the Federal Government must increase its support of full-time, post-high school vocational and technical training.

IV For Youth and Adults Unemployed or at Work Who Need Training or Retraining to Achieve Employment Stability:

TRAINING COURSES MUST BE EXPANDED for the millions of workers who require updating and upgrading — life-long learning — in an era of changing materials, processes, tools, and techniques.

COURSES IN MANY MORE OCCUPATIONS, including the office and service occupations, should be made available to these workers.

MORE EQUIPMENT AND FACILITIES must be provided to extend these opportunities to many more workers, especially those living in communities where training is a critical need.

APPRENTICE AND JOURNEYMEN training opportunities should be expanded by mutual action of employers and unions.

V Services and Facilities Required to Assure Quality in All Vocational and Technical Education Programs:

TEACHER AND LEADERSHIP TRAINING PROGRAMS must be improved and enlarged. Higher educational institutions, especially land-grant colleges and State universities, should provide for the professional growth of vocational and technical teachers.

INSTRUCTIONAL MATERIALS of high quality must be available for all programs. To promote their development, instructional materials laboratories should be established in appropriate institutions. These laboratories should be financed and coordinated through the U. S. Office of Education, Division of Vocational and Technical Education.

OCCUPATIONAL INFORMATION AND GUIDANCE SERVICES must be available for all students. State and national leadership for these programs should be supported and coordinated by the U. S. Office of Education, Division of Vocational and Technical Education.

RESEARCH AND DEVELOPMENT in vocational and technical education should be encouraged, supported and coordinated at the national level. The results of this research and development should be made available on a nationwide basis.

BY 1970, EIGHTY-SEVEN MILLION

Financing Vocational and Technical Education

Support from all sources must expand as enrollments grow, as potential dropouts remain in school, and as adult training and retraining become more general. Local and State governments should increase the half billion dollars they now provide annually for operation, administration, and construction.

The Federal Government should provide at least $400 million in 1963-64 as its investment in the millions of youth and adults who can benefit immediately from vocational and technical education. (This amount would include the $55-$75 million to be expended in the current year.) Future Federal expenditures should be increased as justified by the need for trained manpower. The proposed 1963-64 Federal appropriation should include:

1963-64
School Year

I. For youth in high school who are preparing to enter the labor market or to become homemakers .... $200 million

II. For high school youth with academic, socioeconomic or other handicaps that prevent them from succeeding in the regular vocational education program .... 10 million

III. For youth and adults who have completed or left high school and are full-time students, preparing to enter the labor market .... 50 million

IV. For youth and adults unemployed or at work who need training or retraining to achieve employment stability ..... 100 million

V. For services and facilities required to assure quality in all vocational and technical education programs .... 40 million

(Panel . . . , 1963b, pp. 16-22) .

Vocational Education Act of 1963

Above all the *Panel of Consultants* was concerned to foster new legislation. Many of the Panel's recommendations were incorporated in the Vocational Education Act of 1963. For an account of the drafting of bills by USOE and the American Vocational Association, the influence of agencies such as the AVA and the NAACP, and the history of VEA 1963 from committee to passage, see Kliever (1965).

The Act is contrasted to earlier acts (see Chapter 6) in several ways. In the main, it permitted greater flexibility in local education agencies to serve occupational education needs of a wider range of peoples. The Consultants had insisted that vocational education should no longer be directed at only a few specified occupations and that it should prepare all manner of individuals and groups for work. The Act's declaration of purpose recognizes this:

. . . that persons of all ages in all communities of the state — those in high school, those who have completed or discontinued their formal education and are preparing to enter the labor market, those who have already entered the labor market but need to upgrade their skills or learn new ones, and those with special educational handicaps — will have ready access to vocational training or retraining which is of high quality, which is realistic in the light of actual or anticipated opportunities for gainful employment, and which is suited to their needs, interests, and abilities to benefit from such training (Public Law 88-210, 1963, p. 1).

In addition to maintaining, extending, and improving existing programs of vocational education and to developing new programs, the act provided for part-time employment of youth who need earnings to continue vocational education on a full-time basis.

Elimination of Restrictions

As was indicated in Chapter 6, previous legislation entailed categorical funding. This was eliminated by VEA 1963. Thus, new programs and courses could be introduced as demands changed in the labor market. In some states, priority funding levels were established for emerging occupations. Whereas Smith-Hughes and subsequent acts restricted programs to agriculture, trades and industries, and the like, VEA 1963 provided funding for business education and health occupations programs and myriad other programs initiated at local or state levels.

Groups Served

The Act defines four groups to be served: (1) persons attending secondary school, (2) persons who wish to continue vocational education beyond the secondary school and persons who have left but wish to attend vocational education programs full-time before beginning work, (3) persons already in the labor market who are employed, underemployed, or unemployed and wish to upgrade skills to hold jobs, advance in jobs, or find employment appropriate to their abilities and interests, and (4) persons (for the first time specified by law) with handicaps which have heretofore impeded education for work, e.g., academic, social, economic, physical, mental. VEA 1963 authorized programs for people of all ages and abilities but it gave special attention to those with handicaps.

Kinds of Institutions
The drafters of the Act were careful to assure authorization of programs in a variety of institutions. Some of these are: the several kinds of high schools, secondary area vocational schools, junior and/or community colleges, technical institutes, colleges, and universities. (All programs were to be lesser than baccalaureate.) The Act encouraged the building of area vocational schools and residential vocational schools. It also authorized funding for cooperative education, apprenticeship, and other programs, involving school-employer cooperation.

Advisory Councils and Committees
The Act provided for the regular counsel of several groups. (1) The National Advisory Committee, consisting of the Commissioner of Education, one member each from the Department of Agriculture, Commerce and Labor, and twelve laymen who are familiar with the vocational education needs of labor and management, and with the administration of state and local vocational education (not more than six to be educators). This body was to assure that the Commissioner would have the advice of management, labor, and the public, regarding programming for and administration of vocational education. (2) The National Advisory Council on Vocational Education[1] is appointed by the Secretary of Health, Education, and Welfare. It is charged to evaluate the national program of public vocational education, reporting at least every five years to the Secretary. (See the later section on The National Advisory Council.) (3) Each state and each local education agency was required to establish working relationships with state employment service offices to share information about the

[1]The Act took effect in 1965; the Council reviewed programs, beginning in 1966 and was required to report by January 1, 1968, at intervals of not more than five years.

labor market and students who would be seeking employment. (4) States were required to establish advisory councils consisting of people with recent experience in management and labor. (5) Local education agencies were required to establish avenues which assured regular advice and counsel from people who are knowledgeable of occupational fields.

Special Funding Requirements

VEA 1963 required that ten percent of federal funds be utilized for research. Research, experimental, pilot and developmental programs were to receive earmarked funds, amounting to ten percent of the total funds appropriated for each fiscal year. Here, as elsewhere, the emphasis was to be on youth in economically depressed locales.

The Act also required states to use three percent of their respective allotments of federal funds for ancilliary services. These include (but are not limited to) administration, teacher education, and vocational guidance and counseling.

Amendments to Smith-Hughes and George-Barden Acts

Amendments to earlier acts provided for:

1. Transfer of funds from category to category and law to law.
2. Broadening of vocational agriculture to include occupations related to agriculture and depending upon knowledge of agricultural subjects.
3. Requirement that ten percent of home economics allocations be used for training for gainful employment in occupations requiring knowledge and skills of home economics subjects.
4. Elimination of requirement that trades and industry students spend half of their school day in vocational classes.
5. Funding of full-time distributive education.
6. Permanent funding of area vocational programs.
7. Permanent funding for health occupations, including practical nursing.

Advantages and Shortcomings of VEA 1963

VEA 1963 was obviously not as prescriptive as Smith-Hughes and its amendments. The earlier laws probably had to be prescriptive to assure passage and initiation of viable programs. Long before 1963, local education agencies should have been given responsibility to initiate programs which serve both individual and employment needs. Flexibility under VEA 1963 was a decided improvement but shortcomings remained. (1) There was no provision for funding orientation programs below the level of specialization. (2) The separate administrative structure and reporting procedures which the Act required fostered continued separatism of vocational education (Draper, 1967). Although the intent was to make vocational education a full-partner, a central thread of American education, its special and add-on features remained under VEA 1963. (3) Although the Act introduced the idea of continuous assessment to facilitate programming decisions, it fostered bickering among professionals. Krebs (1966) put in print what many have vocalized, i.e., that given the elimination of categorical funding, vocational educators in one traditional service area are prone to publicly suggest elimination of programs in other areas. The Act could not have prevented this; it is perhaps a necessary evil. In any event, it can be alleviated by accountings of costs and benefits such as employment.

Shortcomings in the Profession

In some senses, VEA 1963 was more than vocational education professionals could manage. Many of the deficiencies of the profession's responses were the result of (1) the slowness and lower-than-authorized appropriations of the Congress and (2) the rapid growth in vocational education. Suddenly there was a dearth of administrators, supervisors and teachers. Many of the "old guard" did not respond as effectively as possible because they were overworked. Many could not adapt to new opportunities. As Maze (1966) points out there were a number of major adjustments for business education people. The repercussions of VEA 1963 and subsequent acts are still felt in the profession. Where they are felt, there is usually vitality and progress.

The Advisory Council on Vocational Education, 1968

As required by VEA 1963, this body conducted an assessment of the effects of the Act. The Council began work in November 1966 and transmitted its report to the Secretary of Health, Education, and Welfare on December 1, 1967. The Council focused on fiscal years 1965 and 1966, using VEA 1963 and issues identified by the Panel of Consultants on Vocational Education as bases for judgments. The summary of its recommendations is couched in the form of a legislative proposal (*Vocational Education: The Bridge Between Man and His Work, Publication II*, 1968b). The numbered statements below are quoted from this document. The comments between the numbered statements are condensed and paraphrased from longer explanations given in pages 372-390 and from a journal article authored by Martin W. Essex (1968, pp. 37-40), Chairman of the Advisory Council.

1. It is recommended that all Federal vocational education acts administered by the Office of Education be combined into one Act.
    [This would simplify administration, facilitate understanding and foster modernization.]
2. It is recommended that a Department of Education and Manpower Development be established at Cabinet level.
    [This would assure coordination of funded occupational programs.]
3. It is recommended that funds and permanent authority be provided for the Commissioner of Education to make grants or contracts to State boards and with the approval of the State board to local educational agencies and other public or nonprofit private agencies, organizations, or institutions for planning, development, and operation of exemplary and innovative programs of occupational preparation.
    [This would establish demonstration and experimental centers for widespread observation and emulation.]
4. It is recommended that funds and permanent authority be provided to develop and operate new and expanded vocational educational programs and services specifically designed for persons who have academic, social, economic, or other handicaps.
    [This is required to do before the fact what remedial programs do after the fact.]
5. It is recommended that the Act provide permanent authority for work-study and include work-study and work-experience programs in the secondary schools and those at the post-secondary levels related to vocational and technical education.
    [This recognizes the benefits of work experience and occupational education in a total educational program.]
6. It is recommended that funds and permanent authority be provided for the Commissioner to make grants to State boards of vocational education, and, with the approval of the State boards, to colleges and universities, and/or to public educational agencies to construct facilities and operate residential vocational schools.
    [The Congress never appropriated funds for this authorization of VEA 1963. (It has not as of this writing.) The intent of residential schools is to account for geographic and socioeconomic barriers to vocational education.]
7. It is recommended that the Act provide for at least 25 percent of the funds appropriated for allocation to the States to be used for the intent set forth in purpose (2), post-secondary schools, and (3), adult programs, of the Vocational Education Act of 1963.
    [This would require emphasis on post-secondary and adult programs.]
8. It is recommended that the Act include vocational homemaking education in a separate section of the act with specific funding authorization.
    [The combination of all acts would otherwise eliminate funding of homemaking.]

9. It is recommended that the Act provide for the distribution of funds to the States on bases which will encourage increased enrollment attendance and improved performance.

10. It is recommended that the Act permit matching of the Federal allotment on a statewide basis.

    [Matching by respective purpose or program works hardships. Matching by total federal allotment would encourage development of new programs and courses.]

11. It is recommended that provision be made for States to receive allotments earlier in the calendar year and expenditure of funds be authorized through the succeeding year.

12. It is recommended the Act provide that salaries and expenses needed for the administration of vocational and technical education be included in the annual appropriation for this Act.

    [This would assure funds to operate the Division of Vocational Education in the U. S. Office of Education.]

13. It is recommended that provisions for developing a State plan in the Act provide that a State shall, through its designated State board for vocational education:

    a. Submit for approval a properly executed legal contract to the Commissioner of Education on such forms and in such detail as the Commissioner deems necessary to assure compliance with the provisions of the Act and regulations;

    b. Submit a 5-year projected plan for administering and operating programs of vocational and technical education. An annual updating of the plan to reflect changes and modifications contemplated would be submitted on or before the beginning of each fiscal year.

    [This emphasizes planning, one of the weak functions identified by the Council.]

14. It is recommended that the Act recognize the need and provide support for professional and paraprofessional staff recruitment, preparation, and upgrading at all levels, including leadership, administration, teacher education, and counseling and guidance, on a State, regional, and National basis.

15. It is recommended that 25 percent of the funds appropriated for Title IV of the Higher Education Act of 1965 be set aside for post-secondary opportunity grants for students interested in entering technical and vocational programs.

16. It is recommended that funds be authorized for pilot projects to study the feasibility of reimbursement to employers for unusual costs of supervision, training, and instruction of part-time cooperative students in publicly supported education.

17. It is recommended that 10 percent of the sums appropriated for the purposes listed in section 4(a) of VEA 1963 shall be used by the Commissioner of Education for the following purposes:

    a. For grants or contracts to colleges and universities and other public or nonprofit private agencies and institutions to pay part of the costs of research and dissemination of research results in vocational and technical education;

    b. For grants or contracts approved by the operating bureau for evaluation, demonstration, and experimental programs in vocational and technical education and for dissemination of results;

    c. For grants to States for paying part of the cost of State research coordinating units, State research, evaluation, demonstration, and experimental programs in vocational and technical education and dissemination of results.

18. It is recommended that the Act provide funds and require the Office of Education to be responsible for collecting data and preparing an annual descriptive and analytical report on vocational education to be submitted to the President and Congress.
[This was to authorize employment of technical specialists, forecasters, and consultants so that data could be collected and used in planning and programming processes.]
19. It is recommended that the Act provide that each State conduct a periodic statewide review and evaluation of its vocational education program.
20. It is recommended that the Act include within the definition of vocational education "pre-vocational" and "employability skills."
[This would permit funding of short-term programs for people who enter occupations that cannot be taught in particular schools or communities. Such people need skills in seeking and applying for work and in adjusting to work.]
21. It is recommended that Section 4(a) of the Vocational Education Act of 1963 be changed to delete the word "area" and that section 8.2 be changed to read: "The term vocational education facilities refers to."[2]
22. It is recommended that the definition of "vocational education" in the act be expanded to include the responsibility of education for initial job placement and follow-up for persons who —
    a. Have completed or are about to complete a program of education;
    b. Require part-time employment to remain in school;
    c. Need work experience which is an integral part of an educational program.
[This is based on evidence of the effectiveness of placement and follow-up services in some of the few schools which offer them. The intent is to assure a full-range of services and to facilitate program evaluation.]
23. It is recommended that in order to meet current needs, authorization levels for administering and operating programs of vocational and technical education under the Act be established as follows:

    I. Grants to States and grants authorized
       by the Commissioner of Education
       (Students served — 8,000,000) $500,000,000

       A. Grants to States (50-50) .... (437,500,000
       B. Grants by Commissioner (100) .... (62,500,000

    II. Work-study program (Students served —
        575,000) (90-10) 350,000,000
    III. Exemplary and innovative programs —
        General and disadvantaged population
        (Students served — 175,000) (100) 200,000,000
    IV. Residential vocational schools (50)
        (Students served — 25,000) (90-10) 200,000,000
    V. Programs for the socially, economically
        and culturally disadvantaged
        (Students served — 175,000) (90-10) 300,000,000
    VI. Vocational homemaking (Students
        served — 2,000,000) (50-50) 15,000,000

        Total Authorization $1,565,000,000
        Note — Total students served — 10,950,000 including 2,000,000
        in home economics.

[2]This change in wording would clarify understanding of the kinds of facilities which could be funded under the Act.

24. It is recommended that there be established 2 to 4 centers for curriculum development in vocational education.
25. It is recommended that the Office of Education provide staff for the National Advisory Committee on Vocational Education and establish guidelines for helping the States make more effective use of State advisory boards.
   [These bodies were establishd by VEA 1963 but had functioned out-of-pocket and rather ineffectively. The intent was to assure that responsible people would have necessary resources to make impact on planning and evaluation of vocational programs at national and state levels.]
26. It is recommended that a learning corps be established on a pilot basis to provide improved learning experiences for economically disadvantaged youth, particularly, inner-city youth. Such corps will arrange for young people to have the opportunity of living in selected homes in rural, small city, and suburban communities and to enroll in the local schools where skill development for employment would be a part of their educational program.

These were weighty recommendations, indeed. This was a loud and clear reaffirmation of the premise that vocational education should become an essential part of education for each individual. Writing in the *National Association of Secondary School Principles Bulletin,* Grant Venn, (then Associate Commissioner for Adult and Vocational Education) concluded:

1. It becomes a responsibility of each level of education to assist the individual in making the transition from the educational system to the work world.
2. Schools and colleges must make learning *how* to work a part of their programs by actually giving work experience (Venn, 1967, p. 34).

Many school principals and others were ready to embrace vocational education when the Advisory Council made its report.

The National Committee on Secondary Education of the National Association of Secondary School Principals

Before describing the 1968 amendments to VEA 1963, it is appropriate to mention what is commonly called "the Draper Report." The National Committee on Secondary Education commissioned Professor Dale C. Draper of San Francisco State College to undertake a fact finding study. His report and the committee's conclusions are milestones in the thinking of school administrators. The conclusions, sans explanatory remarks, are cited below.

1. The public educational system has a basic obligation to aid the preparation of all young people for effectiveness in the world of work.
2. Many traditional definitions and requirements of vocational education need to be modified to allow for expansion and variation.
3. The development of vocational competence involves much more than what is generally called occupational, vocational, or technical education.

4. Vocational education must avoid too-exclusive emphasis on the building of a specific set of skills.
5. Great care should be exercised to protect and strengthen each student's general and liberal education.
6. Special efforts are necessary on behalf of a sizeable marginal group of students.
7. Schools must build a greater range of resources and capabilities into their programs to provide instruction and services needed by the range of students now in school.
8. For the achievement of these multiple objectives the comprehensive high school generally provides a good setting.
9. Planning for vocational education should be comprehensive.
10. There is a great need for research on every facet of the preparation of youth for vocational effectiveness (Draper, 1967, pp. 109-115).

Vocational Education Amendments of 1968

Many of the recommendations of the Advisory Council on Vocational Education, 1968, were enacted into law on October 16, 1968. Seldom does the Congress respond in such good measure in less than a year to the suggestions of a public or private body. It is trite to say that the time was ripe. Experience with remedial programs, beginning with Manpower Development and Training in 1962, had demonstrated that it is much less expensive to prevent push outs and dropouts than to remedy employment and learning disadvantages among young and older adults. Evans, *et al.* (1969) submit that "a small but growing number of Congressmen, social scientists, and educators were dedicated to the notion that major reforms were necessary if education was to be made relevant for the noncollege bound." The literature of education is replete with articles which evidence widespread support for the kinds of changes in programs and services which VEA 1963 had intended. For examples see Sjogren and Gutcher (1969), Ray (1968), Venn (1968), Dittrick (1965), and Haskew and Temlin (1965). It is significant that this bill became law by unanimous vote in both houses of Congress.[3]

Declaration of Purpose

The declaration of purpose of Public Law 90-576 (1968, p. 1) is a sweeping statement indeed:

Sec. 101. It is the purpose of this title to authorize Federal grants to States to assist them to maintain, extend, and improve existing programs of vocational education, to develop new programs of vocational education, and to

[3]For a sketch of the legislative process which lead to passage, see Evans, et al. (1969, pp. 76-84).

provide part-time employment for youths who need the earnings from such employment to continue their vocational training on a full-time basis, so that persons of all ages in all communities of the State — those in high school, those who have completed or discontinued their formal education and are preparing to enter the labor market, those who have already entered the labor market but need to upgrade their skills or learn new ones, those with special educational handicaps, and those in post-secondary schools — will have ready access to vocational training or retraining which is of high quality, which is realistic in the light of actual or anticipated opportunities for gainful employment, and which is suited to their needs, interests, and ability to benefit from such training.

Previous Legislation

With the exception of Smith-Hughes, all previous vocational education acts were repealed. The Smith-Hughes title was maintained for reasons of sentiment. Beginning with Fiscal Year 1970, the $7.2 million continuing Smith-Hughes appropriation is allocated according to the formula in the 1968 amendments. Thus, in effect, the amendments achieved the number one recommendation of the Council.

Funding

Statewide matching was approved. This and the elimination of categorical funding for occupational areas gave the states greater flexibility to honor the statements in the declaration of purpose concerning individual needs, interests, and abilities. Coupled with guidelines prepared by the U. S. Office of Education, the elimination of categorical funding is a mandate to move from emphasis on traditional content areas to programs for new and emerging occupations and clusters.

For the most part, the funding prescriptions of the Act deal with special populations. Fifteen percent of each state's allotment must be spent on programs for the handicapped. Handicapped "means persons who are mentally retarded, hard of hearing, deaf, speech-impaired, visually handicapped, seriously emotionally disturbed, crippled, or other health impaired . . ."

Part "F" is titled "Consumer and Homemaking Education." This provides earmarked annual appropriations for consumer and homemaking programs. The Federal share for such programs is 90 percent. Of this, one-third must be used for programs in economically depressed or high-unemployment areas for programs designed to assist consumers and improve homes and the quality of family life.

Part "G" is titled "Cooperative Vocational Education Programs." It provides annual appropriations for programs which involve learning and experience on job sites. The Act uses the terminology "cooperative work-study programs." The intent is to fund programs which move people to the kinds of jobs they experience part-time while in formal education programs.

Part "H" provides reimbursement for work-study programs for full-time vocational students. Here the intent is to assure income for vocational education students who could otherwise remain in school only with difficulty. Employment must be in the local education agency or another public agency and for no more than fifteen hours per week.

Taken together with the emphasis on the disadvantaged, parts "F," "G," and "H" do much to assure service to individuals; that is, to assure focus on people rather than specified occupations and well-established content of instruction.

Programs, Institutions, and Agencies

The Amendments authorized several of the Advisory Council's recommendations regarding programs.

1. VEA 1968 is much stronger than VEA 1963 on the matter of breadth versus depth. VEA 1968 makes possible preparation for entry into a job cluster rather than a single occupation. (This is not at the expense of programs for specific occupations — licensed allied health occupations, for example.)
2. Whereas previous legislation was concerned with job entry and primarily with programs for grade 10 to adult, VEA 1968 permits states to reimburse pretechnical and occupationally related courses. Experiences which prepare secondary students for post-secondary occupational preparations and experiences which are basic and/or related to occupational competence, e.g., mathematics for technicians, adult basic education, orientation to occupations in electronics, are reimburseable.
3. In addition to vocational education for the peoples identified in the declaration — the same groups identified in VEA 1963 — VEA 1968 provided for the use of Federal funds for guidance and counseling and for ancillary services such as teacher training, supervision, evaluation, demonstration, experimentation, and instructional materials development.
4. VEA 1968 continued the authorization of funds for the construction of area vocational school facilities.
5. The Act provided for vocational education through arrangements with private vocational training institutions in instances wherein such agencies can satisfy objectives

of the State plan at lesser cost or can provide experiences
not available in public institutions.
  6. Residential schools were authorized. The special alloca-
     tion under Part "E" Residential Vocational Education has
     not been appropriated but several residential schools have
     been funded with demonstration monies.
  7. Monies were earmarked for post-secondary vocational
     education. This was the beginning of a mutually satis-
     factory settlement of most of the differences between
     college and secondary school vocational education peo-
     ple. Without earmarked funds, post-secondary programs
     would have been difficult to launch in many states.

Special Projects

Parts "D" Exemplary Programs and Projects, "C" Research
and Training in Vocational Education, and "I" Curriculum Development in Vocational and Technical Education, provided for the many
kinds of study, demonstration, and evaluative projects which were
long needed. Monies appropriated under these titles have done
much to discover needs, propose solutions, and demonstrate success by programs, levels, and populations.

Recommendations of Advisory Council, 1968
Not Incorporated in VEA 1968

The appropriation process was not improved substantially.
The Congress guarded its yearly prerogative. Only funds not used
by one state could be allocated to another for a succeeding year.
There was no mention of professional and paraprofessional recruitment, preparation, and upgrading. The Congress tried to be more
prescriptive regarding research than the Council had suggested
and was, in the end, ambiguous and confusing. Clarification of the
term *area vocation school* was not accomplished. Finally, although
there were attempts to coordinate vocational education planning
across USOE (U. S. Office of Education), USDL (U. S. Department
of Labor), and OEO (Office of Economic Opportunity), labor market
analysts were displeased with the design and excluded this and
other services such as placement from the bill.

That these features of the Advisory Council Report were not
incorporated in the legislation does not indicate that a majority of
the Congress did not favor them, or that they are not desirable, or
that VEA 1968 is not a fully viable and monumental document. The
point is only that some legislative successes remain to be won for
vocational education.

State Plans
In keeping with the Advisory Council's suggestion, state planning became open and long range. The Act specifies procedures and guidelines for preparing, reviewing, and approving state plans. All documents dealing with policies, rules, regulations and procedures must be "reasonably available to the public." This and provisions which state plans must entail were incorporated in the Act so that interested persons, such as local education agency leaders could know how to be eligible for participation, so that programs could serve the needs of people even if similiar things had not been done before, and so that manageable proposals in local agency plans would have to be approved unless expressly prohibited.

National and State Advisory Councils

The Vocational Education Amendment of 1968 established councils as permanent, funded, and essential components of the planning and evaluation processes of vocational and technical education.

National Advisory Council
The Vocational Education Amendments of 1968 created a National Advisory Council on Vocational Education, consisting of twenty-one members appointed by the President for terms of three years and including persons who are: representative of labor and management; knowledgable in varied and sundry occupational fields; familiar with manpower problems and administration of manpower programs; knowledgable about the administration of State and local vocational education programs; experienced in education of handicapped persons; familiar with special problems and needs of disadvantaged; having special knowledge of post-secondary and adult programs; and representative of the general public.

The functions of the Council are threefold:
1. advise the Commissioner concerning the administration of, preparation of regulations for, and operation of, vocational education programs . . .
2. review the administration and operation of vocational programs . . . make recommendations . . . and make annual reports of findings and recommendations . . .
3. conduct independent evaluations of programs . . . and publish and distribute results (Public Law 90-576, 1968, p. 4).

NACVE Reports

The National Advisory Council on Vocational Education has submitted six reports. The *First Report* (1969a) deals with the relationship of vocational education and domestic problems, such as violence and unemployment. It treats three reasons for vocational education's failure to succeed with significant percentages of students. The first is the national attitude "that says vocational education is designed for somebody else's children." The second is inadequacies of vocational programs. This section of the report underscores the need for "exploration of the world of work in the elementary school." The third reason for failure is identified as inadequate funding. The Council challenges the Federal government for spending $4.00 on *remedial* manpower programs for every $1.00 spent on *preventative* vocational programs.

The *Second Report* (1969b) identifies four concerns and makes three recommendations for action. The concerns are (1) for persons flowing into the pool of unemployed, (2) for directing the disadvantaged into the mainstream of vocational and technical education as career preparation rather than into separate programs, (3) that Federal funds be used primarily to cover additional program costs, and (4) for coordination of vocational education and manpower programs. These concerns lead the council to iterate the suggestion that as much money be devoted to reducing the flow of untrained youth as to reducing the pool of unemployed. The three recommendations for action are (1) to require communities to develop coordinated plans for reducing both the flow of untrained youth and the pool of unemployed adults, (2) to focus Federal support for post-secondary institutions on vocational technical education as career preparation, and (3) to place vocational education as high in USOE as manpower is in USDL or to form a Department of Education (as had been proposed by the Advisory Council of 1968).

The *Third Report* (1970) deals with more substantive issues. It challenges American education to better equip the twenty percent of the population who are excluded from effective participation in life by inadequate educational opportunity. To achieve the mandate of equality, the Council recommends four basic steps:

1. Recognize that employment is an integral part of education.
    a. Every secondary school should be an employment agency.
    b. Part-time employment should be a part of the curriculum.

2. Give priority to programs for the disadvantaged without separating the disadvantaged from the mainstream of education.
3. Encourage parents and students to participate in the development of vocational programs.
4. Establish residential schools for those who need them most.

The *Fourth Report* (1971a) deals with five problems of financing and planning vocational and technical education and then recommends new funding and planning techniques. In short, the proposal is to divide federal assistance into a support component of 75 percent of the available funds and an incentive component of 25 percent. The latter component would be used to encourage states to authorize alternative delivery systems, more effective funding formulae for local agencies, and evaluation techniques. This Report makes good fiscal and motivational sense and is an excellent example of the kind of advice and counsel which knowledgeable citizens from many sectors of the economy can make, without disturbing the substance of professional endeavor.

In the *Fifth Report* (1971b) the Council examines forces which prevented adoption of some of the recommendations of the first four reports. In brief, the question was "Is anybody listening?" The obvious answer "No!" leads to the conclusion that advisors to educational policy makers have failed to provide leadership and insight. Leaders from prestigious universities, professional associations, educational associations, educational policy makers at state and local levels, and general education oriented bureaucrats were implored to join the commissioner to reorient education as the early reports had recommended.

The *Sixth Report* (1972) deals with counseling and guidance. Because this report is so directly related to the concern of this book and because it is extremely well written, large portions are quoted below.

Most youth understand full well that education is a key ingredient in preparation for employment. We have passed on to youth the false societal myth that a college degree is the best and surest route to occupational success — and then cautioned them that less than 20% of all occupations existing in this decade will require a college degree. Youth has been told that many more should enter vocational education, but has never been provided with the hard facts that would give them a reasoned basis for choosing to do so.

Given this "adulterated" view of the future and its prospects, coupled with the true complexity of society, is it any wonder that:

Over 750,000 youths drop out of high school each year?

Over 850,000 drop out of college each year?

Fewer than 1 in every 4 high school students is enrolled in vocational education?

Record numbers of high school graduates are enrolling in college during the very time when unemployment among college graduates is at a ten-year high?

The ratio of youth to adult unemployment has risen each year since 1960? Student unrest is a strong and pervasive force among both high school and college students?

Over 75% of all community college students are enrolled in the liberal arts transfer program while less than 25% ever attain a baccalaureate degree?

38% of all Vietnam Veterans are enrolled in vocational programs, while 60% are enrolled in 4-year college programs, in spite of the limited prospects of jobs for college graduates?

When we look beneath the surface, the status of counseling, in practice, looks *shaky* and *shabby*.[4] The following observations summarize some concerns of the Council:

Counselors and counseling are being subjected to criticism by other educators, parents, students, and industry, and there is validity in this criticism.

Some national authorities have recommended elimination of elementary school counselors.

Numerous school boards have reassigned counselors to full-time duties as "economy" measures.

The Veterans Administration has removed the "request for counseling" question from their Application for Education Benefits form.

Adult and community counseling agencies are still non-existent in most parts of the country.

Employment Service and vocational rehabilitation counselors are evaluated in terms of numbers of cases closed rather than quality of service provided.

Counselors are much more competent in guiding persons towards college attendance than towards vocational education.

Job placement and follow-up services are not now being routinely provided as an important part of counseling and guidance programs.

There is a need for the counselor-counselee ratio to be improved in the poverty pockets of the United States.

In almost no setting is the counselor-counselee ratio low enough to justify strict one-to-one counseling, but counselors still persist in their attempts to use this technique, rather than group counseling approaches, as their primary method of helping people solve their problems.

Most counselors know very little about the world of work outside of education.

Counseling and guidance services are being rejected by the hard core disadvantaged as irrelevant and ineffective.

This negative picture is intolerable. Counselors have been more victims than villains in this sorry scenario. Who else is responsible? The answers, we think, are many:

[4]Emphasis added.

School administrators who assign counselors clerical and administrative chores rather than leaving them free to do their professional work.

Parents who pressure counselors to help students gain college admittance and criticize counselors who try to help students study opportunities in vocational education.

State departments of education for not making paid work experience a requirement for counselor certification.

Counselor education institutions which make only one course in occupational guidance required in the graduate programs of counselor preparation.

The United States Congress which has called for counseling and guidance in 19 laws, but in no law now on the books has provided specific funds to support it.

The business and industry community for criticizing counselors rather than mounting forward-looking programs designed to upgrade counselor knowledge regarding the world of work.

Administrators of vocational education for being unwilling to use as much as 4% of their financial resources in support of counseling and guidance services.

The many agencies of government which employ counselors, for failing to unify requirements for counselors.

Professional guidance associations which have not effectively made their voices heard among the decision-makers in our society.

Manpower experts for not collecting and disseminating accurate data to counselors regarding earnings of graduates from occupational education programs.

Organized labor for being neglectful in establishing a closer relationship with education in general and guidance in particular.

The individual counselor whose apparent concerns for those he seeks to serve have not been great enough to cause the counselor to cry out in protest and to struggle for improvement.

We see no magical solutions, but some reforms are obvious and urgent. We urge and recommend that:

State Departments of Education require work experience outside of education for all school counselors who work with students and prospective students of vocational education.

Individuals with rich backgrounds of experience in business, industry, and labor, but with no teaching experience, be infused into the counseling system.

Counselor education institutions require at least one introductory course in Career Education and at least one practicum devoted to an on-site study of the business-industry-labor community.

Responsible decision-makers embark on an immediate major campaign designed to upgrade the vocational knowledge and career guidance skills of currently employed counselors.

Decision-makers in education make extensive provision for the training and employment of a wide variety of paraprofessional personnel to work in guidance under supervision of professionally qualified counselors.

Concerted efforts, including computerized guidance systems, be made to get more accurate, timely data to counselors regarding vocational and technical training and job opportunities.

Increased efforts be made to improve sound counseling and guidance services to members of minority populations and other disadvantaged persons.

Special efforts be made to mount and maintain effective counseling and guidance programs for handicapped persons, for adults, for correctional institution inmates, and for veterans.

Community service counseling programs be established and operated throughout the United States.

Immediate efforts be made to lower the counselor-pupil ratio in elementary, secondary, and post-secondary education institutions to a point where all who need counseling and guidance services will, in fact, receive them, while simultaneously encouraging more guidance in groups.

Job placement and follow-up services be considered major parts of counseling and guidance programs.

Career development programs be considered a major component in Career Education, both in legislation and in operating systems.

The United States Office of Education create a Bureau of Pupil Personnel Services that includes a strong and viable Counseling and Guidance Branch.

The United States Congress create categorical funding for counseling and guidance in all legislation calling for these services.

State Departments of Education and local school boards initiate actions confirming their commitment to the importance of providing sound counseling and guidance services to all individuals.

All those who now criticize counselors be charged with responsibility for making positive suggestions for their improved performance (1972, pp. 2-8).

The National Advisory Council has published other materials, including a special report on employment problems of Vietnam veterans and proceedings of meetings with state advisory councils. The pointedness and weight of council publications is obvious. Professionals hope that the Administration and Congress will respond more forcefully in the future than in the past.

The impact of the Council's efforts on professionals and laymen interested in education has been heavy and is sure to increase in the future. Because the Council is empowered and funded by law, is broadly representative, and consists of influential people, it has many indirect effects: (1) impact on state councils and boards of vocational education, (2) influence on the public and private sectors which its members represent, and (3) influence on professional development, research and other segments of professional education. The council speaks loudly and clearly for education which is at once appropriate to people, to employment, and to improvement of the quality of life.

State Advisory Councils

States participating under VEA 1968 must establish State Advisory Councils. Council members are appointed by the governor or, in states in which the State board is elected, by such board. Councils must include persons familiar with vocational needs and problems of management and labor; representative of industrial and economic development agencies; representative of community and junior colleges and other institutions of higher learning, area vocational schools and other institutions; familiar with the administration of state and local programs; familiar with programs in comprehensive secondary schools; representative of local education agencies; representative of manpower and vocational agencies; representative school systems with large concentrations of disadvantaged; having special expertise with respect to mentally handicapped persons; and representative of the general public.

The functions of state councils are threefold:

1. Advise the State board on the development of and policy matters arising in the administration of the State plan . . .
2. Evaluate vocational education programs, services and activities . . . and publish and distribute results thereof; and
3. Prepare and submit through the State board to the Commission and the National Council an annual evaluation report . . . (Public Law 90-576, 1968, p. 5).

There is already a sizeable literature concerning advisory council composition, organization, objectives, achievements and needs for improvement. Prominent in this literature are Burt (1969) and Clary (1970). Each of the fifty states has established a council. According to Clary (1970) memberships range from 12 to 35 persons. Typically, councils organize into committees which deal with evaluation, public relations, budgeting and funding, legislative liaison, and the like.

In the main, reports of state councils have followed the pattern of the National Council. Most have been brief, pointed, supportive of the ideal of career education-centered schools, negative in their observations regarding current practice, and prescriptive concerning appropriations and expansion of state programs. Some have been exhaustive treatments of respective issues. Many deal with the structure and place of vocational education in respective state hierarchies, services to disadvantaged, articulation of programs and institutions, facilities, problems in kinds of institutions and at various levels, local planning, guidance, placement and follow-up, program planning and budgeting, programs for adults, public relations, research, professional development, and others.

Advisory councils appear to be permanent and, in the main, good features of the educational scene. Their roles and functions are sure to change. Indeed, several state councils are already developing content research facility. That employers, employees, and others are represented on a body which assesses the effectiveness of state and local education agencies seems to be a healthy and democratic development. Councils formalize a very important feedback loop. In the authors' view, they should be expected to benefit substantially the career-oriented segments of the public educational milieu.

National Conference on Exemplary Programs and Projects, 1969

After passage of the VEA 1968, the United States Office of Education was concerned to maximize utilization of funds under Part D, Exemplary Programs and Projects. To that end, USOE sponsored nine regional and one national conference. Bottoms and Matheny (1969) report the contributions of these conferences in a guideline document for planning and conducting exemplary programs and projects. Eight consultants presented conference papers. Of these, two were especially significant: Herr (1969) and Gysbers (1969). Because Part II of this text deals at length with career development theory, these papers are abstracted very briefly here.

The more important of the two papers in terms of influence on the evolution of career education is Herr's. Herr submits that the concept of developmental tasks and current knowledge of career development should be used as the organizing structure of a systems approach to education — from kindergarten into higher education. He advocates a system of education which, in addition to developing marketable skills for all students, would develop directly and systematically students' attitudes and knowledge about themselves, about occupational and educational alternatives, and about decision-making abilities which relate to vocational identity and choice.

Herr abstracts the major theories of career development and gives broad prescriptions for centering career development in the curricula. Above all he argues for appropriate experiences at each level of education. For example: "Because of the importance of early childhood experiences in the family, the school and the community, intervention in career development needs to begin during the first decade of life" (Herr, 1969, p. 8). Throughout, he emphasizes the significance of characteristics of people — the very thing that was causing vocational education leaders to refocus thinking and programming. For example: "In sum . . . the emphases attendant to guidance and the aspects of education which have vocational implications have shifted from a Parsonian model of matching men and job to a model more committed to the clarification of those aspects of self — e.g., interests, capacities, values — which need development for a lifelong process of planning and decision-making" (Herr, 1969, p. 8). Herr is astute to tie his ideas to the behavioral objectives approach which was coming into vogue and to the structure and terminology of vocational education at the specialization levels. He is careful to underscore his theme.

One of the operational goals critical to implementing the Exemplary Programs and Project Section of the Vocational Education Act relates to the need to design behavioral descriptions which would encompass the characteristics of career development, placing these at appropriate developmental levels, and wedding them to educational strategies which will facilitate them (Herr, 1969, p. 18).

No one has put more succinctly the marriage of career development theory, the behavioral objective approach to educational programming and the reorientation of vocational education.[5]

Gysbers' paper (1969) compliments Herr's. He recommends that attempts to facilitate career development be attuned to the characteristics of students at various educational levels. Like Herr and many others before, he advocates turning education around. "The emphasis of career exploration programs at the elementary and junior high levels should be on the individual development of all individuals rather than on the early selection of some to fill certain occupations. The objectives of career exploration activities should be based on and directed toward filling the needs of individuals rather than on meeting the demands of the labor market" (Gysbers, 1969, p. 6). Like Herr's, Gysbers' paper gives broad prescriptions for respective grade levels and abstracts some of the ongoing projects which support the idea that educational efforts which are in keeping with career development theory can, at once, satisfy the goals of vocational education, the purposes of general education, manpower demands, the needs of disadvantaged and other peoples, and economic and societal needs. This may appear to be a sweeping and bold statement. It is, and justly so.

Suddenly for many (but with less shock to those who had been observant for several years) it became clear that VEA 1968 made possible new and vital approaches to educational programming. USOE admits that these and other papers which were used as bases for this conference had great influence on the Exemplary Programs and Services Branch, Division of Vocational and Technical Education. The thinking of many people in USOE and else-

[5]Yet Herr's paper (and Gysbers') is not widely known.

where regarding the form and substance of a reoriented system of education, incorporating elements of general and vocational education and focusing upon people rather than upon (but without losing sight of) jobs they would hold after schooling, is directly traceable to the Herr and Gysbers papers. Propaganda from USOE regarding career education is very much like Herr's paper. It is unfortunate that the seduction was not as thorough elsewhere in vocational education and education at large as it was in the Exemplary Programs and Services Branch. Widespread reading of Herr and subsequent materials would have alleviated much current misunderstanding in the profession.

Conference Recommendations

The summary recommendations of the conference reported by Bottoms and Matheny (1969) are literally loaded statements. They are well-founded and can be taken as the theme of education turned around.

In order to develop exemplary programs or projects designed to broaden or improve vocational education curriculums, the following recommendations are offered.

1. Vocational education should be structured as a developmental and sequential process from elementary through post-secondary and adult vocational programs.
2. The curriculum should be so structured that students can more freely move between academic and vocational education without penalty. Criteria for movement should include the student's needs, readiness, interests, and motivation. This practice would prevent the rigid separation of students into college- and noncollege-bound tracks and makes vocational experiences available to all students.
3. Vocational education should be viewed as the responsibility of the total school.
4. In addition to its emphasis on job skills, vocational education should emphasize other elements of employability essential to job entry and career mobility.
5. Vocational experiences should be incorporated in the teaching of basic academic skills.
6. Each student at the point of separation from school should be provided with a salable skill as well as basic educational preparation.

In order to design exemplary programs and projects to familiarize elementary and secondary school students with a broad range of occupations and to prepare them for a career in these occupations, the following recommendations are offered.

1. Career development efforts should begin at the elementary school level. Significantly more attention must be concentrated at the elementary school level upon attitude development, self-awareness, and decision making.
2. Career development opportunities must be sufficiently varied so as to be suited to the interests and abilities of all students. Experiences that

involve a wide range of students provide an opportunity for students to learn from one another.

3. Career exploration programs should not be seen as a mining operation strictly concerned with the selection of certain talents for the purpose of meeting particular manpower needs, but rather as a farming approach in which all individuals are provided with opportunities to grow and develop.

4. Career information should be expressed in terms of the questions which students are asking themselves and in a format which corresponds to the language system, readiness level, and stage of development of the students to which it is directed. Career information should include not only objective factors but also the social and psychological factors associated with a particular work setting.

5. Career development experiences should be sequentially organized from the elementary grades through high school.

6. Educational technology should be employed to simulate certain career development experiences otherwise difficult to provide; e.g., the use of life career games in which students plan the life of a fictitious student and receive feedback on the possible consequence of decisions made and computer-based information retrieval systems.

In order to develop exemplary programs or projects for intensive occupational guidance or counseling during the last years of school and for special job placement, the following recommendations are offered.

1. Schools should assume responsibility for all pupils until they successfully make the transition from school to work, regardless of the point at which they chose to leave school. Consequently, job placement should be given as much attention as is currently given to college placement.

2. The success of school programs should be measured by the extent to which they prepare students for their next step.

3. Counselors should utilize simulated or direct work experience in assisting students to gain greater self-understanding. To accomplish this, a simulated or direct work experience should be coupled with the process techniques of counseling.

4. Counselors should develop strategies for maximizing the use of school and community resources in promoting the career development of students.

5. Counselors should know as much about job opportunities as they do about colleges in order to serve the needs of noncollege-bound youth.

6. Profiles of major industries and businesses should be developed for terminal students in the same way that college catalogs are now available to the college-bound youth.

7. Vocational guidance must not be separated from the overall guidance function: all counselors should become proficient in the vocational aspects of guidance.

In order to develop exemplary programs or projects which will provide work experiences for students during the school year or during the summer, the following recommendations are offered.

1. Schools should more fully cooperate with business and industry in the development of basic habits of industry on the part of students.

2. Schools should be operated on a full-year basis in order to take advantage of the resulting flexibility in designing work experience programs that best fit the needs of all students.

3. Schools should accept the responsibility for placing and supervising youth in part-time summer jobs for which they receive credit.
4. Schools should allow students to work full-time for a period of weeks and alternate the work schedule with an equal number of weeks in full-time school attendance (1969, pp. 23-26).

Career Education

Credit for coining the term "career education" and initiating the career education movement is often given to Sidney P. Marland, Commissioner of Education. He deserves a lot of credit. But almost a year before the *Career Education Now* speech, Commissioner Marland's (1971) remarks were presaged by Assistant Secretary for Education and U. S. Commissioner of Education James E. Allen (1970).

Allen's speech before the National Association of Secondary School Principals is a little known milestone in the evolution of career education in America. Allen underscored the idea that somnolence regarding education was fast ending because of need, readiness among educators, and emphasis on accountability. He spoke of "a recasting of the entire educational system . . ." He emphasized programming flexibility; serving individuals; and satisfying societal needs, such as environmental maintenance and poverty eradication. The bulk of the speech consisted of a very cogent argument for vocational education, heavily supported by statements from the first two reports of the National Advisory Council on Vocational Education, and evidencing knowledge of career development and its relationship to manpower demands, problems of alienation, the human condition, and school problems. Allen may well have coined the term "career education."

It is the renewed awareness of the university of the basic human and social need for competence that is generating not only increased emphasis today on *career education*[6] but a whole new concept of its character and its place in the total educational enterprise (1970, p. 5).

His speech is evidence of the impact which NACVE reports have on educational leaders and of high-level commitment to career and vocational education centered with all of education on the career development theme. However, the Allen speech was not nearly as forceful or as clear regarding career education as commentary to follow.

As Commissioner of Education, Sidney P. Marland, Jr. has given great impetus to career education. Speaking to the same pro-

[6]Emphasis added.

fessional group which Allen had addressed the year before, Marland
(1971) spoke directly to the point of career education. He opened
with a condemnation of administrators who, like himself, had
relegated vocational-technical education to second class status.
Then he launched an attack on general education, suggesting that
schools be rid of it and arguing that *useful* knowledge is superior
to general knowledge. Then he proposed "that a universal goal of
American education, *starting now*, be this: that every young person
completing our school program at grade twelve be ready to enter
higher education or to enter useful and rewarding employment."
Marland spoke of lifelong learning, humaneness, occupational
exploration, new leadership to States, true and complete reform of
the high school, emphasis on new vocational fields, cooperation
with business and labor, leadership development, and state plan
innovation.

Marland's remarks were iterated in numerous speeches and
articles, among them an address before the State Directors of Vocational Education (1971b). Again, he emphasized the need to affect
80 percent of young people in fundamental fashion via career education, the importance of continuity, and the shortcomings of the
general track. He made very clear the need to focus on two exits,
continuing education or employment, and nothing else. In much
better fashion than in the earlier speech, he linked youth and
female, and disadvantaged unemployment to education. The theme
of his remarks appears to be: "It is flatly necessary to begin to
construct a sound, systematized relationship between education
and work, a system which will make it standard practice to teach
every student about occupations and the economic enterprise, a
system that will markedly increase career options open to each
individual and enable us to do a better job than we have been
doing of meeting the manpower needs of the country." Then he
outlined three model career education programs which had been
developed by Dr. Edwin Rumpf and others of the Division of
Vocational and Technical Education and by Harry Silberman and
others of the National Center for Educational Research and Development. These models, school-based, employer-based, and
home/community-based are treated in a subsequent section.

The thinking of USOE regarding career education is exemplified by Robert M. Worthington, Associate Commissioner for Adult,
Vocational and Technical Education. He has incorporated career
education principles in many presentations. Among these is a
1972 paper presented in Tokyo that contains the basic concepts
of this important point of view.

Career Education is a *revolutionary*[7] approach to American education based on the idea that all educational experiences, curriculum, instruction, and counseling should be geared to preparing each individual for a life of economic independence, personal fulfillment, and an appreciation for the dignity of work. Its main purpose is to prepare all students for successful and rewarding lives by improving their basis for occupational choice, by facilitating their acquisitions of occupational skills, by enhancing their educational achievements, by making education more meaningful and relevant to their aspirations, and by increasing the real choices they have among the many different occupations and training avenues open to them. While it is anticipated that Career Education would increase the opportunities available to the disadvantaged, it is not explicitly designed to involve any particular group or segment of society. It is directed at changing the whole educational system to benefit the entire population.

Career Education recognizes the critical decision points when students must be prepared and equipped to decide whether to pursue a job or further education or some combination of both work and formal study. It is a lifelong systematic way of acquainting students with the world of work in their elementary and junior high school years and preparing them in high school and in college to enter into and advance in a career field of their own choosing. For adults it is a way to re-enter formal as well as informal programs of education at any time to upgrade their skills in their established career field or to enter a new career field. It is similar to vocational education, but there is a fundamental distinction. For while vocational education is targeted at producing specific job skills at the high school level and up to but not including the baccalaureate level, Career Education embraces all occupations and professions and can include individuals of all ages whether in or out of school (1972, pp. 3-4).

Early in 1971, the Division of Vocational and Technical Education prepared a conference discussion paper, *Vocational Education for the 1970's* (Rumpf, 1971). This document is a challenge to vocational educators, guidance and other ancillary personnel, and classroom teachers of all ilks. Starting with the assumption that vocational education should be lifelong career development for each person, this paper presents six objectives of career education:

1. To provide every young person who completes high school with a salable skill and assured entry to further education or training.
2. To provide those students who leave high school before graduating with a salable skill and re-entry opportunities into education or training.
3. To provide career orientation starting in kindergarten and guidance, counseling, and placement services to all students at all levels of education to assist them in career choices in making job changes.
4. To assure every person the opportunity to obtain career-related skills throughout life, within or outside of schools, with employers assuming a greater role.
5. To emphasize and enlarge post-secondary and adult vocational and technical education programs, including pre-technical programs for the academically handicapped, so that a much higher proportion of specific skills training will occur at the post-secondary level.

[7]Emphasis added.

6. To assure that every individual is prepared by education, regardless of curriculum, to lead a productive and self-fulfilling life (1971, pp. 2-3).

. . .

[Then the document presents five platform goals.]
1. Vocational education must become part of the educational experience of all people.
2. Vocational education must be more responsible to the Nation's present and future employment needs.
3. Private schools and private industry must be an integral part of career education.
4. Vocational education is the principle element of a career education program, K - adulthood.
5. Leadership development to effect career education is essential (1971, pp. 3-5).

. . .

[Then the document describes twelve characteristics of the career education model.]
1. Career education will replace general education.
2. Vocational education will give priority to special target groups.
3. Career education will begin in the elementary grades and continue throughout life.
4. Specific skill training will be available for all who choose it at the secondary, post-secondary, and adult levels.
5. Vocational education will make a greater impact at the post-secondary level.
6. Adult vocational education will be emphasized to permit updating and upgrading of job skills, to insure continued employment, and to permit adults to make career changes.
7. Job placement and follow-up will be a continuing school function.
8. Greater involvement of employers and private schools in providing vocational education will be evident.
9. Leadership development for vocational personnel and teacher preparation and upgrading will be required.
10. Vocational education youth groups will be encouraged and their activities supported as an integral part of career education.
11. Effective and continuous evaluation is required.
12. Performance incentives will be utilized to help obtain the most beneficial results (1971, pp. 5-10).

The paper concludes with a brief statement about changes which must be affected in delivery systems. These are treated in more detail in the next section.

Career Education Models

During Fiscal Years 1971 and 1972, the USOE began development of four conceptual models for career education. These were designed to further the trend toward career education. The models are being tested in funded projects and are undergoing constant revision. Following are their major features as described in a USOE (1972) "briefing paper":

Early in the Fiscal Year 1972, the entire directed development Career Education program was placed under the Career Education Development Task Force, directed by a Special Assistant to the Deputy Commissioner of Education for Development (now Deputy Commissioner of Education for Renewal).

By way of clarification, there are several projects which fall outside of the directed development program and still may be referred to as "models." This is accurate in that there are, for example, several school-based Career Education projects throughout the nation which are independent of the directed development projects comprising the R&D initiative of USOE.

In the supervision and monitoring process of the directed development program, USOE is especially sensitive and attuned to:
—Crisp research and development designs, hypotheses and oriented objectives, and
—Complete, concise, candid documentation, chronicling the developmental process.

SCHOOL-BASED MODEL I

Objectives

To insure that students exit school with:
—A sense of purpose and direction,
—Self identity and identification with society (and an idea of their relationship),
—Basic skills and knowledge,
—A comprehensive awareness of career options and the ability to enter employment and/or further education.

The School-Based Career Education model is based on the infusion of career development objectives into comprehensive K-14 educational programs. Specifically, the purpose of this redirection is to acquaint students more intimately with a wide variety of career opportunities through *each* of their school experiences. This infusion must insure that every student receives an education which integrates his academic skills, social development and career preparation so that after high school his options are open for entering the labor market in a productive career or pursuing the post-high school education of his choice. Further, it must provide students with a continuing awareness of educational choices for career planning, which permits them to become fulfilled, productive, and contributing citizens.

Extensive guidance and counseling activities will help the student develop self-awareness, self-confidence, and mature attitudes, and will match his interests and abilities against potential careers. Placement into an entry-level job or further education is one of the ultimate goals for every student in the School-Based Career Education project.

EMPLOYER-BASED MODEL II

Objectives

To insure that students exit school with:
—A sense of purpose and direction,
—Self identity and identification with society (and an idea of their relationship),
—Basic skills and knowledge,
—Specific skills and knowledge to be on a career path.

The Employer-Based Career Education project seeks to serve teen-age students through an optional out-of-school program. Many, of course, are characterized as the "disaffected, alienated and unmotivated." Although this optional program does accommodate such students, it is intended to be a real option for consideration by *all* students.

The Employer-Based Career Education will have as its goal the presentation of a comprehensive set of personalized educational experiences to secondary school students who voluntarily choose to participate in this mode of education instead of the traditional classroom curriculum.

Specifically, Employer-Based Career Education is an attempt to define individual learning elements within the curriculum, either existing or ideal, and to locate actual work or adult activity situations, managed by employers, in which students can learn these specific elements. Materials presented will be composed of all elements in the school curriculum, both academic and vocational in addition to other life skills. A special focus in the Employer-Based Model is the attempt to allow each student to participate in the selection of his own pattern of work or activity situations from a variety of opportunities, so that his learning situations are most relevant to his own interests and needs.

Participation in an Employer-Based Career Education project will provide students not only with the academic skills which are the center of the curriculum, but with familiarity and intimate experience in a variety of work situations of their own selection. It will allow students to function in a *real* adult-centered world. High school educational requirements will still be met, assuring high school graduation and an appropriate range of options upon graduation.

The Employer-Based Career Education projects will be operated by consortia of businesses and other organizations, both public and private. Such consortia are being formed presently under the sponsorship of Research for Better Schools, Inc., Philadelphia; the Far West Laboratory for Educational Research and Development, Berkeley, California; the Northwest Regional Educational Laboratory, Portland, Oregon, and the Appalachia Educational Laboratory, Charleston, West Virginia. They are operating under contract with the Office of Education, and have prime responsibility to develop and pilot test Employer-Based Career Education projects.

HOME/COMMUNITY-BASED MODEL III
Objectives
—To increase the employability and career options of out-of-school adults.
—To develop transportable processes and products.
—To conduct R&D programs aimed at the fractional objectives related to employability and career options.

The Home/Community-Based program is a career-oriented approach to enhance the employability and career options of out-of-school adults. Through the use of mass media, referral centers, individual counseling, and articulated exploitation of community resources, adults will be able to identify their aspirations as they match their capabilities, experience and motivation to move through an adaptive program. The adult population may be reached through mass media; those who are excited into action must be handled by the limited, but expandable, capacities of existing service networks. The need for a central screening and switching mechanism will be met by the establishment of a total systems management entity. This systems management entity will involve representatives of the target populations, service agencies which will accommodate the target population adjustment/education/training/placement needs, employers, and other national/regional/local organizations which will participate in guiding or operating the program.

The program will seek to:
Use mass media to:
—attract the attention of home/community-based populations.
—probe the career education interests of these populations, and generate feedback about their needs.
—provide information about existing career education resources.
—inculcate certain skills related to engaging in career education.
Bring together existing career education agencies to:
—coordinate their efforts to reach home/community-based population.
—tackle problems of accessing the target population.
—identify and attempt to fill gaps in service.
—respond effectively to the emerging career education interests.
Establish a central vehicle (the Career Education Extension Service) to carry out network functions:
—receive and interpret feedback from home/community-based population.
—refer individuals to existing agencies.
—identify problems of access, and aid in their solution.
—identify services gaps and assist in meeting them.
—gather and disseminate information about promising approaches to career education and about the effectiveness of existing approaches to it.
—systemically integrate all of the above.

It is a central theme of the Model to orchestrate, through the Career Education Extension Service, the use of mass media and the existing career education resources in order to help them reach and respond to the career education needs of home/community-based populations.

RURAL/RESIDENTIAL-BASED MODEL IV
Objectives
—To provide rural families with employment capabilities suitable to the area.
—To provide leverage on the economic development of the area.
—To improve family living.

The Rural/Residential Career Education Model is a research and demonstration project which will test the hypothesis that entire disadvantaged rural families can experience lasting improvement in their economic and social conditions through an intensive program at a residential center. The center is designing programs and will provide services for the entire family: day care; kindergarten, elementary and secondary education; career and technical education; young adult, adult and parent education; family-living assistance; medical and dental services; welfare services; counseling; and cultural and recreational opportunities for single and married students and their families.

In addition to the education and social services systems a research and evaluation system, a management system, and a staff inservice training system is being designed and developed at the center. An economic development services plan for the local geographic region will also be designed. This plan will include a program of research on the educational services plan for the local geographic region will also be designed. This plan will include a program of research on the educational services and programs required to improve the economic viability of the region and a program for expansion of regional efforts authorized under existing local, state, and Federal programs in economic development. It is the intent of the project that students be able and ready to find employment in the local (6 state) region after completion of the program. (1972, pp. 2-9).

Position of the National Education Association

At the NEA convention in 1970, Helen P. Bain, then president, appointed a task force to clarify the profession's position and to strengthen and coordinate vocational education. The task force report, *Vocational Education and the Profession in the 70's and Beyond* (Task Force on Vocational Education, 1971), is complimentary of the accomplishments of vocational education and very supportive of its future. The report contains detailed suggestions for how various kinds of professionals may aid and abet vocational education. The official actions on the report are very encouraging to vocational educators.

The NEA Board of Directors meeting in Detroit on June 22, 1971 made the following decisions:

1. To receive the report of the Task Force On Vocational Education; transmit it to the Representative Assembly for information; refer the recommendations to the Executive Committee for beginning implementation; and, further, recommend that the Department of Vocational Education be discontinued.[8]
2. That the report of the Task Force on Vocational Education and the actions taken by NEA be forwarded with emphasis to state education associations and to vocational education bureaus of all state departments of education.

The NEA Representative Assembly adopted the Report and passed the following resolution regarding vocational and career education:

The National Education Association believes that preparation of children for careers, vocations, and productive jobs should be a basic policy of education. Educational programs should be developed for all children which will assure equal opportunity for career and occupational development. A continuing program for training, retraining, advancement, and promotion should be provided to out-of-school youth and adults.

The Association will seek legislation to provide a comprehensive national manpower development policy, as the basic foundation for vocational and career education. It will also assist its affiliates in implementing similar programs and legislation.

[8]The NEA has long had a defunct Department of Vocational Education; this action clears the way for cooperative effort with the American Vocational Association.

Position of the American Vocational Association

The American Vocational Association has established a program for support to and leadership of the Career Education movement. Nearly everyone that aids and abets career education in significant ways is an American Vocational Association member. Furthermore, given a place for skills training and some reason for continuing use of the term "vocational education," almost all AVA members advocate adoption of and action on the principles of career education. At this writing the AVA plans to convene a national forum on education for careers, provide professional leadership to enable affiliated organizations to sponsor similar forums, and prepare and disseminate publications and information on career education.

The AVA also plans to promote a White House Conference on career education and initiate a "major" legislative effort to begin with the second session of the 92nd Congress. The status of professional attitudes toward career education is well-summarized by Kenneth B. Hoyt (1971). His major points are paraphased:

1. Career education involves all kinds of teachers at all levels through the community college. They will do something quite different from past practice.
2. Career education subsumes vocational education as an integral component.
3. Career education must entail active involvement of the business-labor-industry community. Work-experience and observation for students and professionals must become a widespread reality.
4. The career development component of career education means active and continuing assistance to persons all along the educational ladder, including adulthood.
5. The home and family must be involved in career education in new and meaningful ways as a place for work and learning attitudes and values of work.

Dr. Hoyt was careful to point out that career education should not be construed as all of education but only as the preparation-for-work component of education. This appears to be the stance of the American Vocational Association.

Education Amendments of 1972 (P.L. 92-318)

Vocational-technical education is a primary concern of this legislation. Several of the features of the Act bear directly on vocational and career education.

The Act establishes a National Institute of Education, which will study the educational process. Career education and alternate delivery systems seem certain to be early concerns of this agency's research and demonstration systems.

The Act makes two major administrative changes. (1) It establishes an Educational Division in the Department of Health, Education and Welfare, headed by an Assistant Secretary. (2) It establishes a Bureau of Occupational and Adult Education in the U.S. Office of Education. These provisions give new status to education and occupational education specifically. The new bureau will administer programs in adult, vocational, and occupational education, and manpower programs, which are funded under previous legislation. Centering this function in one office and raising it to the deputy commissioner's level are long sought victories for vocational educators.

The Act provides for establishment and expansion of community college occupational programs. Technical institutes, postsecondary vocational schools and junior colleges may participate. States which participate must establish broadly representative commissions, which will be responsible for statewide planning for post-secondary occupational education.

The Act extends six sections of the 1968 amendments through June 30, 1975. These are: exemplary programs and projects, residential vocational schools, consumer and homemaking education, cooperative vocational education, curriculum development, and the National Advisory Council on Vocational Education. It also provides a three-year authorization for grants to strengthen and improve vocational education, counseling and placement in elementary schools, secondary schools, and community colleges. The definition of vocational education is expanded to include training of firemen.

The Education Professions Development Act is extended through June 30, 1975 with the stipulation that 10 percent of appropriated funds be used for vocational-technical education professional development.

The Act permits recognition of industrial arts as vocational education in cases where the Commissioner of Education determines that industrial arts contributes to vocational education objectives. This provision is certain to affect planning in state and local education agencies. Hopefully, it will ameliorate rifts between industrial arts and vocational industrial personnel.

Provisions for disadvantaged, Indian, migratory workers and dependents, and other target groups and many other features of this legislation will have far-reaching affects upon career education. Needless to say, whether annual appropriation levels approach authorization levels is crucial. The Act and appropriate legislation are worthy of thorough reading.

Summary

Career education is a very recent phenomenon. The Manpower Council, the Panel of Consultants, the Advisory Council, the National Advisory Council on Vocational Education, and educational leaders have come rather naturally to the realization that *career development* must be the core, the major thread, of education in a society which is so well advanced technologically that it endangers the human condition. Career education has had its antecedents in "life adjustment" and other approaches to making education meaningful. But it is different in the sense that it is seen as a response to problems accentuated by the economically and socially disadvantaged, to mobility conditions in the world of work, to accumulated knowledge of personal development and the career component of the self concept specifically, and to problems of schooling itself, such as the ineffectiveness of existing instructional and counseling programs. "Basically, we are talking about the fact that in this country we need to have people who want to work, who are prepared to work, and who actively regard work as a meaningful and important part of their lives" (Hoyt, 1971, p. 111).

BIBLIOGRAPHY

Allen, J. E. Jr. *Competence for all as the goal for secondary education.* Address given to the Annual Convention of the National Association of Secondary School Principals. Washington, D. C., February 10, 1970.

Bottoms, G. and Matheny, K. B *A guide for the development, implementation, and administration of exemplary programs and projects in vocational education.* Atlanta: Georgia State Department of Education, and Division of Vocational Education, 1969.

Burt, S. M. *Industry and community leaders in education: The state advisory councils on vocational education.* Kalamazoo, Michigan: The W. E. Upjohn Institute for Employment Research, 1969.

Clary, J. R. *Review and synthesis of research and developmental activities concerning state advisory councils on vocational education.* Columbus, Ohio: ERIC Clearinghouse on Vocational and Technical Education, The Center for Vocational and Technical Education, The Ohio State University, 1970.

Dittrick, A. R. New directions in vocational education. *National Association of Secondary School Principals Bulletin,* 1965, 49(301), 47-53.

Draper, D. C. *Educating for work: A report on the current scene in vocational education.* Washington, D. C.: National Association of Secondary School Principals, 1967.

Essex, M. W. Education for jobs. *American Vocational Journal*, 1968, 43(3), 37-40.

Evans, R. N., Mangum, G. L. and Pragan, O. *Education for employment: the background and potential of the 1968 vocational education amendments.* Ann Arbor, Michigan: Institute of Labor and Industrial Relations, 1969.

Forsythe, J. S. and Weintraub, F. J. Vocational education amendments of 1968, Public Law 90-576. *Exceptional Children*, 1969, 35, 751-754.

Gysbers, N. C. *Elements of a model for promoting career development in elementary and junior high school.* Paper presented at the National Conference on Exemplary Programs and Projects — 1968 Amendments to the Vocational Education Act, Atlanta, Georgia, March, 1969, (ED 045 860).

Haskew, L. D. and Temlin, F. W. Vocational education in curriculum of the common school. In M. L. Barlow (ed.) *Vocational education.* The sixty-fourth yearbook of the National Society for the Study of Education. Chicago: University of Chicago Press, 1965, 64-87.

Herr, E. L. *Unifying an entire system of education around a career development theme.* Paper presented at National Conference on Exemplary Programs and Projects — 1968 Amendments to the Vocational Education Act, Atlanta, Georgia, March, 1969, (ED 045 860).

————. *Review and synthesis of foundations for career education.* Columbus, Ohio: ERIC Clearinghouse on Vocational and Technical Education, The Center for Vocational and Technical Education, The Ohio State University, 1972.

Hoyt, K. B. Excerpts of speech given before Teacher Education Department, American Vocational Association. Washington, D. C.: American Vocational Association Convention Proceedings Digest, 1971.

Kliever, D. E. *Vocational Education Act of 1963: a case study in legislation.* Washington, D. C.: American Vocational Association, 1965.

Krebs, A. H. Vocational Education Act of 1963, vision or mirage? *Agricultural Education Magazine*, 1966, 39(3), 52-53.

Marland, S. P. Jr. *Career education now.* Address given at the Convention of the National Association of Secondary School Principals. Houston, Texas, January 23, 1971. (a)

————. *Career education — more than a name.* Address given before the annual meeting of the State Directors of Vocational Education, Washington, D. C., May 4, 1971. (b)

Maze, C. Jr. Possible side effects of the Vocational Education Act of 1963. *Journal of Business Education*, 1966, 41(8), 314-315.

Mobley, M. D. and Barlow, M. L. Impact of federal legislation and policies upon vocational education. In M. L. Barlow (ed.) *Vocational education.* The sixty-fourth yearbook of the National Society for the Study of Education. Chicago: University of Chicago Press, 1965, 186-202.

National Advisory Council on Vocational Education. *First annual report, July 1969.* Washington, D. C.: U. S. Government Printing Office, 1969. (a)

————. *Second report, November, 1969.* Washington, D. C.: U. S. Government Printing Office, 1969. (b)

————. *Third report.* Washington, D. C.: U. S. Government Printing Office, 1970.

————. *Fourth report, January, 1971.* Washington, D. C.: U. S. Government Printing Office, 1971. (a)

————. *Fifth report, June, 1971.* Washington, D. C.: U. S. Government Printing Office, 1971. (b)

————. *Sixth report, June, 1972.* Washington, D. C.: U. S. Government Printing Office, 1972.

National Manpower Council, *A policy for skilled manpower.* New York: Columbia University Press, 1954.

————. *Government and manpower.* New York: Columbia University Press, 1954.

————. *Improving the work skills of the nation.* New York: Columbia University Press, 1955.

————. *Manpower policies for a democratic society.* New York: Columbia University Press, 1965.

————. *Public policies and manpower resources.* New York: Columbia University Press, 1964.

Panel of Consultants Report on Vocational Education, *Education for a changing world of work.* Washington, D. C.: U. S. Government Printing Office, 1963. (a)

————. *Education for a changing world of work: summary report.* Washington, D. C : U. S. Government Printing Office, 1963. (b)

————. *Education for a changing world of work: appendix I.* Washington, D. C.: U. S. Government Printing Office, 1963. (c)

————. *Education for a changing world of work: appendix II.* Washington, D. C.: U. S. Government Printing Office, 1963. (d)

————. *Education for a changing world of work: appendix III.* Washington, D. C.: U. S. Government Printing Office, 1963. (e)

Public Law 88-210. 88th Congress, H.R. 4955, December 18, 1963.

Public Law 90-576. 90th Congress, H.R. 18366, October 16, 1968.

Public Law 92-318. 92nd Congress, 5.659, June 23, 1972.

Ray, E. M. Social and philosophical framework in vocational, technical and practical arts education. *Review of Educational Research,* 1968, 38(4), 309-325.

Rumpf, E. L. Vocational education for the 1970's. Washington, D. C.: Division of Vocational and Technical Education, 1971, 11 pp., (mimeo).

Sjogren, D. and Gutcher, D. Current and future demands on vocational education. *High School Journal,* 1969, 52(5), 219-227.

Task Force on Vocational Education. *Vocational education and the profession in the 70's and beyond.* Washington, D. C.: National Education Association, May 26, 1971.

Tomlinson, R. M. Implications of (and reflections on) the Vocational Education Amendments of 1968. *Journal of Industrial Teacher Education,* 1970, 7(5), 5-13.

U. S. Office of Education, *Education briefing paper.* Washington, D. C.: U. S. Department of Health, Education and Welfare, June 15, 1972.

Venn, G. Vocational education for all. *National Association of Secondary School Principals Bulletin,* 1967, 51, 32-40.

————. Occupational education for everyone. *National Association of Secondary School Principals Bulletin,* 1968, 52(332), 112-122.

Vocational education: The bridge between man and his work, publication I. Highlights and Recommendations from the General Report of the Advisory Council on Vocational Education, 1968. Washington, D. C.: U. S. Government Printing Office, 1968. (a)

Vocational education: The bridge between man and his work, publication II. Highlights and Recommendations from the General Report of the Advisory Council on Vocational Education, 1968. Washington, D. C.: U. S. Government Printing Office, 1968. (b)

Worthington, R. M. *The implications of career education for adult education in the United States.* Paper presented at the Third UNESCO International Conference on Adult Education, Tokyo, Japan, July 25 - August 7, 1972.

CHAPTER 9

The Function and Place
of Career Education

Introduction

The foundations of career education have been illustrated to be very substantive. They are firmly grounded in technological advance, the nature of psychological, social, and economic man and in career development theory. In the words of Professor Wayne S. Ramp, the authors' sage colleague, "career education is like a big tree falling down." Because it is inescapable, educators had better fit one or another of its branches soon. From time to time during the last five years, one of the authors has refined an explanation of formal schooling's natural evolution to central regard for education concerning work. In a very real sense, this approach to curriculum building is an attempt to deal with the patchwork which has resulted from adding to, while not deleting from, the secondary school curriculum. To begin to deal with curriculum, one has to have a manageable number of categories for labeling the many subjects and areas which have enlarged the offering. The treatise which follows is the result of this labor which has been redirected and encouraged by professional acquaintances.

An Approach to Describing the Function of Schooling

This new way of describing the function of schooling can be confused with residual theory (see Chapter 7) but is readily distinguished from it. Whereas residual theory says "teach what used to be taught elsewhere," this approach says "focus on kids and adults and perform for them the educational functions which other institutions are not doing for the bulk of their kind."[1] That is,

[1]Whether or not the formal school should challenge serious encroachments upon its functions is a controversy not within the concern of this book. Suffice it to say that institutions have far and way too much to do and that the school has such disputes at present.

one way to get at a definition of the function of schooling is to look at institutions in the culture at various periods in history, plotting trends in their functions to the present time and conceptualizing what the school's function might better and legitimately be, presently and in the future.

Description of the formal school's function with relationship to other institutions is facilitated by (1) focusing on the school's function as it has evolved in response to the societal milieu and, at the same time, (2) defining balances of *play, learning,* and *work*[2] in the curriculum at several levels of schooling.

Play, learning, and work are one-word descriptors for broad categories of experiences provided by schools. They are convenient handles for dealing with the entire curriculum in a manageable number of categories and for comparing and contrasting emphases in function.

Play is that part of the curriculum which has to do with the intelligent, healthful, and wholesome use of childhood and adult leisure. One synonym for play is *health and recreation education.* Playground, physical education, recreation, health, clubs and other student activities, much of outdoor education, and much of the instrumental and vocal music programs of American schools are subsumed by this category, which the authors prefer to call "play." This part of the curriculum develops facility with the physical self, play, diet, recreation and leisure.[3]

Learning is that part of the curriculum which begins with the primary abilities; continues with understandings which are important to judicious citizenship, and becomes preparation for college and the scholarly and professional pursuits, typified by those who achieve the doctor's degree. One synonym for learning is *primary abilities, citizenship, and college preparatory education.* Facility with words, numbers, and people is primary. Facility with concepts about the physical world and the world of ideas for purposes relating to intelligent citizenship is secondary. Facility to continue study and research at the collegiate level is tertiary (and occupationally oriented).

Work is the part of the curriculum which deals with understanding the world *of* occupations and with preparation *for* entry

---

[2]Substitute terms might be: leisure, learning and labor. Less appropriate perhaps would be: recreation, rote, and recompense.

[3]When overdone, aspects of the curriculum subsumed by *play* become *work.* That is, done to excess, athletics or music or whatever becomes vocational education. Better, then, that the experience be called "occupational" and that entry, treatment, and exit be managed for such ends to assure minimum failure and disappointment.

into and success in the world of work. One synonym for the work component of the curriculum is *career education*. Occupational information, career guidance and counseling, vocational education, occupational education, technical education, and related services are parts of the work component of the curriculum.

The play-learning-work categorical system has the same limitations which are described in the subsection on intelligence in Chapter 7. These categories are not mutually exclusive or exhaustive. First, it is difficult to decide whether to put health education in play or learning. It is sometimes taught by biology teachers in science departments and sometimes taught by health teachers in health and physical education departments.[4] The authors maintain that the integrity of the categories of play, learning, and work is maintained if health is considered to be part of play. Second, some will argue that there are experiences which nearly everyone agrees should be provided by schools but which do not fit neatly into any one of the categories.

This classification system does serve to sort curriculum elements and does facilitate discussion. Nearly all experiences which are encountered in schooling can be classified easily as one or another of play, learning, or work. Above the elementary level, teachers can be classified just as readily. Furthermore, much of the time students know whether they are engaged in activities about or for play, learning, and work. If these categories were widely understood and utilized, everyone connected with schooling would know better where he is headed.

From the concept that all of schooling may be subsumed under these headings, it follows that the curriculum should entail a proper balance of play, learning, and work. The balance should change over time and by levels on the educational ladder. The balance is defined by a number of factors not the least of which is what other institutions do relative to each of the three functions.

Balances of Play, Learning, and Work Over Time

The history of play, learning, and work in the curriculum is easy to trace in a gross way. As has been illustrated in earlier sections, vocational education predates liberal education. Through colonial times, schools were primarily for members of the elite who would have careers in the professions. There were less elaborate schools for some of the middle class and the poor. But the intent of school was preparation for earning. Only in a few cultural centers could the luxury of schooling for its own sake be afforded.

---

[4]The authors are not interested in perpetuating or destroying existing structures.

Work, learning, and play appeared in that order in the curriculum — play being almost nonexistent in most schools.

By the nineteenth century in many places and by the twentieth century in widely scattered places, the content of instruction was much more formalized and removed from the world of work. The liberal arts and sciences (learning) were king. The classical studies, which earlier had been studied for their value to lawmakers and speech makers, were now studied for ethereal reasons. They were alleged to be liberalizing and whatever else would rationalize their place in the curriculum. For example, Latin was said to be disciplining and other things good, including the key to understanding English. Play was still the loser. Even the very young were expected to sit rigidly and learn. Thus at the turn of the century, the order of significance was learning, work, and play.

During the first four decades of this century, both work and play gained ground on learning. Neither surpassed learning; learning remained king. Three or four years of English, two or more years of science, and one or more years of mathematics were required. But, the rest was elective from a cafeteria of more and more "watered" alphabet soups.

Then, in October of 1957, the country was shocked into a new wakefulness by Sputnik. In short order, learning's dominance in the curriculum was intensified. Unprecedented sums were spent by government, university, and local agencies to upgrade the teaching of the exact sciences, mathematics, and foreign language. Influential people in many fields believed that teaching and learning of these subjects had to be upgraded to new levels of excellence (see Chapter 2) to assure engineering and scientific might in the hot and cold wars of police actions and space conquest. In the period immediately after Sputnik, the ranking was decidedly learning, play, and work. The new myth became: All who can possibly enter universities should be encouraged to do so. Woe be it to those who do not succeed in academic education. Automation will change jobs drastically, and those who do not do well in the sciences will be displaced by technology. Educational facilities must be greatly improved, and many more must go to college. Even though discoveries leading up to the Vocational Education Act of 1963 burst the bubble of the engineering and science myth, educational lag[5] permitted the learning, play, work ranking to continue well into the 1970's.

[5]The primary concern of this book is to lay theoretical ground and practical plans for assuring work's place in balanced curricula — by time, place, and level of schooling — thus to avoid lag.

Balances of Play, Learning, and Work on the Educational Ladder

The other significant way to think of play, learning, and work in the curriculum is to describe how the balance of the three should change during an individual's progress in the schools. The balance should never be such that one of the three is zero. To cite the extremes, even the young should learn something about work and even the very old and infirm should learn about play so that they might be intelligent spectators in their leisure.

Play: Schooling has to begin with play. Play is the natural activity of the young. But, as Dewey (1916) indicated, play should give way to learning gradually during the early years of schooling. Even at the outset, neither work nor learning should be zero in the curriculum. Some experiences should begin to foster learning about work and development of wholesome attitudes toward work. Similarly, experience should create awareness and elementary understandings of physical and social forces in the world which only formal study can develop.

As remaining discussion will illustrate, the balance of play, learning, and work should change. Play should give way during the years of full-time schooling because, after all, a great many other institutions have some responsibility for this function. Curriculum planners should be mindful of recreational enterprises which are sponsored by other agencies when they design specific experiences for boys and girls and adults. Experiences in school should help young and old to evaluate and consume recreational experiences judiciously. The school does not need to supply all, or nearly all, of the experiences. Likewise, an emphasis on the play component of the curriculum should be on healthful living. The special topics which are appropriate to the several age levels are, by themselves, enough to sustain a high place in the curriculum for play.

Learning: Obviously, learning should increase into adolescence. Primary abilities and understandings which depend upon material from the exact and social sciences and the humanities are very closely wrapped up with the function of schooling. Intelligent conduct of free people in an industrialized democracy depends upon widespread intelligibility of forces which shape the physical and social environment. By definition, the liberal arts and sciences — pure and applied — are the storehouses of that intelligence. This should comprise a major part of the schooling of all, at least into adolescence. This is not to say that disciplines should be taught as such but only to say that material from organized bodies of knowledge should be studied by youngsters (and adults) who would understand the world around them.

Learning can be, and is nearly everywhere, overemphasized in the curriculum. Largely because material is removed from the curriculum much more reluctantly than it is added, the emphasis on some aspects of learning is far too great. To understand what is being said here, one has to appreciate how much of learning is the function of the home and other agencies such as mass media. People learn a great deal of speech and other aspects of human knowledge and interchange outside the school. "Sesame Street" and many other attempts at education should be complemented, not duplicated by the schools. But schools continue to teach subjects such as language arts and mathematics year after year well beyond the point when they can be justified for other than baccalaureate-level occupational goals. Thus, many youngsters are denied a balanced educational experience and not enough are provided experiences for job entry with less than baccalaureate degrees. Just as the school assumes functions which other institutions can no longer serve because of the complexities of experience involved, so should it give up functions which other institutions have come to be better equipped to perform.

Work: Schooling about work and, later, for work should gain ground in the curriculum, peaking near the times when young adults move to part-time and full-time work. As Part II, Career Development, illustrated, certain developmental tasks should be accomplished at the several levels of schooling. Presently, many adolescents cry out (in language too few educators understand) for experiences centered around the concept of work because they have not been permitted to learn about work gradually as farm boys and girls often do. If they do not have experience about and for work, some young people express themselves via improper or premature forms of play.

Initiative, responsibility, and creativity cannot be further challenged and enhanced at adolescence unless examples of adult-type work tasks are experienced. Because they know little about work, youngsters think they know all about play and learning. Thus, interest languishes and mediocrity results. Motivation for any pursuit is dependent upon a balance of experiences in the curriculum.

Society has moved as far as it dares to bar adolescents and young adults from first-hand experience with work. Witness the fact that many choose never to work. Many fear to work because work is a big mystery to them. Because the bulk of young people no longer come to understand and participate in work outside the school, it behooves the school to develop programs which will engage youngsters in experiences related to work.[6] Programs should develop understanding of work and jobs along a number of dimensions, such as (1) professional, semiprofessional, skilled, semiskilled, and (2) construction, health, religion, education, government, banking. In-school experiences should deal as deeply as possible with what is known of the role of the two major elements of work, i.e., the human and technical sides of enterprise. Understanding man and technology, coupled for productivity, is the essence of career education.

By adolescence, work should be a major aspect of education for all youngsters. Work should be central, not peripheral in the curriculum. It should not be tacked on. Not only the socially, economically, and academically unfortunate need skills for specified occupations. Everyone needs to understand occupations and many more than most schoolmen suppose need specialized programs in high school and community college.

If, as has too frequently been the case, schools make relevant occupational programs available only to the socially and educationally disadvantaged, the advantaged will become disadvantaged. That is, unless they learn about work, about responsibility, about adult roles, affluent youngsters also become disassociated. Many rioters and other disassociated people do not know about work and the satisfaction of individual achievement. Even if all need not work,[7] occupational education should be required of all adolescents alike, because no one can know long beforehand where he might work and/or study.

Synergistic Effects: Play, learning, and work have synergistic effects. This has often been argued by philosophers and psychologists. Too often educators have forgotten the work part of the system. Play and learning cannot be maximized without work. Play, learning and work aid and abet each other. For example, familiarity with work fosters realizations about how little one knows of adult

[6]Traditional practical arts programs were right for this purpose in their time, but they have lingered too long and now hinder rather than help youngsters and the cause of career education. Broadly conceived industrial arts programs can confuse play and work unless objectives are clearly defined for children.

[7]There are many learned people who prophesy a society which supports a class of people who, by design and without recrimination, only consume. Such theorists espouse the principle that economic goals can be maximized if a major segment of the population makes no direct economic contribution. The authors disagree with this view and submit that environmental maintenance alone is enough to absorb the unemployed if societal needs and goals are sought and realized. However, this controversy is of no consequence to the present concern or the thrust of this book because individuals must be free to move occupationally, geographically, and educationally, according to their peculiar interests and abilities.

play and learning. Motivation to pursue one or another of play, learning or work with new wisdom is difficult if the three have not been experienced in balance. Thus the adage, "All work and no play makes Johnny a dull boy." Other combinations of terms are likewise true. The integrated, wholesome individual is one who engages in an acceptable and appropriate balance of activities in play, learning and work. Witness the facts that many of the idle rich engage in charitable work; many residents in correctional institutions engage in learning, industry, and charitable efforts as they have never done before; and adults of many ilks pursue learning and play as they were never enthused to do in school. The combined and healthy action of informed play, learning, and work is at the essence of balanced societies and individuals. Young people can be motivated to participate as full partners in the society only if the school realizes its responsibilities in each of the three curricular areas. Young people can move happily to adulthood and mature relationships with the economy as farm children did in large measure several generations ago. But, the school must assume increasing responsibility for providing experiences which foster individual understanding of and participation in the world of work. Because of industrialization and urbanization, other institutions have given up this function.

An Individual Matter: In advanced adolescence and early adulthood, the balance of play, learning, and work should be largely an individual matter. As the previous discussion has pointed out, there can be no prescription for adults. The degree of precision in prescribing elements of curriculum is greatest after the very young have been assessed and provided remedial or readiness development experiences. From that point on, precision diminishes until adolescents know better than educators (assuming success in a balanced curriculum prior to adolescence) what balance of play, learning, and work is best for individual interests, abilities, and educational and employment goals.

Furthermore, before the end of adolescence, individual balances will not be the same as the balance for the population. Because individuals are benefited and deprived in different ways and to different degrees by institutions outside the school, they will need differing emphases of play, learning, and work in the school. Consider the child prodigy, the teen-age virtuoso, the physically handicapped, the accident victim, the delinquent, the newly orphaned. These and many more peculiar individuals require special adjustments in the balance of play, learning, and work. Those who, for whatever reason, cannot or need not prepare in public education for work obviously should not be forced to do so. Those who need short-term skills training to achieve earning power to support themselves and perhaps others should be helped to prepare for work, exit, and re-entry to the educational enterprise on a part-time or full-time basis and at will. Easy entry and easy exit should be the mode, not the rarity, for adolescents and adults.

After an individual has achieved whatever is accepted to be the minimum level of intelligence about play, learning and other responsibilities of citizenship, and work and participation in the economy, he should be permitted to strike his own bargain with the world and specific institutions. If he wants great books, fine. If not, fine. If he wants job upgrading, fine. If not, fine. What he experiences of play, learning, and work, and where he experiences them, should be his own affair. This leads to the issue, When should education become specialized?

Age of Specialization

Much of the controversy over what should be taught can be resolved by thorough treatment of the question, When should education become specialized? This question has not been dealt with properly in the literature of educational theory. In the first half of the century, many theorists submitted that specialized education is necessary for only a few of the oldest professions. Others have often submitted that it is appropriate for the children of one or more of the socioeconomic classes. Nearly all contemporary theorists profess tidy theories by concluding that specialization should be reserved for a particular level, usually beyond the compulsory attendance level or beyond the level which all are expected to achieve before leaving. Broudy et al. (1964) are typical of the proponents of a common secondary curriculum for all and specialization for those who want it only at a given level. ". . . Specialized training is so necessary for *everyone* that one layer of our educational system should be devoted exclusively to it rather than treating it as a substitute for, or as an orphan of, common, general education" (1964, p. 182). This viewpoint fails to provide specialized preparation for those who drop out, for those whose attention spans and other characteristics vary from the motivations of those who profit from acquiring knowledge for the sake of pursuit-of-knowledge, and for those who must forego broader educational goals until economic exigencies are satisfied.

Careful analysis of the question, When should education become specialized? is facilitated by three subquestions:

1. What are the educational requirements of the available jobs in the world of work and what will they be in years to come?
2. When can individuals freely and intelligently select occupations for which their interests and capabilities are fitted?
3. How many years of education are necessary to meet the requirements of responsible citizenship in a democracy and what will they be in years to come?

Educational Requirements of Occupations

If formal education is to be responsible for preparing young people for employment, that is, if formal education is to develop some measure of saleable mental and/or manual skill, one must look to the world of work before making decisions regarding when and how that function of the school should be carried out. Educators who are concerned with the saleable skill objective have often looked to the world of work as they have gone about the task of making decisions in this area. Typically they have assessed the employment scene and have come to the conclusions (a) that secondary-school students who have evidenced academic ability and interest in the professions should be enrolled in the college-preparatory program and encouraged to enter a college or university, (b) that those students who have not evidenced academic ability and are interested in immediate employment should enroll in vocational education, meaning by "vocational education" preparation for occupations at the skilled and semiskilled levels (the college-preparatory program should also be classed as vocational because it involves specialization for the professional), and (c) that those who are unable to decide upon a plan of specialized preparation should continue in a program of general education. In practice, these options have not been available in many school districts.

Based upon the saleable skill criterion alone, this plan of specialization has been a pretty good one — at least until recently. In theory, and often in practice, the college-preparatory and vocational-education programs have been good means to their respective and limited ends. There is increasing evidence that the general program is a poor means to no end, that is, that many students from this program do poorly in college and/or the world of work.

Assessment of the employment scene reveals that trends are not as strong or prolonged as predicted a decade or more ago. Primarily because of technological advances which have been spurred by military and other demands upon productivity levels, economic and social theorists predicted that more and more occupations would require higher and higher levels of mental ability. Put each of several other ways, opportunities at the professional, semiprofessional and/or technician levels would increase rapidly whereas opportunities in unskilled, semiskilled and many skilled occupations would decrease rapidly; greater and greater percentages of the available jobs would require longer and longer periods of formal preparation; more and more jobs would require greater facility with the kinds of content elitists would communicate to all youth who could "cut" it.

The rapidity with which these trends would accelerate was variously predicted by experts on automation and cybernetics; industrial psychologists, sociologists, and economists; and employer and employee groups. Now more than ever, assessments of the rate at which these trends will accelerate vary a great deal. That they will accelerate is a commonly accepted idea. But how many organizations which produce goods or provide services will make significant applications of automation is not nearly as clear as early observers of mechanization first thought. Furthermore, the growth of personal service occupations and lower-level occupations in government services such as environmental maintenance, suggests that, counter to what was predicted a decade ago, all who wish to work can do so after rather short preparation.

The complexity of trends in job requirements seriously challenges the thought of permitting specialization at only one level of schooling. Trends suggest that not all of the present high-school population should enroll in the kind of vocational programs now offered in the schools. They also indicate that we must provide a much larger variety of specialized educational opportunities at the grades 13 and 14 levels. They also suggest that specialization should begin after grade eight or nine or ten for some. Educational requirements of a great many of the available jobs suggest that people with great varieties of specialization at many levels can find and hold jobs. Although the average age of entrance into the world of work is continuing to increase, people with training and experience, such as those provided by cooperative education, are employable — even if they tell employers that work is going to be interrupted for further education when economically possible.

Intelligent and Free Selection of Occupations

Those who support the comprehensive high-school ideal have argued that schools with diverse curricula assure equal educational and vocational opportunity. The dominant thinking of educators is that the way to facilitate intelligent and free choice of occupations and equal opportunity to prepare for occupations is (a) to offer an array of programs and courses and (b) to permit students (aided by parents and counselors) to select from among them. From time to time, various critics of secondary schools suggest that the educational program can be improved tremendously if this thinking is abandoned.

The Challenge: Attackers of the comprehensive secondary school argue as follows. In practice, the educational system is, in many respects, compatible with those of fascist or communist states and with earlier ideologies such as those of Marx, Pareto, and Plato who hypothesized, in one language system or another, that each individual should be educated "to his station." As John Dewey charged early in the century, the secondary school which consists of different routes for different kinds of students is undemocratic because it does not facilitate free and intelligent occupational choices.

Such a school prevents students from learning *about* occupations before preparing *for* occupations. Only if the student is permitted to learn about occupations and to try out his capacities and interests can he make decisions freely and intelligently. Decisions regarding one's life work cannot be intelligent unless they are made later in life than some youngsters are expected to make them. A student cannot try out his capacities in many occupations until his intellect nears conceptual maturity sometime in adolescence. It is impossible in many respects for youngsters to become familiar with the highly conceptual activity of professional and semiprofessional occupations until they themselves have a high degree of conceptual ability. A student cannot make the most intelligent decision unless he has all available pertinent data. A student cannot choose a vocation wisely unless he has learned about the multitudinous kinds of endeavor in the pure and applied arts and sciences.

The student cannot become aware of these, let alone understand them, if early in his teens half of his school day is devoted to specialized preparation for one or a small family of occupations. If he is allowed to devote a major portion of his efforts to preparation for work, he can never be sure that he would not have decided upon another career if he had had the chance to explore it. Specialization at immature ages restricts the number of possibilities at later times. The alternative is to prolong occupational choice as long as possible. Occupational choice should be prolonged until economic necessities and other pressures of the society require the student to choose a vocation. Present conditions such as educational requirements of the majority of available jobs, number of years now devoted to formal schooling, and average

age of acceptance into the world of work indicate that occupational choice and preparation should be prolonged at least until the end of secondary schooling.

Fallacy of the Challenge: The faults with this argumentation are obvious. First, people who profess such arguments make the same basic mistake as do many of the traditional vocational educators whom they deride. They assume that people choose an occupation for life, that the choice is extremely important, and that it should be put off as long as possible. All three assumptions are false. In fact, occupations cannot and are not chosen for life by many people and in fact, what one does is not important so long as it is wholesome and dignifying in the worker's view.[8] Secondly, they assume that education and work come before and not during or after employment. In fact, education is never complete. It is hindered when work is missing. Education is more and more sought after by people at all ages for vocational (and avocational) purposes. And third, they fail to realize that healthy people have occupational preferences from early childhood on and that there will always be great variance of ages when preferences can be realized. Some begin work or specialized preparation at one level and many begin at subsequent levels. Fortunately, the trend is up, in keeping with technological advance. But, in recent times, the United States of America has demonstrated that the trend can be artificially accelerated.

Democracy and wise choice are best assured by a system of easy entry and easy exit. So long as people know the bargain they are striking with the world, they should be permitted to strike it. Democracy and wise choice can only be assured by freedom of choice and the availability of full- and part-time continuing education and related services, such as counseling and placement. If the processes of education, training, and wage earning are observed as continuous and manageable under a large variety of relationships, the concept of schooling for individuals comes into better focus than ever before.

Educational Requirements of Citizenship

Democracy requires an educational system which is quite different from that required by other ideologies. Democratic education is unique primarily because democracy is predicated on the existence of an informed and involved populace. That democracy

[8]Any wholesome occupation is inherently dignifying. In large part, the myth of the baccalaureate degree has fostered the concept that some jobs are menial and degrading. There must be an all-out effort to rebuild the status of all manner of work which contributes to the common welfare.

presupposes educated masses is a commonly accepted idea. A government which is "of the people, by the people and for the people" cannot realize its ends if its electorate is not broadly educated. Democratic procedures such as voluntary consent of the governed, choice of candidates for office, social and economic mobility, and equal treatment under the written and unwritten law require that all citizens be intelligent and knowledgeable, that is, that all constituents possess general education. Because democracy cannot flourish unless these procedures are maximized, all should possess education.

Adequate undertaking of the avocational pursuits of responsible citizenship in a democracy involves the use of knowledge from many refined segments of the accumulated culture. As the scope of responsible citizenship expands and/or as more and more refined intellectual and aesthetic materials are developed, more and more time must be devoted to general education. Enough general content cannot be communicated in even twelve years of formal schooling. There are many subjects of concern to those who would understand contemporary objects and events and the people who bring them about. For example, the school does little with astronomy and other fields which are basic to an understanding of space travel. It does little in the social sciences such as political economics which are basic to an understanding of modern industrial and trade blocs. In short, it does little to communicate material from many of the specialties which attempt to explain our world.

From the above, many conclude that education through the secondary school should not involve specialization. But, such people wear the same blinders as were exposed in the previous section. Just as occupational choice cannot be made once-and-for-all, so preparation for citizenship can not be over and done with. Even though other institutions contribute immensely to continuing education for citizenship, the school's responsibility cannot be satisfied and forgotten. Schools and colleges must be prepared to conduct analyses of the social, economic and political scene with students of all ages, not just teen-agers. Continuing education is the key. Governmental and other institutional forms change. Their nature, advantages, and disadvantages can only be understood by the "educated." Thus, to remain educated, the middle-aged and aged need from time-to-time to return to schooling.

Conclusion

The answer to the question, When should education become specialized? has to be: At different times for different people. In a word, the answer is: continual. Of course, the meaning is continual as job and individual needs suggest. Specialization should begin as early as the middle teens for some, and as late as the twenties for others. Specialized instruction should be available throughout employment life for vertical or horizontal movement as indicated by technological change, interest in change or improvement, and other circumstances.

Single or Dual Educational Systems

Implementation of the Smith-Hughes Act at the state level pointed up an issue which had been a recognized controversy in some states prior to that time. The Smith-Hughes Act permitted states to organize and administer vocational education as a part of the common schools or as a separate system. The only requirement was that each state or territory have a board of vocational education. In thirty-three states, boards which were responsible for general education were given the added responsibility of vocational education. In most of the other states, programs were conducted in common schools just the same. Wisconsin is the oft-noted exception. There, independent local boards administer vocational education and many of these have their own taxing power.

At the post-secondary or grade thirteen and fourteen level, a good number of the states have established separate systems. For example, New York and Connecticut have independent technical institutes.[9] The authors are of the opinion that the single versus dual or comprehensive versus separate issue is the same regardless of level. Following are the typical arguments for each.

Dual Systems

Advocates of dual systems present four major arguments: (1) They argue that leaders of the so-called regular school system are too concerned with college preparatory and (in the community college) college parallel education to be troubled with occupational education. (2) They submit that vocational education must be protected (by isolation) from scavengers. Otherwise generalists and academicians will use special monies to do their own things. For example, reimbursement monies are often utilized for improvements in areas such as science education rather than for the programs such monies are intended to support. (3) It is often said that

[9]There is no rhyme or reason to the use of terms at the post-secondary level. Technical institute, area technical school, occupational education, and career education center mean similar and dissimilar things in different states.

adequate funding is much more easily assured for separate occupational education. Taxpayers, legislators, and budget officers need to know clearly what they are buying. They will fund occupational education if it isn't confused with general education. Thus, space, equipment, and staff will be more adequate than they can be in a unified system. (4) A few of the more astute advocates of separate systems argue that career education is so different from college preparatory and general education that it cannot comingle with them.

Single Systems

Advocates of single systems have two basic arguments. (1) The first says that in a state or region, economy can only be maximized if transportation, facilities, auxiliary services, and instructional staff in such fields as mathematics and science are shared by college preparatory, general, and career education students.[10] (2) The other argument says that education must be democratic and that class distinctions arise wherever separate systems are administered.

Current Status

Needless to say, the advocates of each of the two sides to this controversy are able to lay convincing counterarguments and point to examples from practice which allegedly support the respective views. This controversy is far from a sleeping dog. In its contemporary form, the controversy is continued by the United States Department of Labor and the United States Office of Education. Both have been pleased to have Manpower Development and Training Act (MDTA) funds for education administered by USOE, leaving the issue of dual or single systems for remedial education to the states. But, in recent years the USDL has proposed legislation which by its own language would not duplicate what the common schools do, but merely do, at earlier ages than is possible under MDTA, what the common schools will not or cannot do. Put another way, USDL is saying that schools obviously fail to move large numbers of the young to success in wage earning. Therefore, new institutions should be created not to duplicate but rather to complement the common schools, which are not helping given kinds of people, especially in the teens and beyond.

Presently, the USOE appears to have postponed action on the controversy. USOE has arrested the clock for the common schools by promising to (1) promote career education at other levels, (2)

[10]The argument is the same when a general track is not involved.

bring about a truly integrated curriculum which serves all people regardless of exit level or re-entry level and (3) weld new partnerships with employers, homes, and communities to thrust the school into a new and less isolated role in human development.

Meanwhile, people in several quarters propose a cabinet-level human development agency. The authors support this idea. Manpower and public school programs should be articulated. In too many instances struggling programs exist literally side by side. Conducted in an integrated way, they could be stronger in terms of facilities and staff and broader in terms of occupations for which people might be prepared and updated. There is evidence in many local agencies to support the contention that the multiplicity of federal programs too often confuses people and splinters effects. Multiple programs require multiple administrations, grantsmen, and others. This adds to overhead at the expense of service. One way to describe the function of this book is to say that it is an attempt to define the kinds of educational programs and delivery systems which will permit a more articulated educational system to serve diverse peoples who will be free to preserve and develop their individual and peculiar selves. Such a system should be articulated level-by-level and with related agencies such as the family, private schools, and employers. Weber (1971) is correct in his admonishment that vocational education functions in a pluralistic society and in a pluralistic labor market. The plea here is not that one institution but rather that an articulated system of institutions, including the Employment Service, agencies in the labor market, and a variety of educational establishments (as Weber would have it) should serve diverse peoples.

Summary

The summary of this chapter is best presented in the form of principles.

Re Function

1. The curriculum should assure a balance of play, learning, and work.
2. Balances of play, learning, and work are essential to optimum individual and societal development.
3. Because other institutions contribute heavily to play and learning, work should now become the unifying thread of formal schooling.
4. Experiences centered around work are essential to sophistication about play and learning. The three have synergistic effects.

5. Balance of curriculum components is an individual matter, varying a great deal over time. This speaks loudly for continuing education.

Re Age of Specialization

1. Educational requirements of occupations are not nearly as essential to decisions re age of specialization as some maintain. Opportunities and demands for employment shifts and continuing education negate arguments for postponing occupational choice, preparation, and entry until after secondary schooling.
2. Occupational choice cannot be free and intelligent if it is put off. Young people make choices regardless of schools. Schools should intervene to help make choices judicious, knowledge-based, and individual. Continuing education and opportunities to change and adjust choices negate the need to delay occupational education.
3. Good citizenship is assured rather than hindered by education which is centered about career development.

Re Single or Dual Systems

1. The citizenry deserves a planned and integrated educational system which is at once effective and economical.
2. Such a system should be articulated level-by-level and should serve the concerns of individuals and manpower demands. These are not diverse concerns for people who have experienced career education based on sound career development theory.

BIBLIOGRAPHY

Broudy, H. S., Smith, B. O., and Burnett, J. R. *Democracy and excellence in American secondary education.* Chicago: Rand McNally, 1964.
Dewey, J. *Democracy and Education.* New York: MacMillan, 1916.
Weber, A. R. Vocational education in a pluralistic society. *American Vocational Journal,* 1971, 46(2), 26-29.

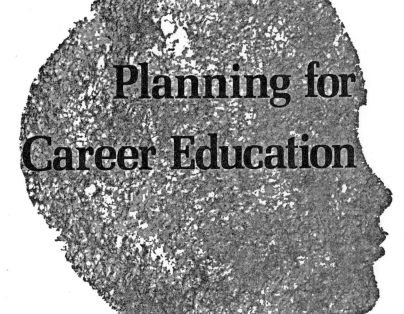

Planning for
Career Education

CHAPTER 10

Fundamentals
of Curriculum Development

Introduction

This chapter was prompted by the authors' concern for the lack of rigorous, systematic thinking regarding curriculum for career education. Disparity exists between the major priority status accorded career education by the U. S. Office of Education and curriculum components being recommended to implement this new concept. To' date, curriculum specialists have been content to develop teaching resource guides which consist primarily of suggested classroom activities and recommended commercial curriculum materials. These activities are, for the most part, loosely organized supplemental instructional units, emphasizing lower-level cognitive behaviors. These activities are not only inadequate to develop the behaviors required for self understanding, career decision-making, and preparation for employment, but are also serious indictments of career education professionals' lack of familiarity with curriculum development fundamentals.

Unlike large-scale curriculum revisions which were done in mathematics and science during the early sixties, career education is seen as a *reorientation* of the total school program. Again, unlike mathematics and science, a traditional program does not exist for career education to build upon, except for selected prespecialized junior high school and specialized high school vocational programs. Career education at the elementary school level is virtually nonexistent.

Before innovative, creative curriculum and instructional materials can emerge, more research and development must be done to translate career education theory into conceptual curriculum models which are manageable in implementation. This chapter presents a broad, analytical review of curriculum development fundamentals. In Chapter 11 these basic principles are applied in the development of a conceptual curriculum model for career education programs.

The Need for Systematic Inquiry

Proponents of career education have a number of reasons for being optimistic about the future, e.g., endorsement by the U. S. Office of Education and large levels of Federal funding. However, affiliation with the Office of Education and dependence on governmental appropriations cause people in many circles to regard career education with some skepticism. With due respect, how many previous USOE initiated programs have been widely adopted?

Successful implementation of career education in the schools will depend in large measure upon how well lessons have been learned from previous attempts to establish educational programs of similar scope and magnitude. Consider the following examples (Goodlad, 1966).

1. Shortly after World War II, child study programs centering on the value of each individual were popularized. Because curriculum was defined as broadly as life itself, however, the content of learning was not significantly influenced. Did this failure teach us that "love is not enough"?

2. With a much narrower definition of curriculum, reformers in the post-Sputnik era changed the content of learning and placed new things of instruction in the classroom. These curriculums have been more successful than many of their predecessors. Serious errors in judgment were made, however, regarding the ease with which teachers could use the materials. Witness the number of teachers who unwittingly destroyed the intent of the new inductive curriculums by teaching them deductively. Like love, the well-designed learning package is not enough.

3. A third example was made obvious in the previous discussion of compensatory education in Chapter 5. It will be recalled that this reform was a massive government subsidized effort to "compensate" for economic, social, and educational ills. The lesson to be learned here (among many others) is that governmental funds and high ideals do not necessarily change a local school program that is steeped in tradition, conservatism, and structure.

These and many other well-known examples manifest education's continuing sin, i.e., vacillating from one curriculum excess to another, indiscriminately applying what is currently fashionable to the whole of formal education with little forethought and planning (Goodlad, 1966). Passion, idealism, subject matter expertise and Federal funds are important ingredients which must be brought to bear on curriculum reform *collectively* rather than *individually.* If career education is going to be anything more than a temporary fad, a thorough appraisal of "functions" (i.e., management by objectives) and disciplined, systematic programs of curriculum development and implementation are required. These are tasks which are made possible through application of the theory and technology of curriculum. It is myopic to infer that curriculum development has matured to the level of some of the applied sciences. Nonetheless, the growing body of curriculum literature provides a substantive base and a scheme of thinking which are adequate for translating career education theory into practice.

The Concept of Curriculum

"Curriculum" and the terms "education," "teaching," "learning," and "school" have many different definitions and usages. And well they should so long as the terms communicate the intent of the user and facilitate communications relative to a given situation or context. For the person who is concerned to translate a particular educational philosophy into practice, a particular concept of curriculum defines the parameters within which he must function. For example, the following might be regarded as possible definitions for curriculum (Oliver, 1965, p. 5):
Curriculum is:

All the experiences the child has regardless of when or how they take place.

All the experiences the learner has under the guidance of the school.

All the courses which a school offers.

The systematic arrangement of certain courses designed for certain pupil purposes, e.g., "college-preparatory curriculum."

Courses offered within a certain subject field, e.g., "the science curriculum," "the language arts curriculum."

The program in a specialized professional school, e.g., "the two-year curriculum in nursing."

Those courses taken by an individual; e.g., John and Peter may both be college-preparatory, but John's curriculum might be different in that he takes French instead of Spanish or that he has a different teacher in English.

These examples demonstrate that a satisfactory concept of curriculum should contain (or at least imply) *a manageable point of view* of organized education. The more practical outlook is suggested by the second statement — curriculum is the part of an individual's day for which the school has direct responsibility.

A second criteria for a minimum concept of curriculum is a *clear distinction* between "curriculum" and "instruction." According to Johnson (1967), curriculum does not prescribe *means*, i.e., activities, materials, or even instructional content to be used in achieving results. Rather, curriculum's role is in guiding instruction; it must be viewed as anticipatory, not reportorial. Curriculum implies intent. (See Fig. 10-1.) In specifying outcomes to be sought, curriculum is concerned with *ends* at the level of attainable learning products.

From these basic criteria a tentative concept[1] of curriculum can be evolved. Authorities in the area of curriculum tend to regard the term as being synonymous with the "educational program." "The term 'curriculum' is simply a name for the organized pattern of a school's educational program" (Phenix, 1958, p. 57). The

[1]No attempt will be made here to provide a specific, arbitrary definition of curriculum. A thorough account of the problems related to a definition of curriculum is contained in Short and Marconnit (1968, pp. 3-50).

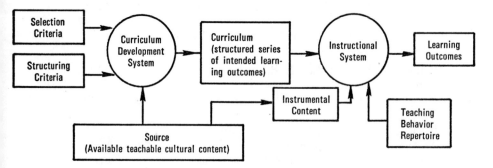

SOURCE: M. J. Johnson, "Definitions and Models in Curriculum Theory," *Educational Theory*, 1967, 17, p. 133.

Fig. 10-1. Model Showing Curriculum as an Output of One System and an Input of Another

educational program generally consists of three basic elements: (1) program of studies, (2) program of activities, and (3) program of pupil personnel services. The distinguishing characteristics and an interpretation of this threefold view of curriculum follow (Oliver, 1965).

Program of Studies

Most elementary and secondary schools obviously function as though they exist to transmit the "cultural heritage." The critical questions for the curriculum developer become "Which cultural heritage?" and "How may it be organized?". Because all man's accumulated knowledge cannot be transmitted, the school must serve as an agency, not only to select, but also to interpret, apply, and organize content in some coherent fashion (Oliver, 1965).

The oldest and prevailing form of organization, especially in the high school, is the subject matter approach. In the secondary schools, most subject organization is according to the "logic" of the pertinent discipline. It is assumed that specified subjects cover important areas of social heritage. Thus, subject matter becomes the central task, exposition tends to be the chief method of instruction, and textbooks are the primary resource. That this pattern of organization is antiquated is made obvious by Taba (1962, p. 392):

1. Subjects alone, *qua* subjects, do not provide a sufficiently adequate basis for developing a scope of well-rounded education, because in themselves they have no inherent criterion for either comprehensiveness or worth, and because subject organization discourages the pursuit of multiple objectives.
2. Subjects alone do not provide a sufficient basis for sequence, especially if they minimize understanding of and concern for analysis of what is learned or of the behavioral objectives.
3. Subject organization, conventionally pursued, practically prevents a pursuit of interrelated learning. It tends toward unnecessary compartmentalization and atomization of learning.

As simple and appealing as subject matter organization may be, curriculum specialists in career education must be willing to think beyond traditional ways of organizing curriculum content. Career educators must take the lead in (1) eliminating the proliferation of course offerings; (2) consolidating subject matter around broad fields, life functions, or unified (core) approaches; and (3) integrating the practical and applied areas of human knowledge with the more traditional academic ones.

Program of Activities

Recognition of the part played by the program of activities and experiences is an important shift in curriculum emphasis, which has occurred during the last several decades. These activities are seen by educators as ways (1) of vitalizing the curriculum, (2) of meeting criticisms of the conventional subject curriculum, (3) of counteracting the passivity and sterility of learning, and (4) of meeting the needs and interests of individual pupils.

At the elementary school level, the program of studies and the program of activities are often blended together. A less integrated program of activities is apparent at the high school level. Regardless of whether certain experiences are scheduled as "activity periods" or as "extracurricular" (Oliver, 1965), they can provide relevant and concrete opportunities for self exploration, development of leisure time pursuits, and the development of career-related interests and abilities. The compatability of career education and the program of activities suggests better articulation of experiences with the program of studies and elimination of negative connotations of "extracurricular" which are held by many advocates of the more formal curriculum.

Program of Pupil Personnel Services

The third fundamental element of our emerging concept of curriculum is direct and indirect, noninstructional services which have come to be called "student personnel services." This program, like the program of activities, reflects an extension of school services beyond formal academic education. Considerable confusion and conflict can be observed in present day schools and colleges regarding the proper role and function of guidance, counseling, placement and other student services. "This problem in semantics may not always seem significant; however, ambiguities regarding goals and methods can lead to many kinds of misunderstandings, such as rivalries among services, poor communication among services and with other school personnel, confused expectancies by lay people, and of most importance, decreased effectiveness in meeting pupil needs . . . Sorting out and clarifying these roles and functions have not as yet reached a mature stage" (Roeber, Walz & Smith, 1969, pp. 52-53).

The confusion of roles and functions is likely to get worse, rather than better, as a result of the needs of career education; e.g., (1) The expansion of career education and career guidance in grades K-14 will create the need for large numbers of teachers and guidance workers. Much of the need will be satisfied by less than adequately trained professionals, who will confuse issues and services. (2) The realization that many career development objectives can better be achieved within the program of studies rather than the program of pupil personnel services will create additional conflicts. Teachers will make all manner of responses. (3) The clear mandate for occupational placement and follow-up at the high school level will face difficult resistance from college-oriented counselors who may be philosophically opposed and/or ill-equipped to provide or develop such services.

These and related requirements of career education have important implications for a concept of curriculum. Career educators can best avoid rivalries with personnel services professionals by assuring that clear statements of educational goals and objectives for career education, guidance, counseling, and placement and follow-up are established *prior* to determination of who will provide the respective services.

Discussion of the three primary elements of the educational program has made obvious the fact that curriculum should provide for the achievement of a wide range of educational objectives. However, as Taba (1962) points out, the possibility of planning learning experiences to attain a wide range of objectives has never been well understood or practiced. The remainder of this chapter defines the task of curriculum development in a way which demonstrates that provision for multiple objectives is not only desirable but practical.

The Technology of Curriculum Development

An exciting new era in curriculum theory and technology has evolved during the last two decades as a result of a phenomenon which Grobman (1970) calls the *developmental curriculum project.*[2] The first group to undertake a systematic, radical change in curriculum through a "developmental process" was the University of Illinois Committee on School Mathematics (UICSM). The UICSM began in 1951 as a cooperative effort, involving education, mathematics, and engineering to improve high school mathematics courses.

It was not until 1957, however, that the modern era of curriculum building and innovation in education began. In that year, the Physical Sciences Study Committee (PSSC) received a multimillion dollar grant from the National Science Foundation to prepare curriculum materials for a "new" high school physics course. The significant features of this project were radically new approaches

[2]Grobman (1970) has written a scholarly, detailed account of the processes and decision points of a number of the more notable curriculum development projects. This book is considered mandatory reading for all who are engaged in curriculum research.

to subject matter and new ways of producing instructional material. A concise description of what constitutes a developmental curriculum project is provided by Grobman (1970, p. 4):

The terms developmental curriculum project and curriculum project are synonymous, and refer to group — in contrast to individual or co-author — efforts to produce some new kind of curriculum, using experimental tryouts of preliminary materials and collecting feedback from such tryouts to be used for the improvement of the curriculum prior to its release for general distribution.

The earliest developmental curriculum efforts were centered primarily on classroom textbooks for students and guides for instructors to permit effective teaching of these texts. A number of projects have since expanded their interests and approaches (they have been concerned with a very broad interpretation of curriculum) to include any activities relevant to student learnings. Some projects work on student text materials; some work on teacher materials in addition to or in place of student materials; some are concerned with supplemental learning materials; and some are primarily process-oriented, to the extent that no student materials are prepared, but instead, the emphasis is on preparing teachers to operate in certain ways.

Thus, the focus of developmental projects varies widely as does the way they go about their tasks. What they have in common is that the effort is not by an individual author, or one or two co-authors, but is broader; there are experimental tryouts of materials or procedures, and feedback from such tryouts is then used to improve the curriculum before it is made generally available.

The mushrooming of developmental curriculum projects, made possible by (1) increasing professional concern for developing alternatives to traditional subject matter courses and (2) large levels of funding by government agencies, private foundations, and commercial textbook publishers, has resulted in an emerging pattern for the curriculum development process. One of the more important discoveries of such projects is that there is no single, best method of achieving project objectives. Considerable variation is possible with respect to the operational conduct of a project. On the other hand, most successful projects are characterized by a rational, systematic process of decision-making and organization. The following discussion of a representative curriculum model has resulted from a synthesis of conventional curriculum theory and technology (for example, see Short and Marconnit, 1968), from application of Grobman's (1970) analysis of the developmental curriculum project, and the authors' personal experiences in directing the Career Development for Children Project (CDCP).

A General Conceptual Model

Every curriculum development effort potentially involves thousands of decisions. Many are of trivial, routine nature and go al-

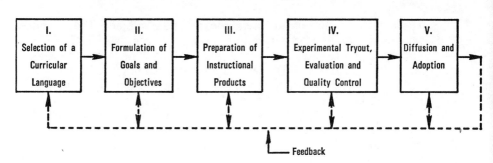

Fig. 10-2. Five Phases in Overall Structure for a General Curriculum Model

most unnoticed. Others have far-reaching effects and may either build restraints into the system or enhance operational "degrees of freedom" (Grobman, 1970). Therefore, some type of conceptual framework is required to help researchers and developers see the entire process, understand the complex of decisions, and assure that certain considerations are not under-emphasized or over-emphasized. Such a framework should be designed to aid careful planning, continual examination, revision, growth, and successful implementation. Emans (1966, p. 327) provides the following additional rationale:

A conceptual framework may be thought to be analogous to a system of light-houses at sea. It does not tell where to go or restrict movement, but it is necessary to guide movement and warn of the danger spots. *American education may be at a point where advance in practice will not come about without a conceptual framework which takes account of all the forces within the curriculum.*[3]

Figure 10-2 provides an example of a type of conceptual framework (or model) which is (1) sophisticated enough to guide curriculum development regardless of level, subject area, philosophy, or specific type of curriculum and (2) reflective of the reality of how curriculum actually evolves in most developmental curriculum projects. Each of these five major phases are now examined in more detail.

Phase I. Selection of a Curricular Language

The area of greatest disparity between conventional curriculum texts and the literature of developmental curriculum projects is in importance attached to the selection of a curricular language.

[3]Emphasis added.

The more conventional texts seldom treat the subject. The implication seems to be that curriculum developers are devoid of feeling, opinions, philosophy, or values. This point of view is challenged by Grobman (1970, p. 64): "Perhaps the most important decisions made by a project are those concerning basic purpose and those involving basic value judgments."

One of the reasons why this initial phase of curriculum development is seldom discussed is that the formulation of basic purpose and the related decisions are often not formalized or identifiable project activities. For many projects, curriculum development is a facet of the director's prior interests. For others, the purpose may be defined by a parent organization or a funding agency. Some define basic purpose after the project has been undertaken and the staff has been employed. Regardless of the degree of formality and regardless of whether the curricular language is stated or implied, all projects can be characterized by their unique "personal idiom." Examine the following examples of curricular language which have been exerpted from descriptive materials of the CDCP.

Basic purpose: The Career Development for Children Project is designed to involve children, beginning in elementary school, in experiences which will facilitate the broad goal of vocational maturity . . . the intermediate goal for the project, at approximately the grade eight level, is to have students formulate a tentative occupational preference which will aid them in making decisions about their choice of a high school curriculum (Bailey, 1971 a, p. 1).

Educational theory: The stimulus for the Career Development for Children Project resulted from a reorientation in the philosophy of vocational education. As a result of the Vocational Education Act of 1963 and 1968 Amendments, the role of vocational education has shifted from an emphasis on filling the requirements of the labor market to meeting the needs of people (Bailey, 1971 a, p. 1).

Learning theory: From a teaching standpoint, CDCP has tried to build into the curriculum concrete activities in addition to vicarious ones. Techniques such as role playing, gaming and simulation, and problem solving will receive high priority in conjunction with personal guidance experiences . . . The important thing for the teacher to keep in mind is that the curriculum is designed to allow the children to participate in various experiences so they will have, on a personal level, an idea of what certain kinds of work are like and will be able to see how these kinds of work 'fit' with their emerging concepts of themselves (Zimmerman and Bailey, 1971, pp. 18-19).

Rationale: While the direction of education is currently in flux, it seems likely that in the future more attention will be devoted to developing flexible approaches to education and career determination. It may be, for example, that middle class children will not be stuck in the go-to-college rut. There may be many alternate routes for them to take, including junior college and paraprofessional level programs. While future manpower forecasts still cite the need for trained personnel, it may not be necessary to have a liberal arts education or a college degree . . . Vocational education in many different forms promises to become education for all types of students (Zimmerman and Bailey, 1971, p. 3).

Moral and value judgments: There is considerable evidence in recent years that this tendency [emphasis on subject matter] is being reversed and that teachers are becoming more aware of the need to emphasize relevant and humanistic education . . . The specific aim is increased personal freedom to make career choices based on an understanding of the tremendously varied opportunities available in contemporary society. We hope to prevent students making choices directed only by custom, geographic accident, or based on race, sex, or social class . . . We believe a vacuum exists in the contemporary school curriculum. A belief shared with many interested citizens, educators, and legislators. This vacuum exists where a bridge should be, i.e., a bridge between the school and a productive, satisfying career (Bailey, Turner, and Van Rooy, 1972, p. 4).

Assumptions: A primary assumption of the project is that career development is one aspect of the continuing and fluid processes of growth and learning. Maturing in a vocational sense involves coping with the developmental tasks of a given life stage, in part, through a series of integrated decisions (Bailey, 1971 b, p. 7).

These examples manifest the nature of the CDCP and reflect the theoretical orientation of its staff. The selection of a curricular language serves to define the "personality" of a project, provides bases for the formulation of goals and objectives, and influences the type of content selected and the type of instructional materials developed.

Phase II. Formulation of Goals and Objectives

Curriculum construction involves the process of moving through descending abstractions from very general and global statements of desired program behaviors to intermediate level statements which indicate the blocks from which the program will be constructed (Krathwohl, 1965). Several levels of description are necessary to judicious planning of educational processes. Obviously, primary levels of description must precede other levels.

Krathwohl (1965) provides a system for describing objectives at three levels of generality:

1. At the first and most abstract level are the general statements most helpful in the *development of programs of instruction* or the laying out of types of courses and areas to be covered. These are goals toward which several years of education might be aimed or for which an entire unit such as an elementary, junior, or senior high school might strive.

2. The second and more concrete level is referred to as *behavioral objectives.* These help to analyze broad goals into more specific ones which are useful as the building blocks for instructional units.

3. Third, there is a level needed to create *instructional materials.* This kind of detailed analysis brings into focus the objectives to be achieved for a specific lesson.

This manner of ordering objectives is representative of contemporary curriculum theory and technology. Although some authors prefer substitute terms such as "performance objectives," "goals," "aims," or "outcomes," there are few substantial differences among those who write about educational objectives. The important thing for the curriculum developer to keep in mind is the necessity for having clear statements of overt behavior for at least three levels of generality.

Additional considerations with respect to program goals and behavioral objectives may now be examined more closely. It will be observed that the authors prefer to think of Krathwohl's Level 2 behavioral objectives and Level 3 instructional objectives as merely "general" and "specific" levels of behavioral outcomes. This rationale will be more obvious in a later discussion.

Specification of Program Goals

The definition of basic purpose in Phase I of the general curriculum model establishes the general parameters for curriculum development. Usually, such statements describe eventual educational outcomes which are to be attained during adulthood. The next step of translating long-term aims into program goals is the curriculum developer's first encounter with defining *concretely* what he means by the basic purpose and global, long-range aims.

In defining program goals for several levels of education (e.g., elementary, junior high, and high school), the authors have found the concept of *developmental tasks* to be particularly useful.[4,5] Havighurst's definition (1953, p. 2) is the most widely accepted interpretation of this phenomenon: "A developmental task is a task which arises at or about a certain period in the life of the individual, successful achievement of which leads to his happiness and to success with later tasks, while failure leads to unhappiness in the individual, disapproval by the society, and difficulty with later tasks." Havighurst goes on to provide examples of major tasks during middle childhood and adolescence:

[4]The authors wish to acknowledge the influence of Herr (1969) in pointing out the utility and validity of this concept for career development.

[5]A case history of the developmental task concept is provided by Havighurst (1953, pp. 328-332).

Middle Childhood (6-12)

1. Learning physical skills necessary for ordinary games
2. Building wholesome attitudes toward oneself as a growing organism
3. Learning to get along with age-mates
4. Learning an appropriate masculine or feminine role
5. Developing fundamental skills in reading, writing, and calculating
6. Developing concepts necessary for everyday living
7. Developing conscience, morality, and a scale of values
8. Achieving personal independence
9. Developing attitudes toward social groups and institutions (pp. 28-41)

Adolescence (13-17)

1. Achieving new and more mature relations with age-mates of both sexes
2. Achieving a masculine or feminine social role
3. Accepting one's physique and using the body effectively
4. Achieving emotional independence of parents and other adults
5. Achieving assurance of economic independence
6. Selecting and preparing for an occupation
7. Preparing for marriage and family life
8. Developing intellectual skills and concepts necessary for civic competence
9. Desiring and achieving socially responsible behavior
10. Acquiring a set of values and an ethical system as a guide to behavior (pp. 111-158)

Developmental tasks reflect three major sources of origin: (1) physical maturation (*biological* basis), (2) the pressures of cultural processes upon the individual (*cultural* basis), and (3) the desires, aspirations, and values of the emerging personality (*psychological* basis). The compatibility of the developmental task concept with career development processes is made obvious by Zaccaria's summary (1965, p. 373):

1. Individual growth and development is continuous.
2. Individual growth can be divided into periods or life stages for descriptive purposes.
3. Individuals in each life stage can be characterized by certain general characteristics that they have in common.
4. Most individuals in a given culture pass through similar developmental stages.
5. The society makes certain demands upon individuals.
6. These demands are relatively uniform for all members of the society.
7. The demands differ from stage to stage as the individual goes through the developmental process.
8. Developmental crises occur when the individual perceives the demand to alter his present behavior and master new learnings.
9. In meeting and mastering developmental crises, the individual moves from one developmental stage of maturity to another developmental stage of maturity.
10. The task appears in its purest form at one stage.
11. Preparation for meeting the developmental crises or developmental tasks occurs in the life stage prior to the stage in which it must be mastered.
12. The developmental task or crisis may arise again during a later phase in somewhat different form.

13. The crisis or task must be mastered before the individual can successfully move on to a subsequent developmental stage.
14. Meeting the crisis successfully by learning the required task leads to societal approval, happiness, and success with later crisis and their correlative tasks.
15. Failing in meeting a task or crisis leads to disapproval by society.

Although the developmental task concept has gained rather wide acceptance in other fields of education, it has seldom been applied to curriculum for career education.[6] This discussion has attempted to alert curriculum developers to the potential for providing a sequential set of developmental experiences. In the next chapter, the authors provide specific examples of how developmental tasks may be translated into program goals for each of several levels of education.

Behavioral Objectives
Having specified program goals derived from developmental tasks, the curriculum developer must begin to elaborate descriptions of observable behaviors which demonstrate successful mastery of a given task. Three important ingredients are brought to bear during this step: (1) Knowledge of the relevant body of theory and research literature (in this case childhood and adolescent vocational behavior and the correlates of vocational maturity). (2) Knowledge of the taxonomies of educational objectives and how they may be used. (3) Proficiency in specifying instructional objectives in behavioral terms. See Fig. 10-3.

Knowledge of relevant theory and research. Why the authors chose to devote a major part of this text to a discussion of career development theory and research will now become more apparent. Research of the type presented in Chapter 4 has important implications for the specification of relevant and valid educational objectives. An example will help to clarify this contention. Bailey (1971 a, b) has described the ultimate goal of the Career Development for Children Project in terms of facilitating "vocational maturity." To translate this construct into measurable behavioral outcomes, it was necessary to analyze the research literature on vocational maturity, e.g., Super, Gribbons and Lohnes, Crites, and Westbrook. Thus, the nature of the *learner* became the object for curriculum study rather than an organized body of content. This is an example of a major distinction between career education and conventional subject-matter- or discipline-centered curriculums. The curriculum

---

[6]One exception is Havighurst's (1964) schema for specifying tasks in terms of a six-stage outline of vocational development. His treatment, however, is only a beginning attempt to relate developmental tasks to career development.

developer in career education must become a specialist in career development theory, vocational psychology, occupational sociology, and related fields if he is to facilitate the requisite outcomes of career education. It is suggested that the reader consult Herr (1972, pp. 110-120) for an additional discussion of "research pertinent to vocationalization."

Knowledge of taxonomies. The Taxonomy of Educational Objectives emanates from three scholarly attempts to organize and classify learning outcomes into three categories or domains: (1)

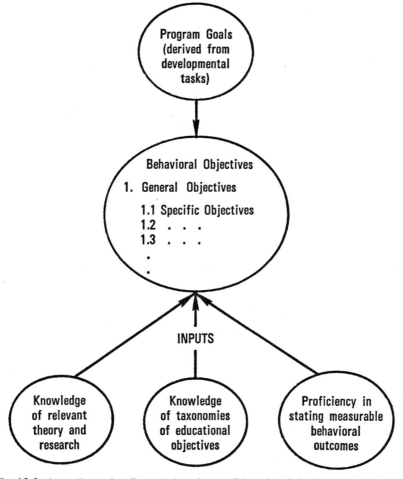

Fig. 10-3. Ingredients for Formulating Career Education Behavioral Objectives

the *cognitive* domain (intellectual outcomes), (2) the *affective* domain (feelings and emotions, such as interests, attitudes, appreciation, and methods of adjustment), and (3) the *psychomotor* domain (motor skills). Within each domain, categories for classifying objectives are arranged in hierarchical order, from the simplest behavioral outcomes to the most complex. Each of the three domains are summarized in Table 10-1.

For the curriculum developer, the Taxonomy is an extremely useful tool during the actual writing operation. Bloom, Hastings and Madaus (1971, p. 40) suggest several ways in which the Taxonomy may be used.

1. The Taxonomy provides illustrative operational statements to help curriculum writers translate broad objectives into operational terms. The Taxonomy provides an additional benefit by serving as a common point of reference for several individual writers.
2. Neophyte curriculum writers often tend to state objectives which deal only with lower level outcomes such as recall of facts. One of the principal values of the Taxonomy is that it provides direction for constructing objectives which deal with more complex behaviors.

TABLE 10-1

SUMMARY OF THE TAXONOMIES
OF EDUCATIONAL OBJECTIVES

Levels in the Cognitive, Affective, and
Psychomotor Domains

Cognitive Domain	Affective Domain	Psychomotor Domain
1. Knowledge 2. Comprehension 3. Application 4. Analysis 5. Synthesis 6. Evaluation	1. Receiving 2. Responding 3. Valuing 4. Organization 5. Characterization by a value or value complex	1. Perception 2. Set 3. Guided response 4. Mechanism 5. Complex overt response 6. Adaptation 7. Origination

SOURCE: Based on Bloom (1956), Krathwohl (1964), and Simpson (1969).

3. Finally, the Taxonomy can suggest classes of objectives not previously covered. Used in this way, it becomes a guide for more comprehensive coverage of desired behaviors.

It was pointed out earlier that the classification of objectives from the Taxonomy and the specification or writing of objectives occurs simultaneously rather than as two separate events. Therefore, discussion of a procedure for stating behavioral objectives, elaboration of the steps in defining objectives, and appropriate examples are in order.

Stating behavioral outcomes. "An objective is an intent communicated by a statement describing a proposed change in a learner — a statement of what the learner is to be like when he has successfully completed a learning experience" (Mager, 1962, p. 3). This statement by Robert Mager, the best known advocate of what are known as "behavioral objectives," represents one of the most significant developments in curriculum and instruction of the last decade. In large part because of the popularization of Mager's *Preparing Instructional Objectives,* most educators readily endorse the rationale for writing behavioral objectives which describe measurable pupil outcomes to be achieved by instruction. Any educator worth his salt quickly recognizes the following as a Mager-type objective:

> Provided with a list of ten occupational establishments, the student will classify their primary goal as either goods or services production. All will be correctly classified in three minutes.

Three elements are contained in this type of objective:
1. A description of the important *conditions* under which the student will be expected to demonstrate achievement of the objective (e.g., time limits, problems to solve, materials, or equipment which will be available, questions to be answered, or special instructions).
2. A description of the type of observable *behavior* which the student will be asked to employ in demonstrating mastery of the objective (e.g., "to write," "to solve," "to classify," "to orally describe").
3. The *criterion* which will be used to evaluate the success of the student's performance (e.g., must get 100% correct, correctly applies three principles, completes the task in fifteen minutes, or correctly identifies eight out of ten).

The centrality of clear statements of behavior for curriculum, instruction, and evaluation are well-documented by leading authorities, e.g., Bloom (1956), Gagné (1967), Krathwohl, et al. (1964),

Tyler (1950), and Bloom, et al. (1971).[7] Although considerable agreement exists regarding the *need* and *importance* of statements of objectives in behavioral terms, some disagreement exists regarding the *form* in which objectives should be stated. Grobman (1970, p. 102) summarizes well a major source of disagreement:

In the last decade, the pendulum has swung from the statement of goals in the most general terms to the statement in highly precise terms. And now it may be swinging back to a midpoint, to a compromise position, where there is a recognition that global objectives are clearly inadequate to set an appropriate framework for curriculum development or evaluation; and precise statements, in terms of immediately observable objectives, may be overly restrictive.

The method of stating objectives which the authors have found to be the most practical and functional is outlined in Gronlund's book on *Stating Behavioral Objectives for Classroom Instruction.*[8] Gronlund's rationale for writing the book reveals the same concern which Grobman has pointed out. "What was needed was an approach that would avoid both extremes, one that would include statements of objectives that were general enough to provide direction, without overly limiting the instructional process, and specific enough to be clearly defined by the behavior that students were to exhibit when they had achieved the objectives" (Gronlund, 1970, pp. iii).

The major feature of Gronlund's method is differentiation between what he calls "minimum-essentials level" (MEL) objectives and "developmental level" (DL) objectives. MEL objectives are those which attempt to shape and modify student behavior to fit a predetermined minimum level of performance. These objectives are frequently stated as tasks to be performed rather than as goals to work toward. Mager is the most prominent proponent of MEL objectives. DL objectives represent a whole class of responses and are not stated as specific tasks to be performed. Objectives in this form are stated as *general* objectives followed by a sample of more *specific* behaviors. Contrasts of the two objectives formats are evident.

Mager-type objective (MEL):

In response to a direct question, the student will be able to name correctly the four principal effects that a career has on an individual's life.

---

[7]For a discussion of the pros and cons of stating objectives in behavioral terms, see Eisner (1969), Ebel (1967), and Hastings (1967).

[8]Though Gronlund's practical guide was written for the classroom teacher, it is equally appropriate and useful to the curriculum developer.

Gronlund-type objective (DL):
1. Understands the importance of choosing a career
    1.1 Explains the four principal effects that a career has on an individual's life.
    1.2 Identifies the relative personal importance of the various factors in identifying career goals.
    1.3 Justifies the importance of systematic career selection.

Following are the major distinctions between instructional objectives stated at the minimum-essentials level and at the developmental level:

1. The most obvious differences between MEL and DL objectives are the ways in which they are written. MEL objectives always contain the three elements of: conditions, behavior, and criterion. Usually, this type of objective also contains a phrase, such as "the student will be able." DL objectives on the other hand, contain only-a statement of terminal behavior. These objectives consist of a two-step process (i.e., general and specific) rather than only one. Each objective begins with an action verb and omits such unnecessary refinements as "the student will be able . . ."
2. Writers of MEL objectives often compile exhaustive lists of specific and completely defined performance tasks. DL objectives are more broadly stated, general goals, defined by a representative sample of specific behaviors. According to Gronlund, from eight to twelve general objectives will usually suffice for an entire course and be both manageable and suitable in terms of level of generality.
3. When MEL objectives are used, teaching and testing tend to focus on the more simple, low-level learning outcomes. More sophisticated outcomes such as the ability to understand, to apply, to interpret, and to think critically are better defined by DL objectives.

The reader may wish to consult Gronlund for more subtle differences.

To the curriculum developer the advantages of using Gronlund's procedure are obvious. Curriculum writers face extremely difficult tasks in formulating program goals and translating them into objectives. Assuring that objectives contain conditions or arbitrary standards of performance, e.g., eight out of ten correct, is an additional and usually unnecessary burden. Curriculum development is a dynamic and evolutionary process. Goals, objectives, and basic purposes change as feedback data are obtained. The procedure which Gronlund recommends not only allows the curriculum developer to define where he is going, but also simplifies evaluation, and is less difficult to revise.

Writing behavioral objectives. How does one go about stating program goals and measurable learner objectives? Two principles are especially relevant. (1) the process consists of identifiable decision points and events, and (2) the process need not necessarily be a linear one, i.e., considerable variance exists regarding the order in which the steps are undertaken, depending on scope of curriculum development, basic purpose, and expertise of personnel. Some steps, which will be obvious, have prerequisites which must be met.

Objectives writing is the epitome of "systems" thinking and practice, i.e., the development-application-evaluation-feedback continuum. Objectives are quite properly emergent. They are subject to continual evolution, evaluation and modification. Together with the knowledge that this is suggested procedure, the following illustrates the major events involved in phase two of the general curriculum model:

1. Think behaviorally. Orient yourself to thinking in terms of observable learner behavior. (If you have internalized the basic principles of career development and accept career education as valid, you are probably already in the groove.)

2. Arm yourself with basic reference material related to developmental tasks (e.g., Havighurst, 1953; and 1964) and recommended goals for education (e.g., Kearney, 1953, and French et al., 1957).[9] Don't expect to "find" existing career education goals; however, they must be deduced. These materials will help you to evolve valid goals and to assure that newly defined goals will be compatible with on-going educational aims.

3. Begin to define tentative educational goals that are consistent with basic purpose. Keep in mind that goals are ". . . something to strive for, to move toward, or to become. It is an aim or purpose so stated that it excites the imagination and gives people something they want to work for, something they don't yet know how to do, something they can be proud of when they achieve it" (Kappel, 1960, p. 38).

---

[9]Do not ignore these even though they are dated. The reader will discover that preparation for a career and related behaviors has long been recommended as a basic educational goal.

4. Once tentative goals are formulated, they must be refined and delimited. Goals which are not compatible with the "curriculum language" must be screened out. Search for inconsistencies which violate basic purpose, educational theory, learning theory, assumptions, and moral and value judgments. Since the curriculum development task is already delimited to career education, a limited number of goals is required for a given level of education.

5. The process of stating and classifying general behavioral objectives is next. These two activities occur simultaneously. Using the Taxonomies of Educational Objectives together with representative behavioral terms[10] as guides (see Tables 10-2, 10-3 and 10-4 for suggested usage), state each general objective that is necessary to accomplish the individual developmental tasks. Initially, formulate objectives for each of the three domains independently. Also, for a given domain, develop the lower order levels prior to moving on to the next highest one. For example, complete the "knowledge" level of the cognitive domain before proceeding to the "comprehensive" level, and so on.

    Not widely understood, but an important consideration to recognize is the relationship between the cognitive and affective domains. As Grobman (1970, p. 93) points out, ". . . achievement of all cognitive objectives requires parallel, concomitant achievement of affective objectives; achievement in the cognitive domain must include achievement in at least the first two levels of the affective domain, and also probably includes some involvement of the third level of the affective domain — the building of values."

6. Next, pause to check where you are going. Did you:
    a. Begin each general objective with an action verb?
    b. State each objective in terms of measurable learner performance?
    c. Limit each objective to only one learner outcome?
    d. State each general objective so that specific types of behaviors are definable?
    e. Include all general behaviors that make up each program goal?

    If so, you are ready to proceed with the next step of stating specific level objectives.

7. Repeat steps 5 and 6 for specific level objectives.

[10]See Gronlund (1970, pp. 53-56) for lists of action verbs.

TABLE 10-2

MAJOR CATEGORIES IN THE COGNITIVE DOMAIN OF THE TAXONOMY OF EDUCATIONAL OBJECTIVES (BLOOM, 1956)

Descriptions of the Major Categories in the Cognitive Domain

1. **Knowledge.** Knowledge is defined as the remembering of previously learned material. This may involve the recall of a wide range of material, from specific facts to complete theories, but all that is required is the bringing to mind of the appropriate information. Knowledge represents the lowest level of learning outcomes in the cognitive domain.

2. **Comprehension.** Comprehension is defined as the ability to grasp the meaning of material. This may be shown by translating material from one form to another (words to numbers), by interpreting material (explaining or summarizing), and by estimating future trends (predicting consequences or effects). These learning outcomes go one step beyond the simple remembering of material, and represent the lowest level of understanding.

3. **Application.** Application refers to the ability to use learned material in new and concrete situations. This may include the application of such things as rules, methods, concepts, principles, laws, and theories. Learning outcomes in this area require a higher level of understanding than those under comprehension.

4. **Analysis.** Analysis refers to the ability to break down material into its component parts so that its organizational structure may be understood. This may include the identification of the parts, analysis of the relationships between parts, and recognition of the organizational principles involved. Learning outcomes here represent a higher intellectual level than comprehension and application because they require an understanding of both the content and the structural form of the material.

5. **Synthesis.** Synthesis refers to the ability to put parts together to form a new whole. This may involve the production of a unique communication (theme or speech), a plan of operations (research proposal), or a set of abstract relations (scheme for classifying information). Learning outcomes in this area stress creative behaviors, with major emphasis on the formulation of *new* patterns or structures.

6. **Evaluation.** Evaluation is concerned with the ability to judge the value of material (statement, novel, poem, research report) for a given purpose. The judgments are to be based on definite criteria. These may be internal criteria (organization) or external criteria (relevance to the purpose) and the student may determine the criteria or be given them. Learning outcomes in this area are highest in the cognitive hierarchy because they contain elements of all of the other categories, plus conscious value judgments based on clearly defined criteria.

SOURCE: N. E. Gronlund, *Stating Behavioral Objectives for Classroom Instruction*, MacMillan, 1970, p. 20.

TABLE 10-2 (Continued)

EXAMPLES OF GENERAL INSTRUCTIONAL OBJECTIVES AND BEHAVIORAL TERMS FOR THE COGNITIVE DOMAIN OF THE TAXONOMY

Illustrative General Instructional Objectives	Illustrative Behavioral Terms for Stating Specific Learning Outcomes
Knows common terms Knows specific facts Knows methods and procedures Knows basic concepts Knows principles	Defines, describes, identifies, labels, lists, matches, names, outlines, reproduces, selects, states
Understands facts and principles Interprets verbal material Interprets charts and graphs Translates verbal material to mathematical formulas Estimates future consequences implied in data Justifies methods and procedures	Converts, defends, distinguishes, estimates, explains, extends, generalizes, gives examples, infers, paraphrases, predicts, rewrites, summarizes
Applies concepts and principles to new situations Applies laws and theories to practical situations Solves mathematical problems Constructs charts and graphs Demonstrates correct usage of a method or procedure	Changes, computes, demonstrates, discovers, manipulates, modifies, operates, predicts, prepares, produces, relates, shows, solves, uses
Recognizes unstated assumptions Recognizes logical fallacies in reasoning Distinguishes between facts and inferences Evaluates the relevancy of data Analyzes the organizational structure of a work (art, music, writing)	Breaks down, diagrams, differentiates, discriminates, distinguishes, identifies, illustrates, infers, outlines, points out, relates, selects, separates, subdivides
Writes a well-organized theme Gives a well-organized speech Writes a creative short story (or poem, or music) Proposes a plan for an experiment Integrates learning from different areas into a plan for solving a problem Formulates a new scheme for classifying objects (or events or ideas)	Categorizes, combines, compiles, composes, creates, devises, designs, explains, generates, modifies, organizes, plans, rearranges, reconstructs, relates, reorganizes, revises, rewrites, summarizes, tells, writes
Judges the logical consistency of written material Judges the adequacy with which conclusions are supported by data Judges the value of a work (art, music, writing) by use of internal criteria Judges the value of a work (art, music, writing) by use of external standards of excellence	Appraises, compares, concludes, contrasts, criticizes, describes, discriminates, explains, justifies, interprets, relates, summarizes, supports

SOURCE: Ibid., p. 21.

TABLE 10-3

MAJOR CATEGORIES IN THE AFFECTIVE DOMAIN OF THE TAXONOMY OF EDUCATIONAL OBJECTIVES (KRATHWOHL, 1964)

Descriptions of the Major Categories in the Affective Domain
1. **Receiving.** Receiving refers to the student's willingness to attend to particular phenomena or stimuli (classroom activities, textbook, music, etc.). From a teaching standpoint, it is concerned with getting, holding, and directing the student's attention. Learning outcomes in this area range from the simple awareness that a thing exists to selective attention on the part of the learner. Receiving represents the lowest level of learning outcomes in the affective domain.
2. **Responding.** Responding refers to active participation on the part of the student. At this level he not only attends to a particular phenomenon but also reacts to it in some way. Learning outcomes in this area may emphasize acquiescence in responding (reads assigned material), willingness to respond voluntarily reads beyond assignment), or satisfaction in responding (reads for pleasure or enjoyment). The higher levels of this category include those instructional objectives that are commonly classified under "interests"; that is, those that stress the seeking out and enjoyment of particular activities.
3. **Valuing.** Valuing is concerned with the worth or value a student attaches to a particular object, phenomenon, or behavior. This ranges in degree from the more simple acceptance of a value (desires to improve group skills) to the more complex level of commitment (assumes responsibility for the effective functioning of the group). Valuing is based on the internalization of a set of specified values, but clues to these values are expressed in the student's overt behavior. Learning outcomes in this area are concerned with behavior that is consistent and stable enough to make the value clearly identifiable. Instructional objectives that are commonly classified under "attitudes" and "appreciation" would fall into this category.
4. **Organization.** Organization is concerned with bringing together different values, resolving conflicts between them, and beginning the building of an internally consistent value system. Thus the emphasis is on comparing, relating, and synthesizing values. Learning outcomes may be concerned with the conceptualization of a value (recognizes the responsibility of each individual for improving human relations) or with the organization of a value system (develops a vocational plan that satisfies his need for both economic security and social service). Instructional objectives relating to the development of a philosophy of life would fall into this category.
5. **Characterization by a Value or Value Complex.** At this level of the affective domain, the individual has a value system that has controlled his behavior for a sufficiently long time for him to have developed a characteristic "life style." Thus the behavior is pervasive, consistent, and predictable. Learning outcomes at this level cover a broad range of activities, but the major emphasis is on the fact that the behavior is typical or characteristic of the student. Instructional objectives that are concerned with the student's general patterns of adjustment (personal, social, emotional) would be appropriate here.

SOURCE: Ibid., p. 22.

TABLE 10-3 (Continued)

EXAMPLES OF GENERAL INSTRUCTIONAL OBJECTIVES AND BEHAVIORAL TERMS FOR THE AFFECTIVE DOMAIN OF THE TAXONOMY

Illustrative General InstructionalObjectives	Illustrative Behavioral Terms for Stating Specific Learning Outcomes
Listens attentively Shows awareness of the importance of learning Shows sensitivity to human needs and social problems Accepts differences of race and culture Attends closely to the classroom activities	Asks, chooses, describes, follows, gives, holds, identifies, locates, names, points to, selects, sits erect, replies, uses
Completes assigned homework Obeys school rules Participates in class discussion Completes laboratory work Volunteers for special tasks Shows interest in subject Enjoys helping others	Answers, assists, complies, conforms, discusses, greets, helps, labels, performs, practices, presents, reads, recites, reports, selects, tells, writes
Demonstrates belief in the democratic process Appreciates good literature (art or music) Appreciates the role of science (or other subjects) in everyday life Shows concern for the welfare of others Demonstrates problem-solving attitude Demonstrates commitment to social improvement	Completes, describes, differentiates, explains, follows, forms, initiates, invites, joins, justifies, proposes, reads, reports, selects, shares, studies, works
Recognizes the need for balance between freedom and responsibility in a democracy Recognizes the role of systematic planning in solving problems Accepts responsibility for his own behavior Understands and accepts his own strengths and limitations Formulates a life plan in harmony with his abilities, interests, and beliefs	Adheres, alters, arranges, combines, compares, completes, defends, explains, generalizes, identifies, integrates, modifies, orders, organizes, prepares, relates, synthesizes
Displays safety consciousness Demonstrates self-reliance in working independently Practices cooperation in group activities Uses objective approach in problem solving Demonstrates industry, punctuality and self-discipline Maintains good health habits	Acts, discriminates, displays, influences, listens, modifies, performs, practices, proposes, qualifies, questions, revises, serves, solves, uses, verifies

SOURCE: Ibid., p. 23.

TABLE 10-4

EXAMPLES OF GENERAL INSTRUCTIONAL OBJECTIVES AND
BEHAVIORAL TERMS FOR THE PSYCHOMOTOR
DOMAIN OF THE TAXONOMY

Taxonomy Catergories	Illustrative General Instructional Objectives	Illustrative Behavioral Terms for Stating Specific Learning Outcomes
(Development of categories in this domain is still underway)	Writes smoothly and legibly Draws accurate reproduction of a picture (or map, biology specimen, etc.) Sets up laboratory equipment quickly and correctly Types with speed and accuracy Operates a sewing machine skillfully Operates a power saw safely and skillfully Performs skillfully on the violin Performs a dance step correctly Demonstrates correct form in swimming Demonstrates skill in driving an automobile Repairs an electric motor quickly and effectively Creates new ways of performing (creative dance, etc.)	Assembles, builds, calibrates, changes, cleans, composes, connects, constructs, corrects, creates, designs, dismantles, drills, fastens, fixes, follows, grinds, grips, hammers, heats, hooks, identifies, locates, makes, manipulates, mends, mixes, nails, paints, sands, saws, sharpens, sets, sews, sketches, starts, stirs, uses, weighs, wraps

SOURCE: Ibid., p. 24.

For convenience in describing the general curriculum development process, this phase may be regarded as completed. Obviously, actual practice is usually not so methodical. The purpose for describing these steps for formulating goals and objectives has been to demonstrate the relationship among developmental tasks, program goals, the taxonomies, and Gronlund's procedure for stating behavioral objectives. *These are offered as strategies to be employed rather than as a blueprint to be duplicated.*

Phase III. Preparation of Instructional Products

"If curriculum is a plan for learning, and if objectives determine what learning is important, then it follows that adequate curriculum planning involves selecting and organizing both the content and learning experiences" (Taba, 1962, p. 266). To this point, concern has been with the *ends* to be attained by curriculum. Now, how these ends may be achieved is to be considered.

Developing instructional products and learning experiences is a central decision in curriculum planning and development. It is imperative that rational criteria be employed. Popham and Baker (1971, pp. 145-148) offer the following general principles that apply to the determination of product, whatever the objectives may be:

1. Supply the learner with appropriate practice during an instructional sequence.
2. The product should provide the learner with the opportunity to obtain knowledge of results.
3. The instructional product should contain provisions for promoting the learner's interest in the product.
4. Avoid the development of an inflexible strategy in approaching product development tasks.
5. If teachers are involved in the instructional process, make their participation as replicable as possible.
6. In general, adopt a "lean" programming strategy.
7. If the product is to be used in the classroom, develop it so that teacher attitudes toward the product will be positive.
8. Selection of the instructional medium should be made in light of the desired instructional objectives, intended target population, cost, and other relevant considerations.
9. The time devoted to the development of the product should be commensurate with the importance of the product.

Whatever the criteria, they need to be applied as a collective set of "screens" for sifting possibilities in order to assure that only experiences which are valid in light of all pertinent considerations get into the curriculum. Use of any one or a limited set of criteria involves the danger of an unbalanced curriculum (Taba, 1962).

Sources of Curriculum Content and Learning Experiences

The most frequently mentioned determinants of curriculum content are: (1) needs of the learner, (2) demands of society, and (3) organized bodies of knowledge or subject matter (Johnson, 1967; Wilhelms 1962; Hanna 1962). It should be obvious to the reader that the authors distinguish between curriculum conceived as the "stuff to be taught" and curriculum conceived as the "stuff to be used in working toward objectives." The general curriculum model discussed on these pages is clearly of the latter type. Content is only selected for its relative ability to achieve previously stated objectives. The needs of the learner and the demands of society are more properly taken into consideration in formulating program goals, rather than in selecting or developing product.

Decisions during the development phase relate chiefly to which raw materials should be utilized to bring about desired behavioral changes. "This does not mean . . . that we do not value specific knowledge and skill; our students will not get less of these because we select materials for their contribution to broad, developmental goals, recognizing that comparatively few particulars of knowledge and skill are *per se* essential" (Wilhelms, 1962, p. 15).

Preparation of Materials

Whereas the tasks involved in the selection of a curricular language and in the formulation of goals and objectives can be described fairly analytically, the preparation of prototype instructional materials is more difficult to characterize. Grobman (1970) explains that there is no single prevailing pattern to previous developmental curriculum efforts. He notes that a possible reason for the lack of pattern may be that projects have not made clear and systematic choices with *knowledge of available alternatives.* Even though it is not possible to provide definitive, tested strategies for curriculum developers to emulate in materials preparation, it is possible to describe the *decision points* which must be met head on.

1. To what degree will the existing subject areas, grade level placement, facilities, and media formats be accepted?
2. Who is the target audience, i.e., which students, teachers, and schools?
3. Will materials be developed as independent units or a sequential course?
4. With respect to personnel: how many and what kinds of people will be involved; who makes the ultimate editorial decision, who reports to whom; how are assignments made and who reviews what; will writers work individually, in pairs, or in teams?
5. How much time will be expended on the writing effort?
6. Are auxiliary staff available to provide supporting services and assistance to writers?
7. How will materials be reviewed for quality control? (Grobman, pp. 119-139).

The difficulties involved in predicting which combination of conditions and personnel will make for the most satisfactory products lead to the following conclusion: *Any alleged curriculum development effort which plunges headfirst into materials development without clear statements of basic purpose, program goals, and behavioral objectives, together with supporting theory and rationale, should be viewed with considerable suspicion.*

Phase IV. Experimental Tryout, Evaluation, and Quality Control

Virtually all curriculum development projects make some provision for tryouts of materials. As might be expected, the compre-

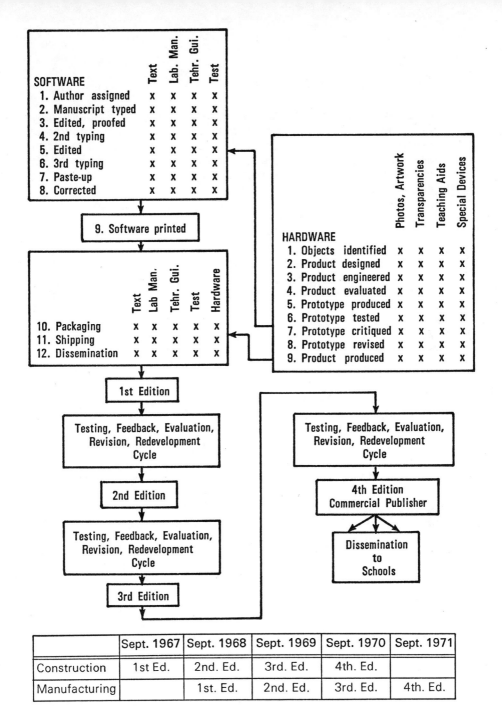

	Sept. 1967	Sept. 1968	Sept. 1969	Sept. 1970	Sept. 1971
Construction	1st Ed.	2nd. Ed.	3rd. Ed.	4th. Ed.	
Manufacturing		1st. Ed.	2nd. Ed.	3rd. Ed.	4th. Ed.

SOURCE: J. J. Buffer, "A Junior High School Industrial Technology Curriculum Project: A Final Evaluation of the Industrial Arts Curriculum Project (IACP), 1965-1971." Final Report, Project No. 70003, Grant No. OEG-3-7-070003-1608, The Ohio State University Research Foundation, August 31, 1971, p. 35.

Fig. 10-4. IACP Materials Development System

hensiveness of experimental testing depends on many factors, e.g., (1) available personnel and financial resources, (2) the degree to which materials depart from conventional practice, (3) amount of advance planning and "inhouse" research and development, (4) the availability and willingness of local education agencies to participate.

A typical model for the tryout and revision of instructional materials is shown in Fig. 10-4. Illustrated are the major events in the development, tryout and revision of materials for two one-year courses entitled "The World of Construction" and "The World of Manufacturing." These were prepared by the Industrial Arts Curriculum Project (IACP) at The Ohio State University. A more detailed breakdown is shown in Fig. 10-5 which illustrates a typical schedule for a year's production. These examples help to demonstrate the complexity of events during the experimental testing, evaluation and quality control phase. The necessity and importance of field testing to the revision and further development of product is made obvious by Buffer (1971, p. 46-47) when he describes the additions and changes which were made in the IACP materials as a result of feedback data collected during tryout:

1. The workbook was discontinued and some of the questions were incorporated at the end of each reading;
2. The review at the end of each period (teacher's guide) was changed to an overview at the beginning of each period;
3. Behavioral objectives were included in the laboratory manual;
4. A list of safety precautions was included in the teacher's guide and laboratory manual;
5. A more detailed appendix list of equipment, teaching aids, and expendable materials was developed;
6. An overall improvement of artwork and photos was made;
7. Time for city and regional planning was reduced from approximately five weeks to two weeks;
8. Time for the unit of housing construction was extended;
9. Numerous activities in construction and manufacturing were changed to make them more relevant, interesting, and exciting;
10. Four sets of readings in construction were combined into two readings;
11. Four sets of readings in manufacturing were combined into two readings;
12. The course design in manufacturing was reorganized;
13. Numerous errors in all the materials were removed;
14. Consistency in the use of materials was improved;
15. The reading level in both courses was lowered for 7th and 8th grade students; and
16. Cover designs on all materials were improved.

This discussion has helped to reinforce the contention that the tryout of materials, like initial planning and development, is an important aspect of ultimate success. Not so apparent, however, is the fact that conditions and circumstances for feedback must be

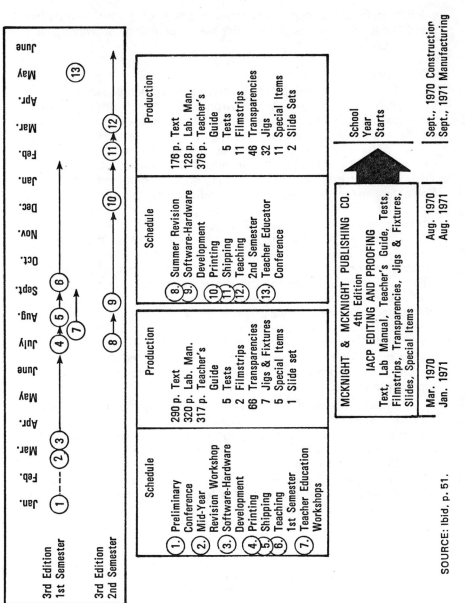

Fig. 10-5. IACP Development of Curriculum Materials

deliberately structured. The entire process of tryout, evaluation and feedback requires a high degree of planning, organizing and controlling.

Evaluation

Curriculum development efforts may be characterized by their purposes, their content, their environments, their methods, and the changes they bring about. Evaluation is a complex process because each of the many characteristics requires separate attention. Evaluation results in a "story," supported perhaps by statistics and profiles. "It tells what happened. It reveals perceptions and judgments that different groups and individuals hold — obtained, I hope, by objective means. It tells of merit and shortcoming. As a bonus, it may offer generalizations . . . for the guidance of subsequent educational programs" (Stake, 1967, p. 5).

In developmental project work, two periods of evaluation usually occur (Grobman, 1970; Scriven, 1967). *Formative* evaluations are undertaken during the period of materials preparation. They may be primarily for the project's use and usually indicate whether the materials are feasible, and if so, how they can be improved. *Summative* evaluation is done after completion of materials. Its focus is on describing the effects of the use of the materials and the student body and circumstances in which their use takes place. Summative evaluation may be directed at audiences in addition to the project staff, including the research community and the target public.

Table 10-5 provides a comparison of selected, major characteristics of each type of evaluation. In actual use, the lines of differentiation between formative and summative evaluation are less clear than they appear on the surface. As Ahmann (1967, p. 87) points out: "It can be argued, nevertheless, that formative evaluation is a kind of intermediate summative evaluation."

Following is an example of a functional system for obtaining and utilizing feedback data for the Industrial Arts Curriculum Project (Buffer, 1971, pp. 52-56). Essential planning decisions were made by IACP concerning five basic questions:

1. What aspects of the program require feedback?
   . . . project personnel identified five areas of the instructional package from which feedback would be desirable. Originally these areas were the textbook, text workbook, teacher's guide, laboratory manual, and achievement tests. Since the text workbook was eliminated as part of the instructional package (because of feedback from students, parents, etc.), feedback was focused on the remaining four areas (p. 52).

TABLE 10-5

SELECTED CHARACTERISTICS OF
TWO TYPES OF EVALUATION PROCESSES

	Formative	Summative
Purpose	— Determine feasibility — Improve materials — Locate errors	— Describe materials — Describe effects of materials — Indicate extent to which goals have been achieved

Emphasis	— Content analysis
	— Classroom tryouts:
	  A. Antecedents: Description of teachers, schools, students and classroom situation
	
	  B. Transactions: What goes on in the classroom
	
	  C. Outcomes: achievement tests attitude tests performance testing
		— Learning gains
		— Product characteristics
		— Opportunity costs
		— Appropriateness of media
		— Diffusion efforts
		— Extent of product use
		— Satisfactions

Instrumentation and Methods	— Objective checklists — Classroom interaction systems — Teacher reports - - written and oral — Ancedotal records — Teacher-made tests — Structured observations — Opinionnaires	— Same as Formative, also: — Standardized tests — Cost benefit analysis — Student follow-up

2. Who will provide feedback?
 . . . about anyone affected by or involved with the program was asked to contribute information relating to particular or overall aspects of the program. Emphasis, however, was placed on obtaining the daily reactions of students and teachers directly involved with the program. Feedback was also obtained from parents, school administrators, program visitors, college and university educators, and substantive specialists associated with manufacturing and construction (p. 52).

3. How will feedback be obtained?
 Five methods were used to accomplish this task and are identified below.
 A. Teachers were asked to complete evaluation feedback forms after each day's activity. They were also requested to make suggestions for improvement of software materials by writing directly on the developmental copy. Examples of the "marked copies" and the daily evaluation forms can be found in Appendix A and B. It should be noted that the daily evaluation form was revised twice during the course of the program.
 B. Achievement tests obtained from the students in the Field Evaluation Centers provided valuable feedback concerning attainment of educational objectives.
 C. Periodic questionnaires completed by students, teachers, parents and school administrators, who were directly involved with the program, were another source of feedback.
 D. Feedback was obtained by soliciting reactions from consultants and other persons associated with the dissemination phase of the project.
 E. Reactions were also solicited from visitors to the field Evaluation Center schools (pp. 52-53).

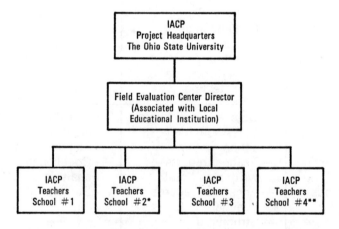

*Signifies Field Evaluation Center Head Teacher, Construction
**Signifies Field Evaluation Center Head Teacher, Manufacturing

SOURCE: Ibid, p. 54

Fig. 10-6. Project Personnel Chart

4. What system will be used to collect and condense feedback?

The major concern here was the *daily evaluation* performed by the teacher. A method was designed to condense the feedback from each Field Evaluation Center so it would be useable upon arrival at project headquarters.

The personnel chart shown in Fig. 10-6 illustrates that the Field Evaluation Center would be the most appropriate point for condensing the feedback prior to arrival at project headquarters.

To accomplish the task of condensing feedback, each Field Evaluation Center held a weekly meeting which involved all IACP teachers and the Field Evaluation Center director. The primary purpose of the weekly meetings was to:

A. Arrive at a consensus concerning problems experienced with the instructional package during the past week.
B. Use group processes to suggest solutions to these problems.
C. Make necessary plans for the coming week.
D. Prepare a written report of the meeting and transmit it, along with daily feedback from the previous week, to project headquarters. The Head Teachers in manufacturing and construction were responsible for preparing their respective reports.

A graphic illustration of the feedback process described above is illustrated in Fig. 10-7.

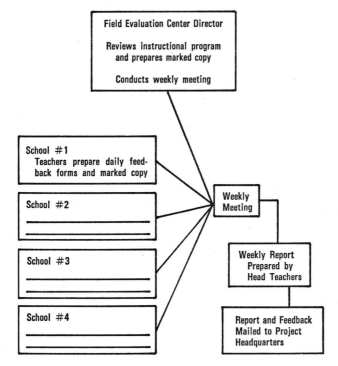

SOURCE: Ibid, p. 55.

Fig. 10-7. Flow of Feedback from IACP Teachers

The structure of the field evaluation test centers also served as an effective means for administering periodic questionnaires to students, teachers, parents, school administrators, and visitors. Instruments of this type were administered through the Field Evaluation Center system and were returned to project headquarters for interpretation.

5. What system will be used to receive, store, and use the feedback for revision purposes?

As the weekly feedback packets arrived from the various Field Evaluation Centers, they were stored, grouped and filed according to the daily instructional sequence listed in the teacher's guide. Thus, when project staff were ready to make revisions of a particular activity, all of the feedback material for that activity from each participating Field Evaluation Center could be found in one folder.

Because of the desire to include Field Evaluation Center teachers in the actual revision process, revision conferences at OSU were scheduled during the middle of the school year and in summer periods so that these teachers could attend. Besides these, selected personnel from the Field Evaluation Centers, project personnel at IACP headquarters and, to some extent, substantive specialists were also involved in the revision conferences. The substantive specialists served primarily as a consultative body and worked closely with project staff in developing and refining the textbooks for construction and manufacturing.

It should be noted that the materials revised during the revision conferences were in rough form only, and considerable effort was still necessary to move the rough copy to a final draft which was typed, edited, age-graded, retyped, proofread, illustrated, and made ready for commercial reproduction.

Concurrent with the revision of the software materials, hardware, mostly in the form of jigs and fixtures, was also being revised and mass-produced by project personnel. Completed production of the revised hardware, transparencies and filmstrips was scheduled to coincide with the arrival of the revised software from the commercial printer. Proper quantities of software and hardware were then packaged at project headquarters and shipped to individual schools within the six Field Evaluation Centers. The process described above generally represents the sequential procedure required to accomplish each revision (pp. 54 and 56).

The practical and functional orientation of this chapter, together with space limitations, prohibits any additional discussion of the processes involved in tryout, evaluation, feedback and quality control of materials preparation. The reader is urged to pursue Bloom et al. (1971), Tyler et al. (1967), and Grobman (1968) for a more comprehensive treatment. In addition, the twenty-one product development reports prepared by the American Institutes for Research[11] should be consulted for a detailed and accurate picture

[11]The twenty one reports were supported by U. S. Office of Education Contract No. OEC-0-7C-4892, entitled "The Evaluation of the Impact of Educational Research and Development Products."

of events in the development of many of the more notable exemplary research and development projects.

Phase V. Diffusion and Adoption

What happens to the materials that have been developed by an externally-funded curriculum development project?[12] The implementation of a curriculum concept must begin the first moment the concept is formulated. One cannot divorce all of the influencing factors that surround a curriculum concept if the goal of implementation is to be achieved. The total thrust of the implementation of curriculum design is dependent upon two main factors:

1. The ability of the (a) creator, (b) producer, (c) marketing agent, and (d) implementer to understand and correlate the significant elements of a message (curriculum content).
2. The ability to communicate the message in an accurate, efficient, and effective manner to influence a positive decision.

Therefore, dissemination of an innovative program cannot be an afterthought of product development. For this reason, the United States Office of Education encourages the involvement of commercial publishers in product dissemination, provided their involvement is accomplished on a competitive basis:

It is the policy of the U. S. Office of Education that the results of activities supported by it should be utilized in the manner which will best serve the public interest. This can be accomplished, in some situations, by distribution of materials without copyright. However, it is recognized that copyright protection may be desirable, in other situations, during development or as an incentive to promote effective dissemination of such materials. In the latter situations, arrangements for copyright of such materials normally for a limited period of time, may be authorized under appropriate conditions upon a showing satisfactory to the Office of Education that such protection will result in more effective development or dissemination of the materials or would otherwise be in the public interest (Dept. of HEW, 1971, p. 13).

The USOE Copyright Guidelines are not applicable to "State-administered formula grant programs." That term, as used in the guidelines, refers to programs in which the appropriations are allotted among the states on the basis of a statutory formula and are administered by the State generally under a "State Plan." Thus, it is the responsibility of the State or some entity other than the Federal Government to determine the circumstances and pro-

[12]Large parts of this section were exerpted with permission from a paper by Dale (1972).

cedures by which such materials will be disseminated under copyright. Following is a brief summary of the steps taken by the State of Illinois to facilitate the dissemination of materials developed under its auspices.

On February 15, 1972 the Illinois Board of Vocational Education and Rehabilitation approved the USOE Copyright Policy published in the *Federal Register* on May 9, 1970 (35 F. R. 7317) as the general policy by which the Division of Vocational and Technical Education (DVTE) could operate to assure that worthwhile educational material developed with public funds will reach potential users. Administrative guidelines (DVTE, 1972) have been pre-

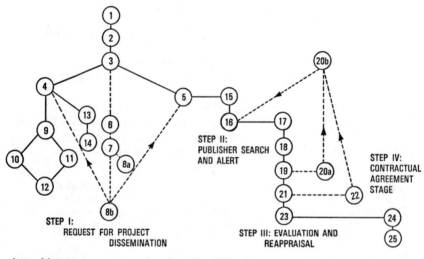

STEP I: REQUEST FOR PROJECT DISSEMINATION

STEP II: PUBLISHER SEARCH AND ALERT

STEP III: EVALUATION AND REAPPRAISAL

STEP IV: CONTRACTUAL AGREEMENT STAGE

1. Letter of Intent	10. Secure Three Written Bids	19. Recommendation of Proposal to Director
2. Onsite DVTE Evaluation	11. Complete Camera Ready Copy	
3. Recommendation to the Director	12. Send to Outside Source to Print	20a. Disapproved
4. Thin Market Material	13. Approval for Internal Printing	20b. Resubmit for Evaluation
5. Mass Market Material	14. Prepare and Send to Material Center (DVTE)	21. Approved by Director; Sent to State Board
6. Request Denied For Dissemination	15. Preparation of the RPA	22. Disapproved
7. Appeal To State Board	16. Responses Received and Acknowledged	23. Approved
8. Approval Denied	17. Review Team Evaluation	24. Completion of Contract
8a. Appeal Denied	18. Negotiate	25. Signing of Contractual Agreement
8b. Appeal Approved		
9. Approved for External Printing		

SOURCE: DVTE, *Administrative Guidelines for Securing Assistance in the Dissemination of Project Materials Arising from Contractual Agreements.* Bulletin No. 37-972, 1972, p. 7.

Fig. 10-8. Process for Disseminating Project Information, Division of Vocational and Technical Education, State of Illinois

pared to assist grantees involved in contractual agreements with DVTE. A four-step process is followed:

1. Request for Product Dissemination
2. Publisher Search and Alert Stage
3. Evaluation and Re-Appraisal Stage
4. Contractual Agreement Stage

Figure 10-8 illustrates a more definitive breakdown of the four-step process. It will be noted that DVTE has provided a mechanism for dissemination of both "thin market" and "mass market" materials. These guidelines should be extremely useful to local education agencies and state education departments which are confronted with similar dissemination problems.

Engagement with publisher-disseminator does not entail sacrifice of goals. It is reasonable and fair for the original developers to expect the following of a producer.

1. A complete and comprehensive plan for strategic achievement of a project's dissemination objectives.
2. Evidence that the strategy for implementation is integrated with and consistent with the producer's total corporate objectives and strategies. The accomplishment of the producer's goals should be dependent upon his ability to accomplish a project's goals.
3. The producer should be willing to commit top priority to the project's program in his marketing strategy and he should reallocate his resources, especially personal sales effort, accordingly.
4. The producer should have a history of performance in the development, marketing, and implementation of curriculum *change.*
5. The producer should provide examples of his ability to successfully implement emerging programs in (a) inner-city schools, (b) suburban schools, and (c) rural schools.

Selling a relevant career development program means selling *change.* People and institutions may resist change; surely they will resist *being* changed. It is, therefore, important that the curriculum planning committee and the producer identify the barriers to curriculum change. Product development and the strategy for curriculum implementation should create solutions to all major barriers (objections) to successful curriculum change. A sample first-year implementation and marketing strategy might take the following form:

1. The producer should begin identifying high-potential adopters during the last year of product development.

2. The producers should utilize experienced teachers from field test centers to conduct in-service workshops to extend the program to teachers and supervisors in high-potential school systems. These workshops should involve college faculty to share in the responsibility of teacher education by extension for in-service and preparation of undergraduates.
3. The producer should concentrate on implementing initial or "try out" programs in school systems that represent high-potential success situations. It is also desirable to locate the initial programs in or around metropolitan areas so they may be used as exhibits for neighboring school systems.
4. The producer should concentrate personal sales attention on local decision makers, on state supervisory personnel, and encourage and facilitate teacher education institutions to establish extension programs in large communities.
5. The producer should develop a plan to retain and stimulate expansion of the established field test and demonstration centers. It is essential to maintain and expand original programs if other schools are to be convinced that the program has validity.
6. Primary personal sales emphasis should be directed to the 193 largest school systems. This represents only 16% of the total school systems in the United States, but a large portion of the national student enrollment.
7. Secondary personal sales emphasis should be directed to the 323 next largest school systems. This represents 9.2% of the total number of school systems in the United States.
8. The producer should plan a method of sales presentation that is efficient in presenting the program information to those schools that are de-centralized.

Chapter 12 deals more specifically with meanings of change, change models, and organizational self-renewal.

Summary

This chapter has attempted to alert the reader to contemporary fundamentals of curriculum development. More specifically, a general curriculum model has been suggested. It provides curriculum specialists with an operational vehicle for developing career education curriculum and instructional materials. The model and related discussion provide strategies which have proven to be successful. The following additional "cautions" should be considered during the planning and policymaking stage of a curriculum development program. One or more of them have been the downfall of many curriculum projects.

> Don't design a program away from the basic school practices such as grade level, length of class time, or the number of days in a semester or year.
>
> Don't forget to utilize existing facilities.
>
> Don't begin product development before a decision-making model has been structured.
>
> Don't involve an unmanageable number of field test centers.
>
> Don't develop a program without valid field testing.
>
> Don't engage in premature publicity.
>
> Don't assume that public domain materials will be used by a large number of school systems.
>
> Don't sell or disseminate test materials to persons or organizations outside the test network.
>
> Don't assume that good program content or methodology is the single ingredient for implementation success.
>
> Don't let theory run away with practice.
>
> Don't omit significant groups such as industry, other disciplines, teachers, minorities, parents, or businesses.
>
> Don't let any single group dominate.
>
> Don't retain program elements that field tests reject because "we have always done it this way," or "it's such a beautiful idea."
>
> Don't be satisfied with "better than it was"; focus on relevant behavioral objectives and instructional goals.

BIBLIOGRAPHY

Ahmann, J. S. Aspects of curriculum evaluation: A synopsis. In Ralph W. Tyler, et al. *Perspectives of curriculum evaluation.* Chicago: Rand McNally, 1967.

Bailey, L. J. Implementing career education. Career Development for Children Project, Southern Illinois University, 1971. (a)

————. A curriculum model for facilitating career development. Career Development for Children Project, Southern Illinois University, 1971. (b)

Bailey, L. J., Turner, K. G., and VanRooy, W. Some questions and answers on career development: an interview with CDCP. Career Development for Children Project, Southern Illinois University, 1972.

Bloom, B. S. (Ed.) *Taxonomy of educational objectives, Handbook 1: cognitive domain.* New York: David McKay, 1956.

Bloom, B. S., Hastings, J. T. and Madaus, G. F. *Handbook on formative and summative evaluation of student learning.* New York: McGraw-Hill, 1971.

Buffer, J. J. A junior high school industrial technology project; a final evaluation of the industrial arts curriculum project (IACP), 1965-1971. Final Report. Project No. 70003, Grant No. OEG-3-7-070003-1608, The Ohio State University Research Foundation, August 31, 1971.

Dale, R. E. Implementation of total package. *Career Ladders and Lattices in Home Economics and Related Areas: Possibilities for Upgrading Household Employment.* Final report for the contract for technical assistance in the development of career ladders; Contract No. 11-1-0406-000. Washington, D. C.: American Home Economics Association, October 15, 1971 - June 30, 1972.

Division of Vocational and Technical Education. *Administrative guidelines for securing assistance in the dissemination of project materials arising from contractual agreements,* Bulletin No. 37-972, Springfield, Illinois, 1972.

Ebel, R. Some comments on educational objectives. *School Review,* 1967, 75(3), 261-66.

Eisner, E. W. Educational objectives: Help or hinderance? *School Review,* 1967, 75, 250-60.

Emans, R. A proposed conceptual framework for curriculum development. *The Journal of Educational Research,* 1966, 59, 327-332.

French, W. et al. *Behavioral goals of general education in high school.* New York: Russell Sage, 1957.

Gagné, R. M. Curriculum research and the promotion of learning. In Ralph W. Tyler et al., *Perspectives of curriculum evaluation.* Chicago: Rand McNally, 1967, 19-38.

Goodlad, J. I. Directions of curriculum change. *NEA Journal,* 1966, 55(4), 33-37.

Grobman, H. *Developmental curriculum projects: decision points and processes.* Itasca, Illinois: Peacock, 1970.

Gronlund, N. E. *Stating behavioral objectives for classroom instruction.* New York: Macmillan, 1970.

Hanna, L. Meeting the challenge. In what are the sources of the curriculum? a synposium. Washington: Association for Supervision and Curriculum Development, 1962, 48-59.

Hastings, J. T. Educational objectives: some comments by J. Thomas Hastings. *School Review,* 1967, 75(3), 267-71.

Havighurst, R. J. *Human development and education.* New York: David McKay, 1953.

————. Youth in exploration and man emergent. In Henry Borow (ed.), *Man in a world of work.* Boston: Houghton Mifflin, 1964, 215-236.

Herr, E. C. Unifying an entire system of education around a career development theme. Paper presented at the National Conference of Exemplary Programs and Projects Section of the 1968 Amendment to the Vocational Education Act, Atlanta, Georgia, March 1969.

Johnson, M. J. Definitions and models in curriculum theory. *Educational Theory,* 1967, 17, 127-140.

Kappel, F. R. Vitality in a business enterprise. New York: McGraw-Hill, 1960.

Kearney, N. C. *Elementary school objectives.* New York: Russell Sage, 1953.

Krathwohl, D. R. Stating objectives appropriately for program, for curriculum, and for instructional material development. *Journal of Teacher Education,* 1965, 16, 83-92.

Krathwohl, D. R., Bloom, B. S., and Masia, B. B. *Taxonomy of educational objectives, Handbook II: affective domain.* New York: David McKay, 1964.

Mager, R. F. *Preparing instructional objectives.* Palo Alto, California: Fearon, 1962.

Oliver, A. I. *Curriculum improvement.* New York: Dodd, Mead & Company, 1965.

Phenix, P. H. *Philosophy of education.* New York: Holt, Rinehart and Winston, 1958.

Popham, W. J. and Baker, E. L. Rules for the development of instructional products. In Robert L. Baker and R. E. Schutz (ed.), *Instructional product development.* New York: Van Nostrand Reinhold, 1971, 129-168.

Roeber, E. C., Wale, G. R. and Smith, G. E. *A strategy for guidance.* New York: Macmillan, 1969.

Scriven, M. The methodology of evaluation. In Ralph W. Tyler, et al. *Perspectives of curriculum evaluation.* Chicago: Rand McNally, 1967.

Short, E. C. and Marconnit, G. D. *Contemporary thought on public school curriculum.* Dubuque, Iowa: Wm. C. Brown, 1968.

Simpson, E. J. The classification of educational objectives, psychomotor domain. *Illinois Teacher of Home Economics,* 1967, 10(4), 110-144.

Stake, R. E. Toward a technology for the evaluation of educational programs. In Ralph W. Tyler, et al. *Perspectives of curriculum evaluation.* Chicago: Rand McNally, 1967.

Taba, H. *Curriculum development: theory and practice.* New York: Harcourt, Brace & World, 1962.

Tyler, R. W. *Basic principles of curriculum and instruction.* Chicago: University of Chicago Press, 1950.

Tyler, R. W., et al. Perspectives of curriculum evaluation. Chicago: Rand McNally, 1967.

U. S. Department of Health, Education, and Welfare. *U. S. Office of Education copyright program information.* Washington, D. C.: Government Printing Office, 1971.

Wilhelms, F. T. Curriculum sources, In *what are the sources of the curriculum? a symposium.* Washington, D. C.: Association for Supervision and Curriculum Development, 1962, 14-25.

Zaccaria, J. S. Developmental tasks: implications for the goals of guidance. *Personnel and Guidance Journal,* 1965, 44, 372-375.

Zimmerman, B. and Bailey, L. J. Teachers guide: career development for children project. CDCP, Southern Illinois University, 1971.

A Developmental Curriculum Model for Career Education

Introduction

This chapter is a culmination of positions and points of view presented in the previous ten chapters. Previous chapters have provided foundations and directions for the curriculum model which follows. Part I, Chapters 1 and 2, reviewed the climate for change in education and the need for substantial modification of the basic characteristics of educational institutions. This part made the significant realization that career education and many of the types of change which are recommended by prominent educational critics and theorists are compatible. Parts II and III described theory and research related to career development and career (occupational, vocational) education respectively. Their purpose was first to demonstrate that career education has *identifiable antecedents* which are *systematically interrelated* and *well-founded* in substance and rationale and secondly to *orient curriculum developers* to purposes, goals, and objectives of career education. The first chapter in Part IV outlined procedures for development of a curriculum framework for career education.

Definition of Terms

Commissioner Marland's commitment to and leadership for career education have been acknowledged and applauded throughout this book. His speeches, public statements and interviews have been widely disseminated and discussed. Predictable and natural by-products of the growing interest in career education are confusion, skepticism, and disillusionment. Following are many of the conditions which have given rise to this state of affairs.

1. Even though career education has identifiable and predictable antecedents and its major purposes have been enunciated throughout the long history of formal education, Commissioner Marland's *Career Education Now* speech caught the educational profession "off guard." Regretably, many of the more naive educators were in fields related to career education, i.e., vocational and practical arts education and guidance.

2. While Commissioner Marland has presented an adequate case for career education, he and his associates have been deliberately nonprescriptive at the level of detail. Pro and con opinions abound regarding the wisdom of this approach. History will be the final judge.

3. The historical proliferation of terminology, such as vocational education, occupational education, technical education, industrial education, has produced skepticism toward new terminology, especially when it's not apparent how newer terms differ from older ones.

4. The central position of the U. S. Office of Education in the career education "movement" causes many to conjure up memories of compensatory education, ES 70, the Right to Read program and other federally-funded programs which have met with relatively little success.

5. Many of the more prominent advocates and "leaders" of career education are viewed by other professionals in light of their earlier reputations and identities in vocational education or vocational guidance. This does not question the expertise of many of the profession's most qualified spokesmen. Rather, it points up the need for clearly illustrating the commonalities and differences between career education and existing programs of vocational education and vocational guidance.

6. One of the greatest single influences on the evolution of career education has been the literature of career development theory and research. This literature and related areas of vocational psychology and sociology are, in the main, unfamiliar to most educators.

7. The recommended shift in emphasis from a *content* based curriculum to a *process* based curriculum has not been fully understood.[1]

8. Finally, whereas career education is a promising alternative to more conventional types of education, all must

[1]For a scholarly account of process education, see Cole (1972).

acknowledge that its major curriculum components do not now exist. A realistic approach to research and development is required. It must account for the magnitude of the changes required and the vast amounts of time, money, and personnel which are needed. Although considerable "action research" is now underway, much of what is being proposed in the way of curriculum is *inadequate, illogical,* and educationally *immoral.*

Even though these conditions are apparent, the authors view the future of career education with considerable optimism. Kenneth Hoyt (1971) puts this well. "I see no way, right now, that we could impede this movement called 'career education', even if we wanted to. It is too popular a concept."

Many observers of career education have expressed concern regarding the absence of a simple and all-inclusive definition of career education. The authors will attempt to shed some light on that concern. Selected definitions of career education have been reviewed and discussed by Herr (1972), Goldhammer and Taylor (1972), and Hoyt, Evans, Mackin and Mangnum (1972). It is obvious that career education has been defined as a *program,* a *concept,* and a *process.* Examples clarify differences.

Career education as a program has been defined in terms of alternate *types of delivery systems* (e.g., school, employer, home-community, and rural-residential based); in terms of *level* (e.g., awareness, orientation, exploration, preparation, specialized education); and in terms of *curriculum components* (e.g., work experience, occupational information, study of technology).

As a concept, career education has been defined in terms of theory and *rationale* (e.g., economic self-sufficiency, self-actualization, preserving freedom of choice, and expanding available career options).

As a process, career education has been described in terms of observable *student behavior* (e.g., development and implementation of a self concept, acceptance of responsibility for career planning, understanding of the American economic system, and development of employable skills).

Whereas all of these usages are technically correct, the authors prefer to differentiate more clearly between *career education,* which they regard as a concept and a program, and *career development,* which is more properly used to describe an individual's career behavior. The authors' definitions follow:

- *Career education* refers to educational programs and curriculums at many different developmental levels, and provided by several types of delivery systems, which provide experiences designed to help individuals become oriented to, select, prepare for, enter, become established, and advance in an individually satisfying and productive career. Basic to the concept of career education is the recognition that preparation for a career role must begin in early childhood if the individual is to develop the concepts, attitudes, and skills which *insure* freedom of choice and *expand* career options. Career education eliminates artificial distinctions between "general" and "vocational" education by fusing the two in a manner which enables the student to better solve personal, social, and career related problems.

- *Career development* is a term used to describe the accumulation of individual behaviors related to work, both before and after entry into an occupation. It is a developmental, continuously iterative process which progresses from infancy throughout adulthood like an expanding spiral. In curricular terms, career development refers to the behavioral outcomes of career education, primarily those related to self development; career planning and decision-making; and work attitudes, values, concepts, and skills.

Purpose

The remainder of this chapter is concerned with the development and description of a career education curriculum model. Description of the model framework parallels the curriculum development procedures suggested in Chapter 10.

Curriculum aims can be regarded in terms of a time dimension, i.e., as eventual outcomes to be achieved during adulthood, or as curriculum goals and objectives for a particular level or grade of schooling (Grobman, 1970; Krathwohl, 1965). The *ultimate goal* of career education may be described in terms of what Tiedeman (1971) has called "career competence" or what Gysbers and Moore (1972) refer to as the "career conscious individual." More specifically, the aim is to develop an individual who can achieve a meaningful career existence in which his individuality functions for both personal and common good.

Thus, long-range curriculum goals are directed to the development of competencies and/or attitudes which will be useful in situations that may not now be predictable; often these are situations for which there are no existing prototypes (Grobman, 1970). Yet, the curriculum developer has the responsibility to define in operational terms what behaviors the individual must develop en route to the appropriate long-range goal. The curriculum developer must turn to relevant bodies of theory and knowledge to (1) identify goals and objectives and (2) make purposes clear and operational. The authors contend that the primary sources of data for conceptualizing a model for career education are the construct of career development discussed in Chapters 3 and 4, and the foundations of vocational education presented in Chapter 7. It now becomes apparent why Herr (1971) has defined career education as "the institutionalization of career development and the marrying of it with occupational education."

Assumptions

Grobman (1970, pp. 104-105) has emphasized the importance of specifying assumptions which guide the formulation of curriculum goals and objectives: ". . . a failure by a project to identify theories of learning and philosophy of education espoused, may result in a dilution of the project's effects. With some noteworthy exceptions, few developmental projects identify a psychology of learning which they accept. Still fewer identify a guiding educational philosophy or the value judgments basic to the curriculum . . . Such philosophies, theories, and value judgments may be implicit rather than stated, but they are present in all curricula, are basic to the curriculum, and are an essential part of the assumptions underpinning the curriculum."

Throughout this book the authors have been careful to identify their orientation toward education and have been deliberate in stating their beliefs and professional value judgments. Following is a synthesis from Chapter 3 of assumptions which reflect their beliefs regarding the nature of career development:

1. Career development is one aspect of an individual's overall pattern of growth and learning.
2. Career development is a long-term evolutionary process, beginning in infancy and extending through adulthood.
3. Career development is the summation of a complex series of career-related decisions made by the individual over a considerable span of time.
4. An individual's striving to arrive at an appropriate occupational goal may be interpreted as an attempt to implement his self-concept.
5. Career development proceeds through a series of (primarily) culturally induced developmental periods or life stages.
6. Each developmental life stage involves meeting and

coping with increasingly complex developmental tasks. The developmental tasks are susceptible to further description and elaboration.

7. Development through the life stages can be guided. The knowledge, skills, attitudes, and motivation essential for coping with the developmental tasks can be fostered and developed. Career decision-making can be done on rational bases.

8. The degree of mastery of a developmental task and the quality of an occupational decision is a function of the type, amount, and validity of data and experiences to which the individual has been exposed.

Limitations

The curriculum model described in this chapter has two limitations. First, it is only an outline for a *school-based* approach to career education. Whereas this model has important implica- tions for *employer-based, home/community-based,* and *rural/resi-dential-based* models, the authors do not wish to imply that their framework is comprehensive enough to encompass the goals of the other three types of career education options.

Second, it has limited scope. An attempt has been made to provide the *nucleus* for an integrated, developmental structure for grades K-12, containing all required, major curriculum goals and objectives which are flexible enough to be adapted to a variety of local school situations and locales. The authors anticipate that the model will be considerably expanded and refined in years to come. One test of the adequacy and validity of the conceptual model will be the extent to which it fosters additional research and development.

Procedure

Subsequent sections elaborate a curriculum framework based on the authors' perceptions and interpretations of desirable career development outcomes. Four curriculum phases have been differentiated. These correspond to the educational levels commonly referred to as primary elementary, intermediate elementary, junior high, and high school. They are:

Awareness Stage	K-3
Accommodation Stage	4-6
Orientation Stage	7-8
Exploration and Preparation Stage	9-12

These stages provide the context for ordering curriculum activities and experiences. For each of the stages, six domains of behavior are identified. These entail the "subprocesses" of career development.

1. Concepts of self
2. Occupational, educational and economic concepts and skills
3. Sense of agency[2]
4. Information processing skills
5. Interpersonal relationships
6. Work attitudes and values

The relationship between the six subprocesses and the four developmental stages is illustrated in Fig. 11-1. Following sections give detailed descriptions of goals and rationale and of representative, integrated objectives for each stage.

[2]Tiedeman (1971) defines "senses of agency" as the sense of responsibility and initiative felt by the individual as he works to articulate his occupational choice.

DOMAINS OF CAREER DEVELOPMENT BEHAVIORS	A. Awareness K-3	B. Accommodation 4-6	C. Orientation 7-8	D. Exploration and Preparation 9-12
1. Concepts of self	A1	B1	C1	D1
2. Occupational, educational and economic concepts and skills	A2	B2	C2	D2
3. Sense of agency	A3	B3	C3	D3
4. Information processing skills	A4	B4	C4	D4
5. Interpersonal relationships	A5	B5	C5	D5
6. Work attitudes and values	A6	B6	C6	D6

Fig. 11-1. A Developmental Curriculum Model for Career Education

Awareness Stage, Grades K-3

The period of schooling spanning the years K-3 is the child's first encounter with a formal learning environment. When a child enters the elementary school, he has long been displaying in recognizable form *inductive* processes of learning (Vinacke, 1972). That is, exposure to objects through manipulation, observation, use, and so on, has led to familiarity on the basis of which the child forms generalizations about them. For example, through ordinary experience with articles in his environment a child learns what things are "clothes," "foods," and "animals." Up to the age of five or six, behavior is to a large degree egocentric, i.e., determined mainly by specific experiences and activities of the child.

About ages six to eight the child begins to shift from inductive to more *deductive* behavior (Vinacke, 1972). Awareness of concrete, perceptually known properties of and relations between objects gives way to grouping and abstract, symbolic behavior. Then, the child begins to employ already formed generalizations to deal appropriately with new objects or with familiar objects in new ways. According to Formanek and Morine (1972), growth in concept formation and cognitive development are generally brought about by the organizing of aspects of the external environment in such a way that classes of objects or concepts are formed. In order to deal with the large numbers of objects in his world, the child must represent them in some way. This representation usually involves some form of grouping or categorizing.

Based on the above, Vinacke (1972) suggests that there are two basic curriculum considerations to be recognized in the early school years. First, *the child needs to be exposed to the ingredients of concepts.* From knowledge of concrete properties of objects and their relations to each other, the child can evolve precise, stable, and complete conceptions. Secondly, since the child is learning how to generalize, how to symbolize, how to apply the same concept to a variety of situations, *he needs practice and guidance in the efficient, harmonious, and productive cultivation of these skills.* The function of career education during the awareness stage thus becomes that of helping the child to perceive the ingredients which are the forerunners or more effective career development concepts and behaviors and to develop skills for differentiating and internalizing new phenomena.

Goals and Rationale:

A1. Awareness of self. In early childhood the individual begins the process of self-concept formation which continues throughout his life. Initially, the child gathers sensory impressions (i.e., "self-percepts") related to his physical configuration and his capabilities (Super, 1963). Gradually, he begins to organize his perceptions into higher-order generalizations and, finally, into simple self-concepts. That is, the impressions he receives from his activities and interpersonal relationships are combined to form mental pictures. Emphasis on self-awareness and differentiation of self from others helps the child develop a repertoire of self-percepts which become the foundation for more accurate and comprehensive self-concepts.

A2. Awareness of different types of occupational roles. The young child perceives people performing different types of work activities, but is not able to conceptualize differences among them (Goodson, 1970, Zimmermann and Bailey, 1971). For example, the child does not distinguish between the work that his parents may do in an occupation outside the home from the "work" that is done within the home, and from hobby and/or volunteer activities done in addition to an occupation. This goal is closely related to A4 which is designed, in part, to help the child develop skills to make such distinctions.

A3. Awareness of individual responsibility for own actions. This goal is related to A1 in which the child begins to recognize his own uniqueness, and to A2 in which he becomes more aware of the types of roles that he and others perform. These perceptions provide the basis for the child's understanding that (1) he is responsible for his activities and (2) controls them by choosing from available alternatives. The child's development of a sense of control is seen as a prerequisite to his later acceptance of responsibility for career planning.

A4. Development of the rudiments of classification and decision-making skills. This goal includes the development of two types of fundamental behaviors: (1) classification abilities and (2) practice in making decisions. With respect to the first type of behavior, research on the nature of concept formation has demonstrated that categorization ability is intimately related to children's cognitive development. Formanek and Morine (1972, p. 154) conclude that "Developing concepts such as 'group,' 'role,' or 'sanction' in the social sciences demands a skill in identifying similarities and differences in human behavior. Consequently, a child's ability to categorize would seem to bear some relation to his ability to understand much of the modern elementary school curriculum." The implications for the understanding of occupational groups are self-evident.

The emphasis on practice in decision-making is designed to acquaint the child with the "logic" of choosing from among alternatives. While most children may not be able to conceptualize decision-making as a process, they will be able to apply such methods to the choosing of alternative courses of action, alternate behaviors, and alternate modes of expression. "From early childhood through adulthood the skills and motives needed for making wise decisions are essential elements in the equipment of the maturing person" (Hill and Luckey, 1969, p. 14).

A5. **Learning cooperative social behavior.** Like previous goals, the need for effective working relationships is a fundamental behavior of childhood that continues throughout life. As Havighurst (1953, p. 31) notes, ". . . the nine- or ten-year-old clearly shows what he will be like, socially, at fifty." The technique of behavior modification notwithstanding, Havighurst's observation is well-taken in that social relationships constitute a *foundation element in later adaptions* to life and its demands. Effective working relationships with his peers is not some frosting on the educational cake that is desirable if it were to come about incidentally. Rather, it is an essential ingredient of the cake itself (Hill and Luckey, 1969).

A6. **Development of respect for others and the work that they do.** Probably at no other time does the individual have as high a regard for work as he does in early childhood. The tendency for children to play at work is well-known. Kabach (1966, p. 167) notes that ". . . the younger the child the greater the interest in the actual job performance itself. Most children are natural born actors; they want to act out in order to understand what it feels like to be a carpenter or a ball player." The question is not one of *should* attitudes toward work be taught in early elementary school. Students *do*, in fact, possess work attitudes. Generally, these are favorable. Rather, at issue is *how to preserve* positive attitudes so they may be used as foundation for more realistic attitudes and understandings (Herr, 1970).

Illustrative Objectives:[3]
1. Begins to form generalizations about self
   1.1 Summarizes ways in which an individual may be described, e.g., emotions, actions, personal information, physical appearance

---

[3]These are provided as samples of desired career development outcomes and should not be interpreted as a formal taxonomy.

    1.2 Provides examples of own self-characteristics and attributes

    1.3 Recognizes uniqueness of own self

    1.4 Differentiates self from others

2. Understands how interests develop
   - 2.1 Explains what is an "interest"
   - 2.2 Describes how people become interested in an activity
   - 2.3 Develops "inventory" (generic sense) of own interests

3. Examines different types of human activity
   - 3.1 Formulates a broad, general definition for what is "work"
   - 3.2 Explains what is meant by "leisure"
   - 3.3 Recognizes commonalities of work and leisure

4. Differentiates types of work and leisure activities
   - 4.1 Defines the term "occupation"
   - 4.2 Describes how an occupation differs from other types of work activity
   - 4.3 Distinguishes between occupations, household chores, volunteer work, and leisure activity
   - 4.4 Associates different types of work and leisure activities with various family members
   - 4.5 Observes and talks to various workers in the school and neighborhood to differentiates occupational roles

5. Examines relationship between interests, occupations, and leisure activities
   - 5.1 Understands how interests may be satisfied in a variety of occupational roles
   - 5.2 Explains why it is desirable to work at an occupation that one is interested in
   - 5.3 Understands how interests may also be expressed in leisure

6. Adopts identity as that of "worker"
   - 6.1 Lists various types of work tasks he performs regularly
   - 6.2 Describes how the role of student is similar to that of employed worker
   - 6.3 Describes how work he does in school can affect him in the future

7. Understands how individual needs are met in work
   - 7.1 Describes how work has a personal meaning for every individual

    7.2 Appreciates how work may enhance self dignity and worth

8. Understands the characteristics of grouping systems
    8.1 Defines what is meant by a "group"
    8.2 Understands how grouping can be used to organize information
    8.3 Understands that objects, events, etc. can be classified in many different ways
    8.4 Understands that groups can be created for different purposes

9. Understands concepts (i.e., economic groups) of goods, services, consumers, and producers
    9.1 Defines what is meant by the term "consumer"
    9.2 Understands that everyone is a consumer
    9.3 Differentiates between goods and services
    9.4 Defines what is meant by the term "producer"
    9.5 Provides examples of people who produce goods and people who produce (i.e., provide) services

10. Understands how goods and service producers are interrelated
    10.1 Examines own family unit to understand the principle of interdependence
    10.2 Explains how specialization leads to interdependence
    10.3 Provides examples to illustrate how goods and services workers depend on each other
    10.4 Recognizes why worker cooperation is necessary in the production of goods and services
    10.5 Describes the individual work habits and attitudes that contribute to cooperative work relationships

11. Understands that production of most goods and services involves a "family" type of effort
    11.1 Identifies different types of job families under the broad headings of goods and services producers
    11.2 For a given occupational family (e.g., leisure, construction, health), describes types of goods produced or services provided

12. Examines the nature of a job family (i.e., occupational group)
    12.1 Recognizes the wide range of different occupations within a single family
    12.2 Understands that many different levels exist within a job family
    12.3 Describes what is meant by the term "job ladder"

12.4 Recognizes that individual occupations may be found in more than one job family
13. Understands that grouping can help in organizing information about interests and occupations
   13.1 Reviews meaning of "interests"
   13.2 Understands that an individual's specific interests may be grouped into a number of general areas
   13.3 Recognizes usefulness of grouping occupations by interest area
14. Understands that information about an occupation can be organized using more than one group at the same time
   14.1 Surveys a variety of goods and service occupations that involve an interest area
   14.2 Surveys one interest area for goods and services occupations
   14.3 Given a description of an occupation, can group it in a two-dimensional system
   14.4 Understands how using more than one grouping system can be useful

Accommodation Stage, Grades 4-6

During the Awareness Stage the child is perceptually orientated; he makes judgments in terms of how things look to him. In the period from about age nine to eleven, certain mental operations begin to manifest themselves, e.g., the ability to be aware of a previous thought. According to Almy (1961), the intermediate years of education, which correspond approximately to Piaget's stage of *concrete operations,* are the time of intellectual development when the child is able to solve problems and give explanations in terms of concrete data. The most important specific changes in cognitive development which take place with increasing age have been summarized by Vinacke (1972, pp. 142-143) as follows:

1. Progression from single to complex concepts. For example, concepts of the structure of society move from the immediate family group to the neighborhood, school, community, and so on.
2. Progression from diffuse to differentiated concepts. Thus, concepts of the self change from generalized awareness of the body and relations to others, to well-organized knowledge of roles, attitudes, traits, etc. in a complex system of needs, social relationships, and activities.
3. Progression from egocentric to more objective concepts. In the first or second grade, for example, a child may assume that a teacher knows much more about his home and parents. Later, of course, he learns to an in-

creasing degree to treat objects and people as distinct from his own experience with them.
4. Progression from concrete to abstract concepts. In this trend, the child tends to become increasingly free from the immediately perceived properties and functions of objects and to deal with them in the classificatory sense mentioned above. For example, a younger person tends to draw pictures of particular persons (himself or his mother), whereas older children can more readily produce a man or a child.
5. Progression from variable to more stable concepts. In earlier school years the rules of a game or a classroom procedure are not treated as having a set form, whereas they come in due course to be regarded as fixed. Words which at first have no stable meaning are increasingly used to signify the same kind of object and characteristics of objects.
6. Progression from inconsistent to more consistent and accurate concepts. A child in the first grade may consider any building with red clapboards to be an instance of a barn.

These changes are continuous and cumulative and are not confined solely to the intermediate level of elementary school education. Certain kinds of concepts, such as those pertaining to self, undergo very extensive development in adolescence and, often, into young adulthood. The significant feature of these cognitive changes in the Accommodation phase of career development is that they occur more rapidly in childhood than in later years.

Goals and Rationale:

B1. Development of concepts related to self. In this phase, the child begins to conceptualize what he formerly only perceived (Antholz, 1972). "Self-concepts are self-percepts which have acquired meaning and which have been related to other self-percepts. A self-concept is the individual's picture of himself, the perceived self with accrued meanings" (Super, 1963, p. 18). Operationally, self-concept development at this level takes the form of helping students develop "self-understanding." Turner (1972) points out that the greater an individual's understanding of the *activities* in which he is interested, his *ability* to participate in those activities, and the *value* of those activities to him, the more accurate will be his choice of a later career.

An additional operational aspect of self-understanding is the provision for periodic assessment of growth and learning, and the assimilation of new information. By becoming more fully aware of characteristics of the process of change which mark growth and development, the child can (1) begin to develop a better understanding of self at a certain point in time, i.e., a *concept of becoming*, and (2) recognize that his understanding of self is constantly changing, i.e., he is in a *process of becoming*.

B2. Development of concepts related to the world of work.
At this level, the child moves from perceptualization of work activities and simple generalizations, such as goods and services workers, to more sophisticated concepts. If the child is to differentiate among thousands of occupations, he must be helped to develop a "cognitive map" which will serve as a conceptual framework for later occupational orientation and exploration. The emphasis should be on learning (1) *what* is the world of work and *how* it has evolved, (2) *why* occupations exist, (3) *what* is work, and (4) *why* people pursue various types of work activity (i.e., occupations) (Van Rooy and Bailey, 1972).

B3. Assuming increased responsibility for planning one's time.
Awareness of individual responsibility for one's activities acquired in the previous stage now gives way to greater independence and a certain degree of authority to make decisions for oneself. Antholz (1972, p. 30) states, "He has developed a sense of agency: he knows he can master parts of his environment." The cultural desirability of extending a child's sense of agency has been emphasized by Havighurst (1953, p. 39): ". . . every society recognizes the growth of personal independence and initiative as desirable during middle childhood. The American society sets greater store than most by personal independence and starts training for independence at a relatively early age."

B4. Application of decision-making and classification skills.
Learning how to meet change, to adapt to it, to acquire the new skills demanded by occupational change, must begin early in the child's education. Students in grade six face at the end of the year an important change: transfer to junior high school. Increasingly they are looking beyond their immediate world. The changes that are taking place become more significant in their conscious behavior. Therefore, it is important for children in the later elementary school years to develop behaviors and make decisions which will provide them with the greatest potential for occupational fulfillment under varied circumstances.

B5. Development of desirable social relationships. This goal relates very closely to B1 and is concerned with developing greater "social self" awareness. Self-understanding is nourished and enhanced by impressions or reflections of self received from others. Conversely, self-understanding contributes to the development of desirable social relationships. Turner (1972) maintains that the ability to communicate and cooperate with others is facilitated in proportion to the degree that an individual understands himself.

B6. Development of work attitudes and values. During the previous stage, the child manifests work attitudes and values by *taking the role* of various workers. As the child becomes better able to conceptualize, his basis for choice becomes more rational. "Since living requires choosing between values, which are more or less desirable objects or modes of action, and since many important life situations require a choice between two or more values, the growing child must develop a scale of values which will enable him to make stable choices and to hold himself to these choices" (Havighurst, 1953, p. 36). According to Antholz (1972), if the value of work is not internalized, it becomes very difficult for the individual to achieve self-direction. The probability that he will work only because and when others want him to remains high. This, in turn, has a deleterious effect on his ability to achieve the discipline of work or a positive self-concept.

Illustrative Objectives:

1. Understands the terminology used for self-appraisal and self-understanding
   - 1.1 Reviews what is meant by interests
   - 1.2 Knows what is meant by aptitudes and abilities
   - 1.3 Describes what is meant by values
   - 1.4 Differentiates among interests, abilities, and values
2. Understands that interests may vary at different points in life
   - 2.1 Provides examples of how interests may change as a result of growth, learning, new experience
   - 2.2 Recognizes the tendency of interests to become more stable as he grows older
3. Analyzes how abilities shape interests
   - 3.1 Describes what is meant by the term "ability"
   - 3.2 Differentiates between general ability (primarily scholastic ability) and special abilities (e.g., art, music, manipulative skills, leadership)
   - 3.3 Describes the role of abilities in relationship to interests
4. Analyzes how values shape interests
   - 4.1 Understands that values determine how an individual "feels" (i.e., importance, worth) toward an activity
   - 4.2 Differentiates own values toward various activities from those of peers
   - 4.3 Describes the role of values in relationship to interests
5. Demonstrates an awareness of the continuing process of change that characterizes maturation

5.1 Describes a number of ways of "growing"
5.2 Identifies commonalities in individuals growth and development
5.3 Differentiates own patterns of growth and development from others
6. Formulates present self-identity reflecting knowledge of own interests, abilities, and values
    6.1 Summarizes primary areas of interest
    6.2 Compares present interests with those characteristics of earlier periods
    6.3 Provides examples of individual aptitudes and abilities
    6.4 Recognizes assets and limitations
    6.5 Provided with a list of activities, expresses the importance (value) of those activities to him
7. Judges the validity of own self-identity
    7.1 Recognizes that he has several identities
    7.2 Understands that the "me I see" may be different from the "me others see."
    7.3 Becomes aware of how others characterize him
    7.4 Compares own self-identity with the self others see
    7.5 Explains how knowledge of his "social self" contributes to more accurate self-understanding
8. Becomes more aware of a "social self"
    8.1 Identifies ways he relates to other persons
    8.2 Attempts to characterize self as others see him
    8.3 Expands his capacity to understand the feelings of others
    8.4 Describes how a better understanding of self leads to better relations with others in group activity
9. Analyzes the ways his self-understanding helps him relate to others
    9.1 Identifies activities which depend on cooperative relationships
    9.2 Infers the effect of cooperation on the ability of people to work and play together successfully
10. Understands how man's basic requirements (needs) result in the development of a culture
    10.1 Provides examples of basic human needs: food, shelter, clothing
    10.2 Describes how a culture develops to meet basic human needs
    10.3 Explains how a culture in turn generates its own

needs and requirements necessary to continue the culture

11. Understands that the world of work is composed of occupational units (factories, institutions, enterprises) designed to meet cultural needs

    11.1 Explains why various occupational units have evolved

    11.2 Illustrates by example how a particular type of occupational unit, e.g., construction company, meets a specific cultural imperative

    11.3 Explains why more industrialized cultures have a greater variety of occupational units

    11.4 Describes why more industrialized cultures have a greater variety of service and leisure occupations

12. Categorizes various occupational units in relationship to three types of cultural needs

    12.1 Identifies those occupational units concerned with the *replenishment* of culture (primarily goods and services occupational units)

    12.2 Identifies occupational units concerned with the *management and maintenance* of culture (governmental and regulatory agencies)

    12.3 Identifies those occupational units concerned with the *transmission* of culture (primarily education)

13. Examines work in relation to the environment in which it takes place

    13.1 Understands that work is physical and mental activity undertaken primarily within an occupational unit

    13.2 Explains how the various jobs within an occupational unit contribute to the goal of the enterprise

14. Understands that people engage in occupations for a variety of reasons

    14.1 Recognizes that a person works to satisfy various *social, economic,* and *psychological* needs

    14.2 Explains how work satisfies both individual needs and the needs of society

15. Engages in a wide range of occupationally related and leisure activities

    15.1 Has opportunities to express interests and to develop goals and aspirations

    15.2 Plans experiences, in and out of school, to capitalize on strengths and to strengthen weaknesses

16. Becomes aware of individual responsibility for orderly development
    16.1 Understands that the future is built on the present
    16.2 Lists ways in which individual actions can affect progression toward a preferred career
    16.3 Assumes personal responsibility for the consequences of his choices
    16.4 Relates the importance of education to planning one's own future
    16.5 Understands that different kinds of occupations require varying degrees and types of educational preparation

17. Demonstrates that he is in charge of becoming himself
    17.1 Explains why he is responsible for his own behavior
    17.2 Identifies ways he can take responsibility for his own behavior
    17.3 Identifies times in his daily life when he makes decisions on his own
    17.4 Proposes why only the individual can develop his potentialities

18. Understands that career development is an ongoing, continuously patterned process
    18.1 Recognizes the fact that some day he will have to make an occupational choice
    18.2 Recognizes life in the future as being continuing education and preparation for work
    18.3 Lists the wide range of factors that influence behavior and development

19. Develops increased abilities for making educational, occupational, and personal decisions
    19.1 Understands how a decision has important implications for future decisions
    19.2 Gains a knowledge of the process of decision-making

Orientation Stage, Grades 7-8

Career developmental tasks at the elementary school level have been little researched. Therefore, in the treatment of the previous two stages it was necessary to infer such behaviors from the writings of child development authorities such as Piaget, Erickson, and Havighurst. A much clearer picture of career development at the junior high school level can be drawn. This situation is primarily the result of the work of Donald Super and his colleagues.

Adolescence is seen as a period in which young people explore the world in which they live, the subculture of which they are about to become a part, the roles they may be expected to play, and the opportunities to play roles which suit their personalities, interests, and aptitudes. It is at the same time a period in which the adolescent through experience and self-examination *clarifies his self concept*[4] and begins to put it into words, finds out what outlets exist in society for one who seeks to play a given role, and modifies his self concept to bring it in line with reality (Jordaan, 1963, p. 51).

. . . .

Vocational exploratory behavior refers to activities, mental or physical, undertaken with the more or less *conscious purpose* or hope of eliciting information about one's self or one's environment, or of verifying or arriving at a basis for a conclusion or *hypothesis which will aid in choosing*,[4] preparing for, entering, adjusting to, or progressing in, an occupation (Jordaan, 1963, p. 59).

The authors' decision to designate this stage of development as "orientation" rather than "exploration" follows from Jordaan's discussion of exploratory behavior. To be exploratory, an act should include aspects of (1) search, (2) experimentation, (3) investigation, (4) trial, and (5) hypothesis testing. "If these elements are not present, we propose that the term orientation be substituted for exploration. In other words, we would distinguish between becoming oriented to a situation and exploring it" (Jordaan, 1963, p. 56). While many of the tasks involved in achieving the goals of this stage do indeed involve exploration and would meet Jordaan's criteria, the more insightful and purposeful acts of trial and hypothesis testing are *more characteristic* of the next career development stage.[5]

The crucial point in the orientation stage is at the end of junior high school, when the student is confronted with the necessity of making a curriculum decision prior to entering high school. The intimate relationship between education and career, and the potential effects of this decision on later available options, suggest that choice of high school curriculum is, in a very real sense, as much a "career choice" as an educational one. As Katz (1963, p. 33) points out, when ". . . the adolescent is prompted by cultural expectations (especially the educational system) to think and act in terms of becoming, a becoming which will progressively be subjected to reality testing, then the occupational choice process has been put in motion. The eighth or ninth grade curriculum decision is the first of these formal choice-points. Like a stereoscope, it

[4]Emphasis added.
[5]The authors are merely re-emphasizing the contention that career development is a continuous rather than a discrete process.

provides a means to bring perceptions of self and perception of alternatives for choice into the same field of vision, with one set of perceptions superimposed upon the other."

Behavioral changes in grades seven and eight are not nearly so much cognitive as they are affective and social. According to Piaget, the early adolescent is in the stage of *formal operations* and can reason similarly to an adult. He can examine the consequences of various combinations of factors in systematic and orderly fashion. He is able to devise theories, state them verbally, and then test them in actual practice (Almy, 1961). Thus, according to Piaget's theory, most adolescents should be capable of dealing *intellectually* with the tasks which they confront during the exploration stage.

The more important problem of adolescence has been described by Erickson (1968) and Asubel (1954) as that of establishing an identity. In adolescence, the individual experiences a period of "developmental disequilibrium." At this time, he must exchange "derived status" (i.e., role of parent satellite) for "primary status" (i.e., becoming a person in his own right). In this process, the formulation of a career objective plays a crucial role. "The chief agent in promoting these developments [shift in role] is exploration which furnishes the adolescent with opportunities to make choices and independent decisions, to play different kinds of adult roles, and to establish his own identity" (Jordaan, 1963, p. 47).

Goals and Rationale:
    C1. Clarification of a self-concept. This goal relates to the process of organizing lower-order self-perception into newer, more comprehensive pictures of self. Super (1963, p. 18) points out that ". . . the concept of self is generally a picture of self in some role, some situation, in a position, performing some set of functions, or in some web of relationships." Formulation of a "career hypothesis," which is an expression of a career objective, based upon self data and information related to preferred occupations, is the end result of clarification. Behavior in this area is largely verbal. It becomes instrumental at the point when the career hypothesis is implemented via choice of high school curriculum.
    C2. Understanding of the structure and interrelatedness of the American economic, occupational and technological systems. The desired outcomes for this goal involve *discovery, new knowledge,* and *orientation* to occupations, economics and technology. These behaviors and concepts are interrelated with the previous goal and are essential inputs to the formulation of a career hypothesis. An activity-oriented setting such as is found in the more

progressive industrial arts laboratories is *one* of the more desirable "in-school" environments for (1) orientation to technological processes; (2) acquiring familiarity with occupational roles; and (3) developing vocabulary and understandings of the structure and organization of business, service, and industrial enterprises.

C3. Assuming responsibility for career planning. A sense of responsibility and initiative (i.e., sense of agency) in approaching the career planning tasks of this stage is the desired outcome of the present goal (Tiedeman, 1971). This behavior grows out of (1) recognition that career development is a longitudinal process, requiring planning in earlier years and (2) understanding that planning helps to preserve freedom of choice and expand available options.

C4. Development of individual inquiry and problem-solving skills. Formulation of a "career hypothesis" during the latter part of the orientation stage depends upon the application of previously learned decision-making skills. Because career decision-making is an individual act, the type and amount of personal, occupational, and educational data that each individual requires will vary. Therefore, students must be helped to learn (1) the *characteristics of data* (e.g., interest classifications, occupational and industrial classifications), (2) *where* data may be obtained, (3) *how to use* occupational files and resources, and (4) *which* types of information best meet their needs at the appropriate stage of career development. Thus, curriculum for developing these behaviors becomes "processes" of inquiry and problem-solving rather than only "content," e.g., interest profiles and occupational information.

C5. Development of socially responsible behavior and more mature social relationships. The importance of adolescent social development to later life adjustment has been underscored by Havighurst (1953). Of equal importance and related to later occupational adjustment is the need to provide students with opportunities to *learn to work together* as peers. Long ago, John Dewey argued that if children are to live democratically, they have to experience the living process of democracy in the classroom. The authors maintain that the same can be said for cooperative work behavior.

C6. Appreciation of work as a valued and enduring social institution. Appreciation of work at this level is primarily manifested in an attitude that work has potential for meeting various types of personal needs. The goal is not to dictate to students common sets of work values, but to help students recognize that considerable variation in work values is normal.

Illustrative Objectives:

1. Understands the importance of the need to begin career planning
   1.1 Explains why it is necessary to begin early career planning
   1.2 Explains the principal effects that a career has on an individual's life
   1.3 Identifies the relative personal importance of various factors in identifying career goals
   1.4 Justifies the importance of systematic career selection
   1.5 Describes the consequences of not planning for a career
2. Participates in class discussion on the role of work in individual personality development
   2.1 Discusses types of basic values, i.e., work as: a key to independence, as an outlet for energy, as a means of achieving satisfaction, and as a means of channeling hostile and aggressive drives
   2.2 Explains the concept of individual differences in work values
   2.3 Discusses the need to sometimes invest present time or energy for future benefits
   2.4 States personal attitudes toward work
3. Evaluates the role of work in satisfying physical and psychological needs
   3.1 Describes ways personal needs may be satisfied
   3.2 Relates fulfillment of needs to occupational goals
   3.3 Relates fulfillment of needs to job satisfaction
   3.4 Examines structures (e.g., Maslow) for identifying basic needs
4. Understands fundamental economic concepts
   4.1 Identifies the three major components of economics, i.e., technology, resources, and institutions
   4.2 Describes the circular flow of economic activity
   4.3 Recognizes the role technology plays in economic change
5. Understands basic principles of the manpower market
   5.1 Analyzes the effect supply and demand have on the manpower market
   5.2 Describes the changing nature of the manpower market
   5.3 Identifies major trends in the labor force

5.4 Discusses the social and economic effect of greater labor force participation of youth and women

5.5 Understands basic causes of individual unemployment

6. Traces the changing nature of the manpower market

6.1 Summarizes changes that have taken place in the labor force since 1920

6.2 Projects which industries and occupations will have the greatest employment potential in the future

6.3 Discusses implication of employment trends for own career planning

7. Understands the changing meaning of work

7.1 Compares the meaning of work in an economy of abundance with an economy of scarcity

7.2 Discusses the dual role of women in society

7.3 Acknowledges that the work roles of women may be as socially significant as those of men

7.4 Recognizes that many women desire the stimulation and rewards of a work role in addition to a family role

8. Relates the importance of education and training to American economic growth

8.1 Explains what is meant by the phrase "education is a form of investment in human resources."

8.2 Interprets the positive correlation between education and lifetime earnings

9. Analyzes the social and psychological aspects of work

9.1 Defines what "success" means for him as an individual

9.2 Provides examples of noneconomic rewards of work

9.3 Discusses the relationship between job satisfaction and good mental health

9.4 Discusses how needs may be met through work

9.5 Discusses nonwork (leisure) activities for meeting needs

10. Recognizes the need to effectively use occupational resources to maximize self-evaluation

10.1 Describes how occupational information can enhance career decisions

10.2 Describes how information may affect his view of certain occupations

10.3 Identifies the resource tools to use in studying an occupation and to find information quickly and accurately

10.4 Describes available resources in terms of their accuracy, recency, and completeness

10.5 Formulates criteria for evaluating occupational information

10.6 Identifies factors which may contribute to mis-information about occupations

10.7 Evaluates adequacy of occupational information

10.8 Discusses different ways that occupations can be classified

11. Exhibits goal-seeking behavior in quest of occupational information

11.1 Increases the range of occupations of which he has a knowledge

11.2 Accumulates information about the many available occupations within a preferred occupational family

11.3 Studies preferred occupations to determine future employment outlook, worker functions, and job requirements

11.4 Analyzes preferred occupations in terms of re-quired aptitudes, abilities; and educational level

12. Understands that self-evaluation is a necessary element in career decision-making

12.1 Identifies possible sources of information for self-appraisal

12.2 Interprets the role of interest assessment as an aspect of self-appraisal

12.3 Understands types of interest inventories

12.4 Gives examples of work activities related to peo-ple, ideas, and things

12.5 Appraises mental aptitudes and abilities

12.6 Describes ways of classifying mental abilities

12.7 Rates own mental aptitudes and abilities

12.8 Appraises physical and social aptitudes and abil-ities

12.9 Rates own grooming and physical characteristics

12.10 Identifies special abilities or limitations

12.11 Rates own social abilities

13. Shows awareness of what constitutes personality

13.1 Differentiates between personality and character

13.2 Identifies characteristics of others that make them "attractive"

13.3 Gives examples to illustrate that attractiveness has more to do with the way you feel about yourself than with the features you inherit

13.4 Recognizes that growing up is essentially the same for everyone

14. Displays new self-perspectives and understanding
    14.1 Explains how individuals have control over their own personal behavior
    14.2 Describes the importance of individual differences
    14.3 Accepts own personal limitations
    14.4 Develops plan for strengthening own self-image

15. Demonstrates correct usage of the decision-making method
    15.1 Explains what is meant by a "good decision"
    15.2 Describes the steps in the decision-making process
    15.3 Recognizes the importance of considering many different factors before making a decision
    15.4 Uses the decision-making process in interpreting case studies

16. Formulates a tentative career hypothesis
    16.1 Accepts responsibility for career planning
    16.2 Rejects earlier occupational choices which were based on childhood fantasies or unrealistic expectations
    16.3 Understands the principle that the satisfaction an individual obtains from his life work is related to the degree to which it enables him to implement his abilities, interests, values, and other self-characteristics
    16.4 Eliminates from consideration those occupational areas for which he clearly lacks basic qualifications
    16.5 Formulates own criteria for choice of an occupation
    16.6 Identifies major obstacles or impediments which may affect progress toward career goal
    16.7 Describes means of coping with these factors

17. Evaluates how tentative career hypothesis meets his goals
    17.1 Lists components of his desired career
    17.2 Identifies those components which are included in his hypothesis
    17.3 Describes how he can fulfill goals not included in his plan
    17.4 Identifies goals which are not compatible with his plan

18. Exhibits planfulness in choosing a high school curriculum
    18.1 Identifies the important elements needed to prepare for his career objectives
    18.2 Recognizes that life in the future will become a matter of continuing education
    18.3 Knows that there are certain basic educational skills important for all areas of work
    18.4 Knows the kind, length, and general cost of education or training for occupations in which he is interested
19. Develops a projected high school program compatible with educational requirements and tentative career hypothesis
    19.1 Identifies academic courses where completion may aid in achievement of goals
    19.2 Identifies extra-curricular or nonschool activities which may aid in achievement of goals
20. Pursues courses of implementation
    20.1 Selects coursework compatible with his career hypothesis
    20.2 Engages in extra-curricular activities compatible with his career hypothesis

Exploration and Preparation Stage, Grades 9-12

During the four years of high school the adolescent is expected to *crystallize* an occupational choice and evidence commitment to that goal by embarking upon a specialized educational or training program or by taking an entry level job upon leaving school. Behaviors in this stage differ from the previous ones in *degree* of intent and purposefulness *rather than in kind or type*. At the end of the orientation stage, the typical student formulates a "career hypothesis." This serves as a symbol for a number of preferred occupational activities and life goals. Although this act is an important prerequisite to subsequent selection of more specific goals, two characteristics tend to be lacking: *reality testing* and *commitment*. Whereas behavior in the orientation stage is generally characterized by *search, experimentation,* and *investigation,* behavior in the exploration and preparation stage deals more with *trial* and *hypothesis-testing.* "By hypothesis-testing we mean behavior which is engaged in for the purpose of checking the validity of some more or less clearly formulated belief, hypothesis, or expectation concerning the self or the environment" (Jordaan, 1963, p. 56).

The tasks at this stage, then, require the student to expand and refine behaviors of earlier stages. "At this level, the concepts which students hold about self, the work world, and career preparation become internalized and form the basis for more specific generalizations concerning career life identity. Students at this level begin to take on certain features of real occupational roles related to their visualized career life" (Gysbers and Moore, 1972, p. 226). Above all, it is important to acknowledge that the stakes are considerably higher at the end of this period than at the end of previous ones.

Guidance at the eighth or ninth-grade choice-point could look ahead to student development under the continuing shelter of the secondary school . . . change would generally involve some loss: [the student] learned that the rules of the decision-making game required him to play 'for keeps.' But the stakes were low . . . the institutional protection of the school and its guidance program provided him with a benign climate for inexpensive exploration and try-out . . . Now, at grade 11 or 12, both thought and observation are presumed to be ready for a more severe test (Katz, 1963, p. 42).

Goals and Rationale:

D1. Crystallization and implementation of a self-concept. The process of career development involves the formulation and reformulation of the self-concept throughout the life stages. Super *et al* (1963) have repeatedly pointed out differences in the level of complexity of the self-concept. For example, in the orientation stage, behavior was predominately verbal as the individual clarified a career hypothesis. In the exploration and preparation stage the behavior becomes more instrumental as the self-concept is (1) tested and reformulated through occupational exploration and (2) implemented through commitment to a preferred occupation or educational option. Thus, as Super (1963, p. 18) points out, "The complex self-concept is organized within the framework of a role."

D2. Executing plans to qualify for career objectives. The relation of this goal to D1 above is obvious. The crystallization and implementation of the self-concept is a gradually evolving one, pieced together from bits of experience acquired during this stage (and beyond). The purpose of the student's present goal is to *qualify* for his preferred career objectives through appropriate study and occupational experience. Two sub-goals are involved: (1) In grades nine and ten the students will explore several occupational clusters to (a) test the career hypothesis formulated in the earlier stage and (b) narrow the range of his occupational interest. (2) The outcome of occupational exploration in grades nine and ten will be the reformulation of a career hypothesis and the selection of *one* occupational cluster for preparation in greater depth in grades eleven and twelve. The type of course work pursued in the last two years will of necessity depend on whether the student opts for (a) entry level employment, (b) post-high school technical education, or (c) post-high school baccalaureate education.

D3. Commitment to implementation of a career plan. "Exploratory behavior may be systematic and planful or it may be random, haphazard, and diffuse" (Jordaan, 1963, p. 65). An attitude essential to systematic career behavior is the individual's commitment to plan. Super (1963) points out that the attitude, not the act, of commitment is a key factor in the specification of an occupational preference. The outcome at this level is what Morrill and Forest have called an *active agent.* "The focus . . . is to provide the individual with the view of himself as having the 'power' to make a commitment and to influence and create his future" (Morrill and Forrest, 1970, p. 303).

D4. Application of problem-solving skills. This goal requires the student to use decision-making and problem-solving skills in the execution of his career plans. Three subgoals are involved. In grades nine and ten the student begins to (1) relate the feasibility and appropriateness of his self characteristics to the occupational roles he is exploring. During the grade eleven and twelve period, the student (2) acquires knowledge of alternative educational and occupational paths and (3) obtains initial employment or enters an appropriate post-high school education or training program. Thus, as Martin (1971, pp. 30-31) states, "The goal at this level is to insure that the complex interrelationship of specific factors, including personal, social, economic, and educational, provides an appropriate and realistic motivational basis to enable the individual to apply his concepts and knowledge regarding work-life selection in planning and decision-making and determine for himself appropriate action to achieve his intended adult work-life goals."

D5. Understanding the dynamics of group behavior in a work situation. Opportunities for students to work together in group situations, which was the focus for goal C5, should be continued at this level. Students should develop expanded awareness of the factors that facilitate or inhibit group functioning. Reports from employers repeatedly underscore the fact that failure of an employee is due more often to lack of cooperative work relationships than to actual job skill performance. Peters and Farwell (1967, pp. 275-76) describe many different roles that are indicative of various levels of operation within a functional group. These are examples of types of roles with which students should become acquainted. Group experiences should help students discover how each individual can contribute to or detract from satisfaction of group needs and goals.

D6. Acquiring the discipline of work. Preparation for employment is often only regarded as the mastery of job skills and related knowledge. The concern of goal D2 is, in part, for the individual to acquire skills to qualify for one of three career paths. The type of skills to be developed varies in relation to the chosen career objective. The present goal, however, is considered to be important for *all* students to acquire in order to be able to function effectively with various life demands. The individual who has internalized a value to work displays a drive to act out that behavior. He approaches work and other tasks in a systematic manner, completes tasks at or beyond the level of proficiency required, and derives satifaction from the products of his efforts.

Illustrative Objectives:
1. Shows awareness of the importance of continuing own education
    1.1 Describes the reasons why many individuals drop out of school
    1.2 Understands why employers prefer high school graduates
    1.3 Characterizes the career pattern of dropouts, i.e., last hired, first fired, lower pay, and poorer jobs
2. Recognizes the future implications of dropping out of school
    2.1 Illustrates how automation will change the number and type of available jobs
    2.2 Outlines opportunities available for those who prepare themselves for the future
    2.3 Identifies ways that dropouts may complete a high school education
    2.4 Recognizes the responsibility of each individual for "making it"
3. Relates economic benefits to level of education
    3.1 Identifies three ways an individual's economic future is affected by his level of education, i.e., amount of income, ability to compete, and job stability
    3.2 Explains the relationship between job market competition and the level of education completed
    3.3 Explains the relationship between holding a job and level of education completed
    3.4 Compares potential earning power to level of education completed

3.5 Interprets graphical relationship between education level and unemployment
4. Explores occupational clusters to verify interests and aptitudes
    4.1 Engages in representative, sample work experiences
    4.2 Completes task specifications for a given activity
    4.3 Conducts self evaluations of the products of his work
    4.4 Recognizes that occupational clusters offer various types of jobs at several different levels
    4.5 Discovers the level of responsibility associated with various work roles
    4.6 Narrows down his interests to one occupational cluster (reformulates a career hypothesis)[6]
5. Demonstrates success in coping with work tasks
    5.1 Follows prescribed job instructions
    5.2 Completes assigned job tasks on time
    5.3 Practices assigned job standards
    5.4 Practices stated and accepted ethics on the job
6. Understands the social nature of an occupational enterprise
    6.1 Describes typical personnel organizational structure
    6.2 Understands the level of responsibility associated with various work roles
    6.3 Describes how workers at all levels make a valuable contribution to the goal of the enterprise
    6.4 Describes the factors which contribute to vertical movement within an organization
    6.5 Identifies the physical, mental, social and educational requirements associated with different levels of authority
7. Performs in a given work situation in a manner which indicates he understands that work effectiveness depends not just on proficiency but on quality of interpersonal relations as well[7]
    7.1 Demonstrates in a group task that completion of the task depends on cooperation as well as individual proficiency
    7.2 Describes the effect of pleasant or unpleasant relationships on his ability to work effectively

[6]Many of the objectives in the previous stage related to the formulation of a career hypothesis would be repeated during this stage.
[7]The authors wish to acknowledge the assistance of Mary Antholz in formulating objectives 7, 9, and 10.

7.3 Identifies similarities in his relations with other students and in adult workers relations with co-workers

7.4 Identifies factors which contribute to success or failure in a work situation

7.5 Describes his performance in a given situation as successful or unsuccessful and asks for constructive criticism

7.6 Describes knowledge gained in failure to complete a task which might not otherwise have been gained

8. Analyzes the social roles and demands required for successful performance in a work situation

8.1 Describes human relations skills that are useful in a work setting

8.2 Demonstrates sensitivity to the needs of employers and co-workers

8.3 Understands the extent to which command of the fundamental processes of communication is necessary in a group-oriented work setting

9. Shows a genuine concern for his fellow workers and expresses a shared responsibility for success or failure of the work group

9.1 Describes how the performance of any member of a work group can affect the group's performance

9.2 Identifies the effects of his actions on other workers and describes his responsibilities to them because of these effects

10. Contributes positively to group effort in a work situation by demonstrating ability to both compromise and exercise influence in the achievement of group goals

10.1 Lists group goals in a given situation and identifies reasons why he may have to compromise to reach those goals

10.2 Describes how his influence might help to achieve group goals

10.3 Identifies advantages and disadvantages of compromise and influence in a given situation

10.4 Identifies ways in which he is dependent upon the work of others

10.5 Identifies ways in which others depend upon work he does

11. Evaluates reality of educational-occupational preference (i.e., reformulated career hypothesis)

11.1 Solicits assistance from counselor to help validate preference

11.2 Reviews cumulative record to help confirm areas of greatest strength

11.3 Realistically assesses weaknesses

11.4 Completes diagnostic tests, interest inventories or other selected instruments for additional self data

11.5 Summarizes why he qualifies for preferred educational-occupational objectives

12. Examines contingencies affecting implementation of educational-occupational preference

12.1 Understands that personal compromises may have to be made in order to attain a chosen career goal

12.2 Identifies *personal* (ability, aptitudes), *situational* (illness, finances) or *social* (race, religion) factors which may affect educational entrance or advancement in preferred career field

12.3 Lists factors which may influence own job stability in preferred occupational field

12.4 Acknowledges that many careers require postponing immediate rewards for later long-range rewards

12.5 Identifies skills and/or knowledge utilized in preferred occupation which may transfer to another

12.6 Makes career plans which take into consideration the fact that technology, automation, or manpower surpluses may eliminate preferred occupation

12.7 Describes how different occupations vary in the degree of personal freedom to define one's role and activities

13. Prepares to embark on chosen educational-occupational path

13.1 Compiles information which an employer might require for a job interview

13.2 Practices filling out sample job application forms

13.3 Practices appropriate behavior for an employment interview

13.4 If further education is desired, completes required application and/or entrance requirements

14. Obtains initial employment

14.1 Demonstrates the ability to assess the performance requirements of a preferred occupation

14.2 Eliminates from consideration those occupations for which he clearly lacks basic qualifications

    14.3 Demonstrates appropriate job-seeking behavior
    14.4 Learns about the opportunities offered by employer and/or unions to advance in his chosen career
    14.5 Knows about related educational programs which may facilitate advancement in career field
15. Enrolls in appropriate post-secondary school or college
    15.1 Is informed concerning the kind, length and cost of training for the occupation he has an interest in
    15.2 Knows the content and requirements of courses that may facilitate occupational goal
    15.3 Knows sources and requirements for obtaining needed financial aid
    15.4 Knows the employment opportunities available in the occupational role for which he is training
    15.5 Understands how advanced degrees may facilitate or impede progress in chosen career field

Issues and Projections

This chapter is a *beginning* step in the creation of a comprehensive and integrated career education curriculum. The authors are fully convinced that the ultimate acceptance of career education is in no small way related to the degree to which it can be demonstrated to be an integral component of education. The climate for acceptance of career education has been shown to be favorable and widespread. However, professionals should not be seduced into believing that career education will be warmly received by all constituencies within education. *Serious theoretical questions remain and many operational problems persist.* Goldhammer and Taylor (1972, pp. 283-293) have enumerated a number of critical factors which have to be taken into consideration by advocates of career education. The major issues have been paraphrased as follows:

1. The centrality of work in determining an individual's future life style is well known. However, how do we prepare people for work roles and also accommodate those for whom a career may not be the sole or major determiner of life style?
2. Career education challenges the concept that the basic function of the school is transmission of knowledge. However, this does not negate the importance of providing a base of knowledge and skills to support an individual's preparation for a career and to enable him

to deal effectively with the problems which confront
him. What bodies of knowledge are of the most importance? How do we develop a truly interdisciplinary curriculum?

3. What will be the role of vocational education within the
   broader career education scheme? Will all students be
   provided with employable skills at the end of high school
   (or when they exit school)? What "employability skills"
   should be taught to ensure maximum future adaptability
   and potential?

4. Should career education only devote itself to the development of "economic man"? This issue is closely
   related to number one. What about social, aesthetic,
   recreational, and moral interests; needs, and obligations?
   There is much overlap. What are the most desirable
   relationships?

5. Career education mandates that guidance will be part of
   the total curriculum program. How? Will teachers or
   guidance personnel provide instruction for career education?

6. How will career education be administered to assure that
   students are not penalized by traditional standards for
   high school graduation and by college or other post-high
   education entrance requirements?

7. How realistic is it to propose that every high school
   student be equipped with an entry level job skill? Is it
   possible, for example, for a student to enter the health
   occupations at an assistant level and move up the career
   ladder to become a physician? Are there more direct
   ways of assuring student mobility and advancement?

8. A basic premise of career education is that students at
   the elementary level must begin career planning at an
   early age if they are to be adequately prepared later for
   making more specific occupational choices. How will
   programs be organized to provide continual reassessment of choices at increased levels of maturity to insure
   that decision-making is a continuous process of clarification while at the same time an expansion of available
   options?

9. Vocational education has a negative image among many
   educators and members of minority groups. Will career
   education be able to demonstrate, by example, that it
   deserves the prestige accorded the academic subject

areas and that it offers more hope for all groups than does the present educational program?

10. Career education is too large an undertaking to be achieved solely within the confines of a single public agency. It is important that career education pioneer cooperative relationships among school, home and community. What are the primary roles of each? How will cooperation and participation evolve?

11. Many critics see career education as a move to indoctrinate students to fit into the "system." In Chapter 1 it was pointed out that in the future, education will in all probability be much more humanistic. In what ways will career education facilitate exploration of values and life styles?

The authors have not intended to end this chapter on a somber note. Partial answers to many of these issues are already available. The purpose of examining issues is to focus needed research and development and to promote meaningful dialogue in the educational community. The confidence in career education exhibited by leaders in government and education indicates that career education professionals are equal to the challenge. This book underscores the strength of that capability.

BIBLIOGRAPHY

Almy, M. Wishful thinking about children's thinking? *Teachers College Record,* 1961, 62, 396-406.

Antholz, M. B. Conceptualization of a model career development program, K-12. Unpublished research paper, University of Minnesota, 1972.

Ausubel, D. P. *Theory and problems of adolescent development.* New York: Grune & Stratton, 1954.

Cole, H. P. Process education: the new direction for elementary-secondary schools. Englewood Cliffs, New Jersey: Educational Technology Publications, 1972.

Erickson, E. *Identity: youth and crisis.* New York: Norton, 1968.

Formanek, R. and Morine, G. Categorizing in young children: two views. In A. R. Binter and S. H. Frey (eds.), *The psychology of the elementary school child.* Chicago: Rand McNally, 1972, 146-158.

Goldhammer, K. and Taylor, R. E. (eds.) *Career education: perspective and promise.* Columbus, Ohio: Charles E. Merrill, 1972.

Goodson, S. Children talk about work. *Personnel and Guidance Journal,* 1970, 49, 131-136.

Grobman, H. *Developmental curriculum projects: Decision points and processes.* Itasca, Illinois: Peacock, 1970.

Gysbers, N. C. and Moore, E. J. Career development in the schools. In G. F. Law (ed.), *Contemporary concepts in vocational education.* Washington, D. C.: American Vocational Association, 1971, 218-229.

Havighurst, R. J. *Human development and education.* New York: David McKay, 1953.

Herr, E. L. *Decision-making and vocational development.* Boston: Houghton Mifflin, 1970.

————. What is career education? Paper presented to the Career Education Conference for Cochise County School Administration, Casa Grande, Arizona, August 1971.

————. *Review and synthesis of foundations for career education.* Columbus, Ohio: The Center for Vocational and Technical Education, 1972.

Hill, G. E. and Luckey, E. B. *Guidance for children in elementary schools.* New York: Appleton-Century-Crofts, 1969.

Hoyt, K. B. Paper presented at the American Vocational Association Annual Convention, December 6, 1971.

Hoyt, K. B., Evans, R. N., Mackin, E. F., and Mangum, G. L. *Career education: What it is and how to do it.* Salt Lake City: Olympus, 1972.

Jordaan, J. P. Exploratory behavior: The formation of self and occupational concepts. In D. E. Super et al. *Career development: Self-concept theory.* New York: College Entrance Examination Board, 1963, 42-78.

Kaback, G. R. Occupational information for groups of elementary school children. *Vocational Guidance Quarterly,* 1966, 14, 163-168.

Katz, M. *Decisions and values: A rationale for secondary school guidance.* New York: College Entrance Examination Board, 1963.

Krathwohl, D. R. Stating objectives appropriately for program, for curriculum, and for instructional material development. *Journal of Teacher Education,* 1965, 16, 83-92.

Martin, A. M. *The theory and practice of communicating educational and vocational information.* Boston: Houghton Mifflin, 1971.

Morrill, W. H. and Forrest, D. J. Dimensions of counseling for career development. *Personnel and Guidance Journal,* 1970, 49, 299-305.

Peters, H. J. and Farwell, G. F. *Guidance: A developmental approach.* Chicago: Rand McNally, 1967.

Super, D. E. *Career development: Self-concept theory.* New York: College Entrance Examination Board, 1963.

Tiedeman, D. V. The agony of choice: guidance for career decisions. In R. C. Pucinski and S. P. Hirsch (eds.), *The Courage to change: New directions for career education.* Englewood Cliffs, New Jersey: Prentice-Hall, 1971. 121-130.

Turner, K. G. A conceptual model of the functional self. Career Development for Children Project, Southern Illinois University, 1972.

Van Rooy, W. H. and Bailey, L. J. A conceptual model of the world of work. Career Development for Children Project, Southern Illinois University, 1972.

Vinacke, W. E. Concept formation in children of school ages. In A. R. Binter and S. H. Frey (eds.), *The psychology of the elementary school child.* Chicago: Rand McNally, 1972, 135-145.

Zimmermann, B. and Bailey, L. J. Children's conceptions about work and play. Career Development for Children Project, Southern Illinois University, February 1971.

Implementing Change
in Education

Introduction

This book has described the foundations, theory, goals, and objectives of a kind of public education which would be different in significant ways from previous experience. The prescription is for a total reorientation of schooling, focusing on individuals, with career development the central experience of the curriculum. This is *change* in large measure. *In The Courage to Change: New Directions for Career Education,* Pucinski speaks of restructuring public education and creating new institutions. He obviously assumes planned change: ". . . preparing young people for adulthood involves *turning around the system,*[1] recognizing the rightful role of all citizens in shaping that system, and exercising leadership with extraordinary vision at all levels of educational input" (Pucinski, 1971, p. 19). Turning around the system is drastic change. Because these are the words of the chairman of the House of Representatives Committee on Education and because the real rate of change in career education theory and practice has never been greater, it behooves knowledgeable professionals to understand change in education. The concern is not with change in career education alone but, rather, with change in *education* because career education entails changes in all aspects of public education. As Hoyt, *et al.* (1972) point out, career education is a packaged deal which can be maximized only if teachers, counselors, the business-labor community, and other groups are involved in and committed to it.

In the United States of America (and much of the world), there is talk of planned change. In the early decades of this century, social reformers who advocated deliberate planning and inter-

[1]Emphasis added.

vention in socioeconomic development and the evolution of institutions were offset by a declining majority which placed its trust in the *laissez faire* principle of automatic adjustment. As Bennis, *et al.* (1969) demonstrate, by the 1960's, planned interventions involved both the products and the methods of social research across wider and wider segments of the social fabric. Planned change is now accepted as necessary not because it stems from one ideology or another but because it is essential to political and physical survival and traditional values such as liberty and equality of opportunity.

Even though social change has not been as dramatic as technological change and although large-scale curriculum modifications have come on the scene several decades after planned change in other institutions, the need for planned change in education has now been long accepted. Lifton (1970) concludes that there is tremendous lag between schooling and available resources, i.e., that schools have been greatly resistant to change. The past is bleak. The future can be bright only if systematic change becomes ubiquitous in education. Fortunately, there is already a large body of literature on change in education. In relatively recent times, the theory and practice of planned change in education has matured to the point of being generally and widely applicable.

In the hope that change in education will improve rather than complicate curriculum, in the hope that change will be planned and pointed rather than for its own sake, in the hope that change will be meaningful to students rather than frustrating and senseless, in the hope that the function of schooling will be identified and realized rather than obscured and muddied, the authors offer the principle that *professionals in education must be intimately familiar with the change process and the role and function of the several agencies who effect it.*

The Meanings of Planned Change

It is important to understand that the word *change* is to be differentiated from its synonyms. Webster's (1967, p. 139) makes rather clear distinctions.

CHANGE implies making either an essential difference often amounting to a loss of original identity or a substitution of one thing for another; ALTER implies a difference in some particular respect without suggesting loss of identity; VARY stresses a breaking away from sameness, duplication, or exact repetition; MODIFY suggests a difference that limits, restricts, or adapts to a new purpose.

Chin (1967) delineates five levels of change. These are paraphrased in very brief form and illustrated with career education examples.

Substitution

The simplest form of change involves replacing one element with a new element. Adopting a new drafting textbook, installing new ovens, updating a filmstrip about community helpers, and myriad other improvements (?) in the on-going educational enterprise are exemplary of substitution. Not much is threatened by this low level of change.

Alteration

Alterations are a little more basic than substitutions and have greater potential for impinging on the form and substance of the enterprise. Alternate content and new methods of instruction can have far-reaching effects on learning and on the professional status and reward system. Altering a course so that it includes occupational information and/or involves resource people from the working community can have a variety of effects on a school or a school district. Even if the intent of instruction is not altered, new approaches, i.e., alternatives of many kinds, to similar goals can have more impact on the social system than can simple substitutions.

Perturbations and Variations

By definition, this level of change entails temporary shifts or oscillations in a system. Distributing copies of brochures which depict technicians who utilize principles of science and mathematics in their work has varying effects on professionals and students. But, for many possible reasons the effects are temporary. For example, brochures are readily out of supply or out of date, time to relate occupations to textbook mathematics seems always to be too short, teachers come and go, many teachers cannot relate mathematics to semiprofessional occupations.

Restructuring

Restructuring means modifying and reorganizing a system and is thus a more fundamental level of change. Restructuring is basic social change. Restructuring the curricular system to give career development its own place on the main trunk rather than a tacked-on, catch-as-catch-can, or tangential place is a different level of change from the previous levels. This and the next level of change is what Pucinski and Hirsch (1971) and many others prescribe for public schooling.

Value Orientation Change

Many examples of this form have been depicted in previous chapters. Change of the greatest magnitude is dependent upon understanding and adopting the idea systems, thought models, or conceptual frameworks and assumptions which underlie the proposal. The better career education theorists are saying that they have proposals of this magnitude. They are asking practicing educators to reform the total school from concern to maximize the number and success of university students to concern for individual, career development regardless of where, when, how, or why (or even if) one will be employed. As Chapter 1 demonstrated, many of education's contemporary critics propose changes of this magnitude. Most of these proposals do not concern career development. Some do. But the point is: they call for a revaluing of schooling.

So much for change. What is planned change? To these definitions of changes of several magnitudes must be added the concept of *plan*. Planned change is change which occurs by design. (Design can come from within and/or without a system.) Design connotes model. Planned change proceeds (when all goes well) according to the model or design of the planner — insofar as the planner understands change models, agents, and obstacles.

Decision Models

Before models of change in education are examined, it is necessary to examine the more general phenomenon of individual thought or decision-making. Although it is not well to draw sweeping generalizations about these developing areas of social science,

TABLE 12-1

FIVE-STEP ANALYSIS OF THE
COMPLETE ACT OF THOUGHT

1	2	3	4	5
Situational milieu	Defining the problem(s)	Researching	Action/ initiation planning	Action/ initiation testing

it seems safe to conclude that decision models deal with individual thought and adoption and that change models deal with innovation in organizations.

Five-Step Analysis of Complete Decision Process

The following decision model has been developed by the authors. They first began thinking about decision models because of exposure to John Dewey's *How We Think* (1933). Only his concept of a five-step process and perhaps some insights are borrowed here (see Table 12-1). This five-step analysis of the complete act of thought is a general model, applicable to any kind of thought above the motor-chaining level, e.g., creative thinking, adoption of new ideas.

1. Thought begins and ends in the situational milieu. Problems can be presented by others, found in nature, or sought out. Normal, healthy people encounter some problems in each way. The mind is continuously active (even in sleep) perceiving and structuring problems. What is perceived is modified by the receiver variables which are identified by Rogers and Shoemaker (see Fig. 12-1). Characteristics internal to the perceiver qualify stimuli. The healthy mind does not wait for emergencies to occur, but rather seeks them out.

2. Problem definition also involves features not in the situation itself. The perceiver looks within his mind to consider such matters as his purposes as he goes about the task of clarifying the problem. Like the other four steps, clarification involves judgments. Here, as elsewhere, judgments may be wise or otherwise. The major judgment that people make when clarifying problems is a twofold one. People attempt to define (1) how much effort is involved in affecting solution(s) and (2) how much value will result — cost-benefit, if you will. This is nothing more or less than the principle of least effort in operation — not in the hedonistic or pleasure-based sense but the information-based sense. This step has impact on the next step. During clarification, one decides what quality of answer or solution will be acceptable. The self-concept comes into play in problem definition. One decides whether the problem is the type one usually deals with, whether it will enhance the self or not and so on. Put another way, definition of self is an intermediate stage of problem solving.

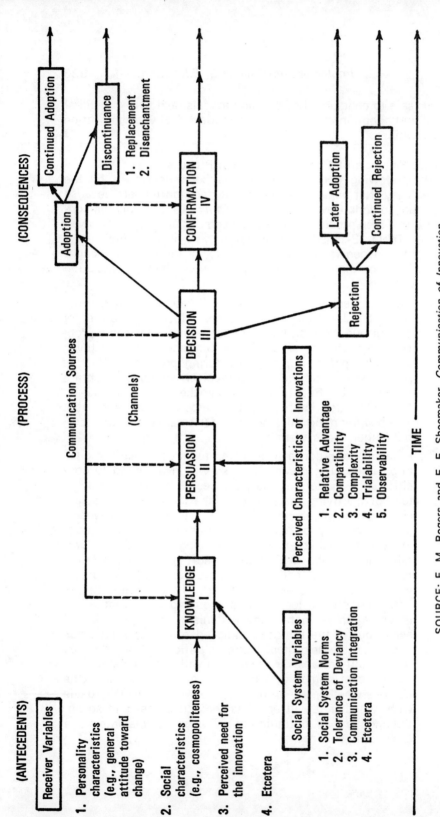

SOURCE: E. M. Rogers and F. F. Shoemaker, *Communication of Innovation.*
Free Press, 1971, p. 102.

Fig. 12-1. Paradigm of the Innovation-Decision Process

3. The third step involves research in anticipation of formulating an hypothesis. One draws upon known generalizations about the world (or conducts new research — a special kind of thought) in his mind and/or other information resource systems, to establish alternate solutions.

    It is well to note at this point that problems which are classified as important to one's purposes result in different kinds of research than do problems such as memorizing State capitals. That is, life problems and many school problems are distinguishable. One way to describe what career education people are asking of schools is to say that the suggestion is to engage learners in activities which they can relate to real life interests. People who talk about intrinsic and extrinsic motivation appreciate the distinction between institution purposes and learner purposes. Career education people are saying (a) that youngsters are unable, for long, to relate life purposes to the traditional college preparatory *or* general education stuff, (b) that the life purposes of youngsters and purposes of institutions should be coincident, (c) that the major and thus central overlap, the core of education, is career development, preparation and updating, and (d) that intelligent professionals should appreciate this and revitalize schooling accordingly.

4. The research step suggests plans for action or inaction. These range from the simple idea that the problem will right itself if no action is taken to very involved plans for multifacetted solutions which take many years. Obviously, most plans involve do's and don'ts. That is, most situational milieus are analyzed as requiring some positive actions *and* avoidance or curtailment of some other actions.

    In the planning step, one attempts (a) to align action with what is known about solution of similar problems and (b) to establish a new solution(s) which will be useful in the future. Put another way, the decision-maker tries to establish valid and reliable schema for solving problems. Although each situation is peculiar, people try (a) to make the most of prior knowledge and (b) (quite naturally) to plan not just for immediate problems but for similar problems of the future.

5. The final step in a complete decision-making sequence is the action/inaction test. The plan is tried out. The do's and/or don'ts decided upon in the planning step are

tested. This results in two judgments (a) whether the solution has been successful and (b) whether the chain of events justifies new conclusions about the way similar problems should be solved. Examples of decisions in career education will clarify this step and others in the decision process.

Suppose that an elementary school curriculum director receives a piece of literature on career education from the State education agency. The situation is readily understood. From the return address on the envelope and the document itself, it is obvious that this is a dissemination problem like many which are solved each week. The matter is quickly defined as "What use shall be made of this publication?" In the research step, a wealth of information about the publication and the school system is utilized to lead the decision-maker to an action/inaction plan. Past practice suggests whether the publication should be reviewed and responded to in writing, whether it should be filed, catalogued, circulated, destroyed, and so on. If the publication deals with financing career education programs, the research step might lead to the decision to (a) write a thank-you to the sender, (b) circulate the piece to the district finance director, and (c) file the piece with materials which are used in the drafting of annual plans for submission to the state agency. The test of this plan involves the actual routing, monitoring possible responses from the finance director, observing the letter going into the mail, observing the filing of the publication (or assuming this and finding it in the appropriate file at plan writing time), and finding the piece useful in annual planning.

One other typical and more involved example should help the reader to consider many examples of decision-making. Suppose that during the course of the school year, a classroom teacher comes to a point where career development principles and the progress of students (situational milieu) suggest the problem: What experiences will foster awareness and appropriate levels of understanding of working conditions in vehicular repair occupations? The teacher will consider peculiarities of students, curriculum materials available in the district and elsewhere, desired learning outcomes, and district policies before defining the problem. (Problem definition.) The problem might be defined: What establishments should be visited during a two-hour field trip that is intended to serve as a springboard for reading and discussions about the characteristics of vehicular repair occupations? After recalling what she knows of establishments within easy access to the school, consulting files, talking with an advisory committee member, and using many other data gathering techniques (research) she comes to a point where she is prepared to settle on a plan of action/inaction. The plan would involve a step-by-step sequence of departures, arrivals, questions to ask of workmen, and the like. (Action/inaction planning.) Testing would involve the actual field trip, many checkpoints concerning timing and nature of the experience, and responses in later discussions.

Several additional features of the decision-making process are important to understanding individual change agents. As many others point out when describing their paradigms, the decision process can be interrupted at any point. Research alone can take a long period of time and lead to blind alleys. Some problems are rightly and wrongly ignored or abandoned at various points. Some cannot be resolved.

Then, there is the matter of decisions within decisions. The teacher had to decide many minor issues during the planning of the field trip, e.g., which establishment should be visited first? Where should the children visit washrooms? Any complex act of thought is composed of smaller acts of thought at each of the respective steps. The paradigm is only a paradigm.

Nevertheless, it has great value. Educational change agents must use a paradigm of decision-making to understand their own actions and to understand others. Researchers need to ask questions on the order of: Are we defining these problems properly? Have our colleagues discovered all available research evidence? Are we considering the full array of plausible alternatives? Are we giving new experiences fair and thorough tests? Are we getting all possible kinds of feedback? As promoters of new instructional material, developers have to ask: Are we presenting concepts and materials in ways which are motivating rather than threatening? Are we giving people opportunity to redefine issues in light of local conditions? Are they able because of time and resource limitations to examine practice and the literature before setting a course for themselves? Are they giving instruction and learning a fair chance by conducting several kinds of short- and long-range follow-up analyses?

Innovation-Decision Process

Rogers and Shoemaker (1971) are highly regarded experts on the specialized decision-making process called *adoption of innovations*. They describe a four-stage model of "the innovation-decision process." This is "the mental process through which an individual passes from first knowledge of an innovation to a decision to adopt or reject and to confirmation of this decision" (Rogers and Shoemaker, 1971, p. 99). Unlike the two models described in the next section, this is a model of what takes place in an individual mind. Diffusion in a social system is a different phenomenon. The four stages or functions of the innovation-decision process are knowledge, persuasion, decision and confirmation. See Fig. 12-1.

The model has three divisions: antecedents, process, and consequences. The antecedents and consequences parts of the paradigm are rather self-explanatory and, remarkably, they contain nearly as much information as the text. The four stages of the process are better defined by:

1. *Knowledge.* The individual is exposed to the innovation's existence and gains some understanding of how it functions.
2. *Persuasion.* The individual forms a favorable or unfavorable attitude toward the innovation.
3. *Decision.* The individual engages in activities which lead to a choice to adopt or reject the innovation.
4. *Confirmation.* The individual seeks reinforcement for the innovation-decision he has made, but he may reverse his previous decision if exposed to conflicting messages about the innovation (Rogers and Shoemaker, 1971, p. 103).

It should be noted (1) that this is the second model developed by these authors and (2) that it is designed to account for deficiencies noted by rural sociologists and many other scientists during the 1960's. The examples which Rogers and Shoemaker use to illustrate detailed descriptions of the four stages are very helpful to understanding. Yet, the paradigm is, by itself, very understandable.

Rogers and Shoemaker are very thorough scholars. They have examined more than 1,500 publications and synthesized them into 103 generalizations about the diffusion process. Their Appendix A (1971, pp. 346-385) lists these generalizations and studies which support or do not support them. This monumental book is essential reading for curriculum innovators in instructional enterprises, education agencies, and publishing houses.

Change Models

It seems appropriate to call innovation in organizations *change* and to speak of *change models* rather than something as unwieldy as "models of collective decision-making."

Social scientists use a great many terms to describe steps in the change sequence. Wall (1972) compares a number of representative models and illustrates well facts such as: (1) There is a lot of agreement and a lot of disagreement among model designers. (2) Models have different characteristics, depending upon the field of interest of the designer, i.e., on what the designer wants to account for in the model. (3) All models have a series of rather similar steps.

One of the models which is widely known and used in education is the Guba-Clark (1965) schema, Table 12-2. Unlike many others, Guba and Clark depict a series of processes. Progression from *research* through *development* and *diffusion* to adoption is logical and can easily be seen to parallel other change models. Guba and Clark are wise to use terms which apply to people and to innovation in education. This is their intent and is the major advantage of their model. Another advantage of this model is that it facilitates dealing with lags and gaps between theory and practice. Guba and Clark were careful to point out the obvious limitations of their model. (These apply to any model.) Not all dissemination-implementation problems in education (or anywhere else) start with a research step. Effort at any one step can suggest questions for any other step. For example, adoption usually suggests research questions. Wall (1972) is wise to point out that this seems to justify the contention that the client system, the change agent, and research development agency should have continuous interaction. This is to say that curriculum research, development, diffusion, and adoption cannot occur (for any large block of experiences) in isolation; that once begun, the total process cannot go forward without interruption and reversal; that several problems will progress at different rates in the total process and subprocesses; and thus, that this model is like any other paradigm, an honest attempt to depict an aspect of human endeavor, while admitting to the impossibility of a thorough and accurate description.

Gideonse (1968) submits an "output-oriented model" (a) to show essential differences between development and research and (b) to relate the two to each other and to educational systems. (See Fig. 12-2.) He emphasizes the point that each of the three subsystems can have different objectives, outputs, concerns regarding interaction, and the like. He speaks of the three subsystems as planes of research, development and operations activities. Circles depict initiatives and triangles depict outputs. Research is initiated by "C" and results in new knowledge. Similarly, development is initiated by "B" and results in hardware and software, i.e., materials and processes. Operations in a school are all oriented toward production. New production is initiated by "A" to install new materials and processes. All manner of interactions between the three planes are possible. Gideonse uses a number of examples

TABLE 12-2

A CLASSIFICATION SCHEMA OF PROCESSES RELATED TO AND NECESSARY FOR CHANGE IN EDUCATION

	Research	Development		Diffusion		Adoption		
		Invention	Design	Dissemination	Demonstration	Trial	Installation	Institutionalization
OBJECTIVE	To advance knowledge	To formulate a new solution to an operating problem or to a class of operating problems. i.e., to innovate	To order and to systematize the components of the invented solution: to construct an innovation package for institutional use. i.e., to engineer	To create widespread awareness of the invention among practitioners. i.e., to inform	To afford an opportunity to examine and assess operating qualities of the invention, i.e., to build conviction	To build familiarity with the invention and provide a basis for assessing the quality, value, fit, and utility of the invention in a particular institution. i.e., to test	To fit the characteristics of the invention to the characteristics of the adopting institution. i.e., to operationalize	To assimilate the invention as an integral and accepted component of the system, i.e., to establish
CRITERIA	Validity (internal and external)	Face Validity (appropriateness) — Estimated Viability — Impact (relative contribution)	Institutional Feasibility — Generalizability — Performance	Intelligibility — Fidelity — Pervasiveness — Impact (extent to which it affects key targets)	Credibility — Convenience — Evidential Assessment	Adaptability — Feasibility — Action	Effectiveness — Efficiency	Continuity — Valuation — Support
RELATION TO CHANGE	Provides basis for invention	Produces the invention	Engineers and packages the invention	Informs about the invention	Builds conviction about the invention	Tries out the invention in the context of a particular situation	Operationalizes the invention for use in a specific institution	Establishes the invention as a part of an ongoing program; converts it to a "non-innovation"

SOURCE: E. Guba and D. L. Clark, "A classification Schema of Processes Related to and Necessary for Change in Education," *Strategies for Educational Change Newsletter*, 1965. 1 (2), p. 25.

which illustrate such phenomenon as good and bad outputs, reversals, and suggestions for work in one plane that result in another. These examples and Gideonse's entire commentary are well worth the reader's time.

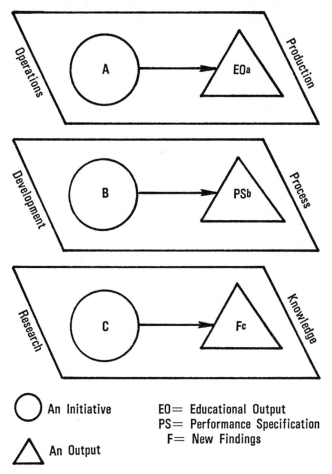

An Initiative

An Output

EO= Educational Output
PS= Performance Specification
F= New Findings

SOURCE: H. D. Gideonse, "An Output-Oriented Model of Research and Development and Its Relationship to Educational Improvement." In Herbert J. Klausmeir and George T. Hearn (eds.), *Research and Development Toward the Improvement of Education*, Madison, Wisconsin: Dembar Educational Research Services, 1968.

Fig. 12-2. An Output Model of Educational Research and Development (Gideonse, 1968)

Wall (1972) submits that change is a cyclical process because of the ever-present need for evaluation. Thus, it is well to view change models as beginning with the evaluation/assessment step. This is the widely accepted point of entry into the cycle. Wall (1972) concludes that nearly all change models have a number of similar features. His broad conclusions are paraphrased below. His commentary is recommended to the reader.

1. Change models usually begin with some form or forms of evaluation, assessment, survey, and the like.
2. A problem definition step or phase comes after evaluation. This may be called "elaboration" or "clarification" and is a crucial step.
3. Determining alternative approaches or solutions is the next step. Judgments have to be made about these.
4. Data gathering and analyzing is next. This step can be complicated and cannot rely on readily available information alone.
5. The decision involves selection from among all recognized possibilities.
6. Once made, decisions should be programmed into the organization's priorities and budget.
7. Finally, control, coordination, and adjustment must assume that innovations correspond to plan definitions.

Decision Models and Change Models

A case could be made that decision models and change models describe the same phenomenon. This will start a chicken-and-egg kind of argument. It is better to understand them for what they are, i.e., attempts to explain what their designers have observed. The authors have observed decisions in many organizations from the vantage point of human relations in industry. Rogers and Shoemaker have studied the diffusion of innovations and adoption decisions specifically. Guba-Clark and Gideonse have modeled the planning process, focusing on instructional innovation from research through development to adoption. All of these models (and many more) aid understanding of the progress of ideas from inception to action in individuals and in organizations.

It can be argued that decision models describe shorter range acts of thought than do change models. (Surely, change models entail many levels of decision-making.) On the other hand, it can be argued that change is only a special kind of decision — the kind which is the opposite of inaction. Perhaps each of these plausible arguments is true. At this junction, it is best to understand thought or decision-making and planned change as well as possible. To this end teachers, instructional hardware and software developers, and curriculum researchers are admonished to monitor the literature of planned change, utilizing what works for them and for the good of children and adult learners.

Barriers to Educational Change

Herr and Cramer (1972) outline personal and organizational resistances to change.

A. Resistance in Personality
 1. *Homeostasis.* It is hypothesized that there are stabilizing forces within an individual that cause him to return to a previous state.
 2. *Habit.* Once a habit is established, its operation is often satisfying to the individual and is therefore difficult to change.
 3. *Primacy.* The way in which an individual first successfully copes with a situation sets a pattern which is unusually persistent.
 4. *Selective Perception and Retention.* Situations may be seen as reinforcing an original attitude when they actually are dissonant.
 5. *Dependence.* Agreement with early authority figures may carry over into adult life.
 6. *Superego.* In a dependence sort of way, the super-ego may act as a tradition-serving agent
 7. *Self-distrust.* Individuals tend to distrust their own impulses and thus are fearful of change.
 8. *Insecurity and Regression.* Individuals tend to seek security in the past and thus be cautious about the future.
B. Resistance to Change in Social Systems
 1. *Conformity to Norms.* Norms are to a social system what habits are to an individual. Because norms are shared by many participants, they cannot easily be changed.
 2. *Systematic and Cultural Coherence.* It is difficult to change one part of a system without affecting other parts of the system.
 3. *Vested Interests.* Change is frequently perceived as a threat to the economic or prestige interests of individuals.
 4. *The Sacrosanct.* It is easier to change technology than to change what people hold to be sacred.
 5. *Rejection of "Outsiders."* Most changes come from the outside. Outsiders tend to be distrusted; hence change is difficult (1972, p. 339).

From the literature of research on resistance to change, only a few of the major categories of resistance can be described here. The reader is encouraged to begin more detailed examination with Bennis, et al. (1969, pp. 486-524) and Miles (1964).

University Dominance

Although this barrier is seldom mentioned in the literature of educational change, the authors are of the view that power along the educational ladder is the most forceful barrier to educational renewal. Professionals at each level of schooling look to the subsequent level for many clues. Elementary teachers fear to introduce new curricula lest something which is alleged to be important to performance in high school will be deemphasized. Secondary school governing boards and professionals resist innovations in curriculum structure and content which challenge specified liberal arts and science entrance requirements for budding professionals. Finally, undergraduate faculty evaluate proposals which allege to make studies relevant to student and community in light of the policies and practices of graduate departments and the professional schools. Thus, the system is content-oriented. Content has little plasticity; it can be labeled and defended. It has all the characteristics of a defensible political unit: boundaries, integrity, structure, and self-indoctrinating characteristics. Groups and individuals who are compelled to entrench rely heavily on the content, discipline, college entrance defense mechanism.

Ideologies and Institutional Orientation

Organizations and individuals can be slow to alter ideologies. Evidence of resistance to vocational education and career development on the part of vested interest groups abounds. One of the authors has done consulting work in several community colleges which began as college parallel institutions and now harbor vocational education only because of state law. Similar situations exist in thousands of secondary schools, which were (perhaps properly) at one time exclusively preparatory schools and have since come to serve a population which is primarily noncollege bound.

Individuals use ideologies as a defense mechanism in a special way. Many American teachers fall back on professional autonomy and academic freedom when they wish to repel innovations. Moreso in the United States of America than any other country, teachers have been encouraged to maintain that the self-contained classroom is inviolate. This contrasts very much to education in even the countries who are very much like the United States politically. In most countries, ministries of education have a great deal of control over day-to-day instructional affairs. Teachers in the United States are prone to insist on their professional rights and accept innovation only if they have been involved in the adoption process.

Cost

Little need be said to substantiate that much of the resistance to educational change is the result of cost factors. In the private sector, most technical and social innovations are subjected to economic scrutiny before they are adopted. If benefits can be projected on the profit and loss sheet, innovations are much better received. The cost-benefit picture is not as clear in public agencies as in private and for-profit agencies. Furthermore, it is dimmer in education than in agencies such as public works and environmental control. Educational innovations must satisfy one or both of two conditions: (1) greater efficiency, i.e., more students will experience more learning situations at less expense than heretofore and (2) learning experiences of higher quality (against old or new objectives) than heretofore. Whereas education enjoyed a more or less blank-check condition in the post-Sputnik era, it is now required to show beforehand what innovations will do with development dollars which are diminished by rising operating costs and inflation.

Established Standards

Standards are probably more restrictive in education than they are in building construction. It is not permissible to build windowless schools in most large cities.[2] But, at least it is known that glazers' unions have had great impact on building codes. The matter of educational standards is much more difficult to understand and alter. This is true in no small part because change agents run amuck of the "they" complex. They is reduceable to *accreditation, certification* and *examinations*. Regional and professional accrediting associations are responsible to their memberships. Most memberships are interested to maintain rather than to update standards. Thus, even though many accrediting agencies are designed to evaluate local agencies in light of local goals and processes, individuals and organizations feel comfortable in saying *they*, the accrediting agency, will not permit this or that.

Certification of professionals in education has mostly negative effects on innovation. Certification requirements are function-oriented for ancillary personnel and subject-matter oriented for instructional personnel. Thus, established standards are barriers to new subjects and to new orientations for all schooling at any level. Certification affects teacher education; it insists that teachers have certain kinds and numbers of credits. Coupled with the fact that most people teach the way they have been taught and that change in teacher education has been more gradual than anywhere else in education, certification can be seen as a barrier if not an out-and-out impediment to change.

[2]Air conditioned and windowless schools are cheaper than conventional schools.

Standardized examinations have a very real influence on teachers. Published achievement tests and state regency examinations are deployed as barriers by the individual teacher much more often than are accreditation and certification. The little add-ons to curriculum, such as the evils of alcohol and drugs, fare badly because the social studies or science teachers, who are assigned to specialized instructional tasks, want their students to do well on standardized tests in established subjects.

Teacher and Student Turnover

Educational innovations are resisted because one out of five students changes schools each year. Professionals argue (and rightly so) that it is disruptive for youngsters to move from one innovative curriculum to another.[3] The movement of teachers is probably a larger barrier to change than is student mobility. Adopted changes are greatly jeopardized by staff turnover. One of the best examples of this fact is evidenced by idle equipment in vocational education laboratories. New teachers are often unfamiliar with the hardware or software of innovations introduced by their predecessors. Too often, the unfamiliar is feared and ignored.

Characteristics of the Innovation

Miles (1964) reports a number of studies which demonstrated resistance to characteristics of innovations themselves. Some of the more obvious of these are cost, technological complexity, and availability of associated materials. Innovations which are associated with thorough-going teacher and student materials requiring only readily available hardware, and costing relatively little are most likely to be adopted. A less obvious barrier is what Miles (1964) calls innovation/system congruence. Innovations are more likely to be adopted if they are novel but not too novel. If a costly innovation is not too different from current practice, it has little chance of adoption. Conversely, if it is far out of line with organization goals and practice, it will be ill-received. Thus, innovations have to appeal to organizations as to individuals. Healthy organizations want novelty at rates they can manage comfortably.

Population Increases and Knowledge Explosion

It is a matter of fact that schools have too much to do. All too little money and effort can be invested in research and develop-

---

[3]The authors submit that it would be least disruptive for youngsters to move from one *student*-oriented school to another. Focus on content makes for difficulty of movement.

ment by an overworked organization. On the one hand, most schools have been overburdened with students. Perhaps the only truism about education is that parents will supply children. Even though the population increase has abated in some regions and at some age levels, inadequate financing continues to hamper educational improvements.

On the other hand, schools have been pressured by literally hundreds of agencies to teach more and more things. The knowledge explosion has prevented focusing on students and has tended to direct available resources at teaching more of the same kinds of things rather than at total curriculum renewal. Even though it has been obvious for decades that only samples of knowledge from a few disciplines can be learned in school, educators continue to try to teach more in given disciplines and to add disciplines to the curriculum. Education is too busy with the forest to see the trees. Overcrowding and content worship compel teachers and curriculum directors to work on immediate problems and forego long-range planning and development.

This barrier is nowhere more effective than in career education. Many teachers whose background of experience has been in traditional areas such as home economics and trades and industry are resistive to innovations which would move young people to employment in sales and personal service occupations. They are too busy "tending the store" to plan new programs and adopt new procedures. Even minor changes such as working with advisors from the business community, or working with cooperative education coordinators to place youngsters at work stations in industry, or working with ancillary personnel to establish placement services are resisted because of the press of long-established duties.

The reader is admonished to recall that this section on barriers to change is not exhaustive. The literature of change and, specifically, educational change is replete with studies on barriers and strategies. A great deal is known about receptivity to innovations in agriculture, medicine, and education. The references in the bibliography of this chapter are fascinating reading and musts for the educator who would affect community members and professionals in the interest of curriculum renewal.

Horvat (1968) identifies three major reasons why change and improvement are slow to come in education. (1) The magnitude of the enterprise, the sheer numbers involved. (2) Change is hard work; it doesn't come easy. (3) Lack of knowhow. The authors submit that subsequent pages of this chapter illustrate that some good progress has been made on the latter of these to make the second a lesser impediment to serving the multitudes indentified in the first.

Gateways for Educational Change

The formidable barriers to change in educational enterprises can only be dealt with successfully by innovators who use well-designed strategies. Gateways to change are rarely open to developments which are undertaken without clear plans for introduction, testing, and institutionalization. Lawler (1970, p. 16) speaks of *"developing strategies* in relation to our *unique combat area, the school system and the individual schools within the system"* as the focus of concern. Miles (1964) emphasizes the same forces in his definition: "Strategy is defined here as a means (usually involving a sequence of specified activities) for causing an advocated innovation to become successfully (durably) installed in an on-going educational system" (Miles, 1964, p. 18-19).

Career education is fortunate to follow a history of (a) innovation in elementary and college preparatory education, (b) a developing science of change in education, and (c) a history of research on the diffusion of innovation.[4] Most of the barriers have been coped with successfully; the matter of change is more widely accepted in education than it was a decade ago. And the conditions which career education is challenged to right are widely evident and hard felt. In sum, the conditions for career education's advance will probably never be better. But, its advance must be according to especially good design because it proposes more fundamental change of educational enterprises than they have experienced to date.

McNally and Passow (1960) list ten principles of curriculum improvement based on case studies.

1. Curriculum improvement was viewed as a process of changing teacher's behavior.
2. Extensive participation of teachers in curriculum development could be encouraged by committee organization.
3. A free flow of communication was necessary so that proposals for change might emerge from almost any place in the system and community.
4. The local school building was viewed as the basic unit of participation.

[4]For a brief and readable history and status report on diffusion research, see Katz *et al.* (1963, pp. 237-251).

5. The responsibility for curriculum change was assigned to one person, but leadership within the organization was encouraged to emerge.
6. System-wide coordination was essential for curriculum improvement.
7. The organization for change in each system was determined by its own particular purposes, size and resources.
8. Participation of lay persons in the community was encouraged.
9. Experimentation was an integral part of the process of curriculum improvement.
10. It was a major responsibility for the school administration to provide time and resources (1960, pp. 293-308).

Lawler (1970) states twenty-one guidelines for developing strategies for curricular change. These are paraphased below.

1. The innovator must be knowledgeable of these areas of pupil encounter: content, methods of a discipline underlying a subject area, language behavior of the teacher, other classroom behavior, learning environment, instructional materials, organization of time, space, personnel, and evaluation.
2. Content should be selected with attention to the two goals (a) transmission of our cultural heritage and (b) quality education for all.
3. Planners must deal with how to order or sequence content in keeping with current educational thinking and research.
4. Teaching strategies and teaching materials must be designed to achieve the goals of teaching.
5. Teaching materials must help the teacher to examine his language behavior through self-analysis; this requires long-term in-service programs.
6. The action-behavior of teachers and instructional team members must be similarly analyzed; video tape and interaction analysis are important.
7. Innovators must anticipate problems which teachers may encounter in developing supportive environments.
8. A wide range of materials must be available for all learners.
9. Teachers should be trained in the use of these materials; students must be aided in intelligent uses of whatever they are to encounter.
10. The proper use of time, space, and personnel must be considered.

11. Evaluation via student feedback must be incorporated and not added on to instruction regiments.
12. There must be provision for (a) developing awareness and assessing acceptance of the goals of the innovation by behavior commitment rather than verbal commitment, (b) redesigning goals, (c) long-term budgeting, and (d) reassessing priorities of an achievable range of innovations.
13. There must be provision for many forms of healthy communication forms and systems about the innovation.
14. Power must be equitably distributed in the organization so that experimentation and action involve rather than impose on professionals.
15. Wise staff utilization should assure (a) that professionals do not spend inordinate time on tasks such as public relations (b) that they receive paraprofessional assistance, (c) that they have time for updating professional understandings.
16. Staff must be involved in general feedback.
17. Innovators should use all forms of feedback to discover ways of improving staff morale.
18. The enterprise should be helped to move through change, stability, and maintenance of instituted innovations.
19. Autonomy of individuals, instructional units, and the school system should be examined and understood by strategists.
20. The security of parents and staff depends on feedback linkages with the community.
21. Procedures for feedback and problem solving must be publicly agreed upon (1970, pp. 20-45).

Lawler's guidelines are remarkably similar to the seven requirements for successful implementation outlined by Dale (1971, p. 1). These are used as headings for the following discussion.

Identification of Present Instructional Situation

For obvious reasons, innovation at any level must begin with assessment of the on-going instructional milieu. Even if an alternate institution is being considered, the planners must know how parents and children respond to extant educational experiences. Wall (1972) supports this contention when he notes that models of change begin with some form of evaluation or survey. The assessment should be done in terms of the eight categories of student encounter identified by Lawler (see item 1 above) and the additional categories of finance, public relations, and institutional resources.

Identification of Instructional Goals

The Center for Coordinated Education (1966) was careful to emphasize the importance of levels of change.

> The highest form of change, and the only kind that is likely to make a significant difference in education, is change that results from a reconstruction of rationale.
>
> It is because we seek a teacher who is a creative artist, who can dance to the nuances of the learning situation, and who can continuously plot his own betterment, that we quarrel with the efforts at school improvement which consist only of giving the teacher a preconceived method of instruction or a new system (1966, pp. 7-8).

As Part III indicated, career education begins with a new rationale for the whole of education. Curriculum innovation cannot be accomplished unless people at several levels are involved in reestablishment of educational goals. Involving people in the identification of goals saves the embarrassment of admitting that existing goals have not been adequately achieved, that current experiences and methods are not good enough. Given a new rationale which is in keeping with societal and individual needs, most people can be expected to consider new experiences and instructional strategies fairly. Needless to say, the authors offer the material of Part III and especially Chapter 8 as basic to goal setting.

Identification of Transitional Instructional Goals

During periods of change, students, parents, professionals and administrators should be given opportunity to evaluate innovations on relatively short-term bases. Old ways cannot be given up immediately. Space and equipment and staff will not change overnight. Furthermore, innovations may not be possible in all classrooms or for as large a time block as originally designed. Therefore, innovators must be willing to *negotiate*, i.e., give and take, in the establishment of intermediate goals. Schools will not participate in all-or-none partnerships. Schools and their supporting communities must somehow be permitted to try new experiences. If they are willing to set some old experiences aside, they might remove them totally after a successful experience with the innovation.

Identification of Realistic Behavioral Objectives

Behavioral objectives are advantageous to all parties concerned. They are the contract which binds students, professionals, outside consultants, and community members to the implementation project. Needless to say, objectives should be written by system professionals and consultants with fair and measureable time and quality of learning stipulations. Stabilization and maintenance, i.e., institutionalization of innovations, is much more sure to occur if there are regular and thorough assessments of progress. Assessments of both professional (see Lawler's principle 6 above) and student performance can only be meaningful if it is undergone according to agreed to objectives. This is trite but easily forgotten. Innovators have the onus of more careful scrutiny than established practice. Therefore, innovators must assure that fair behavioral objectives are clearly established.

Identification of a Rationale for Professionals, Administrators and Governing Boards for Changing the Status Quo

School board members, administrators, all faculty members, and individual teachers who are intimately involved with innovations must have a rationale, a reason or reasons, for changing the status quo. Career education is a big switch in direction; it looks different and feels different to students and various adults. Because it requires basic changes in orientation, career education cannot be successful unless various adults, i.e., change agents, are involved first to develop and eventually to internalize a rationale for its introduction and maintenance in the district. This book has introduced ample concepts and literature for such an educational task. Subsequent sections of this chapter describe techniques for sharing them with change agents.

Identification of Instructional Tools that Support the Teacher-Educator, Classroom Teacher, and Student

The literature of educational change and renewal is very supportive of this contention.[5] Innovations which do not satisfy each of the three parts of this statement are doomed to failure. Especially, where teacher turnover is significant, teacher education institutions must graduate people who will use new materials instead of old. The quality of materials, ease of use, and like considerations are important to teachers and student acceptance. Materials must be thorough and high quality because youngsters encounter many good learning experiences in the out-of-school world. Furthermore, students and teachers are familiar with a wealth of high quality materials which communicate traditional content. New curriculum concepts which ask all parties to internalize a new rationale require materials which are as good as or better

[5]See Miles (1964, pp. 636-637) for a review of supporting research.

than extant materials for traditional learnings. A significant change should not be ventured unless this condition is met. To attempt change without the strength of good materials is suicide.

Identification of Benefits that Related Businesses or Industries Can Receive by Supporting the Development and Dissemination of the Program

This is obviously a principle for career education innovation and not for improved instruction in Latin. Because career education depicts occupations and jobs and because it is maximized by functioning in a variety of ways with employers rather than in isolation, it is essential that implementation and dissemination of information about the program not be undertaken until employers have had opportunity to learn about and be involved in the planning and staging of the program. Part III outlined some of the ways in which employers and others may be involved in career education. But Community members will shun projects which concern them, but are introduced before they know of it. They will support programs in which they have had some hand from inception.

Miel (1970) provides a very forceful summary for this section on gateways and an introduction to the next section:

> Developing appropriate power in the community, fashioning an organiza-
> tion that facilitates productive efforts, giving attention to all phases of the
> process of building an innovation into the system, making a careful study of
> the innovation itself to get a full picture of its peculiar requirements, and
> taking a thoughtful and sympathetic look at the people of whom the innovation
> will require the greatest adjustments — all these are equally important leader-
> ship activities. All go to make up a complete strategy of planned curricular
> innovation (1970, p. 159).

A Strategy for Planned Educational Change

Miller (1967) defines strategy as a planned and systematic attack on a problem. There are a great many strategies for diffusing innovations. Many of these have been developed for political, commercial, medical and other purposes. Some rely on force and some rely on knowledge. Many are marginally applicable to education. Fortunately, Havelock (1970) has developed a very useful guide for use by change agents in education. Havelock (1970) believes "that the focus of innovation has to be the *USER*, himself: his needs and his problems must be the primary concern of educational reform . . . our orientation is PROBLEM SOLVING BY AND FOR THE USER THROUGH EFFECTIVE USE OF RESOURCES" (1970, p. 11). The Havelock model satisfies one of the characteristics identified by Chin (1967, p. 336): "a system model allows for change to come from components inside the system through invention and innovation."

According to Havelock (1970) change agents may work from inside or outside of organizations, from line or staff positions, and from any level of the hierarchy. He submits that any of the following may act as change agents.

Curriculum Coordinators
Directors or Coordinators of Federal Programs
State Department Curriculum Consultants
Regional Laboratory Dissemination Staff
County and Intermediate School District Consultants
Supplementary Center Staff
Continuing Education and Extension Instructors
Professors in Schools of Education Who Do Field Consulting
Salesmen of Educational Products and Publications
Superintendents and Other Administrators (at least part of the time)
Teachers (at least part of the time)
Counselors (at least part of the time)
Board of Education Members (at least part of the time)
Students (at least some of them some of the time)
Concerned parents and other citizens (Havelock, 1970, p. 11).

Havelock devotes the bulk of his excellent *Guide* to description of a very manageable six-stage strategy for innovation in education. These serve as headings for the remainder of this section. Note that these chronological steps are compatible with Dale and Lawler.

1. *Building Relationship*

A viable relationship with the client system is the basis of a helping role. The change agent must establish himself firmly as part of or consultant to the client system. This relationship must be expanded to segments of the community which relate to the innovation. Havelock uses cases and narrative to show how the relationship may be built and maintained.

2. *Diagnosing the Problem*

Diagnosis is a systematic effort by the change agent and the client system to understand needs and delineate problems. The purpose of need identification and problem delineation is to establish goals and objectives. Havelock makes the same stipulations as Dale and others, i.e., that these be stated in terms of inputs and outputs and that they be diffused to all concerned parties.

3. *Acquiring Relevant Resources*

After problems are well-defined, the system must be able to identify and obtain relevant resources. Havelock provides a very good appendix of sources of materials for curriculum change

(1970). By acquiring resources, Havelock means discovering what is available, not deciding on which ones to incorporate in an educational plan. He defines six major purposes for resource acquisition: diagnosis, awareness, evaluation before trial, evaluation after trial, installation, and maintenance. The chapter on acquisition contains a very sound strategy for establishing a permanent resource acquisition system. Of course, resources may be identified and procured at any step in the strategy.

4. *Choosing the Solution*

Solutions are decided upon only after the waterfront has been surveyed and relevant aspects of available resources have been carefully examined. Choosing is done by a four-step sequential process: (a) deriving implications from research, (b) generating a range of solution ideas, (c) feasibility testing, and (d) adaptation. Client system people should be involved in the later steps; the change agents' responsibility is greatest for step one. In the end, assessments must be made of benefits to the client system, workability, and acceptability.

5. *Gaining Acceptance*

This is the stage where intention is transformed into action. Because of myriad ways individuals and groups accept innovations, it is important to choose communication strategies which are (a) effective with respective clientele and (b) permit flexible programming for gaining acceptance. Great skill is necessary in the execution of this step. A wealth of research on educational change and diffusion in the private sector bears on this step. For example, it is known that peer group influence can be employed to reduce adoption time. ": . . every attempt should be made to prepare a schedule which is both flexible and schematic—a difficult balance to strike, but a crucial one" (Havelock, 1970, p. 123). Communication to all relevant audiences must be clear and accurate and should incorporate indications of support for and approval of their inputs to the innovation.

6. *Stabilizing the Innovation and Generating Self-Renewal*

Acceptance is not the end of the change process. The change agents' responsibilities must continue until the innovation is stabilized, i.e., internalized. Innovations are best internalized in organizations which are helped to continue recently installed innovations and to become change agents for themselves. Continuance can be assured by helping client systems to (a) perceive continuing rewards from innovations, (b) become accustomed to them, (c) adjust innovations to system structure, (d) continue evaluation, (e) continue maintenance, and (f) continue adaptation capability for the innovation. In other words, the client system should be helped to understand that innovations die unless they are nurtured. They need continual renewal like any other program in the system.

The best way to assure that a system will continue an innovation is to help it to become a change agent, i.e., infused with the quest for appropriate change and self-renewal. To become a self-starter, the client system must have (a) a positive atmosphere, (b) an internal subsystem devoted to change, (c) an active inclination to seek external resources, and (d) perspective on the future.

The Self-Starting Organization

Even minor changes are short-lived in organizations which are not committed to change. Something as significant as career education cannot properly affect organizations unless they are fully sensitized to (1) the form, substance, and benefits of career education and (2) change and its sociopsychological benefits. This section describes one way of focusing organizations on change and uses career education examples to illustrate the process. Carl Rogers (1969) puts the matter well:

> A way must be found to develop, within the educational system as a whole, and in each component, a climate conducive to personal growth, a climate in which innovation is not frightening, in which the creative capacities of administrators, teachers, and students are nourished and expressed rather than stifled. A way must be found to develop a climate in the *system* in which the focus is not upon teaching, but on the facilitation of self-directed *learning* (1969, p. 304).

As readers who know Roger's work can foretell, his charge and prescription are compatible with this book. Focusing on organization so that it will be self-innovative requires commitment to change at all levels, especially top administration, and time and other resources to concentrate on change instead of (but not at the expense of) the on-going productive effort of the enterprise. As stated earlier administrators, teachers, and students who are overworked with traditional school responsibilities have no time to innovate. Furthermore, innovation in education is different from innovation in agriculture, medicine, and industry (Lippitt and Colleagues, 1967). Moreso than other kinds of enterprises, education is not readily reducible to the physical and numerical. More kinds of individuals and groups are involved in successful change in education. Thus, planning for basic change in people is paramount. Indeed, ". . . responsibility for an effective school curriculum for children from infancy to adulthood lies with all members of our society" (Fish, 1965, p. 328). Moving a local education agency to become an organization which generates its own renewal depends upon creating a climate of openness and problem-solving. Shepard and Blake (1962) put it well: "The first change problem is to create conditions in which people can shift their own interpersonal relationships from win-lose defensiveness to openness with the increased possibility of relations which are on an 'everyone can win' basis . . ." (1962, p. 90).

Glines (1972, pp. 230-246) says similar things in a chapter titled "Magic 69 Glossary." He lists sixty-nine elements or short statements which describe features of self-starting or innovative schools. These are categorized under philosophy, instruction, learning, structure, technology, and reporting. This chapter and the rest of Glines book, *Creating Humane Schools*, are well worth reading. He is careful to point out that the sixty-nine elements which successful innovations in the 1960's left as their legacy for schools will be added to and deleted from in the 1970's and 1980's. The authors submit that career education is already the major feature of innovation in the 1970's. What this book has been saying is compatible with Glines (1972): ". . . to be successful in change and to truly develop a significantly different program, the schools must engage in massive retooling. Everything in the school is affected. Most schools have tried to make only a few changes at a time. But now it is known that a dramatic amount of quantity as well as quality will be included in the effort" (1972, p. 231).

A plan for focusing a local education agency on innovation in career education should have the following parts:
1. Sensitizing and informing administrators, governing board members, and influential citizens.
2. Sensitizing and informing teachers, related professionals, and parent representatives.
3. Sensitizing and informing students

Administrators and Community Leaders

Although change can be generated from any point in an organization, ideally administrators will be committed to the new development — career education in this case — and work with professionals to install innovations. Because career education is a proposal to turn educational agencies around, it is especially important that administrators be the first to become knowledgeable about and committed to it. The authors advocate the kind of intensive group experience which has been advocated by Carl Rogers and other behavioral scientists for many years. Administrators, representatives of the governing board, and representatives of employers and employees in the community should be brought together for intensive sessions which focus at the same time on establishing better communication and on the form and function of career education. Such sessions should be retreats, i.e., they should be conducted for periods of several days or a week's duration and in out-of-the-way places, removed from firing-line work and telephones.

A community college, secondary school district or attendance center, unit school district, or elementary school district or attendance center, which wishes to initiate career education programs, should begin by employing a change facilitator. This is a person expert in group dynamics and the encounter group specifically. This person should be complemented by a person expert in career development theory and practice and in career education. Together, these two people should plan the retreats and other activities.[6] Outcomes of these activities should be evident in the behavior of administrators and teachers. Administrators, for example, should be more willing to give up old constructs and beliefs, less threatened by innovative ideas, quicker to make decisions, better able to communicate to superiors, peers, and subordinates, more person-oriented and democratic, more straightforward, and more analytic of their own behaviors.

Once administrators and their links with the community are involved in and informed about career development and schooling's role in education about and for work, a plan for moving the educational enterprise toward self-renewal in the career education function will unfold almost by itself. As Sayles (1962) submits, educational managers must somehow balance the aspects of their jobs which require stabilized utilization of proven methods and change toward new methods. Balance can only be achieved if many kinds of relationships result in feedback, cooperation, and high morale. Morale, motivation, change, and stability of purpose and productivity can have circular effects.

Professional and Parent Representatives

Encounter-group sessions, similar in every way to the ones provided for leaders in the local education agency and the community, should be provided for professionals, paraprofessionals, representative (and influencial) parents and, if possible, some representatives of the governing board and employers and employees. These encounter groups should be on "company time." School must somehow keep while professionals and their publics are re-orienting themselves. Rogers (1969) recommends that encounter groups for teachers should be voluntary. It would be well

[6]See Rogers (1969, pp. 306-314) for descriptions of procedures and behavioral outcomes for administrators, teachers, and students, which will foster basic change in educational organizations.

to have them so. In a large system, several tens of initial volunteers might influence others to volunteer for subsequent sessions. But, in a small system — say a high school with forty staff members — the expense of two consultants might be too great to permit the volunteer system. No matter what the scheme, not all professionals will become acclimated to change and to career education. Many will. Others will have to be shown. All will have to have updating experiences because (a) they will slip back into old ways of doing and (b) career development theory and career education practice will be changing.

The response of teachers to encounter group sessions should do much to aid and abet innovation in career education. Teachers should show many of the changes demonstrated by administrators. They should also be more receptive to student attitudes and ideas, more appreciative of innovation, professional problem solving, less concerned with "covering the material," more concerned to deal with interpersonal relationships than with rules, and more interested in creativity and participation of students.

Because teaching is primarily a relationship (Combs, 1965), it is important that teachers and students be directly involved in planned, educational change. Teachers must be recognized as central to both change and to maintenance of the education enterprise (Frymier and Hawn, 1970).

Students

Youngsters should also be involved in the turning around of a local education agency. Class groups should have some of the same experiences as teachers and administrators. The students' concerns, attitudes, and opinions regarding employment, study, and the future should be sought and recorded during encounter group sessions for use in planning the agency-wide career education program. The function of encounter group sessions is to generate receptivity to both change and to career education. *Students are as important as professionals and community leaders in establishing the tone and direction of educational agencies.* They should be involved from the start so that they will be more free to contribute, vent energies continuously instead of spontaneously, realize the benefits of evaluation, be responsible for career and preparatory program planning, adept at utilizing a widened array of communities and institutional resources, and able to define the quality of life.

The Educational Experiences

As programs of encounter groups are carried on, teachers should be involved in the several steps of the strategy for planned change. The substantive planning and implementation of curricular components should parallel the on-going sensitizing activities. The focus of the total effort must be on the teachers, the professionals. As Miel (1970) points out, teachers will be innovative when:

1. They know that individual differences are expected and respected and that their best will be recognized.
2. They have an organization within which to work.
3. They are encouraged to discover better ways of teaching.
4. They have sources of new ideas.
5. They can select, plan, and time the specifics of their own changes.
6. They have help in making changes (resource persons and materials).
7. They are informed of others' attempts to improve teaching and, if a change is adopted on a wide scale, they understand and feel ready (Miel, 1970, pp. 163-164).

The Future of Career Education and Change

It behooves local education agencies to organize for planned change and for career education specifically because several levels of government are doing so. Moreso than for any previous educational program, the United States Office of Education and many state-level education agencies are tooling up for a prolonged effort in the interest of career education. As Chapter 1 indicated, laymen of all ilks are widely aware of the incongruence of schooling and society. They expect change. Furthermore, legislators now focus on educational institutions in much the same way that they have focused on transportation, health, and other public agencies. Talk about new delivery systems, new institutions and life-long career education and placement is not idle professional arm flaying. A final quotation is used because it (1) summarizes the charge laid by this book and (2) is taken from a magazine which is circulated to laymen. Francis A. J. Ianni, Director, and Barbara D. McNeill, Staff Assistant in the Division of Education Research in USOE, said in *Saturday Review* what professionals and laymen alike must internalize if schools are to be viable members of their communities.

We must have an orderly means for shedding out-worn educational practices, dismantling outmoded educational structures, and creating new and better relationships for experimentation and innovation. What is needed within federal, state and local programs is a means and a willingness to test the results of research, to put into practice the best of tested innovations, and to view the school as the logical place for such testing. And, since we live in an era where change has become a constant, we cannot depend on a single, crash program of innovation. We need a system designed to accomplish its own continuous renewal through a constant process of experimentation and innovation (Ianni and McNeill, 1965, p. 55).

All parties to the educational enterprise should be intelligent activists instead of uninformed and complaining passivists. Hopefully, education will respond so fully to external demands for change that change will be internalized in revitalized enterprises, committed to self-renewal. Career education is not just another concept developed in the United States Office of Education; it is a kind of education which is advocated by individuals and groups in diverse segments of the population. Educators can do little else but embrace it and the support which the employer-employee community gives it.

Career education is, afterall, a response to the life needs of individuals. To focus learning and ancillary services of public education enterprises on individuals is inevitably to center schooling on career development, i.e., on the occupational information, self-understanding, preparation, employment, placement, continuing education function which has been the theme of this book.

BIBLIOGRAPHY

Bennis, W. G., Benne, K. D., and Chin, R. (eds.), *The planning of change.* New York: Holt, Rinehart, and Winston, 1969.

Center for Coordinated Education, *Strategies for school improvement — the nurture of teacher growth.* Santa Barbara: University of California, May, 1966.

Chin, R. Some ideas on changing. In Richard I. Miller (ed.), *Perspective on educational change.* New York: Appleton-Century-Crofts, 1967.

Dale, R. E. Implementation of total package. Paper presented to AHEA Exploration Conference for Career Development of Household Employment Opportunities, 1971 (mimeographed).

Dewey, J. *How we think.* New York: D. C. Heath, 1933.

Fish, L. D. Curricular change involves people. *Educational Leadership,* 1965, 23, 49-51.

Frymier, J. R., and Hawn, H. C. *Curriculum improvement for better schools.* Worthington, Ohio: Charles A. Jones, 1970.

Gideonse, H. D. An output-oriented model of research and development and its relationship to educational improvement. In Herbert J. Klausmeir and George T. Hearn (eds.), *Research and development toward the improvement of education.* Madison, Wisconsin: Dembar Educational Research Services, 1968.

Glines, D. E. *Creating humane schools.* Mankato, Minnesota: Campus Publishers, 1972, (mimeographed).

Guba, E. and Clark, D. L. A classification schema of processes related to and necessary for change in education. *Strategies for Educational Change Newsletter,* 1965, 1(2), 5.

Havelock, R. G. *A guide to innovation in education.* Ann Arbor, Michigan: Center for Research on Utilization of Scientific Knowledge, Institute for Social Research, 1970.

Havelock, R. G. and Collaborators. *Planning for innovation through dissemination and utilization of knowledge.* Ann Arbor, Michigan: Center for Research on Utilization of Scientific Knowledge, Institute of Social Research, January, 1971.

Herr, E. L. and Cramer, S. H. *Vocational guidance and career development in the schools: toward a systems approach.* Boston: Houghton Mifflin, 1972.

Horvat, J. J. Major impediments to educational change and improvement. In *The teacher and his staff: differentiating teaching roles.* Report of the 1968 Regional TEPS Conference. Washington, D. C.: National Commission on Teacher Education and Professional Standards, 1969.

Hoyt, K. B., Evans, R. N., Mackin, E. F., and Mangun, G. L. *Career education — what it is and how to do it.* Salt Lake City, Utah: Olympus, 1972.

Ianni, F. A. and McNeill, B. D. Organizing for continuing change. *Saturday Review,* 1965, 48(26), 55.

Katz, E., Levin, M. L., and Hamilton, H. Traditions of research on the diffusion of innovation. *American Sociological Review,* 1963, 28(2), 237-252.

Klohr, P. R. and Frymier, J. R. Curriculum development: dynamics of change. *Review of Educational Research,* 1963, 33(3), 304-321.

Lawler, M. R. Guidelines for developing strategies for introducing planned curricular innovations. In Marcella R. Lawler (ed.), *Strategies for planned curricular innovation.* New York: Teachers College Press, 1970.

Lifton, W. M. Planning for tomorrow. In Walter M. Lifton (ed.), *Education for tomorrow.* New York: John Wiley, 1970.

Lippitt, R. and Colleagues. The teacher as innovator, seeker, and sharer of new practices. In Richard I. Miller (ed.), *Perspectives on educational change.* New York: Appleton-Century-Crofts, 1967.

McNally, H. J. and Passow, A. H. *Improving the quality of public school programs.* New York: Teachers College, 1960.

Miel, A. M. Developing strategies of planned curricular innovation: A review with implications for instructional leadership. In M. R. Lawler (ed.), *Strategies for planned curricular innovation.* New York: Teachers College Press, 1970.

Miles, M. B. Innovation in education: Some generalizations. In Matthew B. Miles (ed.), *Innovation in education.* New York: Teachers College, 1964.

Miller, R. I. Some observations and suggestions. In Richard I. Miller (ed.), *Perspectives on educational change.* New York: Appleton-Century-Crofts, 1967.

Pucinski, R. C. and Hirsh, S. P. (eds.). *The courage to change: new directions for career education.* Englewood Cliffs, New Jersey: Prentice-Hall, 1971.

Rogers, C. R. *Freedom to learn. Columbus, Ohio:* Charles E. Merrill, 1969.

Rogers, E. M. and Shoemaker, F. F. *Communication in innovations.* New York: Free Press, 1971.

Sayles, L. R. The change process in organizations: an applied anthropology analysis. *Human Organization,* 1962, 21(2), 62-67.

Shepard, H. R. and Blake, R. R. Changing behavior through cognitive change. *Human Organization,* 1962, 21(2), 88-96.

Wall, J. E. *Review and synthesis of strategies for effecting change in vocational and technical education.* Columbus, Ohio: ERIC Clearinghouse for Vocational and Technical Education, The Center for Vocational and Technical Education, The Ohio State University, April, 1972.

Webster's seventh new collegiate dictionary, Springfield, Massachusetts: G. and C. Merriam, 1967.

Index

Behavioral objective —
  as approach to learning, 225-227
  and career development, 264-265
  in curriculum development,
    311-326
  identifying for curriculum
    implementation, 403-404
  ingredients for formulating
    (figure), 315
  MEL *vs.* DL, 318-320
  stating outcomes of, 317
  terminology for affective domain
    (table), 325
  terminology for cognitive (table),
    323
  terminology for psychomotor
    domain (table), 326
  writing, 320-326
Behavioral science, 190
  and vocational education, 207-216
Biological basis, of developmental
    tasks, 313
Biological control, and career
    education, 185
Black race, and vocational choice,
    109-111
Blacks, education gap of (table), 153
Black studies, as basis for relevance,
    40
Budd, Thomas, 172
Budgeting, and program planning, 194
Bureau of Occupational and Adult
    Education, 277

Calvinism, and work, 209
Canada, and apprenticeship teaching,
    171
Capacity stage, in occupational
    choice, 66
Capitalism, and work, 209
Career development —
  and age factors, 115-117
  assumptions regarding, 348-349
  as core of education, 278
  definition of, 347
  factors affecting, 97-128
  history of, 59-65
  and learning theory, 85-86
  needs of the disadvantaged,
    148-163
  needs of women, 132-147
  organizing approach to, 264
  review of major theories, 86-93
  and sex differences, 112-114
  and social structure, 104-117
  summary of research on, 127-128
  theories of, 57-93
Career Development for Children
    Project (CDCP), 310-311
Career education —
  accommodation stage in model,
    356-362

and accountability, 50-52
and the American Vocational
  Association, 276
answer to culturally disadvantaged,
  162-163
answer to relevance, 43
for antipoverty, 214
awareness stage, 351-356
and community education, 20
as a concept, 346
and curriculum development
  fundamentals, 301-341
curriculum model for, 344-380
definition of, 346-347
definition of terminology, 344-346
and developmental tasks, 312-314
domains of curriculum model, 350
and economic foundation of,
  193-207
exploration and preparation stage,
  370-377
factors in emergence of, 235-278
functions of (summary), 297
function and place of, 281-298
future of, 412-413
as information on employability,
  216
initiation of, 268-271
long-range goals, 347
major issues of theory, 377-379
models of, 271-275
and the National Education
  Association, 275
and the National Manpower
  Council, 235-240
need for focusing on, 3-4
objectives of, 270-271
orientation stage of model, 362-370
psychology and, 216-232
and relevance, 40
to resolve critical issues, 6
response to contemporary
  criticisms, 26-27
and roles of professionals, 306-307
and school-society partnership, 25
see also Vocational education
single or dual systems (summary),
  298
and sociology, 207-216
and specialization, 289-295
stages of curriculum model, 349
to teach dignity of work, 212-213
and technology, 184-186
and theoretical foundations,
  186-193

Career Education Now, 345-346
Career guidance, of culturally
  disadvantaged, 158-163

Career Pattern Study (CPS), 70,
  99-102
Carnegie Study, 16-17

Engineering, educational, 49-50
Enterprise, education as competitive, 46
Environment —
  and career education, 185
  and intelligence, 217
  and occupational choice, 72, 73
  and the preschool years, 150-155
Environmental model, and vocational choice (table), 80
Equal educational opportunity, 8-12, 18
  contemporary criticism, 7-8
  recommendations for, 238
Equal Pay Act of 1963, 138-139
Equal Rights Amendment, 139
Establishment, and work, 210-211
Establishment stage, in self-concept theory, 70
Ethnic backgrounds, and vocational choice, 109-111
Ethnic groups, and employment, 213-215
Etiology, 158
Europe —
  influence on education, 32-34
  role in vocational education, 171, 172
Evaluation —
  in cognitive domain, 322
  in curriculum development, 332-337
  formative and summative, (table), 332, 333
  in school structuring, 16
Evans, Rupert, 199
Every Kid a Winner: Accountability in Education, 48
Examinations, standardized and change, 398
Excellence —
  and education, 30-39
  thesis of, 31-39
Exemplary Programs and Projects, 264-268
Expenditures, for public and vocational education (table), 36
Expense-earning ratio, of vocational education (table), 196
Exploration stage —
  of career education model, 370-377
  in occupational choice, 67
  in self-concept theory, 70

Facilities —
  and educational excellence, 34
  recommendations for improvement of educational, 238
The False Ideology of Schooling, 20
Family, and career development, 104-111

Family income, and women's employment, 134-135
Fantasy, and occupational choice, 66
Father-son relationship, and career choices, 104-105, 108
Feasibility study, on voucher system, 46
Federal legislation, and vocational education, 176-180
Federal Register, 139, 338
Feedback —
  in curriculum development 330-337
  IACP (figure), 335
Field testing, *see* Evaluation of curriculum
Ford Foundation, founder of National Manpower Council, 235
Forecasting of manpower, 202-207
Foreign language, and educational excellence, 34
Formal instruction, in vocational education, 171-173
Formation stage, of self-concept, 71
Foundations, of vocational education, 183-232
Foundations of Behavioral Research, 98
Freedom —
  in individualized education, 9
  and work, 209
Free schools, 7, 16, 25
Function —
  of career education, 281-298
  of schooling, 50, 187-193
  summary of career education, 297
  of theory, 58-59
Funding —
  and accountability, 45
  of early vocational education, 181-182
  of projects for the culturally disadvantaged, 150
  under VEA of 1963, 247
  for vocational education, 244, 251, 254-255

General Aptitude Test Battery (GATB), 61-62
George-Barden Acts, amendments to Title I, 178
George-Barden Acts, Amendments to by VEA of 1963, 247
George-Deen Act, 178
George-Ellzey Act, 178
George-Reed Act, 177
Ghetto —
  awareness of, 9-11
  escape from, 160-161
Giest Picture Interest Inventory, 116

Instruction —
  formal, 171-173
  ineffective use of, 5-6
  quality of vocational
    education, 228-229
Instructional materials —
  in curriculum development, 312
  and educational excellence, 34
  preparation of curriculum,
    326-328
Instructional system, and change, 402
Integration —
  and intelligence, 218-219
  of society through education, 40
Intelligence —
  definition of, 217
  emphasis on, 60
  and vocational education, 216-217
Interests —
  guideline to students, 120
  and higher education, 119
  inventory to career, 57
  and vocational choice, 101,
    118-121
Interest stage, 66

Job clusters, as curriculum
    approach, 229-230
Job Corps, 156
Job Values and Desires Card, 125
Job Values and Desires Checklist, 125

Kennedy, John F., 240
Knowledge —
  in cognitive domain, 322
  in contemporary education, 8
  and curriculum development,
    314-317
  in decision-making processes,
    385, 390
  in education curriculum, 12-15
  explosion of and change, 399
*Kuder DD Occupational Interest
    Survey*, 118
Kuder Preference Record, 106-107,
    118

Labor —
  forecasts of needs of, 203-207
  and industrial education, 175
  local market, 204, 205
  see also Work
Laboratory learning, 228
Labor force, women in, 133-138
Language —
  and the culturally disadvantaged,
    151
  foreign and excellence, 34
  selection of curricular, 309-311
Learning —
  the concern of schooling, 14
  imitation as process to, 169-170

  see Important learnings
  laboratory, 228
  as life's purpose, 9
  process of, 225-227
  vs. teaching, 41, 45
  types of, 226-227
  work and play, 282-289
Learning theory, and career
    development, 85-86
Legislation —
  and educational accountability,
    44-45
  and vocational education, 176-180,
    245-271
Lehman Vocational Attitude Quiz, 112
Leisure industries, and career
    education, 184
Life adjustment, 32
Life planning —
  components of (table), 144
  need for total, 143-147
Life stages, 65
  review of, 87-89
  and self-concept theory, 70

Maintenance, in self-concept theory,
    70
Management, of performance
    contracting, 47
Manpower —
  competence of professional, 202
  forecasting and vocational
    education, 202-207
  national council findings,
    235-240
  recommendations for researching,
    238, 239
Manpower Development and Training
    Act (MDTA), 10, 180
*Manpower Policies for a Democratic
    Society*, 239
Manual arts, in vocational education,
    172, 174
Manual training, 173-174
Marland, Sidney P., 268-269,
    344-346
Marriage-career conflict, 140-143
Massachusetts Commission, 174-175
Materials, instructional, 34
Mathematics, and educational
    excellence, 33
Maturation, and career development,
    115-117
Mechanical schools, public and
    private, 173-174
Mechanization, and work in society,
    215
Memory and drill, *vs.* involvement
    and relevance, 10
Men, and vocational choice, 112-114
Mental ability, and vocational
    choice, 121-123

423

424

Reformation, and work, 209
Relevance —
    and education, 30-31, 39-43
    personal, 41-42
    social, 40-41
Relevance and involvement vs.
    memory and drill, 10
Religion, and formal instruction, 171
Renaissance, and work, 209
Request for proposal (RFP), 47
Research —
    on benefits of vocational education,
        197-198
    in career development, 314-317
    in change process, 391-392
Research Conference on Education
        and Cultural Deprivation, 149
Research and development, and
        performance contracts, 47
Residual theory, 188-189, 281
Resources —
    need for future, 194
    recommendations for strengthening,
        236-237
Responsibility, developing social, 11
Restrictions, eliminating in
        individualized education, 9
Restructuring, as planned change, 383
Revolution —
    against educational excellence,
        37-38
    of women workers, 133-138
Richards, Charles R., 175
Runkle, John D., 173
Rural/residential based model, of
        career education, 274-275
Rural-urban environment, and
        vocational choice, 107-109
Rush, Dr. Benjamin, 172
Russia —
    influence on American education,
        31-34
    role in vocational education, 173

Salaries, men's vs. women's, 135-136
School-based model, of career
        education, 272-349
School-society relationship, 15-25
    as education issue, 7-8
    in individualized education, 9
School-work, gap between, 154
Schooling —
    describing function of, 281-289
    see Education
Schools —
    and accountability, 43-52
    changing structure for culturally
        disadvantaged, 152, 159-163
    economic foundations of, 193
    free, 7, 16
    functions of, 187-193

future, 186
    history of agricultural and
        mechanical, 173-174
    see also Education
    in United Kingdom, 15
Schools Where Children Learn, 15
Schools Without Failure, 10-11, 43
Science Advisory Committee, 5
Science —
    and career education, 184-186
    and educational excellence, 33
Secondary education, recommenda-
        tions for strengthening, 237
Segregation, and funded education
        programs, 38-39
Self-appraisal, and vocational
        maturity, 101
Self-awareness, goal of education, 11
Self-concept —
    in awareness stage, 351-352
    development of, 57
    development through education, 14
    theory of, 69-71
Self-development, in elementary
        school, 57
Self-image, and the culturally
        disadvantaged, 151
Self-perception, and ghetto escape,
        161
Sex, and vocational choice, 112-114
Sexism, and career development,
        132-147
Sex-role, and career choices, 145-146
Signal learning, 226
Single educational systems, 296-298
Skills —
    and career education, 270-271
    salable and education for, 290
    and vocational education, 206
Sloyd, in schools, 174
Slums and Suburbs, 150
Smith-Hughes Act, 176, 177, 254
    amendments to by VEA of 1963,
        247
    and educational systems, 295
Smith-Lever bill, 176
Social adjustment, of culturally
        disadvantaged, 160
Social movements, and decentrali-
        zation of school systems, 45-46
Social problems —
    and educational excellence, 37-38
    including in curriculum, 42
    and ineffective education, 10
    and relevance, 40
Social responsibility, developing
        through education, 11
Social structure —
    and employment of women,
        145-147
    and interest in education, 119
    and occupational choice, 72-73
    and vocational choices, 104-117

425

426

of conceptual framework for
   occupational choice, 71-74
definition and function of, 58-59
early determinants of vocational
   choice, 81-84
learning, 85-86
personality of vocational choice,
   79-80
of psychoanalytic vocational
   development, 77-79
self-concept, 69-71
Thesis, of excellence, 31-39
Thought, five step analysis of, 384
Trades —
   analyzing and teaching, 173
   teaching vocational, 171-173
Trait theory, 59, 60-62
   deficiencies in, 63-64
   review of, 87
Transition stage, in occupational
   choice, 66
Translation stage, of self-concept, 71
Turnover, of staff and students, 398

Underground, student movements, 25
Unemployment —
   among culturally disadvantaged,
      154
   and NACVE reports, 258-259
   study of, 61
United Kingdom, characteristics of
   schools in, 15
United States Department of Labor,
   133-136, 203
United States Employment Service
   (USES), 61
United States Office of Education,
   and educational accountability,
   45
University dominance, barrier to
   educational change, 395-396
University of Illinois Committee on
   School Mathematics (UICSM),
   307
Urban-rural environment, and
   vocational choice, 107-109

Value complex, in affective domain,
   324
Value orientation change, 384
Values, and vocational choice,
   101, 123-126
Value stage, in occupational choice,
   66
Variables —
   definition of, 98
   in employment (table), 213
Verbal association, type of learning,
   226
VISTA, 23
Vocational behavior —
   and childhood relationship, 81-84

review of theories, 86-93
and self-concept theory, 70
theory of, 65
Vocational choice —
   early determinants of, 81-84
   interaction among variables,
      126-127
   and mental ability, 121
   personality and environment
      theory (table), 80
   and the personality theory, 79-80
   and psychological factor, 118-126
   and race, 109-111
   see also Occupational choice
   and sex differences, 112-114
   and values, 123-126
   of women, 132-147
Vocational development —
   characterizations of (table), 76
   and model of decision-making
      (table), 76
   psychoanalytic framework for,
      77-79
   and the self-concept, 69-71
Vocational Development Inventory,
   114
Vocational education —
   agenda for action, 242-245
   apprenticeship as, 170-171
   and categorical systems, 219-223
   as college preparation, 199
   and content organization, 223-225
   defense of, 192
   delivery systems questions,
      200-201
   and development of skills, 239
   economic foundation of, 193-207
   expenditures for (table), 36
   foundations of, 183-232
   funding of, 244, 251, 254-255
   graduates in labor market, 198
   historical perspectives of, 169-182
   and individual career performance,
      227-228
   legislation on, 176-180
   and manpower forecasting,
      202-207
   to meet special needs, 230-232
   model of learning, 226-227
   and motivation, 230-232
   and the National Manpower
      Council, 236
   occupational adaptability, 229-230
   panel of consultants on, 240-245
   process of, 226-227
   psychological foundation for,
      216-232
   quality of instruction in, 228-229
   see also Career education
   shortcomings of early, 181
   sociological foundation for,
      207-216
   summary of limitations of, 241

427

Vocational Education Act of 1963, 150, 245-248
   advantages and shortcomings of, 247-248
Vocational Education Amendments of 1968, 253-257
Vocational Education Association, 175
Vocational Education: The Bridge Between Man and His Work, 241
Vocational Education: Innovations Revolutionize Career Training, 154
Vocational Education for the 1970's, 270
Vocational guidance movement, 59
Vocational Interest Blank, 118
Vocational Preference Inventory, 91
Vocational maturity —
   concept of, 98-104
   definition and dimensions of, 99-102
   goal of career education, 314
   and psychological factors, 118-126
Vocational Maturity of Ninth Grade Boys, 100
Voucher system, 18, 27, 44, 46

Warfare, and career education, 185
War on Poverty, 150
Withdrawal, failure of education, 11
Womanpower, 135
Women —
   equal educational opportunities for, 146-147
   needs for career development, 132-147
   reasons for increased employment of, 134-135
   relevant factors in career development of, 140-143
   and salary discriminations, 135-136
   and vocational choice, 112-114
Women: A Bibliography on Their Education and Careers, 146
Woodward, Calvin M., 173
Work —
   and awareness stage, 352
   and career education, 278
   future role of, 215-216
   learning, and play, 282-289
   meanings of, 208-213
   need of youth, 286-287
Work-school, gap between, 154-155
Work values, 124
Wright, Caroll D., 175

Index to Quoted Authors